Roger Macdonald is a historian, journalist and television producer. He studied modern history at Hertford College, Oxford, where his special subject was the French *ancien régime*.

Praise for *The Man in the Iron Mask*

'A delight for anyone who has rooted for the secret prisoner with an iron face.' *Oxford Times*

From: *The Sign of Four* by Arthur Conan Doyle

First serialized in *Lippincott's Magazine*, February 1890

Sherlock Holmes to Dr John Watson:

'How often have I said to you that when you have eliminated the impossible, whatever remains, *however improbable*, must be the truth?'

THE MAN IN THE IRON MASK

THE TRUE STORY OF THE MOST FAMOUS PRISONER IN HISTORY AND THE FOUR MUSKETEERS

ROGER MACDONALD

CONSTABLE • LONDON

To Jeannie
and our own Three Musketeers:
Sarah, Simon and Timothy

ᘒ ᘒ

Constable & Robinson Ltd
3 The Lanchesters
162 Fulham Palace Road
London W6 9ER
www.constablerobinson.com

This edition published by Constable,
an imprint of Constable & Robinson, 2008

A copy of the British Library Cataloguing in Publication
Data is available from the British Library

ISBN: 978-1-84529-300-0

Printed and bound in the EU

1 3 5 7 9 10 8 6 4 2

CONTENTS

ACKNOWLEDGEMENTS

My particular thanks are due to:

My indefatigable literary agent, Jonny Pegg of Curtis Brown International; my genial commissioning editor at Constable & Robinson, Andreas Campomar; David Bloomfield of Hertford College Oxford, for the strategic thinking he brought to the story; Claire Trocmé for her knowledge of every nuance of the French language; and Jessica Cuthbert-Smith, for her sharp eyes and deft streamlining of the text.

The staff of the following, who showed endless patience: the University of Oxford Faculty of History; the Bodleian Library Oxford; the British Library; the London Library; the Bibliothèque of the Voltaire Institute and Museum in Geneva; and four libraries in Paris: the Service Historique at Vincennes, the Bibliothèque Nationale, the Bibliothèque Sainte-Geneviève and the Bibliothèque de l'Arsenal, particularly on the occasion when a box of papers, opened for the first time in over a century, created a mushroom cloud of dust.

And to: John Armstrong, Laetitia Audumares, Burcu Baikali, John Beare, Stéphane Bibard, Jean-Pierre Boudet, Barbara Brindlecombe, Stanislas Brugnon, Jeanne du Canard, Leonardo Giannini, Genna Gifford, Becky Hardie, Camille Lebossé, Anthony Levi, Andrew Lownie, Sarah Macdonald, Simon Macdonald, Tim Macdonald, Felix Markham, Peter Mills, Carol O'Brien, Claire Sauvrage, Catherine Walser and Dominique Wells.

PROLOGUE

THE FACTS BEHIND THE FABLE

Louis XIV was not called *dieudonné*, 'god given', solely because his arrival after more than twenty barren years of marriage between Louis XIII and Anne of Austria seemed to be the answer to a nation's prayers, a direct heir at last to the throne of France. His conception – or at least the official version of his conception – was also little short of miraculous, said to be the outcome of a single stormy night when the estranged king and the queen were forced to share a bed. However, the incidents that led up to this bizarre happening in history show that Louis XIII was almost certainly not the father of the future Sun King. But for the singular importance of the occasion, his candidacy would have been dismissed long ago, not as merely unlikely but as hugely improbable. From birth Louis XIV and the main Bourbon line faced the constant risk of exposure as illegitimate, leaving the identity of his true father as dangerous a piece of knowledge as ever existed in France.

One man who knew the Sun King's secret paid a heavy price: not only incarceration without hope of release but also forced to hide his own identity by means of a cruel and unusual punishment. The Man in the Iron Mask has fascinated historians, novelists and film makers alike, blurring fact and fiction.

Indeed, few things in this story are what they once seemed. The Three Musketeers, Aramis, Athos and Porthos – immortalized by Alexandre Dumas – existed outside the great writer's imagination and their famous duel against Cardinal

Richelieu's Guards, when they fought alongside the young Charles d'Artagnan on his first day in Paris, really did take place. The Musketeers and their captain, Tréville, were also inextricably linked in real life to the Iron Mask, whose tragic fate was far more extraordinary than anything even Dumas could devise.

This book begins decades before the confinement of the Mask but this was the time when the events took shape that drew him inexorably into danger. These were the almost superhuman effort of the dying Cardinal Richelieu to defeat his enemies and the low cunning shown by his successor, Cardinal Mazarin in desperately trying to prevent France descending into chaos. Then there was Queen Anne, now regent, prepared to take any risk to ensure that her son Louis would inherit the throne; the fall through hubris of Louis' over-mighty minister, Fouquet; the scheming of the royal mistresses to remain in favour; the ring of sorcerers and poisoners plying their evil trade in Paris.

The trail of torture, murder and betrayal that leads to the Mask's entombment in the sinister French prisons of Pignerol, Exilles, Sainte-Marguerite and the Bastille, takes us deep inside the corrupt and glamorous court of Louis XIV. Nonetheless, it is exceptionally well documented. We can still read the avalanche of orders sent to his perpetual jailer, Saint-Mars, by the king's minister of war, Louvois, on how the Mask was to be transported, confined and treated.

This book bases its findings on this wealth of original documents and histories, some of which have never been properly assessed. The most important sources are identified whenever needed within the text and further notes appear on the interpretation of source material in each chapter in the Notes and Sources section beginning on page 330. There is a complete list of all the relevant works in the Bibliography at the end of the book. The Notes start with an explanation of the various denominations of French money in seventeenth-century France and a calculation of what they might be worth today. The principal characters in the book are listed on page xi and a chronology of important dates appears on page xv. The reader may look at any of these and the chapter-by-chapter notes up to and including Chapter 13 safe in the knowledge that they will not reveal prematurely whose face was to be found behind the mask.

Some of the original documents, covered in dust and yellowing with age, had been either missed or misunderstood by previous investigations. None of the fifty-odd names previously put forward as the most famous prisoner in history survived this re-examination of the evidence. It quickly became apparent that the Man in the Iron Mask was not Louis XIV's twin brother nor even the one credible candidate previously suggested, Eustache Dauger or Danger, who at last emerges from the shadows. Even the few purported facts on which historians seemed largely agreed, such as the start of the Mask's imprisonment and the date of his death in the Bastille, also proved to be incorrect. It finally became possible to resolve the four key unanswered questions:

Why was the Man in the Iron Mask not simply disposed of?
What vital knowledge did he possess that condemned him to
    perpetual imprisonment?
Why was he forced to wear a metal mask?
Who was he?

The absolute regime of seventeenth-century France went to unprecedented lengths to conceal the truth about the Man in the Iron Mask, even to deny his very existence. The truth has been successfully hidden for centuries behind smoke and mirrors. However, the explanation put forward in these pages is the only one consistent with all the facts. The door into the Sun King's world of plots and paranoia is far from open fully; but this key alone undoubtedly fits the lock.

Welcome to Hell: the remote Alpine fort of Exilles, prison of the Man in the Iron Mask

Principal Characters

Anne of Austria: wife of Louis XIII
Aramis, Henri d'Aramitz: one of the Three Musketeers
Athénaïs *See* Montespan, Athénaïs de Rochechouart de
Athos, Armand de Sillègue: one of the Three Musketeers
Barrail, Henri de: friend of Lauzun
Barbezieux, Louis Le Tellier, marquis de: son of Louvois
Besmaux, François de Montlézun, sieur de: Musketeer and
    governor of the Bastille
Brienne, Henri-Auguste de Loménie, comte de: confidant
    of Anne of Austria
Carlisle, Duchess of *See* Percy, Lucy
Chanlecy, Anne-Charlotte de: wife of d'Artagnan
Chevreuse, Marie de Rohan, duchesse de: perennial plotter,
    Richelieu's enemy
Cinq-Mars, Henri Coffier de Ruzé, marquis de: favourite
    of Louis XIII
Colbert, Jean-Baptiste: minister of Louis XIV
Courtilz, Gatien de: soldier and biographer
Cyrano de Bergerac, Hercule-Savinien: poet and duellist
D'Artagnan, Charles-Ogier de Batz-Castelmore: captain of
    the Musketeers
Dauger or Danger, Eustache *see* Martin, Étienne
Du Junca, Étienne: King's lieutenant at the Bastille
Fouquet, Nicolas: finance minister under Louis XIV
Gaston d'Orléans: Louis XIII's younger brother
Grande Mademoiselle, Anne-Marie-Louise d'Orléans, the:
    wilful cousin of Louis XIV
Hautefort, Marie de: lady-in-waiting to Anne of Austria

Henrietta Stuart: Louis XIV's sister-in-law, Charles II's sister

Jussac, Claude, comte de: expert duellist in Cardinal Richelieu's Guard

La Porte, Pierre: servant of Anne of Austria

La Reynie, Gabriel Nicolas: Paris chief of police

La Vallière, Louise de: mistress of Louis XIV

La Voisin, Catherine Montvoisin: notorious poisoner

Lauzun, comte de: captain of the royal bodyguard

Le Tellier, Michel: Louvois' father, minister of Louis XIV

Lionne, Hughes de: minister for foreign affairs under Louis XIV

Louis XIII: King of France

Louis XIV: King of France

Louvois, François Michel Le Tellier, marquis de: minister of war under Louis XIV

Maintenon, Madame de: mistress, later wife, of Louis XIV

Mancini, Olympe, duchesse de Soissons: niece of Mazarin

Maria-Theresa, Queen: Louis XIV's wife

Marie de' Médici: mother of Louis XIII

Martin, Étienne *alias* Eustache Danger/Dauger: fixer, poisoner, valet

Mattioli, Ercole: Italian count who double-crossed Louis XIV

Mazarin, Cardinal Jules: First minister to Louis XIV

Milédi *See* **Percy, Lucy**

Mirabeau, Honoré-Gabriel, comte de: revolutionary orator

Montespan, Athénaïs de Rochechouart de: mistress of Louis XIV

Montespan, marquis de: husband of Athénaïs de Montespan

Montvoisin, Catherine *See* **La Voisin**

Ormesson, Olivier Lefèvre d': judge in the Paris Parlement

Percy, Lucy: English aristocrat, Richelieu's spy, known as Milédi

Peyroz, Marguérite de: Besmaux's wife

Philippe d'Orléans: younger brother of Louis XIV

Porthos, Isaac de Portau: one of the Three Musketeers

Prignani, Abbé Guiseppé: Catholic priest and secret agent

Renneville, Constantin de: prisoner in the Bastille

Reynie *See* La Reynie

Richelieu, Jean-Armand de Plessis, Cardinal: First minister
  of Louis XIII

Saint-Mars, Bénigne d'Auvergne de: jailer of the Man in the
  Iron Mask

Saint-Mars, Marie-Antoinette de: wife of Saint-Mars

Scarron, Françoise *See* Maintenon, Madame de

Séguier, Pierre: Chancellor of France

Sévigné, Marie, Madame de: letter writer *extraordinaire*

Soissons, comtesse de *See* Mancini, Olympe

Stuart, Henrietta *See* Henrietta Stuart

Tallemant, des Réaux, Gédéon: court diarist

Three Musketeers, the *See* Aramis, Athos, Porthos

Tréville: captain of the King's Musketeers

Trois-Villes, Jean-Arnaud de *See* Tréville

Vallière *See* La Vallière

Visconti, Primi: diarist and soothsayer at court of Louis XIV

Voisin *See* La Voisin

Voltaire: firebrand philosopher, born as François Marie Arouet

CHRONOLOGY

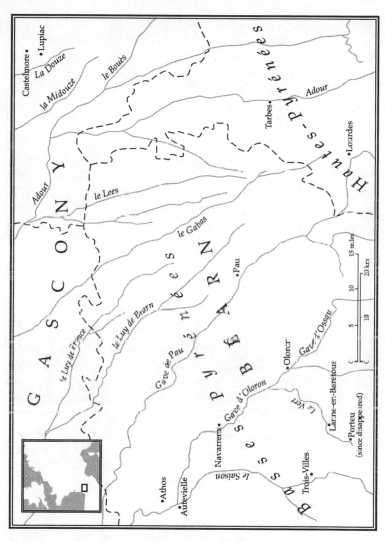

Béarn and Gascony — Musketeers' territory

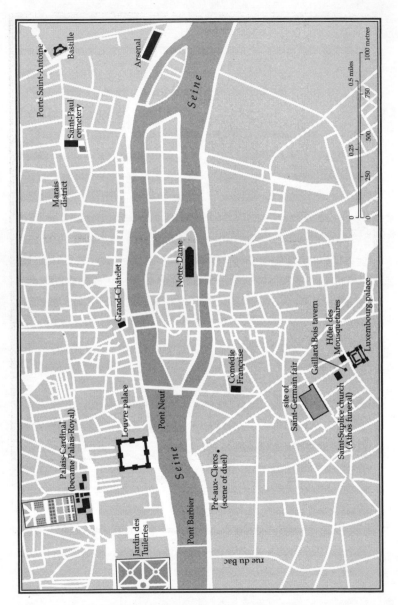

The untamed Paris of the seventeenth century

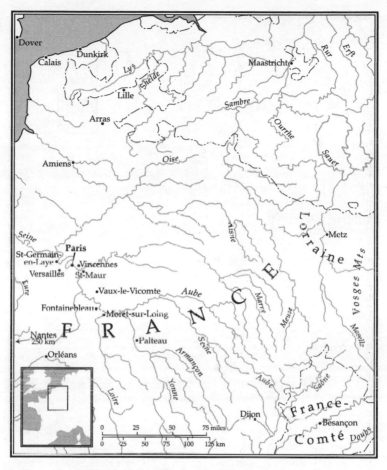

Northern France and the early campaigns of Louis XIV

Southern France and the journeys of the Man in the Iron Mask

1

THE QUEEN'S LOVER

The man in Anne of Austria's bed was not the French queen's husband, Louis XIII. He had easily avoided the patrol of King's Musketeers at the palace of Saint-Germain-en-Laye near Paris because he knew their every move; and even if by some misfortune he had been seen and challenged at the main gate, they would simply have saluted and allowed him to pass. In the early hours, once the last flickering candle was extinguished, he had entered the queen's apartments via the backstairs passages used by scurrying servants during the day; he knew their every twist and turn. Long before first light, when the lowliest kitchen maids began to rake the embers and relay the fires, and the keeper of the royal hounds went to wake his pack, Anne's clandestine companion would be gone: silently retracing his steps to disappear, like some will o'-the wisp, into the night.

When Alexandre Dumas made Queen Anne and her imprudent gift of diamond studs to the Duke of Buckingham the central theme of *The Three Musketeers*, he was following a well-trodden path in romantic fiction, in which queens were invariably trapped between two narrative models: maternity or adultery. An adulterous queen was almost always barren, or at least supposedly unable to bear the son that the royal dynasty required. In the realpolitik of seventeenth-century France, the harder Anne tried to escape from the role defined by her womanhood through becoming politically active, the greater the likelihood that charges of adultery would be levied

against her to weaken her supporters and to prepare the way
for divorce or repudiation; in extremis she might even be put
on trial for treason. The French queen must have been aware
of this and knew she was closely watched; yet in the autumn
of 1637 she risked taking a lover and being discovered and
disgraced, a decision born out of desperation. It spawned an
extraordinary sequence of events and provides the key to the
most unfathomable secret of all, the identity of a mysterious
state prisoner, the Man in the Iron Mask.

Had she been almost anyone but the queen, Anne's adultery
would have been tolerated, even quietly applauded. A husband
was expected to meet his conjugal obligations, and after
twenty-two childless years of marriage, in this Louis XIII had
conspicuously failed.

The court of Louis' parents, Henry IV and Marie de Médici,
did not prepare the king well for manhood and marriage. Wife
Marie and institutionalized mistress Henriette d'Entragues
lived in uneasy proximity with Henry IV at Saint-Germain and
the Louvre. Both women first became pregnant within weeks
of one another, and their many children, heirs and illegitimate
children, were brought up together. An insatiable womanizer,
Henry was enormously proud of his sexual performance and
showed his considerable, erect penis to Louis at the age of three,
telling him this was what ruled the kingdom and ensured its
future. His courtiers took their cue from their sovereign and,
even after Henry had been assassinated before Louis was ten
years old – leaving his mother to rule France – they continued
to make Louis' genitals the focal point of his upbringing. When
they were not manipulating the boy king's penis to see if it had
begun to show signs of a life of its own, they were mischievously
threatening to cut it off. As historian Geoffrey Regan commented,
'What passed for child rearing in seventeenth-century France
could have provided material for a whole psychiatric conference
on infant trauma and personality disorders.'

The Queen Regent, Marié de Médici, daughter of the
Grand Duke Francis of Florence, was bigoted, dim-witted

and overweight, with poor eyesight and even poorer French. However, she was a devout Catholic who instinctively, if unrealistically, wanted to bring together the two great Catholic powers, France and Spain, to subdue the Protestants and their faith. In Marie de Médici's uncomplicated and self-centred mind lay a conviction that French Catholic interests and her own were best served by making a Habsburg princess the next Queen of France. The marriage driven by Marie de Médici and celebrated by proxy in October 1615 between Louis and Anne, a Spanish princess of predominantly Austrian descent, was supposed to begin in earnest on 25 November when the couple came together in Bordeaux. They were both fourteen, not considered particularly young for wedlock at the time. The consummation of a diplomatic marriage was of great importance, as it was expected to presage the arrival of an heir from the union; so reports of what took place that first night are pruriently detailed.

One of the principal accounts comes from the *Historiettes*, the work of Gédéon Tallemant des Réaux, a Huguenot lawyer distantly related to Catherine de Vivonne, marquise de Rambouillet, whose Paris mansion was an important social and literary centre for nearly forty years. Madame de Rambouillet and her set gave Tallemant impeccably sourced stories of the reign of Louis XIII from their wide contacts at court. Tallemant originally intended to publish them in 1660 but, perhaps fearing for his own safety, drew back from doing so. These succinct and unsparingly candid descriptions of prominent people remained unpublished for more than 150 years; two centuries elapsed before some of their more salacious detail saw the light of day. Richelieu's biographer, Anthony Levi, concludes that Tallemant was 'studiously well informed'. One of Tallemant's editors, F.J. Barnett, refers to his 'impressive degree of accuracy' and adds that 'he did not hesitate to doubt or dismiss as unreliable much that he was told.' Philippe Erlanger, the most prolific expert on seventeenth-century France, notes that Tallemant 'draws his facts from eyewitness informants that he never fails to name . . . His realistic accounts . . . should often be preferred to other ornate descriptions'.

According to Tallemant and other independent testimony, despite his father's clumsy attempts to stimulate in his son an early interest in sex, Louis was by no stretch of the imagination an eager bridegroom. On the first night he had to be forcibly carried to Anne's bedchamber in an almost farcical procession that included his mother, his doctor, two nurses and sundry members of the wardrobe, with Louis' *premier valet de chambre*, Henri de Beringhem, solemnly leading the way with a lighted candle.

As was expected of her, in the morning the Queen Regent held up the stained bed sheets and coarsely asserted that her son had penetrated Anne with his 'gland rouge'. Jean Héroard, the royal physician, noted in his journal that Louis twice had sexual intercourse with his young wife in less than three hours, but the doctor distorted the testimony of the two nurses, who alone remained in the room. The curtains around the royal bed were drawn, making it impossible for them to tell what was really going on. It seems most unlikely that in such a goldfish bowl the couple succeeded in having penetrative sex on their wedding night. As for the bed sheets, Louis' own reported comment on what happened strongly suggests that he had actually urinated into the queen's vagina, under the misapprehension that this was what was expected of him.

Nor did things improve. For as long as he could, Louis slept alone, 'shrinking from any physical contact with the queen', even avoiding meals with his wife for seven months. Exceptional measures were taken in an effort to stimulate the king's appetite for sex, even – perhaps prompted by what had really transpired on his wedding night – to show him first hand the basic technique of intercourse. In January 1619 Louis' illegitimate half-sister, Catherine-Henriette de Vendôme, married the duc de Lorraine, Charles II d'Elboeuf. The couple invited Louis to the bridal chamber to watch them make love, naked, on top of the sheets. Louis stood right beside the bed, poking his head through a gap in the closed curtains. According to the Venetian ambassador, 'the act was repeated more than once, to the great applause and general pleasure of the king.' Catherine, clearly an uninhibited young lady, even by the relaxed customs of the day, then said, 'Sire, you do the same with the Queen, and you will feel the better for it.'

It was all to no avail. The following week, the Queen Regent ordered Louis to be taken, by force if necessary, to Anne's bedroom. The weeping, struggling king was again put to bed with Anne, whereupon Dr Héroard unpromisingly recorded that Louis 'compelled himself' to have sex with her. The King of Spain was still far from convinced that the marriage had been consummated and Père Joseph, the court's *éminence gris*, was given the task of persuading him. Soon he reported back to Madrid that the couple had spent a night together and that 'several things show clearly the work of God.' The unworldly Capuchin monk was perhaps delicately referring to another tentative, and unconvincing, inspection of the sheets.

Louis was known to be capable of an erection, displaying one to the master of the wardrobe as he entered his bath, not long before Louis began to rule in his own right, aged sixteen. In recording this, Tallemant suggested the king's arousal was due to flagellation, of being willingly beaten. His informants named the potential candidates who might have performed this unusual task, among them Louis' head coachman Saint Armour and Haran, keeper of the royal kennels. They featured in Tallemant's long list of the men who became the king's lovers and he left no room for any misinterpretation of the nature of their relationship. According to Tallemant, the king engaged in a wide variety of sexual acts with a succession of male companions.

As a Spanish princess far from home, Anne might have accepted her dismal lot but for the influence of the duchesse de Chevreuse, Marie de Rohan-Montbazon. Marie, the daughter of a duke, lost her mother when she was only two years old and she had been brought up, a wild tomboy, by one of her father's mistresses. At fifteen, when she became a maid of honour to the queen, she already had ravishingly good looks: golden hair, blue eyes and long eyelashes. Her vivacious free spirit 'animated her voice and her gestures . . . and imparted to her whole personality an irresistible charm'. Louis, amused by her skilful repartee, made her superintendent of the queen's household shortly after her eighteenth birthday. He quickly regretted this prestigious appointment and was soon rather less amused by Marie's frivolous references to his sexuality. When the court ladies visited the French army besieging Montauban and stayed much later than planned, the king objected to their sleeping in the camp, claiming there were no beds available. Marie shouted out, 'Surely the king has a bed,' provoking spontaneous laughter from those who knew which sex usually occupied it.

The same age as the queen, Marie became Anne's closest and most attentive companion, and soon her most intimate friend. Men fell at Marie's feet; she manipulated them ruthlessly by means of sexual favours that were not coquettish but deeply carnal. The only contraceptive device in regular use in France was a sponge soaked in brandy to prevent semen reaching the uterus. This was far from reliable, so inevitably from time to time the promiscuous Marie fell pregnant, only to give birth to illegitimate children with equal aplomb. Conversations in the queen's inner circle were highly salacious and Marie introduced Anne to the *Cabinet satyrique*, a notorious book full of pornographic verses devoted to the full repertoire and appeal of heterosexual sex. The queen, sensuous, lazy and indolent, with few ideas of her own, simply sailed in Marie's licentious wake. It would have taken strength of character that Anne did not possess to play with fire as incessantly as she did, without eventually being scorched by the flames.

Encouraged by Marie to have affairs, Anne was frequently seen in the company of male courtiers and, in particular, of handsome black servants from the French colonies, a novelty at court. The queen was rumoured to have given birth to a baby having 'the colour and visage of a blackamoor', who died within a month. There were more reliable stories of three miscarriages, one particularly well documented. In the early hours of 15 March 1622, Anne returned with Marie from a party and, although pregnant, went 'romping like a schoolgirl' in the Louvre, where she slipped on the polished floor of the long gallery and fell heavily. For a full week news of her subsequent miscarriage was withheld from the king, renewing speculation that the child was not his and that Anne was happy to get rid of it if she could. Louis was furious at being kept in the dark and dismissed Marie from court.

So far the royal courtiers had suppressed any scandal but the arrival in France of George Villiers, Duke of Buckingham, the charismatic favourite of England's James I, changed all that. Early in 1623, Buckingham embarked on one of the madcap adventures that characterized his mercurial career. He persuaded the Prince of Wales, the future Charles I, that his best interests lay in marriage to the Infanta Isabella of Spain, Anne of Austria's sister; and that Charles should break every diplomatic convention by wooing her in person. Together they made their way to Madrid, travelling through France incognito, though scarcely unrecognized, via Paris, where they were able to see Anne and nineteen of her ladies dancing in a masque and a ballet. Buckingham may have glimpsed rather more than that. The queen allowed him into her bedroom, which provoked an outburst of anger from Louis.

The prince and the duke, predictably rebuffed in Spain, eventually returned to England 'in the mood of the disappointed suitor who demonstrates the depth of his devotion by cutting the ungrateful loved one's throat' – as the great historian Richard Henry Tawney memorably put it. War with Spain quickly followed and Buckingham, having thrown the levers of diplomacy into reverse, persuaded the declining James I that a French marriage had more to offer his son. Charles was duly betrothed to Louis XIII's fifteen-year-old sister, Henrietta Maria.

In May 1625, two months after the death of his father, Charles I dispatched the Duke of Buckingham to France to bring home his bride. The *Mercure de France* reported that Buckingham travelled 'with more pomp and glitter than if he had been king'. He was rowed up the Seine in his personal barge by twenty-two oarsmen decked out 'all in sky-coloured taffety', followed along the bank by three coaches lined with padded velvet and adorned with gold lace, each pulled by eight horses, with six coachmen riding pillion.

Buckingham's arrival in Paris with his huge entourage caused a sensation. He was accompanied by 600 people, including thirty chief yeomen, twenty-four outriders, twenty-two cooks, twenty gentlemen, twelve pages, seven grooms of the chamber, assorted footmen, huntsmen and watermen, and twelve other lords, no doubt all a-leaping. When asked to sit for Rubens, the duke could not make up his mind which costume he should wear for the portrait out of the twenty-seven included in his baggage train. One suit of purple satin was 'embroidered all over with rich orient pearls'; another of 'white satin uncut velvet' was 'spangled with diamonds' that broke off his shoulders as he strode through the corridors of the Louvre and left onlookers scrabbling for them on the marble floors.

The duke had another motive for his return to Paris: he was bent on seducing the French queen, seen by many as the ultimate conquest. Anne may not have been truly beautiful, as some of her admirers claimed; more objective observers thought her nose was too long, her green eyes too big for her head and her complexion poor. But under Marie's tuition she knew how to make the most of her assets: flowing chestnut hair, large breasts and white slender hands. For his part, Buckingham, aged thirty-two, was at his most handsome. The attraction was mutual from the start. One of Anne's officers observed that 'from the first day the freedom between them has been as much as if they had known each other for a long time.' Marie, realizing this was a love match, arranged a rendezvous between the queen and the duke in the secluded little walled garden of the Louvre. Marie kept watch a discreet distance away. The queen was sufficiently concerned by what had transpired to send her confidante the next day 'to ask Buckingham if he was quite certain she were not in danger of becoming pregnant'.

On 2 June the intended Queen of England, Henrietta Maria, left Paris for London, escorted by Buckingham and his retinue. Members of the French court, including Anne and the Queen Mother, travelled with them as far as Amiens. Louis, piqued by rumours that Anne had lost her heart to Buckingham, sourly claimed he was unwell, and stayed in Paris. The British and French entourages were separately housed, the queen in a fine building overlooking the Somme, where Marie made sure that Buckingham and Anne were 'left alone in a trellis garden' by the river. The gold lace on his tunic left telltale marks on the queen's bosom and the best that her cousin the Princess de Conti could say of this episode was that she could vouch for Anne's virtue from the waist down but not from the waist up. Two days later Buckingham reluctantly took his leave of the queen and travelled on with Henrietta Maria to Boulogne. However, finding a gale blowing that would keep all ships in port, the same night he seized his chance to return, galloping back to Amiens in the dark. He burst unannounced into the queen's bedroom and swore to Anne that he loved her. When Louis heard what had happened, he dismissed the four male members of the queen's household, and gave orders that Buckingham was never to set foot on French soil again.

Soon, on the eve of a military expedition to relieve the Huguenot enclave of La Rochelle, besieged by royal troops – Buckingham's first step towards fulfilling the impossible dream of claiming the Queen of France for himself – the duke would be assassinated by a disgruntled English officer passed over for promotion. His death may have saved Anne from the serious consequences of one major indiscretion but, for the queen, thanks to Marie, there were always others. The more the duchesse de Chevreuse had the ear and other parts of the anatomy of the not so good and the great, the more she believed her schemes could overturn the established political order of things. This put Marie on a collision course with Cardinal Richelieu, the real ruler of France, whom the queen was already inclined to dislike. Marie saw to it that mere inclination was quickly turned into a living force. Before long Anne showed her contempt for the cardinal by describing Richelieu as 'Cul Pourri', 'Rotten Arse', in her private correspondence among her allies at court. This was a spiteful epithet because it was widely known that Richelieu suffered severely from haemorrhoids and often could not sit down without acute discomfort; a bungled operation to remove his haemorrhoids had resulted in a near-fatal abscess. As almost nothing escaped the cardinal's spies, it was the most injudicious of ways to ridicule Richelieu, but Anne made few concessions to common sense.

In 1626 Marie de Chevreuse, for good reason called 'the arch intriguer of the century', entangled the queen in a plot to remove the cardinal and replace Louis with his seventeen-year-old brother Gaston d'Orléans, another of Marie's many lovers. Anne's marriage was to be annulled on grounds of non-consummation so that she could marry Gaston. The plot predictably failed, in part because Anne did not find her brother-in-law at all attractive. Gaston was a great fidget, always making faces, which exaggerated his least endearing features: huge staring eyes, a drooping lower lip and a perpetually open mouth. In August Gaston, despite Marie's exhortations to decline the match, agreed under duress instead to wed the wealthy Princess Marie de Montpensier. Louis' support for the marriage was a strong indication that, even at twenty-five, he had already resigned himself to not having children, and to his brother's descendants inheriting the throne. Nonetheless on 9 September Anne was questioned by Richelieu in front of the royal council about her part in the abortive scheme to marry her to Gaston in place of Louis. The queen brazened it out, replying scornfully that she 'would have had too little to gain in the exchange'. Louis was far from convinced. He issued an order, countersigned by Richelieu, forbidding anyone not attached to Anne's household to enter her apartments and compelling her to seek the cardinal's approval in advance for every private audience.

Marie de Chevreuse took flight to the independent duchy of Lorraine but was allowed to return to Paris in November 1628. Referring to Marie's prominent role as a lovers' go-between, Gaston contemptuously observed she had 'been brought back so that the queen might have more opportunities of bearing a child'. Although in his memoirs Richelieu would describe this as 'a devilish idea', it seemed that Louis' weak, indecisive and disloyal brother might be correct when Anne was visibly pregnant in January 1631, only to suffer another miscarriage in April. Throughout her most likely month of conception, September 1630, the king had lain dangerously ill with chronic dysentery in Lyon, making it highly improbable that Louis was the father. Some courtiers believed that Richelieu himself had insinuated his way into the queen's bed; he was also said to be sleeping with the superintendent of his household, his niece the Duchess of Aguillon. He was certainly not above the pleasures of the flesh. An inveterate womanizer since his teens, he had been treated by the king's physician for a severe case of gonorrhoea; his initial rise to power was attributed in some quarters to Marie de Médici having taken him as a lover. If true, it went some way to explain the torrent of abuse Richelieu received from the Queen Mother at the Luxembourg Palace on 11 November 1630, when he slipped through an unbolted back door and successfully interrupted her secret meeting with the king, in which she had hoped finally to persuade Louis to remove him from office. By the end of what became known as the Day of Dupes – the dupes being those in the Médici camp who wrongly believed the cardinal was finished – Richelieu had turned the tables.

The Queen Mother soon went into exile in the Spanish Netherlands, never to return. She left behind the youngest of her *filles d'honneur*, Marie de Hautefort, a precocious fourteen-year-old, with flowing blonde hair and a dazzling smile. Mademoiselle de Hautefort's extraordinary charm concealed a steely determination; she had been brought up in difficult circumstances. Her father, a field marshal and gentleman of the king's bedchamber, had died less than a month after she was born and her mother not long afterwards. In 1628 she was found a new place at court among the ladies of the queen through the influence of her elder brother Jacques-François, who looked after Anne of Austria's household budget. He was admirably suited for such a task, as his parsimony was legendary, and he would become the inspiration for Molière's play, *The Miser*.

Several members of the queen's entourage were already in Richelieu's pay and the cardinal took it for granted that he could suborn Mademoiselle de Hautefort. He was unpleasantly surprised when she rejected his overtures out of hand and showed a fierce loyalty for Anne from the start. Louis, by contrast, found the teenager enchanting and used every excuse to be in her company, ostensibly visiting the queen but instead spending his entire time with her ladies-in-waiting. But if there was any doubt that the king's admiration for her was purely platonic, Mademoiselle de Hautefort dispelled it in one bold stroke. One day, seeing that Louis was clutching a letter he was about to send to Richelieu, she snatched it from him. When the king tried to retrieve it, she slipped the parchment down the front of her dress between her ample breasts, held her arms open wide, leant forward and said wickedly to Louis, 'Take as much as you want, right now.' The king hastily declined.

Louis soon switched his innocent affections to a rather less forward member of Anne's entourage, sixteen-year-old Louise-Angélique de La Fayette, who had been introduced at court by her uncle, the bishop of Limoges, and by Richelieu himself. Louise, a pretty brunette, tried her best to accommodate the king's every mood; she sang to him and played games, though not the kind with sexual connotations favoured by Mademoiselle de Hautefort. Historian Louis Auchincloss aptly described the relationship by observing that Louise's 'terror of losing her virginity was delightfully flattering to a lover who had no intention of taking it'. But if one day the king could be persuaded to change his mind, a fertile teenager seemed much more likely to produce an heir than his still-barren wife.

Even if Louis died childless, a union with his brother Gaston, whose first wife died young, for Anne proved to be only briefly an option: in January 1632 the widowed prince remarried, his new bride a petite princess, eighteen-year-old Marguerite of Lorraine. No doubt Richelieu hoped that the prospect either of being set aside in favour of one of her own ladies, or of becoming superfluous to requirements at the accession of King Gaston, would concentrate the queen's mind wonderfully on a means of procreation. Aided and abetted by Père Joseph, the cardinal was said by the pamphleteers to be selecting a suitable candidate to give Anne the male child needed to follow Louis XIII and preserve the stability of the kingdom.

Richelieu's preferred choice for this delicate task was almost certainly his eventual successor, the Italian Guilio Mazzarini. Jules Mazarin, as he would be known in France, came from humble origins, the son of a major-domo to a rich Roman family. Educated in Spain, he spoke fluent Castilian, the queen's native tongue. Mazarin, a year younger than Anne, arrived in Paris in that same month, January 1632, as a member of a papal diplomatic mission. Richelieu presented Mazarin to the queen, saying, one can imagine in his most sardonic way, 'Madame, you will like him. He looks like Buckingham.'

Although the cardinal was convinced of the chemistry between them, and saw to it that Mazarin met Anne again on a return visit to court in November 1634, unfortunately for the eager nuncio, a recommendation from Richelieu was not at all likely to smooth the passage to the queen's bed. In January 1636, while based at Avignon, he was dismissed by Pope Urban XVIII for having too much regard for the interests of France and returned temporarily to Paris to offer Richelieu his services. His demeanour impressed Louis XIII, who gave him lodgings at the Louvre. Such powerful patrons left Mazarin firmly in the enemy's camp as far as the queen was concerned. Seen as a creature of the cardinal, he was unlikely to appeal to her as a reliable confidant, let alone as a suitable candidate to sire the next king of France.

In 1637 Richelieu sent Mazarin to Rome, to represent France at the Vatican. Although in his biography of Louis XIV Anthony Levi makes a powerful case for Mazarin being the Sun King's father, citing a letter written by Mazarin from Paris to a British diplomat on 16 September of that year as proof that he was in the right place at more or less the right time, unfortunately it does not quite ring true. Mazarin may indeed have returned to the French capital to brief the cardinal but Rome was his base. Had he remained in Paris beyond mid-October, the journey across the Alps would have been more or less impossible for several months during the winter snows, and there is no mention of Mazarin being absent from Italy for any significant period.

The proposition also fails to take into account Mazarin's character, in particular his conspicuous lack of personal courage. One of his siblings said of him contemptuously, '*Mio fratello e un coglione,*' 'My brother has no balls.' The fate of Henry II de Montmorency, a peer of the realm guillotined in October 1632 after an abortive coup, was still fresh in everyone's mind. Louis XIII refused all appeals for clemency for Montmorency, who was widely believed to have been Queen Anne's lover and when captured was found to be carrying her portrait on a diamond bracelet. Whatever their subsequent relationship after Louis' death, it is almost inconceivable that in 1637 Mazarin risked his neck by having illicit sex with the queen.

The suggestion seems equally untenable in the light of events in the second half of the year, when Anne became embroiled in another conspiracy inspired by Marie de Chevreuse. From her latest place of banishment, the Château de Milly near Tours, the high priestess of conspirators wove intrigues of love and lust seamlessly with plots of assassination and revolt; the acquiescent queen never distinguished between them. Although France and Spain were at war, with Marie's encouragement Anne secretly corresponded with the former Spanish ambassador to Paris, the marquis de Mirabel, who had become a senior diplomat in Brussels. By any yardstick of cloak-and-dagger activities, it was ridiculously amateur. The queen regularly retired to the convent of Val-de-Grace, south-west of Notre Dame, ostensibly for meditation. If a casket stood on the terrace, this was a sign that a letter had arrived for her. It would be brought to Anne's devotional cell at the convent, where she waited with Pierre La Porte, whose official duty was to be responsible for her portmanteau. The skills of this confidential secretary of noble blood evidently ran to codes as well as clothes, as La Porte both decoded Mirabel's dispatches and encoded the queen's replies, which he then slipped through a grille and into the safe hands of secretary Ogier at the British embassy, who would forward them to Brussels in the diplomatic pouch.

Alerted by his agents to what might be happening, Richelieu reported his suspicions to the king. The convent was raided, but nothing significant was found. Louis then decided on 'his own accord' to arrest La Porte and sent his Musketeers to spring the trap. On 10 August five Musketeers led by ensign Goulart, their tabards hidden beneath their cloaks, seized the queen's manservant in the street without warning and bundled him into a coach. Reinforced by another fifteen Musketeers, they escorted him to the Bastille. When La Porte was searched, he was found to be carrying a letter from Anne to Marie de Chevreuse. Once alerted, Richelieu decided to question La Porte himself in the equally forbidding environment of the Palais-Cardinal. The letter referred to Marie's intention to make a secret visit to Anne in Paris, damaging but not damning, and despite the cardinal's best efforts, no amount of threats or bribes could induce La Porte to betray his mistress. After five hours of interrogation he was taken back to the Bastille, at one o'clock in the morning. La Porte was shown an order from the king to put him to the Question, a brutal form of interrogation that began by forcing gallons of water down the victim's throat and ended with their bones being crunched in a wooden casing. A sergeant, La Briere, escorted La Porte to the lowest level in the prison and confronted him with the hideous apparatus: its planks, wedges and cords. But he still refused to talk and the order was never carried out.

La Porte had usually resided at the Hôtel de Chevreuse, Marie's grand house in Paris. When his rooms were searched, another partly encoded letter was found in a hiding-place behind the plaster, addressed to Mirabel in Brussels. Its contents were innocuous but showed clearly that Anne was in regular communication with several different parties in the Spanish government.

The king, hunting at Chantilly, north of Paris, summoned his queen to the chateau there but then declined to see her. Anne, in a state of terror, could neither eat nor sleep and was twice bled by physicians. The highest law officer in the land, Chancellor Pierre Séguier, arrogant, ruthlessly opportunistic, the cardinal's unquestioning vassal from top to toe, arrived to question the queen. No sooner had she denied corresponding with the Spanish than he produced the intercepted letter to Mirabel. Anne, muddle headed at the best of times, impulsively seized the parchment and hid it in her bosom, whereupon Séguier sprang forward to retrieve it. He searched Anne 'like a common criminal' for further documents, his hands lingering on her breasts far longer than was necessary. That the chancellor dared to violate the queen in such a fashion showed Anne the danger she was in.

On 15 August the queen received Holy Communion, and sent her principal secretary, Le Gras, to tell the cardinal that she swore by the Blessed Sacrament she had not had any dealings with foreign courts. She gave similar assurances to the king's confessor, Père Caussin. However, the cardinal already knew differently; another letter from Anne had been intercepted. It warned that a certain priest in Richelieu's employ was on his way to Spain. It was not of course 'authentic proof' of her 'treacherous correspondence with the enemy', but in matters of state Richelieu thought 'persuasive inference must sometimes be held to be sufficient.'

The cardinal told the queen that, if she would confess

everything, the king would forgive and forget. But after Anne reluctantly made further admissions, Louis showed no signs of doing either. He wanted the queen arrested on a charge of high treason and had to be dissuaded by Séguier, who said such a move 'would damage the prestige of the monarchy and be prejudicial to the dignity of the crown'. Louis reluctantly settled for much less. On 17 August, upon his specific instructions, Anne had to write out a full confession exactly as it was dictated to her, culminating in a promise to cease all such treasonable activities. However, the king showed his continuing distrust by forbidding the queen to visit Val-de-Grace or other convents, or to write any more letters except in the presence of one of her ladies-in-waiting, the marquise de Lansac, who was in Richelieu's pay.

The king now turned his attention to Marie de Chevreuse. The duchess, interviewed at Tours, was offered a pardon in return for a full confession, but gave little away. The queen, back in Paris, had arranged to warn her if she faced arrest. The signal was to be the gift of a copy of the Book of Hours. If it had a green binding, all was well, but if the binding were red the duchess should look at once to her own safety. With rumours rife of Anne's own imminent disgrace, Mademoiselle de Hautefort sent her distant relation, the baron de Chambelay, to Tours. On 5 September Marie de Chevreuse received from him the book with a red binding, the fatal colour, and a verbal message from the queen that said starkly 'she must escape, somehow or other; if she did not, she was lost, and would be arrested the following morning.'

In the parlance of the time, Anne was *deux doigts de sa perte*, a fingertip or two from disaster. What may have prompted her to take the huge risk of alerting the duchess was the fear that she would be forced to reveal far more about the queen's treasonable communications with Spain. Marie de Chevreuse took heed of Anne's warning and left Tours immediately. After an adventurous journey south, mainly on rough tracks, she escaped across the Spanish frontier dressed as a boy. She made her way to Madrid, and found a warm place of safety: the King of Spain's bed.

François VI, duc de La Rochefoucauld, an ally of the queen and one of Marie's many lovers, acknowledged that the duchess' dramatic disappearance 'inspired the king and the cardinal with the gravest suspicions that they had not, after all, fathomed her majesty's treachery'. Hearing rumours that she was about to be repudiated, or worse, and confined at Le Havre, the queen suggested to La Rochefoucauld that he should 'kidnap' her and Marie de Hautefort and carry them off to Brussels. La Rochefoucauld, however, soon had problems of his own. Under well-founded suspicion of helping the duchesse de Chevreuse to escape from Richelieu's clutches, he was summoned to Paris in late October and sent to the Bastille for eight days.

Already languishing in the Bastille was another of the queen's allies, the chevalier de Jars, the discomforts of his stay alleviated by regular gifts from his family, brought by a serving maid. None of the guards noticed when the maid's role was assumed by Mademoiselle de Hautefort, dressed in a shabby hooded cloak and disguised with theatrical make-up. She carried a series of letters for La Porte from the queen, passing them on each occasion through the visitors' grille to Jars, whose room was directly above La Porte's dark cell, but with two floors and ceilings between them. Jars knocked a hole through to the room below and persuaded its inmate to do the same, thereby gaining access to La Porte on the still lower floor. But on Richelieu's orders, La Porte was carefully watched day and night by a guard who even slept in his cell. Just one brief interval occurred daily, when the guard empted the earthenware pot containing La Porte's *nécessités naturelles*; each time the turnkey was absent from the cell, tipping the contents of the chamber pot over the Bastille's outside wall and no doubt taking the opportunity to answer a call of nature of his own, the queen's messages were lowered and La Porte's replies raised on a rope.

By this stratagem, Anne and La Porte got their stories straight but the queen was still in great danger. Marie de Chevreuse's last advice to her before taking flight had been succinct and to the point: '*sois enceinte*', 'become pregnant'. As the mother of a dauphin, Anne would be safe. However, this was far easier said than done. She would not contemplate a relationship with anyone in Richelieu's orbit, or, as past events had shown, with someone whom she did not find physically attractive. But by November 1637, even though surrounded by spies, the queen had acquired a paramour. This was quite different to her fleeting liaisons of the past. At thirty-six, judged by the infant mortality rates of the time, Anne was generally thought past child-bearing age. In order to conceive, to satisfy the burning biological urge to procreate, she needed to find a sexual partner and, according to a widely believed old midwives' tale, to reach orgasm in the process.

This recurring image of concupiscence, of eager passionate intercourse with a secret lover, has been difficult for some historians to accept, even when confronted with the circumstantial evidence of Anne's past indiscretions and the likelihood of her subsequent extramarital sexual relationship with Mazarin. Antonia Fraser observed that if it were indeed true, 'this apparently pious woman who continued to take communion frequently was an outrageous hypocrite', as this compounded what was already considered to be a mortal sin. Anne would not have seen it that way. The French ruling classes had always been able to compartmentalize their actions so effectively that they fervently believed even their most extreme breaches of God's law could be assuaged afterwards by prayer and repentance. Was it not the queen's duty to provide France with an heir, however far the means transgressed the most sacred rules of the Catholic Church? Given Anne's undeniable willingness on different occasions to swear by all that was holy that she had not committed potentially treasonable activities (which alas were proven facts), such a flawed rationalization – what Levi calls the 'baroque . . . casuist case' – probably would have come easily to her.

The queen's real difficulty was not spiritual but practical.

If she were to produce a child, the king's physical proximity was essential around the moment of conception in order to legitimize it. However, as far as royal protocol permitted, they were leading separate lives, often in separate palaces. Even while nominally together, their waking hours were as if they occupied different time zones: the king would go to bed early and rise at dawn to go hunting; the queen would eat close to midnight after the Spanish fashion, stay up for several hours more, and remain asleep for most of the morning. When the quasi-official court *Gazette* reported the couple's arrival at Saint-Germain on 9 November, it omitted to mention that the queen would occupy the old chateau and the king the new. Perhaps such an oversight occurred because this was not at all unusual: Louis had consistently opted for the new chateau for most of his reign, preferring the wonderful view across the valley towards Paris, its cool breezes, lack of formality and proximity to the stables. No one close to the king and queen believed they ever shared a bed at Saint-Germain during 1637. Indeed, the idea of Louis suddenly one winter night deciding to sleep with Anne was almost unthinkable and would have caused chaos. Protocol would have demanded that his Swiss Guard turn out at the new chateau long after they had gone off duty, hand over their sovereign to the care of the Musketeers, then hurry ahead of the escort, uphill for more than 500 metres, in order to receive him back into their charge on the solitary bridge across the moat, the only entrance to the old chateau. The king would also have needed to negotiate by candlelight the excrement-ridden bumpy ground between the chateaux, regularly used by those too lazy to walk to the latrines.

On 1 December the queen returned to the Louvre, while Louis travelled south-west to Crosne, an attractive riverside chateau in the middle of forest land, one of his favourite hunting grounds. Here he remained for five days, oblivious to the fact that during his absence, for Anne, in Paris, the critical moment had arrived. The tiny circle who probably knew of her efforts to conceive included Henri-Auguste de Loménie, comte de Brienne, always willing for her to take 'as a lover a cavalier at court'. Brienne was a master 'of diplomacy and intrigue', 'in constant and often intimate contact with the highest affairs and some of the deepest secrets of the realm'. He also had a reputation for making, with apparent impunity, candid remarks to kings and queens that others dared not make. Seeing Anne's 'demeanour and the look in her eyes', at the 'beginning of December' he blurted out, 'Madame, it occurs to me you might be pregnant: is it true?' Considering her constant need to dissemble, the queen had the singularly unfortunate habit of blushing wildly whenever someone hit upon the truth. Her face went bright red, leaving Brienne in no doubt that she was.

It was now imperative that Anne shared a bed with her husband to legitimise the pregnancy, and here she received help from an unexpected quarter, Louise de La Fayette. Buffeted from every side in the power struggle at court, Louise found the pressure too much to bear and decided to take the veil. On 19 May she had entered the Paris convent of Sainte-Marie de la Visitation as Sister Angélique. The king, however, was not ready to relinquish completely the fruit he found so reassuringly forbidden. According to the marquis de Monglat, grand master of the royal garderobe, the king visited Louise once a week for many months, so frequently that the mother superior misread his intentions and invited him in vain to attend upon the novice privately in the convent's inner sanctum, the clausura. On 5 December Louis went to see Louise at the convent, passing on the way to Paris his intended overnight destination, Saint-Maur-des-Fossés, a village standing on a loop in the river Marne. Its nondescript chateau overlooking the river belonged to the Condé family, with whom Louis was not always on the best of terms, and his plan to return there that particular evening may have been influenced by the weather. In accordance with the custom of the time, the king's furniture, baggage, butlers and cooks – *'officiers de sa bouche'* – moved from venue to venue; and the road north of Crosne was particularly slow for wheeled traffic. They could reach Saint-Maur that day, but no further.

Anne, meanwhile, was starting from Paris in the opposite direction, hopeful perhaps that the chateau's limited facilities would compel Louis to spend a night in the same apartment as his queen. La Porte, who had been moved to a more comfortable cell at the Bastille, heard a drumbeat outside his window. A turnkey told him the drummer was marking time for the Musketeers on escort duty, marching beneath Sainte Antoine's Gate, and that the court was to visit Saint-Maur. This was so rare a happening that La Porte believed its main purpose could only be to incarcerate Anne en route, in the prison of Vincennes. Allowed to exercise in the roof garden of the Bastille, La Porte immediately went aloft and caught sight of the queen's coach in the rue de Sainte Antoine, directly opposite the convent of Sainte-Marie de la Visitation. Anne briefly alighted under some pretext, and was able to signal surreptitiously to La Porte that all was well, and perhaps more besides.

Whether the queen was turned back on the orders of the king, or persuaded by her courtiers that the deteriorating conditions made the journey dangerous, her cortege did not get far from Paris; before long, she returned to the Louvre. Louis, meanwhile, had reached Sainte-Marie de la Visitation on horseback and spent three hours there in conversation with Sister Angélique. When he emerged from the convent in the gloom of late afternoon, the weather had taken a turn for the worse. Driving snow and gusts of wind were making it impossible to keep lit the flares needed to light the way. The king decided to take shelter and wait for the storm to pass. He felt he could not go to the Louvre: his own apartments had not a stick of furniture and the roof immediately above them leaked badly.

Anne heard of the king's predicament and seized the opportunity. She sent the captain of her guard, François de Comminges de Guitaut, to see Louis. Guitaut, 'who was accustomed to speaking freely with the king', suffered badly from gout. He also had a painful leg injury caused when a pistol had misfired, so Louis may have been unusually patient with him. The king received Guitaut no fewer than four times, at first politely declining his persistent suggestion that His Majesty join the queen at the Louvre, where 'he would find in her quarters supper and lodging prepared.' On the fourth occasion, with the storm still showing no signs of abating, Louis objected with rather less conviction, on the grounds that the queen took her dinner much later than he did. When Guitaut assured him that Anne would dine much earlier than usual that evening, the king gave way. He was in no position to refuse, already chronically sick with tuberculosis, the illness that would prove fatal six years later.

Of the night that legitimized the future Louis XIV, nothing is known beyond the fact that the queen's servants arranged for a double bolster to be placed on the bed shared by the royal couple. As Anne was already pregnant, it seems unlikely that she tried to stimulate Louis or encourage him to attempt intercourse, for which the only circumstantial evidence was of past unremitting failure; it is equally implausible that the ailing king took the initiative himself. Louis continually ostracized his queen, seeing her as a traitor to France; and he was an active homosexual, with no interest in intimacy with women. Historian Auguste Bailly made a particular study of the relationship and concluded that Louis had for Anne a 'prodigious physical coldness bordering on repulsion'.

This bizarre episode at the Louvre was the fig leaf that Anne needed. It could no longer be proved that Louis was not the father of her unborn child. However tempted he may have been to repudiate it, Louis' desire to prevent Gaston's succession at all costs eventually prevailed. He may also have preferred the humiliation of being cuckolded to the humiliation of being thought of as the monarch who would never be a man.

When the campaigning season began in 1638 the king once again joined his troops fighting the Spanish on France's northern frontier, but returned from Picardy to Saint-Germain three times in the first half of August in anticipation of the imminent birth. Anne's child was originally expected by 10 August, rather too early for it to have been conceived on the previous 5 December. The most likely date of conception was between 14 and 17 November. Told by the doctors it would be healthier for the infant, Louis' only concession was to hand over his cherished new chateau at Saint-Germain for use by the queen. On 20 August, as Anne still showed no sign of contractions, Louis decided to visit Versailles, then a small hunting lodge. From there he wrote a letter of complaint to Richelieu about the delay in Anne going into labour, as though the cardinal could somehow alter the natural process of nature. 'I am out of sympathy with all women,' he told the cardinal, 'it doesn't matter who they are.' The king remained at Versailles for three days before resuming his vigil at Saint-Germain; upon finding the queen apparently no further advanced, thereby preventing his return to the front, he sent another ill-humoured missive to the cardinal and shouted at Anne in the presence of her ladies-in-waiting. On 25 August Mademoiselle de Hautefort reported that the queen was 'excessively large and uncomfortable', indicating that she was well past her term.

Three days previously, Gaston had arrived at Saint-Germain with a heavy heart. To keep his spirits up, Gaston's cronies confidently forecast the infant would be a girl and under the French rules of succession unable to claim the throne. For a fortnight, with the child still awaited, Gaston hid his private agonies behind a veneer of calm and good cheer, his thick black eyebrows rising and falling as he joked with the queen's ladies.

Anne finally began her contractions shortly after 5 a.m. on the morning of 5 September. Gaston and the other designated witnesses to the royal birth, including Chancellor Séguier, the Princess de Conti, the comtesse de Soissons and the duchesse de Vendôme, were abruptly awoken. They assembled in the ante-room of the queen's chamber, knowing that their role would subsequently be to testify, if necessary, that no changeling had replaced the royal infant. Anne's labour was hard but gave no real cause for concern until shortly before the birth, when the king callously told Marie de Hautefort, 'I shall be happy if the child can be saved. You, Madame, can worry about the mother.' The royal midwife, Dame Perronet, was under instructions to ensure that Gaston stood beside the queen's bed and saw what she could see, in all its gynaecological detail. As the child emerged from its mother, at 11.22 a.m., the midwife held him high and triumphantly drew the displaced heir's attention to the tiny penis of the future Louis XIV. Gaston reluctantly professed himself satisfied that the infant had indeed emerged from between the queen's bloodstained thighs but added spitefully, as a parting shot, that he did not know who the Devil had put it in.

After shedding floods of tears at his chateau of Limours in the Ile de France, Gaston seriously considered challenging the parentage of the dauphin but, as always, lacked the courage to act. With the future of France at stake, everyone who knew the truth had a vested interest in concealing it. La Porte may have been among the very few who possessed every piece of the jigsaw. His courage never failed him, and he had been released from the Bastille on 12 May, on condition that he went into exile at Saumur. Anne's son was indeed, as La Porte wryly observed, 'the child of my silence'.

Richelieu took care not to be around during the anxious wait for the child's arrival, residing successively at Abbeville, Amiens, Ham and Saint-Quentin. The cardinal wrote a congratulatory note to the king and queen from Saint-Quentin but, the *Gazette* reported, did not put in a personal appearance at Saint-Germain until 2 October. After the birth the king also spent as much time away from Saint-Germain as he could, visiting Chantilly, Versailles, Saint-Maur successfully at last, Grosbois and Richelieu himself at his country house at Rueil. Even judged by the traditions of the time, by no stretch of the imagination could this be described as the normal conduct of a new and devoted parent.

Richelieu's informants were everywhere and the ban on outsiders entering the queen's apartments, introduced back in 1626, had never been rescinded, all but eliminating most of the plausible candidates to be Louis XIV's real father. Anne's household chamberlain, the comte de la Rivière, and the captain of her guard, Guitaut, were briefly mentioned by court gossips as possibilities, but both were elderly men that possessed little physical appeal. Only the sharp eyes of La Rochefoucauld noticed the one man who was stationed at the palace of Saint-Germain around the time of her conception, was almost above suspicion, could come and go as he pleased and had the charisma to make him, for the queen, a worthy successor to Montmorency and Buckingham. He was none other than the captain of the King's Musketeers, Tréville.

Unless caught in flagrante, Anne was now untouchable, but her household was not. Richelieu rewarded his ally the marquise de Lanzac with the post of governess to the dauphin, 'precisely because he knew this would anger the queen'. He had the comte de Brassac made superintendent of her household, and his wife Catherine first lady of honour, the senior position among the fourteen ladies-in-waiting, both with instructions to report to him almost daily. Louis willingly created the vacancy by removing Marie de Hautefort from the court, sending a servant to her with a terse note of dismissal, for daring to make common cause with the queen. Like La Porte, she was dispatched to Saumur, then to stay with her grandmother in Metz, followed by a posse of eager suitors despite her disgrace.

No one knew more about the queen's pregnancy than Mademoiselle de Hautefort and within weeks of her departure, her sister, Mademoiselle d'Escars, became a *fille d'honneur* to the queen and her younger brother, le comte de Montignac, a cadet in a leading regiment, was promoted to King's Musketeer. Two simultaneous favours for her family, one from Anne, the other from Tréville, were highly significant and represented something of a risk: Richelieu was not noted for believing in coincidences.

2

A GASCON GOES TO PARIS

The queen's secret lover, Jean-Arnaud de Peyrer, called
Tréville, came from Béarn, the most distant province of
France, a sparsely populated land beneath the western
Pyrenees. It was rugged country of fierce rivers, mountain
passes, spectacular gorges and dense forests of oak, which
superstitious peasants believed to be inhabited by werewolves
and vampires. The real wolves, though, were hazard enough,
hunting in packs and relentlessly picking off domestic animals
or small children unwise enough to stray. At night, man and
beast huddled together inside their bastides, fortified hamlets
with earth walls, linked by rough tracks.

The poorest peasants existed barely above subsistence level,
amidst dirt and stench in windowless hovels of cob, dried mud
and thatch. They were constantly hungry. Their cultivated
ground, created by hewing back the trees, was hard and poor,
producing crops only by dint of backbreaking effort. Even many
skilled workers, like the potter, the miller or the blacksmith,
were oppressed by taxes and almost destitute. If that were
not bad enough, discharged mercenaries, 'the flotsam of war,
riddled with pox and fit only for the gibbet', terrorized the local
population and stole their meagre possessions.

For their own safety, the lords of these wretched manors lived
high above their domains, in ancient chateaux that had seen
much better days. Constantly repaired rather than rebuilt, their
walls were a bizarre patchwork of masonry, the cracks filled and
refilled with sub-standard mortar, their red, light-tiled roofs

constantly leaking through the gaps left by missing slates. No larger than modest modern country houses, they were bolstered by a series of higgledy-piggledy appendages such as a barn or a bake house, a wine press or a butter store. The ground floor consisted of a gloomy, damp, open space, with a long oak table and chairs, and tiny rooms leading off where cooking pots were stored and servants slept. Their aristocratic masters spent most of their lives on the sparsely furnished but drier upper floor, reached by an oak staircase.

Oak, and the labour to carve it, was cheap. It needed to be because many nobles, though spared the abject poverty of many of their subjects, were themselves miserably poor, forced to sell off land and titles to survive. They found willing buyers among the local artisans and petty bourgeoisie when, under Henry IV, the first Béarnais king of France, commerce expanded rapidly. Among these people was Jean de Peyrer, who came from a humble family of millers and stonemasons. He established himself as an architect, building several fine houses in Pau, and later as a prosperous trader. In September 1607 he secured for 15,000 livres the *seigneurie* of Troisvilles. These grand-sounding 'trois villes' or 'three towns' in the Soule valley were in fact three tiny hamlets, Alcabéhéty, Etchebar and Lichans; but if insignificant in size, they gave Jean de Peyrer a place on the bottom rung of the French aristocracy.

Under French law the oldest male child inherited everything left by his father and Peyrer's youngest son, Jean-Arnaud, born at Oloron in Béarn late in 1598, knew that he had to make his own way in life. In 1616, at the age of seventeen, he resolved to claim the single privilege granted him by virtue of his father's meagre title: to be received at court. Jean de Peyrer, however, wanted him to remain in Béarn and seems to have made the journey north as uncomfortable as possible for his son. Jean-Arnaud left for Paris *pédestrement*, that is, without any kind of horse, carrying on foot a battered small valise and wearing a borrowed sword that was too long for him and kept bumping against his calves. On his arrival at Saint-Germain, courtiers mocked his patched clothing, his chronic lack of funds and his heavy Béarnais accent: the way Jean-Arnaud de Troisvilles pronounced 'Troisvilles' ensured that his name quickly and permanently became 'Tresville' or 'Tréville' to everyone else. It said a good deal for Tréville's resilience and persistence that he was eventually accepted as a gentleman cadet in one of the Régiments des Gardes. He saw his first action on 24 March 1617, at the opening of the siege of the Château de Pierrefonds, near Soissons.

Lacking any alternative means of advancement, Tréville took almost suicidal risks to be noticed. Promotions were rarely rewarded after military reverses, but in September 1621, when the forces of the king failed to take the Huguenot stronghold of Montauban, Marshal François de Bassompierre was so struck by Tréville's courage under fire that he recommended him to Louis XIII for a commission as ensign in the Navarre regiment. To their surprise, Tréville turned down the offer, gambling that he would achieve the same promotion in the Guards before long, which he did in October 1622, after the fall of Montpellier. But he already had his eye on an elite force formed that year and armed with muskets – the King's Musketeers. Mindful that his father Henry IV had died by an assassin's dagger in a Paris street, Louis created the Musketeers to ensure his safety, if needs be at the expense of their own lives. They accompanied the monarch on official visits, escorted him on military campaigns, and manned the perimeter night and day wherever he slept.

It took Tréville three years to gain a place in the Musketeers, with the rank of cornette. He fought with them during the fourteen-month siege of the Huguenot stronghold of La Rochelle from August 1627 to October 1628, receiving both a promotion to sous-lieutenant and a serious injury – possibly incurred during an unwise picnic under fire – that obliged him to convalesce in Béarn.

Tréville returned to active service in 1629 just in time to join a French expedition across the Alps, led personally by Louis and Cardinal Richelieu, with the object of seizing control of the key passes into Italy. On 6 March the king, delayed by a fierce storm near Grenoble, rode all night to join his army and watched his Musketeers lead the main attack at dawn on the Pas de Suze, the gateway to Savoy. They achieved almost complete surprise and Tréville had an audience of both monarch and cardinal for his latest feat of arms. Pushing ahead at a furious pace in the snow and ice, he almost captured the opposing commander, the Duke of Savoy himself. One of the duke's senior officers, Jean Cerbelloni, captain-general of the Spanish artillery, tried to intervene and Tréville left him bleeding on the frozen ground after a fierce exchange. Tréville, although also wounded, resumed his pursuit of the duke, who was lucky to escape. For this glittering exploit, Tréville was feted at court and promoted to lieutenant.

During the French invasion of Lorraine in 1632, Tréville again led a charge by the Musketeers, overwhelming a much larger force, two Spanish regiments defending the town of Rouvroy, with the ferocity of the attack. According to Bassompierre, it was this spectacular success that decided Louis XIII to make Tréville captain of his Musketeers, following the death of the incumbent, the marquis de Montalet, from wounds received at the battle of Castelnaudry in September. There was predictable opposition at court, where several nobles wanted the post, normally for sale at 200,000 livres, a huge sum completely beyond Tréville's means. As an expedient the king appointed Vieilchastel, the head of the royal household who had little experience of military matters, as acting captain of the Musketeers; but in October 1634, after the fuss had died down, Vieilchastel was consoled with a governorship and Louis confirmed Tréville in the post.

The official historiographer, Scipion Dupleix, hastened to provide an explanation for what was by any yardstick an extraordinary departure from tradition: 'This favour astonished nobody,' said Dupleix, 'for M. de Troisvilles, by his own merit, has acquired a splendid reputation in the army.' However, Dupleix was in his dotage and deaf as a post, the least likely to spot the obvious. As at the very least Louis' 'sexual orientation was the subject of widespread comment', most courtiers firmly believed Tréville had gone to bed with the king to secure his high office, but Tréville already had an illegitimate daughter and there is no evidence that he remained anything other than resolutely heterosexual. The once penniless petitioner from Béarn now had a formidable salary of 16,800 livres a year, to which in 1635 Louis added the governor's stipend from three small towns in Picardy, purely titular posts. Thirty-six years old, a handsome and wealthy bachelor, Tréville was seen as a considerable catch, particularly among the queen's ladies-in-waiting. Shrewdly, he chose not the best looking but the one with the largest dowry and an impeccable noble pedigree, Anne de Guillon des Essarts, whose father was a king's counsellor and controller general of artillery. They married on 3 February 1637 and thereafter, courtesy of his plain, innocent and unsuspecting wife, Tréville had easy access to Anne of Austria; as effective head of royal security, he was one of the few whose presence near her palace apartments could easily be accounted for. Louis does not appear to have harboured any suspicions that by the autumn his own captain of Musketeers might be a welcome visitor to his wife's bed. On 25 October he wrote to tell Tréville how satisfied he was with the services 'Monsieur de Trois Villes' was rendering him.

Tréville's favoured status at court had its roots in the complex relationship between the king and Cardinal Richelieu. Louis wanted to be seen as a great monarch and recognized, however grudgingly, that this could only be achieved with Richelieu at the helm. But he did not have the temperament to accept this gracefully and was subject to periodic unpredictable displays of jealousy and petulant resentment. The cardinal knew that his power flowed from the king and was the master of earnest, or perhaps not so earnest, protestations of humble devotion to his majesty. For all his outward tact and subtlety of speech, however, Richelieu could never completely suppress his sense of irony and his effortless air of superiority that infuriated almost everyone, including Louis himself. The Musketeers were for the king his one outward manifestation of independence from the cardinal. By choosing in Tréville a captain who owed everything to the monarch and nothing to Richelieu, and whom Richelieu, given the opportunity, would never have chosen, the king could maintain the illusion that it was he who was really in control.

If the cardinal had been content to allow Louis to keep the sense of majesty and unique privilege that came from possessing and parading an elite bodyguard, all might have been well. Instead, Richelieu set out to emulate and surpass it, thereby placing himself on a dangerous collision course with the king. He may have been driven at first by a genuine fear of becoming a victim of violence, a serious risk from August 1624, when he took over the running of the royal council. By 1626, at least three plots to assassinate him had been discovered and foiled. Louis reluctantly recognized this by granting the cardinal the right 'to keep close to his person fifty men on horseback together with their officers, all chosen by him'.

However, Richelieu also realized that he urgently needed his own men to enforce the ban on duelling, a subject of passionate interest to the cardinal, profoundly affected by the death of his own brother in a duel that he fought on Richelieu's behalf. But the cardinal also believed it was central to the issue of state authority. Duelling in seventeenth-century France was a way of life and, for those lacking skill or luck, also a way of death. It had become endemic, a part of the national psyche, and had spiralled out of control. 'Do you know who fought yesterday?' was the most common opening topic of conversation. Laws against duelling, created in successive reigns, were disregarded by the dissident nobility with 'insolent distain'. In 1626 Richelieu persuaded Louis to issue a fresh edict, one that was much more specific and more easily enforceable. It made two particular circumstances punishable by death: duels where a fatality occurred, and multiple duels – increasingly commonplace – where the seconds assisting the principal protagonists also duelled with one another.

As the cardinal anticipated, the nobles saw duelling and its code of honour as one of their few remaining privileges and would not relinquish it easily. François, comte de Bouteville-Montmorency, self-styled champion dueller of France, soon put Richelieu's resolve to the test. The arrogant, handsome and daring count, the darling of the nobility, had won at least twenty-one duels in thirteen years. He ran a fencing school from his house in Paris and had given his name to an ingenious reverse sword-thrust of his own creation, against which there was no known defence. On 12 May 1627 he fought a duel against François d'Harcourt, baron de Beuvron, not, as was traditional, early in the morning in the secluded meadows of the Pré-aux-Clercs on the south side of the Seine, but at 2 p.m. right under the cardinal's own windows in the place Royale, the newest and most fashionable square in Paris. Their seconds fought as well, and one was fatally wounded, ending the duel prematurely and thereby making it a capital offence on both counts.

Beuvron fled to England. Bouteville was soon arrested but believed that Richelieu would not dare to execute a Montmorency, one of the leading families in France. He was wrong. The cardinal persuaded an anguished Louis, who would have preferred to avoid a decision, to refuse clemency, much to the outrage of his family. At 5 p.m. on 22 June, Bouteville was publicly beheaded in another Paris square, the place de Grève. Richelieu took extraordinary precautions to prevent a rescue. Chains were stretched across the adjoining streets, and the cardinal's new bodyguard controlled the checkpoints, with orders not to 'allow any man on a horse to pass'.

As with everything else, Richelieu set exacting standards for his personal troop. They had to be more than twenty-five years old, and to have served at least three years in the army. Unlike most soldiers, who went home between campaigns, each recruit was given a full-time indefinite contract. They were all professionals, not gentlemen, and extremely well paid. A captain received a stipend of 10,000 livres per year, a lieutenant 6,000, a man in the ranks more than 2,000. Père Joseph, charged with finding suitable officers, with perhaps unconscious irony told a friend they were 'worth their weight in gold'.

The cardinal did not keep to the limit on his bodyguard set by the king. He trained at his own expense another thirty men, 'put under arms for reasons of state', whose only task was to protect him 'from the hatred of many enemies'. In 1631, having survived the Queen Mother's attempt to remove him from office, the cardinal won a further concession from the king, the right to raise a company of light horse, 120 strong. These were the direct equivalent of the Musketeers, recruited from the ranks of the lesser nobility. Unlike the Musketeers, however, they were not exposed to the hazards of the war with Spain. Within a year Louis gave permission for Richelieu to recruit an additional 100 men at arms, who would fight for him at the front during the summer campaigns. This led to complaints to the king that while Tréville and his Musketeers huddled under fire in the trenches, the Cardinal's Guard 'sat in the shade at their barracks', or 'at the door' of Richelieu's bedchamber. Any caller upon the cardinal had to pass five separate checks by his men.

Richelieu went everywhere with a large escort, and even ordered his Guards to accompany him into the main courtyard at Saint-Germain. This was a serious breach of protocol when visiting the king, which the Musketeers at first prevented by drawing their swords. Eventually, however, a small phalanx of Richelieu's Guard was allowed to follow on his heels as far as the *cabinet du roi*, passing between two lines of glowering Musketeers. This annoyed Louis, but he was much angrier when one evening he visited Richelieu in his new Palais-Cardinal, down the street from the Louvre, and saw the huge panoply of Guards scurrying about in their new uniforms. The cardinal's personal vanity ensured that he spent lavishly on full-length scarlet tunics with white crosses, while the Musketeers still had to make do with blue tabards decorated with silver crosses, worn over their ordinary clothes. 'Go ahead of me,' Louis snapped at the cardinal, who was trying to give him precedence. 'You are evidently more king here than I am.' Richelieu, seizing a burning torch from one of his retainers, saved the day with a quick-witted reply. 'I will, sire, but only to light your way.'

In 1634 the cardinal responded to Tréville's controversial appointment by making an equally controversial one of his own as captain of his Guard, François Dauger de Cavoie. At one time Cavoie had seemed destined for a life of obscurity as the chamberlain to the Montmorency household in Paris. He saw at first hand the execution of its most flamboyant member, Bouteville, for flouting the edict against duelling. Far from abandoning his sword, however, over the next few years Cavoie took part in several duels himself, assuming Bouteville's mantle. He was fortunate that Richelieu was looking for a firebrand to force the Musketeers into a fight. There could be no doubt that Richelieu knew all about his activities. Cavoie's formidable skill with the sword had left his most recent opponent, a certain Valençay, disarmed and helpless, and perhaps as a subtle way of seeking revenge, Valençay wrote to the cardinal recommending his services.

Cavoie and Tréville had much more in common than just a turbulent temperament. Both were the younger sons of minor nobles, both had distinguished themselves in army campaigns and each married a lady-in-waiting to the queen. In Cavoie's case, however, it was an undoubted love match: he captured the heart of a young widow, Marie de Lort de Serignan. After his elevation by the cardinal, they lived next to the Palais-Royal in a grand apartment on the rue des Bon-Enfants, an appropriate enough address for the eleven baptismal certificates in the parish of Saint-Eustace recording the birth of their eleven children, nine of whom, six boys and three girls, survived into adulthood. Like Tréville with his absentee governorships, Cavoie was benefiting from the power of patronage. In March 1639, at Richelieu's behest, Louis granted Cavoie, in partnership with the marquis de Montbrun, who ran the actual business, a monopoly on sedan chairs. This was a far more lucrative favour than it might initially appear, because sedan chairs had recently been introduced from England, and were in huge demand among the aristocracy, especially in Paris.

As Tréville's influence at court increased, Richelieu tried to make his life as uncomfortable as possible. The cardinal poached the Musketeers' head cook, offering him 400 livres a year, at least three times the going rate, to prepare meals for his own men instead. He encouraged the comte de Chavigny to propose that the cardinal's mounted Guards should protect the king instead of the Musketeers whenever he went hunting or elsewhere on horseback, and berated the count for his timidity when Louis rejected the idea out of hand. In June 1639, having persuaded the king to send most of his Musketeers ahead of him to the siege of Hesdin, Richelieu wrote to the French commander, the marquis de La Meilleraye, suggesting that Tréville and his troop could be deployed in a dangerous part of the siege lines.

The cardinal put forward his own protégé, Henri Coiffier de Ruzé, marquis de Cinq-Mars, hoping he would replace Tréville in the king's favour. Cinq-Mars was the son of one of Richelieu's most reliable supporters, and after his father's death he had been brought up in the cardinal's household, where he seemed devoted to his patron. Richelieu knew exactly what he was doing by introducing the handsome young marquis at court. Sure enough, Louis fell for Cinq-Mars and in November made him Grand Écuyer, responsible for the wholesale movement of the court from one palace to another, at the absurdly young age of nineteen. Tallemant reported that the king loved Cinq-Mars '*éperdument*', 'to distraction', could not keep his hands off the pretty young man and that they spent the afternoons naked in bed together.

Unfortunately, the title that went with the job, 'Monsieur le Grand', also went to Cinq-Mars' head and in some respects to his feet, as he used gifts of money from Louis to buy 300 pairs of boots. Cinq-Mars took advantage of the king's slavish attachment to him and made increasingly outlandish demands. They even began to exchange formal notes regulating their behaviour towards each other, as though they were equals, ignoring the proprieties of courtly etiquette. Whether this provoked the queen to resume her relationship with Tréville, or whether it had simply continued undetected, by December Anne had once again conceived. With much less at stake now that France already had an heir, there were no frantic efforts afterwards to ensure that Louis could claim the credit. When he wrote to Richelieu on 23 January 1640, it was to say he was going hunting. Louis gave the cardinal news of his wife's pregnancy – 'we have reason to believe she may be with child' – almost as an afterthought, all but confirming it had nothing to do with him. Five days later, no doubt prompted by Richelieu, the *Gazette* casually announced that the queen was pregnant and that the king had made a conjugal visit on Christmas evening, after 'ordering his pillow' to be placed on her bed. The interval between the alleged conception and its promulgation was suspiciously short and 25 December was probably chosen because it was one of the few days when king and queen both resided at Saint-Germain, as usual in separate châteaux. Anne rarely left the palace, spending all her time with the dauphin; while Louis scarcely went there, dividing his time between various hunting estates and his refurbished apartments at the Louvre. His obsession with Cinq-Mars made any kind of concurrent marital relations with the queen highly unlikely.

Mazarin was also otherwise engaged. On 14 December he left Rome for good, setting out for the French capital via Genoa, by sea. At Civitavecchia, the port of Rome, he embarked fifty 'marble statues and other agreeable objects . . . gifts for his Christian Majesty [Louis XIII], Seigneur Cardinal Richelieu and other grandees at court'. On the journey to Paris, where he arrived on 5 January 1640, conclusively ruling out any contribution on his part to the queen's condition, Mazarin probably had only one kind of naked female form on his mind: inanimate and in a box.

Richelieu may have suspected that Tréville was responsible for Anne's second pregnancy, so restricted was her circle and so few the eligible men that had access to her. But he could do nothing that might also call into question the legitimacy of the dauphin, on whom the future stability of the kingdom depended. Tréville's personal standing with Louis, however, was a different matter entirely. It relied heavily on the reputation of his Musketeers, against whom the cardinal determined to deal a near-fatal blow: nothing less than public humiliation at the hands of his Guards. The confrontation was not difficult to stage-manage, as they were already at each other's throats. With Tréville and Cavoie making little effort to restrain their men whenever they returned to Paris at the end of the campaigning season, incidents involving them multiplied. 'Such was the jealousy between the company of musketeers and that of the guard of Cardinal de Richelieu, that they came to blows every day.'

As the rivalry between Guards and Musketeers intensified, both Tréville and his opposite number, Cavoie, knew it could only end in some kind of duel. However, they must have realized the cardinal could not possibly be seen to condone it and that as a consequence neither of them personally could take part. They both began seeking out men with a reputation for swordplay.

The Guards' newest lieutenant was François de Jussac d'Ambleville, a young noble noted for his aggressive seduction of women. He had a haughty, proud demeanour and a quick and violent temper. Jussac was regarded as intractable and tyrannical by his subordinates but enjoyed considerable success as a duellist. After killing his opponent in a duel early in 1636, Jussac had fled to Brussels to escape arrest, before Cavoie brought him back with the promise of a pardon.

Tréville needed a champion of his own and inevitably looked towards his native Béarn. Here, the frustrated sons of his father's friends, relations and rivals, deprived of any obvious opportunities for advancement, were devoting most of their time to the usual sports of hunting and wenching. A safe distance from the capital, they were also making a considerable name for themselves at the forbidden pursuit of duelling.

Tréville summoned Athos, Aramis and Porthos and made them Musketeers.

Tréville's father, Jean de Peyrer, at one time employed his pretty niece Nicole in his business. She caught the eye of the prosperous Adrien de Sillègue d'Autevielle, whose family owned the tiny riverside villages of Autevielle and Athos. Their son Armand became Athos the Musketeer. Peyrer's brother-in-law Charles had inherited the small village of Amaritz and its chateau. His only son, Henri d'Aramitz, was Aramis the Musketeer. So Tréville and Aramis were first cousins, while Athos was Tréville's first cousin once removed. Isaac de Portau, Porthos the Musketeer, also had family connections with Aramis, another of whose first cousins, Gédéon de Rague, was married to Anne d'Arracq, Porthos' second cousin. They all moved in the same circle of bourgeoisie who had bought their way into the petty nobility. Porthos' father, also called Isaac, notary general of the provincial parliament and a councillor to the king, had joined their social rank by purchasing land further north at Porteu, a hamlet, long disappeared, on the River Vert near Castelfranc, which gave Porthos his name. Porthos kept very quiet the fact that his grandfather Abraham came from the humblest of origins and had been one of Henry IV's cooks.

Tréville sent word first to his blood relatives, Athos and Aramis, probably through a fellow captain, Jean de Rague, who was attending his grandson's baptism in Béarn. All the local nobility were invited to this important social event on 14 April 1640 and Aramis' parents, Charles and Catherine d'Aramitz, had agreed to act as godparents to the child. After receiving Tréville's summons, Aramis and Athos wasted little time; they arrived in Paris in early May. Tréville had discovered that Porthos was already in the capital: a few months earlier Porthos' influential father had arranged for him to enlist in one of the companies of Guards. Tréville would have found little difficulty in detaching him temporarily from his regiment, as Porthos' captain was Tréville's brother-in-law, Alexandre des Essarts.

The majority of Musketeers not from Béarn hailed from

Gascony, the next most distant province of France. To all but themselves, a Gascon was indistinguishable from a Béarnais. They were both easily recognizable, short even in an age of short men, swarthy and sunburned. Most spoke Bernes, an offshoot of the Occitan dialect. Vigorous, shrill and largely incomprehensible to anyone else, it was a language as far removed from French as Dutch or Danish. Together, the Gascons and the Béarnais also had an unsurpassed reputation for embroidering the truth, so much so that *gasconner* became the French word meaning to boast, and a *gasconnade* was the tallest of tall tales.

Gascony, too, had its share of ambitious entrepreneurs with ideas above their station, and impecunious nobles who were prepared to swallow their pride and accept the lower classes as sons-in-law in return for a source of ready cash. These men included Bertrand de Batz, a tax collector and butcher, who in the spring of 1608 married Françoise de Montesquiou d'Artagnan, from one of the great noble families of France. Not that the Montesquious had much option: the wilful Françoise silenced them by becoming pregnant before the ceremony. In all she would have eight children, five boys and three girls: the youngest boy, Charles-Ogier de Batz-Castelmore, would be known to posterity as d'Artagnan.

In June 1635, Bertrand died suddenly, leaving large debts. Françoise was determined not to lose Château Castelmore, the family home, even if this meant that her seven children would have to start earning their keep. D'Artagnan's idyllic childhood, which had included endless fencing matches with his older brothers whenever they returned from the wars, came to an abrupt end. Françoise made him help in the family abattoir at Lupiac and showed him how, in heavy ink-stained ledgers, she reconciled payments received with payments due under the monopoly they enjoyed to levy local taxes. An incurable romantic, dreaming of adventure and glory, d'Artagnan did not see himself in the mundane role of butcher or tax collector, especially as he had come to realize that any commercial occupation demanded at the very least a rudimentary grasp of mathematics. D'Artagnan was hopeless at figures, and could scarcely read or write. Fearful that his wings would be permanently clipped, he decided to fly the nest.

In mid-February 1640, d'Artagnan, aged about seventeen, left his native Gascony for the French capital. It was less of a grand departure, more of an escape at dawn, because he did not have the blessing of his mother, who was implacably opposed to his plan to enlist in the army. Despite that, d'Artagnan's excellent contacts offered him every prospect of a successful military career. Two of his brothers had already served in the Musketeers, and his uncle, Henri de Montesquiou, the newly appointed governor of Bayonne, had been a senior officer in one of the other leading regiments of guards. Henri delighted in undermining his sister's authority and was almost certainly the source of the ten livres d'Artagnan took with him, sufficient to ease the discomfort of his journey.

Like his brothers before him, d'Artagnan borrowed his distinguished noble name from his mother's side of the family, although he had no right to do so. His means of transport, however, undermined his determined efforts to be seen as a person of consequence. His small, yellow steed, the only horse that could be inconspicuously removed from Château Castelmore, was better suited to life before a plough than beneath a bold cavalier. D'Artagnan barely held his fiery Gascon temper in check as the size, shape and colour of his mount provoked frequent ridicule on his expedition north.

This was to have unfortunate consequences at Saint Dié, near Blois, where to save time d'Artagnan had planned to join a barge sailing up the Loire, which was a deep and navigable river in the seventeenth century. Among his prospective fellow passengers waiting on the bank stood the comte de Rosnay, returning from some disreputable mission for Richelieu. Rosnay, anxious to report to the cardinal without delay, made several disparaging remarks about the suitability of d'Artagnan's little horse for long-distance travel when, so tired 'it could hardly raise its tail', it declined to cross a row of planks to reach the barge. The young Gascon could contain himself no longer: he rashly unsheathed his sword and demanded satisfaction. Rosnay had no intention of being drawn into a fair fight, and at his sign d'Artagnan was promptly knocked unconscious by a blow from behind by one of the count's henchmen. He awoke to find himself in a cell, nursing a bloody head wound, charged with assault and deprived of horse, saddle, weapon and money. Unable to pay his fine, d'Artagnan languished in the local jail for two and a half months, with not so much as a spare shirt to his name. He was extremely fortunate that a passing Orléans gentleman called Montigré, who had had his own past differences with Rosnay, heard who was responsible for d'Artagnan's misfortune and took pity on him. Montigré paid for his release and generously bankrolled his onward travel to Paris, including the loan of a rather bigger horse.

If his journey from Gascony had been less eventful, d'Artagnan would still have taken nearly three weeks to reach the French capital, on roads that were little better than tracks and almost impassable in the rain. As it was, three weeks became three months, and he arrived about the middle of May. To a country boy such as d'Artagnan, Paris, with its half a million inhabitants, must have looked like somewhere from the world of fairy tales. The creaking sails of a dozen windmills, some ingeniously built into the decaying city walls, all turned in unison, as though a giant were winding a great handle to grind his corn with their primitive machinery. Beyond them, it seemed to d'Artagnan that roof after roof merged as one, their endless tiles gleaming in the sun. Hundreds of smoking chimneys cloaked the more densely populated districts of Paris in a perpetual haze. In every direction that d'Artagnan turned, there were new marvels to behold. On the skyline rose the stupendous steeples of Notre-Dame and Saint-Germain-des-Prés, the crenellated ramparts of the royal palace of the Louvre and the sinister towers of the prisons known as Le Châtelet and the Bastille.

Even on horseback, d'Artagnan would not have found it easy to pass through the southern gate, the Porte Saint-Jacques. An unceasing stream of mules, donkeys, cows and pigs blocked his progress as the carriages of noblemen jostled with the carts of peasants for the remaining space. Hundreds entered the city every day to sell their produce directly to the populace. Once inside, they soon found themselves in a maze of narrow alleys, lined by tiny shops. Whether offering charms or cooking pots, stepladders or second-hand clothes, these primitive establishments allowed their wares to spill over the cobbles, creating a precarious obstacle course for the unwary. Most streets were barely five feet wide, and the taller buildings on opposing sides almost touched at third-floor level, creating a claustrophobic passage of perpetual twilight.

D'Artagnan arrived not long before dusk. Preparations had already begun to close the city gates. When the heavy wooden crossbeams were lifted, ready to be dropped into their slots, this was the signal for all the shops to shut. As d'Artagnan passed by, their oak shutters were closing one by one, the iron bars reverberating as they were forced hastily into place. Within half an hour the hubbub had been replaced by an eerie silence, broken only by the scurrying footsteps of law-abiding citizens anxious to reach the safety of their houses before dark.

Now Paris became the dangerous domain of the vagabonds of the night. Its underworld drew on an endless supply of labour, both men and women, who existed barely above starvation level. Opportunist 'cloak-snatchers' sold their plunder at the thieves' market, whose dingy backstreet location was widely known but where dealers and fences nonetheless operated openly without fear of arrest. The city did not have an organized police force: it was patrolled half-heartedly by yeomen, still called *hoquetons* or 'archers', although they carried concealed batons in their smocks rather than the crossbows of earlier times. When these yeomen went home to bed, gangs of cutthroats emerged from the shadows and roamed the capital's unlit streets. More than three hundred unsolved murders took place each year, the corpses of the victims left to lie where they fell, until they could be casually collected by a municipal cart.

Prudent Parisians ventured out only in daylight hours. Those men who could afford to buy boots wore them right up to the thigh, an essential protection against the mud kicked up by animal hooves or splattered by the wheels of coaches. It was mixed with human waste, from receptacles emptied out of upstairs windows, in a city where sanitation did not exist and where the odour was unpleasant in winter and unbearable in summer. Known locally as *la crotte*, this nauseating effluent was swelled by animal droppings, decaying vegetables and entrails thrown into the street from the butchers' shops. Lacking the scented gloves that were essential wear for every well-dressed citizen, d'Artagnan had nothing to relieve the stench and would have been almost overwhelmed long before he could see what was causing it. 'Paris was perhaps the dirtiest city in France, and . . . Paris mud could be smelt two miles outside the gates.'

No doubt sensing that there were many sound reasons to find safety indoors as quickly as possible, d'Artagnan made his way through the gloom to an inn called the Gaillard Bois. *Gaillard* meant 'merry' or 'ribald', and *conter des gaillardises* was 'to tell risqué stories'. *Une gaillarde* was also a 'wench' or a 'hussy', so it is easy to see why d'Artagnan might have found such an establishment attractive. *Bois*, however, indicated here not simply 'wood' but *les bois de justice*, the wooden gallows. The Gaillard Bois was located in the unwelcoming rue des Fossoyeurs, Gravediggers' Street, so-named to reflect the predominant local profession. With the hangman and the gravedigger as fellow patrons, this particular tavern was clearly not a place to choose to knock over a stranger's drink.

According to his earliest biographer, Gatien de Courtilz de Sandras, d'Artagnan could only afford a tiny room off the inn's main courtyard, used by its noisy customers for torch-lit boule; so the Gascon probably rose late, short on sleep. To make a positive impression with the Musketeers, d'Artagnan realized that he needed to improve his bedraggled appearance, and he resolved to spend his remaining francs on a new feather for his hat and a coloured ribbon for his cravat. This was easy for d'Artagnan to accomplish because the clamour of bargain hunters on the nearby Pont Neuf was unmistakable, an irresistible magnet to every visitor to Paris.

Pont Neuf, the so-called 'New Bridge', built in stone by Henry IV, was new no longer, but in thirty years its status as the epicentre of the capital had been steadily reinforced. It was an incongruous combination of principal thoroughfare and open-air market, with dozens of stalls set up along the parapets. Here passers-by could obtain anything from an oil painting to an ointment that allegedly shifted the worst constipation, though a drink from a communal cup provided by one of the 600 watercarriers in the capital, who extracted their supply from the faeces-ridden Seine, was probably a more rapid remedy for this condition. Pimps, pedlars and so-called painless 'withdrawers' of teeth, whose main instrument was a crude pair of pliers, all competed unsuccessfully for the dwindling contents of d'Artagnan's pockets as he made his purchases and pushed through the throng.

Re-crossing the river to the south side, the Gascon found his way to the Hôtel des Mousquetaires, the headquarters of the King's Musketeers. An hôtel was a mansion or town house, not yet an establishment where anyone with the necessary means could choose to stay. D'Artagnan's immediate impression would have been of chaotic activity, for despite a single-minded approach to their responsibilities, those Musketeers not rostered on any particular guard duty treated the hôtel as though it were an unruly gentlemen's club, practising with razor-sharp swords up and down the stairs and along the corridors.

Tréville, like many with the power of patronage, received at his daily levée an unceasing procession of petitioners hoping for his favour. However, d'Artagnan was too late for the levée and never reached Tréville's suite. Nor was he given an opportunity to pick the quarrels that committed him to fight three duels, at one-hour intervals, as in Dumas' *The Three Musketeers*. In real life, d'Artagnan progressed no further than the first Musketeer he came across at their hôtel, who happened to be Porthos. If Porthos did not already know d'Artagnan personally, he quickly recognized him from his accent as a kindred spirit. Porthos told d'Artagnan that he and his friends, Athos and Aramis, were due to fight the Cardinal's Guards at 10 o'clock that very morning in the Pré-aux-Clercs, across the river from the Louvre, at the end of the rue Saint-Germain. By pure chance, d'Artagnan had arrived at Tréville's headquarters a little over an hour before the long-standing feud between the Musketeers and the Guards was due to be settled by a clandestine duel involving three of the best blades from each company. The Cardinal's Guards, far from trying to enforce their master's strict edicts against duelling at the expense of the Musketeers, were just as bent on breaking them.

Porthos, a natural leader, gave d'Artagnan some well-intentioned advice: he should quickly prove his bravery or return to Gascony. D'Artagnan's instant reaction was to invite Porthos out in the street, if he doubted his courage. Porthos laughed heartily and said if d'Artagnan wanted to fight, he would see that his wish 'was gratified before long'. Ordering the slightly bemused d'Artagnan to follow him at a discreet ten paces, Porthos paid a surprise call on Jussac at the Guards' headquarters in the Hôtel d'Aguillon, close to the Gaillard Bois inn. Porthos made it a point of honour that Jussac should produce a fourth Guard to fight the young Gascon. Jussac was furious but, with d'Artagnan watching, he had little option but to agree. Porthos chose to involve d'Artagnan, not because he was aware of his ability with a sword, but to wrong-foot Jussac. Instead of resting ahead of the engagement, Jussac was obliged to race around Paris seeking one of his men sober enough to fight a duel in less than an hour's time.

Jussac had selected as his fellow duellists Cahusac and Biscarat, two brothers from the Rotondis family. Jean de Badarat de Rotondis, sieur de Cahusac, was one of Cavoie's junior officers. Jacques de Biscarat de Rotondis, noted for his courage, was the lieutenant in charge of the mounted division of the Cardinal's

Guards. Together they visited five or six different taverns in Paris without finding a suitable opponent for d'Artagnan.

Jussac added to his difficulties by insisting on taking his personal coach. These symbols of prestige had increased in such numbers that more than four thousand five hundred were crammed into the centre of Paris, and by the time Jussac's gilded conveyance forced its way through the crowded streets, news of his mission to find a fourth duellist had reached the off-duty Guards. All but those too drunk to stand rapidly made themselves scarce, leaving by the back door of each inn just as Jussac's compatriots entered hopefully through the front. By now it was close to eleven o'clock, an hour after the appointed time for the duel. Afraid that the Musketeers would not wait much longer, Cahusac and Biscarat shanghaied their own younger brother, Armand-Jean de Rotondis, who far from being a professional soldier, was a novice about to enter the Church. Protesting in vain, he was pushed into Jussac's carrosse.

Porthos, meanwhile, had his own problems. The subtlety of his scheme to tire out the opposition was wasted on Athos and Aramis. When the other Musketeers discovered what had happened, they were as angry as Jussac. They did not expect d'Artagnan to last long against the Cardinal's Guards and this would leave them, according to the prevailing rules of engagement, as three to fight four.

The exact location in the Pré-aux-Clercs was a convenient hollow that could not be seen from the river or the road. The atmosphere was highly charged, to say the least. After their bitter exchange with Porthos, Aramis and Athos probably practised together, barely acknowledging d'Artagnan's embarrassed presence. It was only after the defiant Porthos had put d'Artagnan's skill to the test, that they realized he was a natural swordsman of rare talent. Instead of a sacrificial lamb, Porthos had conjured up a tiger.

Jussac and the three brothers Rotondis finally arrived on foot, leaving their coach, coachman and other servants some distance away, for fear of witnesses. It was becoming warmer by the minute. They were all sweating, mainly from their exertions, but Armand-Jean surely from mind-numbing fear. A sword was put in the cleric's hand and he stood there, white and still as death, scarcely able to credit his predicament.

Porthos and Jussac were sorting out the individual duels when a man with an enormous moustache unexpectedly appeared. Jussac had left a desperate message for Bernajoux, a captain in the Navarre regiment and a friend of Biscarat, asking him to be his fourth duellist. Bernajoux gently disarmed the shaking cleric and took his place. Divine intervention, perhaps, had saved Armand-Jean at the last possible moment. Many years later, as bishop of Béziers, he would embellish the story from the pulpit for the benefit of his awestruck parishioners, claiming that the famous d'Artagnan had barely escaped with his life.

Bernajoux, from a family of regular duellists, should have proved a formidable opponent for d'Artagnan. However, with no opportunity to get his eye in and having run to the rendez-vous, Bernajoux was in the worst possible condition to take on the Gascon. He also completely underestimated d'Artagnan, scornfully asking Jussac whether a joke was being played on him because so far as he could see, he was expected to fight a child. D'Artagnan gave Bernajoux the best possible answer.

The duellists touched swords, circled and closed. Bernajoux lunged, d'Artagnan easily parried. Bernajoux finessed, all subtlety of invention: d'Artagnan again countered, although this time, it seemed to Bernajoux, with much more difficulty. Lulled into a false sense of self-confidence, he attempted to deliver the *coup de grâce* but struck only air. D'Artagnan swayed tantalizingly out of reach, turned away Bernajoux's weapon with a twist of hilt upon hilt, and having created the perfect opening, impaled him with a sinuous thrust beneath the armpit. Bernajoux staggered, dropped his sword and fell heavily to the ground four paces away. The duel ended in less than a minute.

Bernajoux, bleeding furiously, pleaded with d'Artagnan to help bind his wound, which he chivalrously agreed to do, raising Bernajoux to a sitting position and tearing long strips off the end of his shirt. As he wrapped the improvised bandage tightly around Bernajoux's bloodied chest, the other duels continued about them in grim earnest, blade on blade, back and forth, back and forth.

D'Artagnan broke off his efforts at first aid only when he saw Jussac wound Athos in the arm and prepare to deliver a fatal blow. Not wishing to strike a man from behind, d'Artagnan called out to Jussac to turn and face him. Jussac assessed the situation in a moment. He was isolated from his fellow Guards. Athos was hurt but still fighting and d'Artagnan had just dispatched Bernajoux after a breathtaking display of his ability. *In extremis*, Jussac found that he cared more for his skin than his reputation and promptly surrendered. Cahusac and Biscarat, faced with odds of four to two, needed little persuasion to give up their swords to Aramis and Porthos. The indefatigable d'Artagnan ran to fetch Jussac's coach, in which they placed the wounded Bernajoux. 'In this way he was taken home, where he remained for six weeks on his bed before he was cured.'

The following day, d'Artagnan turned this defeat of Richelieu's Guards into a full-scale diplomatic incident. The Three Musketeers were excused duties by Tréville as a tacit reward for their success and they decided to play tennis on a court near the stables of the adjacent and empty Luxembourg Palace. D'Artagnan, with nothing better to do, went with them. He grew bored with watching and tried to take part but did not know the rules. His efforts were mocked by a spectator, another of the Cardinal's Guards, who derided him as an 'apprentice musketeer': an ill-advised insult that inevitably led to a challenge and a duel. While the Three Musketeers watched with unconcealed admiration, d'Artagnan repeated his devastating attack of the previous morning. In four or five exchanges, he achieved three hits, wounding the hapless Guardsman in the arm, the thigh and finally through the lungs.

The lawned gardens of the Luxembourg ran down to the Hôtel de Trémouille. Unlike Tréville's faded but functional headquarters, this hôtel was a grand mansion with luxurious furnishings. The majority of hôtels were occupied on an intermittent basis by leading nobles whenever they came to Paris. The most prestigious stood in or near the place Royale, a square dominated by a statue of the monarch and surrounded by tall residences, set back behind covered arcades. Others had been built close to the lovely garden of the Tuileries, with its symmetrical avenues of elm trees. A few, including the Hôtel de Trémouille, could be found in the more rural environment of the rue Saint-Germain. Each hôtel employed a vast number of poorly and erratically paid staff that often took their wages in kind: wine, meat or even furniture. They earned their keep by looking after endless visitors who consumed vast quantities of food and alcohol and, with the incentive of free board and lodging, invariably stayed on for years. Such guests, known as '*les domestiques d'un grand seigneur*', more often than not were the younger sons of other noble families without prospect of a good inheritance, hoping their host would put in a good word for them in the upper echelons of the army or at court. In return they would pledge, sometimes literally, their sword, taking their patron's part in any quarrel, irrespective of whether it was lawful or just.

D'Artagnan quickly discovered for himself the considerable resources of the Hôtel de Trémouille. His latest opponent had a cousin, who happened to be *écuyer*, chief steward, to duc Henri-Charles de la Trémouille himself. Hearing the Guardsman's cries for help, the duke's household, armed to the teeth, poured out of every doorway in response. They would have soon overwhelmed d'Artagnan and the Three Musketeers had not another Musketeer, seeing what was happening, already dashed the short distance to Tréville's headquarters for reinforcements. When about twenty more Musketeers suddenly arrived, swords in hand, the street outside the hôtel became a scene of multiple combats and wild confusion. The duke's *domestiques* quickly lost their enthusiasm for the fight and retreated indoors, carrying two of their number, wounded by Athos and Aramis, as well as the seriously injured Guardsman. There was some discussion among the enlarged group of Musketeers about how best to set fire to the hôtel to smoke out their opponents and a half-hearted attempt was made by throwing an incendiary device through one of the windows; but, in the end, wiser counsels prevailed.

Meanwhile, news of the duel in the Pré-aux-Clercs had reached the king, who feigned indignation and summoned Tréville to the palace. The captain of the Musketeers assured him glibly that the affair was not prearranged but a chance encounter provoked by Biscarat and Cahusac, resulting in only minor injuries. He then called on Bernajoux at his lodgings to make sure he was indeed on the mend from d'Artagnan's sword-thrust, only to find on returning to his headquarters that he now had a full-scale battle to explain away. His opposite number, Cavoie, had visited the duc de la Trémouille and made much of the throwing of an incendiary device at his hôtel. He asked Henri-Charles to ally himself with Richelieu, 'to obtain satisfaction for an injury done to both'. Tréville, however, persuaded the duke to interview the injured Guardsman lying prostrate in his servants' hall; close to death, the Guardsman whispered that d'Artagnan was not to blame.

Trémouille, many of whose relatives were Protestants persecuted by the cardinal, had no love for Richelieu, and the next day he went to Louis XIII to support Tréville's version of events. The duke was evidently determined not to waste such a rare chance to wrongfoot His Eminence because despite arriving home from a ball at 2 a.m., he missed his breakfast in order to be in good time for the king's levée. Consequently, when Cavoie returned to make sure of Trémouille the following morning, much to his consternation he found that the duke had already left for the palace.

Unaware of Cavoie's miscalculation, Richelieu was confident that the king, however reluctantly, would take his part. He warned Louis by letter that if the Musketeers went unpunished, 'a thousand insolences' would occur unchecked. Lacking any supporting witnesses, however, the cardinal's imperious sermon was ignored. It was not often that Louis had an opportunity to anger the cardinal by simply doing nothing. Far from reprimanding Tréville and his Musketeers, he discreetly summoned Aramis, Porthos and Athos to his closet, 'up the little hidden staircase' in the palace. They were told to bring d'Artagnan with them. The four were alone with Louis for an hour and after listening intensely to d'Artagnan's account of his eventful arrival in Paris, the king gave him fifty newly minted gold louis.

D'Artagnan, Tréville and sixteen of his Musketeers celebrated the double defeat of the Cardinal's Guards over supper at their regular haunt, the Bel Air tavern near the Luxembourg. Taking advantage of d'Artagnan's unusually heavy purse, they drank copiously *pichets du vin d'Anjou*. The Musketeers' triumph was the talk of Paris and d'Artagnan the hero of the hour.

D'Artagnan had ample money left to rent the garret at the Gaillard Bois, where his newfound fame had preceded him. The innkeeper's wife invited him into her bed. At the time her eccentric husband was away on a tour of Burgundian vineyards, but d'Artagnan, having tasted this new nectar, continued his trysts after the innkeeper's return. Suspecting the worst, the landlord hid in his own bedroom closet. Hearing d'Artagnan and his wife making love, he flung open the closet door and fired a pistol at him at point-blank range. Whether the rapid movement of the naked entwined bodies put off his aim or he subconsciously aimed high to avoid his spouse, we shall never know, but the bullet missed its target. For the first time, although by no means the last, d'Artagnan was to show that, whenever in danger, he was blessed with a charmed life.

3

CYRANO DE BERGERAC

    ⚭ ⚮

D'Artagnan soon discovered that the bells of 100 churches rang early and unmelodiously in the French capital. Each morning their cacophony would wake him, sleeping the sleep of the just, if no longer of the innocent, in his garret at the Gaillard Bois. Whenever d'Artagnan emerged bleary-eyed from the tavern, he was surprised to find himself instantly recognized and applauded. The Three Musketeers, though, did not approve of his bedraggled appearance: they felt that as the toast of Paris, their young friend needed to look the part. Mindful perhaps that a bag of gold pieces from the king would not last forever, they took him to Antoine's, a kind of Moss Bros of the day, which sold fine clothes and later bought them back at half price if their owner fell on impecunious times. Here d'Artagnan could outfit himself in the finest fencing fashion whilst in funds: a hat with a heron's long black plumes, a red rounded doublet, gloves with green satin revers at the wrist, outlandish stockings known as 'amorous desire' and a gleaming new blade with a *petite oie*, a knot of bright ribbon, tied flamboyantly at its hilt. Two tall assistants were ready to hold him aloft and drop him straight into his new breeches to keep them free of wrinkles.

As d'Artagnan and the Three Musketeers paraded insolently around the streets, brandishing the swords surrendered by his Guards, inside Richelieu's opulent Palais-Cardinal, the temperature was close to meltdown. The immediate object of the cardinal's fury was Cavoie, his commander-in-chief, hitherto the favoured subordinate who brought Richelieu's visitors in to see the great man himself. It was unbelievable and quite inexcusable, he ranted, that his most senior officer could have 'carried out his orders so badly'. Cavoie had failed to make certain that the duc de la Trémouille would support the cardinal's vociferous complaint about the conduct of Tréville's Musketeers. Richelieu thought that Cavoie should have waited outside the duke's residence all night, if needs be, to avoid missing his departure for the palace to see the king. After his relentless dressing-down by the cardinal, Cavoie returned home deathly pale and close to collapse. His wife, Marie de Sérignan, put her husband to bed and sent for the doctor. Marie then showed herself to be as resourceful as she was beautiful. She had little difficulty in persuading one of the royal physicians that Cavoie was at death's door, although there was nothing seriously wrong with him. Four days later, dressed in widow's weeds, Marie called on the cardinal, fuelling the already strong rumours of Cavoie's demise. Richelieu, fearing he was about to be blamed by a hysterical woman for her husband's death, hastily invited her into his inner sanctum, took the initiative and spoke of Cavoie in glowing terms. Marie then informed the cardinal that Cavoie, though ill, had not yet died, and said she was sure her husband would recover quickly when he heard Richelieu's true opinion of him. Marie held her breath. She knew that the cardinal was capable of violent and unpredictable changes of mood and that when he lost his icy self-control, his anger could be terrible. Richelieu, realizing that he had been tricked, nonetheless burst out laughing and told Marie that he 'knew of no better actress than she'.

D'Artagnan would have been equally amused to discover that single-handedly he had put at serious risk Cavoie's monopoly of sedan chairs, a favour engineered by the cardinal; what Richelieu had given, he could just as easily take away. As news of d'Artagnan's exploits reverberated around the city, these numbered conveyances for the wealthy began to arrive at the insalubrious Gaillard Bois, with preening footmen clutching invitations from the leading noble families of France and bidding him to enter. Fawning flunkeys who a week earlier would have unhesitatingly preferred to throw d'Artagnan into the street rather than admit him to their hôtel, rushed to make him welcome. He was an object of intense curiosity, the fashion accessory of the moment. Many of those who had suffered abuse and humiliation at the hands of the cardinal wanted to see at first hand the young man who had got the better of him.

Desperate as Cavoie was to settle the score, the cardinal's Guards were constantly outmanoeuvred. The Musketeers had an uncanny knack of materializing in great numbers at the slightest sign of trouble. More often than not d'Artagnan, at a loose end in Paris, fought alongside them. When on one occasion at least a dozen Musketeers forced two of the cardinal's men into an undignified flight, shorn of weapons and clothes, news of the fresh incident reached the king, who could not resist poking fun at Richelieu. The cardinal tartly observed that the Musketeers 'were brave enough when they found themselves twelve to one', whereupon the king, nettled, said that was the sort of odds to suit his Guards, because 'they were only the scum of all the bullies of Paris.' For one moment, until a courtier stepped in between them, it looked as if king and cardinal would actually come to blows. Somewhere at the back of Richelieu's mind must have been a feeling that once again d'Artagnan, not even a Musketeer, was the invisible catalyst behind his embarrassment. As the ruler of all France, Richelieu could guillotine great nobles with impunity and have princes of the blood at his beck and call but a young Gascon had unwittingly shown that the cardinal was not invincible.

Meanwhile, with a nod from Louis, Tréville took on the task of finding a less controversial use for d'Artagnan's sword. D'Artagnan had set his heart on becoming a King's Musketeer but, like all eager aspirants, he first had to serve an apprenticeship in another regiment. Tréville asked another favour of his brother-in-law, Essarts, to accept d'Artagnan into the royal household guards as a gentleman cadet. As part of the bargain Porthos, however, had to relinquish his Musketeer's mantle and return to Essarts' company, which would not have pleased Porthos at all.

Essarts was happy to accommodate Tréville because, according to custom, a cadet was an unpaid volunteer. Indeed, Essarts was said by his cynical fellow captains to have received three new recruits for the price of none, as Athos and Aramis took turns to watch over d'Artagnan whenever he mounted guard alone at his windswept sentry position before one of the gates of the royal palace. This was no idle gesture. For an enemy of the cardinal, in a France lit only by fire, at night Paris was a pitch-black, dangerous place. Candles were a currency in themselves, an expensive commodity; and such were the strains on the royal budget that most of the Louvre and its grounds remained in complete darkness. The occasional flickering candle punctuated the gloom, appearing and disappearing, like a glow-worm in the dark. Courtiers and their servants had to illuminate their own way from one apartment to another, skirting the shadows where muggers often sought out their prey.

D'Artagnan placated Porthos and rewarded Aramis and Athos for their night vigil by inviting his three friends to join him in his off-duty hours on a reckless spending spree. During his brief flirtation with high society, d'Artagnan had come across a gambling den in the Louvre itself. Wealthy aristocrats, including the duc de Saint-Simon, father of the famous memorialist, were playing for stakes way over d'Artagnan's head, but with typical luck, he emerged on the throw of the dice richer by several times the reward given to him by Louis XIII. His windfall made him the ideal client for the cabarets, up-market inns with billiard rooms, musicians, courtesans and comfortable beds, open from dusk to dawn. For those with the immediate means to pay, these exclusive establishments served the best cuts of fresh meat on silver dishes, offered fine wine in goblets and supplied white tablecloths and napkins. Promissory notes, however, were treated with disdain. Accustomed to the unscrupulous ways of noblemen, the cabarets displayed an uncompromising sign on the front door that applied to all-comers: '*Crédit est mort!*' 'Your credit has expired!'

The best-known cabaret was Durier's at Saint-Cloud on the outskirts of Paris, a rabbit warren of interconnecting rooms with luxurious furnishings and a reputation for debauchery. Its proprietor, the merry widow Durier, was also the buxom mistress of Jussac, lieutenant of Richelieu's Guards. It may well have been here that Athos and Aramis, unable to afford a drink until d'Artagnan and Porthos arrived at the end of their relief, tried to take over the billiard table from some of the cardinal's men, a dispute that led to an exchange of insults and threatening hands on cape-draped rapiers protruding behind like the tail of a cock. It could easily have been worse, in this era:

> close shaves and unbridled sword play . . . someone looked at you – instantly a duel; someone did not look at you – another duel; the one had insulted you, the other underrated you; and all that . . . with . . . admirable nonchalance as if one were merely concerned with drinking a glass of wine.

In the cabarets and at formal occasions elsewhere, gentlemen were expected to conform to certain rules of etiquette, which included sitting down for meals still wearing their hat, sheathed sword and cloak. This cumbersome combination had one unintentional benefit: quarrelling diners found it difficult to start a fight while seated at table. A cloak also served many useful purposes, as d'Artagnan discovered soon after meeting François de Montlézun, sieur de Besmaux, another of the seemingly inexhaustible supply of Béarnais soldiers. Besmaux came from Pavié, a tiny riverside village east of Pau, where his father, Manaud de Montlézun, farmed an unwanted *métairie* in the middle of a thick wood. Its complete lack of a view prompted the name Besmaux, in the local dialect '*y besi mau*', which meant '*j'y vois mal*', 'I see nothing there'. The smallholding was held under a *métayage* agreement, enabling rent to be paid as produce, because Manaud had hardly any money. Such humble origins suggest that Manaud had been born on the wrong side of the blanket and d'Artagnan, whose adoption of his own noble name was not exactly beyond reproach, provocatively claimed that Manaud's son Besmaux was not entitled to call himself Montlézun.

D'Artagnan had little time for Besmaux and thought him 'a man of quite different disposition [whose] vanity surpassed imagination'. It certainly exceeded his means. Besmaux belonged to a mounted household brigade whose members wore their sword in a grand shoulder belt embroidered with gold, costing from eight to ten pistoles. His finances did not quite run to that amount, so he had a belt made with gold embroidery in front, leaving the back quite plain. Besmaux hid the belt's plain side under his voluminous red cloak, which for a while fooled his compatriots.

The flaw in Besmaux's harmless deception was that regulations prevented a mounted soldier on guard duty from wearing a cloak. Suspicions were aroused when Besmaux always came on guard in a different, inferior belt, only to reappear with gold belt and cloak the following day. After a great deal of alcohol-fuelled speculation, one evening several of Besmaux's companions, egged on by d'Artagnan, without warning seized Besmaux at the supper table and forcibly removed his cloak from his shoulders. Much to Besmaux's discomfort, his little secret was exposed. Thereafter d'Artagnan's new acquaintance was ridiculed among his fellow guards as 'shoulder-belt Besmaux', and d'Artagnan would discover that out of this seemingly trivial affair he had made a dangerous foe.

Besmaux and d'Artagnan's misuse of their noble names was but a mere trifle in comparison with the deception of one Hercule-Savinien Cyrano de Bergerac. This manic young poet and playwright of Italian descent was not born in Bergerac, never lived there and even a small piece of land in Bergerac owned by his father, the basis of Cyrano's very tenuous title, had been sold in 1636. Cyrano also described himself as a Gascon but was brought up at the Château de Mauvieres in the Dordogne, beyond the borders of Gascony. For Cyrano, however, these were inconvenient details to be brushed aside. He lived for the duel, sometimes fighting 'two or three in the same morning' and regarded himself as the most famous swordsman in France, *'le démon de bravure'*, 'the devil of the duel', a title that d'Artagnan was in danger of usurping. Cyrano needed something spectacular to restore his previous pre-eminence.

According to Edmond Rostand, who wrote his heroic comedy *Cyrano de Bergerac* after 'long research' into actual events, Cyrano's chance came when d'Artagnan went to the theatre, on possibly his twentieth day in the capital. D'Artagnan's invitation to a run-of-the-mill performance at the Hôtel du Bourgogne rather than a premiere at the more fashionable Théâtre du Marais was a sign that his initial impact on Parisian society had already waned. The Bourgogne was a decrepit converted tennis court, long and narrow, with a balcony at one end and a crude stage at the other, standing five feet above floor level. A tall iron grille acted as a further deterrent to unruly spectators in the *parterre* in case they became tempted to jump from the pit on to the stage.

Cyrano had forbidden the leading actor Champfleury, who had offended him, from performing for a month; so, as Champfleury was due to appear in defiance of the poet's interdict, the audience waited with keen anticipation to see what would happen. While d'Artagnan hobnobbed with the upper classes in the expensive seats, the Musketeers, having intimidated the doormen into allowing them to enter the theatre without paying, stood in the *parterre*. They threw their weight around and provoked their macaroon-munching, wine-swigging neighbours into a brawl that soon involved almost everyone. By the time the curtain went up at 2 p.m., the struggling mass of lackeys, liveried servants, pages and soldiers had lost interest in the performance. This emboldened Cyrano, not that he needed much encouragement, to interrupt the play, an indifferent work called *Clorise* by Balthazar Baro. Pushing his way into the pit, Cyrano loudly ordered Champfleury to get off the stage. At first the actor ignored him, whereupon

Cyrano, applauded by d'Artagnan, effortlessly leapt over the iron barrier and reinforced his demand at the point of a sword. Champfleury fled for his life and when the theatre manager protested that without his leading man he would have to abandon the performance altogether and return the audience's money, Cyrano contemptuously tossed his purse on to the boards. His cronies, knowing that this was all he had in the world, afterwards scolded him for his foolishness. Cyrano retorted: *'Mais quel geste'*, 'But what a gesture'.

Despite appearances to the contrary, Cyrano was not fully fit, having returned to his native Paris to recuperate from an injury received at the siege of Mouzon near the Ardennes, where a musket ball had burned a furrow across his chest. After leaving the theatre, however, Cyrano ostentatiously escorted a fellow poet, Lignière, to his lodgings on the far side of the Porte de Nesle, the eastern gate of Paris, knowing full well that the comte de Guise had put a large price on Lignière's head for insulting him in an epigram. Fearing the worst, Cyrano's friends, d'Artagnan probably among them, went on ahead and disposed of most of the hired thugs lying in ambush for Lignière near the Seine, leaving an unmistakable trail of abandoned knives and cudgels on the bloodstained cobbles. Of the battered survivors, Cyrano killed two and wounded seven, but the story, like Cyrano's long nose, grew in the telling and by the following day it was widely believed that he had prevailed single-handed despite odds of 100 to one. Perhaps with some surreptitious help from his generous new rival, Cyrano could once again claim to be the supreme duellist in Paris.

Cyrano and d'Artagnan first met because Cyrano was exploiting an enthusiastic amateur poet, Ragueneau, the owner of a successful *traiteur* on the corner of rue de l'Arbre Sec and rue Saint-Honoré, not far from the Louvre. On their way to report for guard duty at the palace, d'Artagnan and other soldiers often bought takeaway dishes from Ragueneau, who was famous for tarts, pastries and especially his ragout stew.

He was also liberal with his hospitality and Cyrano, who as a result of his show-stopping gesture had become one of his more impoverished customers, helped him to write sonnets and ballads in return for unlimited free meals.

By the end of June 1640 d'Artagnan found that his winnings were all but exhausted. Cyrano de Bergerac was also completely broke. Like many gentlemen soldiers in a similar predicament, they hoped to escape their irate creditors by being sent to the front. However, Essarts' company had yet to mobilize fully and Cyrano's captain was still away recruiting replacements for his all-Gascon brigade. So the two intrepid duellists took matters into their own hands and joined a band of 1,400 volunteer nobles raised by the Prince of Condé, the king's cousin.

This would have been tantamount to desertion in a modern army, but in those days, it was not as risky a move as initially it might appear. Noblemen were expected to fight for their king but enjoyed considerable discretion as to how they went about it. The French army still operated under an old feudal system, making it easy for all but the common soldier to change allegiance. The state paid the wages of its troops but did not recruit them; that was the business of each captain, who bought the rights to his regiment. It was like a gamble on a stock market, a potential liability in times of peace, a heaven-sent opportunity to make a fortune in times of war by exaggerating the regiment's complement of men.

The scam worked like this. In the *passé volant* or false muster, a captain receiving the going rate for, say, one hundred men might pay and maintain fifty, pocketing the difference. Inspections were prominently advertised in advance, enabling a corrupt captain – which almost all of them were – to muster for the day a collection of servants and peasants who could barely hold a musket, to bring his contingent temporarily up to strength. This might be noticed but the alternative ploy, impossible to detect, was for two captains to collaborate by lending each other soldiers for the appropriate muster parade. No captain using such fraudulent devices to line his own pockets was in a strong position to complain if a few of his genuine recruits, like Cyrano and d'Artagnan, also went missing.

Most nobles who acquired a company either went home rich or in a wooden box, because the seventeenth-century wars were not isolated events but a way of life, 'as much part of European culture as the weather'. The Thirty Years War, involving a large slice of Europe, still had eight years to run. Nearly all the protagonists were exhausted, but France and Spain continued to fight each other tenaciously over disputed territory in the north, south and east. The northern French frontier with the Spanish Netherlands ran broadly along the Somme, uncomfortably close to Paris. Each summer France usually made strenuous efforts to push the border further back by investing one or more of its line of fortified towns.

In 1640 the principal target was Arras, the key to Spanish Picardy. When the French arrived at Arras on 13 June, its citizens showed their contempt for the besiegers. They suspended two huge white wooden cut-outs from the city walls, depicting a mouse in pursuit of a cat. The sardonic message of this unusual tableau was that mice would begin to eat cats before Arras fell to the French.

For a while, it looked as though the defenders were correct in their assessment. Richelieu deliberately kept the French army divided, to reduce any potential threat to his own authority. His three commanders outside Arras could not agree among themselves how the siege should be conducted, and before long they were under attack in their turn by marauding Spanish reinforcements. Cut off from their source of supplies, the hungry French troops were reduced to fishing for minnows in the river Scarpe and catching sparrows, the only wildlife to survive earlier scavenging expeditions.

Richelieu organized a relief column from Paris and on discovering from captured Spanish dispatches that their cavalry planned to intercept it, he asked the Prince of Condé's irregulars to provide an escort for the convoy. Many of its 6,000 carts were filled to overflowing with highly unstable artillery shells, bringing home to d'Artagnan and Cyrano the wisdom of the old soldier's adage that one should never volunteer. When the ammunition finally got through, the French heavy guns pounded the outer defences of Arras; mortars, whose shells had crude, delayed fuses, exploded as shrapnel inside its walls. One of Rostand's characters at Arras is a 'Gascon Cadet' green enough to stand directly behind a siege gun while it was being loaded and fired. It would have been typical of d'Artagnan after a narrow escape from the recoil, covered from head to toe in grey gunpowder residue, to complain with all the insouciance of youth, like Rostand's Cadet, that cannons in Gascony 'never roll backwards'.

The fresh bombardment of Arras led to its surrender on 9 August, but only after its garrison had been allowed to withdraw with all the honours of war, even taking with them four cannon and a mortar. The direct attacks all failed, resulting in many French casualties, including Cyrano, whose neck was cut open to the bone by a defender's sabre, causing a festering wound from which he never fully recovered. His best duelling days were already over but he went on to defeat in all more than 1,000 opponents, killing only ten of them. Ill luck continued to dog Cyrano. Almost fifteen years later he would be badly hurt in a freak accident in Paris when a plank of wood, dropped by a careless servant at the home of his patron, fell on his head. Cyrano lingered on for fourteen months but, to the grief of his adoring public, never recovered.

Louis had hoped that Cinq-Mars would make a name for himself at Arras but Richelieu refused to let him lead the relief convoy of munitions and when the favourite's horse was shot from beneath him on the battlefield, the soldiers jeered, suggesting he should stick to ballroom dancing, a reference to his vast collection of footwear. The editor of the *Gazette*, Théopraste Renaudot, still printed an eulogistic account of Cinq-Mars' part in the siege, whereupon the cardinal forced him to retract it and substitute a report in which Cinq-Mars did not even get a mention. As a consequence, despite the fall of Arras,

at the end of August both the king and favourite returned to
court in ill humour. One of Anne's ladies-in-waiting, Madame
de Motteville, said that for Louis, the dauphin in particular
'appeared to be a source of vexation and resentment'. When
the little prince, told to expect Louis, caught sight of him in
the guardroom, he sprang forward and tried to lead him by the
hand towards Anne. The king froze. Cinq-Mars then tried to
embrace the dauphin, who pulled away and howled. Another
incident occurred a few days later, recounted tearfully by the
queen to her ladies. On the evening of 7 September, baby
Louis was startled and began to cry when the king suddenly
appeared next to his bed in his nightgown and bonnet. Instead
of comforting him, Louis flew into a rage, and made the child,
barely two years old, ask on his knees for forgiveness for crying
in his presence. He accused Anne of encouraging her son to
hate him, saying 'The dauphin cannot stand the sight of me.
You are educating him in a strange way that I intend to put
right.' He wrote to Richelieu, 'I am very ill-satisfied with the
dauphin . . . he must be removed from the queen as soon as
possible'. This was no whim arising from a moment's anger.
As early as January 1640, when the dauphin was aged sixteen
months, Louis wanted to send him and his governess to live at
the chateau of Amboise in the Loire valley, leaving his pregnant
mother behind, and had to be dissuaded by Richelieu.

The queen's second child arrived more or less when expected,
on 21 September, the last day of summer, much to the king's
irritation, as he had to postpone for a few days his visit to
Monceau to hunt wolves with Cinq-Mars. In the afternoon
the sun shone, and Anne was walking with her ladies in the
gardens of Saint-Germain when she felt the first sharp pains
of childbirth and her waters broke. With a press of courtiers
outside the door, just before ten o'clock in the evening the
queen produced another healthy son, Philippe, her delivery
attended by the usual court grandees, including the Princess de
Conti and the duchesse de Vendôme. This time, though, there
was no Gaston, whose prospects of inheriting the kingdom

legitimately had all but vanished. However much Louis hated the queen, however much he loathed Richelieu's encroachment on the royal prerogative, he was soon forced to concede that with a disenfranchised brother on the loose, Saint-Germain, protected by the King's Musketeers, was the safest place for the heir and the spare. But from now on Louis and Richelieu wanted 'every possible precaution taken for their safety'. They could not decently prevent Gaston from visiting Anne and the two princes at Saint-Germain but Tréville and his Musketeers were ordered to stay 'very close' to Louis' brother and to 'refuse Monsieur entry if more than three men accompanied him'. These were treacherous times.

The war with Spain rumbled on, indecisive and costly. Both sides had a chronic shortage of cash and modern artillery, but plenty of men. Generals regarded their lower ranks as expendable, like pawns on a giant chessboard. In this age of horse and musket, the musketeer usually dismounted and fought on foot because it was almost impossible to fire his unwieldy weapon on the move. Cheap, mass-produced muskets took a long time to prime and load, lacked sights to guide the aim and had an effective range of less than 100 metres. As a result, most skirmishes took place at frighteningly close quarters. Exchanging musket shots at a distance of fewer than fifty paces, when armour offered no protection, could result in appalling carnage; a frontal assault on a prepared defensive position was such a desperate enterprise that its participants were known as '*les enfants perdus*', or 'the lost children'. Before each attack the conscripted rabble, the dregs of society, were given large tots of rum in the ranks and, if despite this injection of Dutch courage they were still disinclined to fight, they were threatened with wholesale hangings on the spot. Any severe injury in combat led almost inevitably to death: soldiers with bullet wounds or mangled limbs succumbed quickly to septicaemia or to the shock of unanaesthetized surgery carried out by, quite literally, professional butchers plying their trade on the battlefield. Some of the injured even died in anticipation of the knife, overcome by a whirlwind of black terror. Cholera accounted for many soldiers accommodated in unsanitary makeshift bivouacs, especially those already weak from dysentery, accentuated by eating rotten meat heavily spiced to disguise the taste and ladled out as huge pots of bouillon. In eight years of campaigning in Flanders, France lost 18,000 of the 26,000 deployed, a fatal casualty rate of almost 70 per cent.

Despite such grim statistics, d'Artagnan survived the Arras siege without a scratch, and after rejoining Essarts' company he noticed with contempt how Besmaux cunningly kept out of harm's way. With Porthos at his side, d'Artagnan, like Tréville before him, took risk after risk to be noticed by his superiors. Not far from Calais, at Aire-sur-la-Lys, which fell to France on 26 July 1641 after a siege of sixty-eight days, 190 of his comrades were killed in a single attack, but again d'Artagnan emerged completely unscathed. North-west of Arras, at La Bassée, taken a month later, a shell landed at his feet but failed to explode. The odds against him remaining uninjured were as high as the odds against survival while charging the enemy's machine guns over the very same ground in the First World War, perhaps even higher. Nor were the territorial gains any more durable. Just over three months later, on 7 December, the Spanish recovered Aire and on 13 May 1642 they regained La Bassée, after bombarding its defenders with more than 12,000 cannonballs.

In the south, the French armies were faring rather better. Fearing the loss of Roussillon, Spain stirred up yet another conspiracy to undermine their advance. It included all the usual suspects: Gaston, the self-exiled Queen Mother and Marie de Chevreuse, and Queen Anne. But for the first time it also involved two strange bedfellows, Tréville and Cinq-Mars.

The royal favourite was unchallenged at court because of the king's extraordinary obsession with him, which he exploited outrageously. Despite his background, he had no thought of loyalty towards the cardinal. As Cinq-Mars saw it, only Richelieu stood between him and more tangible rewards. The first minister refused him a seat on the royal council, reducing its serious agenda to trivialities on the occasion when the king dared to bring his favourite to its deliberations. Richelieu gave his ruling with contemptuous laughter, reminding Cinq-Mars of his youth and humble beginnings.

For Tréville, the choice was simple. He must have known that the confrontation between his Musketeers and the Cardinal's Guards, which so far had played out in his favour, could only have one conclusion. Richelieu had 420 men under arms; Tréville barely 150. Even if Louis allowed it, Tréville could not afford to equip more. The king was fickle: his support would ebb away if Richelieu's Guards gained the upper hand. And the cardinal's vast network of agents was always capable of exposing Tréville's relationship with the queen, which Louis could scarcely have ignored.

From the beginning of 1642 Tréville and Cinq-Mars plotted in Paris at the Hôtel de Venise, where Gaston had his stables. On 27 January all three came together at the Château de Chilly, where the king spent the night. 'It was a veritable hotbed of conspirators.' They were emboldened by Louis' hostility towards Richelieu. He drew a perverse satisfaction from public attacks on his principal minister and made no effort to curtail them. Cinq-Mars mimicked Richelieu's infirmities in front of the king, and Louis laughed. Encouraged by Tréville, Cinq-Mars suggested having Richelieu assassinated and said the surest way 'was to surprise him' when he came unguarded to his [Louis'] rooms'. Louis' response, to say the least, was ambiguous: he demurred solely on the grounds that the pope would excommunicate anyone involved in such a crime because Richelieu was both a priest and a cardinal – scarcely a vigorous objection on principle to the proposed murder. Tréville then dramatically raised the stakes and said, 'provided he had His Majesty's authority, he would not worry about excommunication, even if he had to go to Rome on foot to obtain absolution.' Louis, offered the opportunity to quash such reckless talk, did not answer. Afterwards Tréville thought he had persuaded Cinq-Mars that the king's silence amounted to tacit approval to act. On 17 February, when both Louis and Richelieu were due to meet at Lyon, he waited in an ante-room with his brother-in-law Essarts for the cardinal's arrival and for the favourite's signal to strike. But Richelieu entered with his captain of the guard and Cinq-Mars' nerve failed him at the critical moment.

From that moment on, the paths and priorities of the plotters significantly diverged. Tréville, interested only in removing Richelieu, remained loyal to Louis. The rest entered into a secret treaty with Spain, signed on 13 March, which had as its equal objective the overthrow of the king. At the very least Louis was to be deposed and his brother Gaston made regent. Anne, ignoring Brienne's advice, impulsively gave the conspirators several blank sheets of paper bearing her signature, to be used to gather support in her name. Richelieu, suspecting everyone but unable to penetrate the conspiracy, decided that the queen was the weakest link. He encouraged Louis to send his wife to Fontainebleau and threaten once more to remove Anne's children from her keeping. On 30 April Anne wrote in anguish to Richelieu: 'The idea of having my children removed from me at such a tender age is unbearable.' The cardinal did not respond. Fearing his vengeance even if the plot succeeded, she arranged a place of safety in Sedan for herself and her two sons 'after her husband's death', in case Richelieu survived the coup. It might have been Tréville, unwilling to see the children he had surely fathered at Richelieu's mercy, who suggested to the queen a desperate gamble: the wholesale betrayal of the conspiracy to the cardinal. One of those who knew the truth was a Béarnais captain, and friend of Tréville, called Abraham Fabert. Much later, in 1659, Fabert said he would not reveal who had told Richelieu until after a certain person had died, who by then could only have been the queen.

Louis went to visit his troops, Porthos and d'Artagnan among them, who were besieging Perpignan, the capital of Spanish Roussillon. Richelieu, suffering from an ulcerated arm, followed a day or two later but felt too ill to travel beyond Narbonne. By the end of May, aware of Cinq-Mars' involvement but lacking any hard evidence against the royal favourite, even the cardinal was in despair; he dictated his will, seventeen pages long, but was unable to hold the pen to sign it. However, on 8 June Le Gras, from the queen's household, arrived with a bundle of papers. They almost certainly included a copy of the secret treaty itself and of a letter to Cinq-Mars from the Queen Mother that spelled out Gaston's future role as regent. The cardinal realized this damning proof of the full extent of the conspiracy would force the king to come down on his side and cried out gleefully: 'O God, you take great care of your poor servant!'

Richelieu was correct. Not even the king could ignore incontrovertible evidence of a plot against him personally and felt compelled to sign a warrant for the immediate arrest of Cinq-Mars. Warned by friends, Cinq-Mars tried to leave Narbonne to evade capture but found the gates of the town closed against him. He hid in the roofs of a row of houses and had to be winkled out of successive attics by the King's Musketeers, like some desperate deathwatch beetle. 'What a fall for Monsieur le Grand', Louis kept repeating to anyone who would listen, as though this would somehow make people believe that the entire conspiracy had come as a terrible shock to him.

The king gave the queen 'the thing she most desired'. On 15 June she was allowed to return to Saint-Germain and to keep her children with her. Marie de Chevreuse, although unaware that her messages to Anne were now being intercepted, sensed something was wrong and stayed out of harm's way. Gaston saved himself as usual by betraying everyone; as Richelieu scornfully observed, 'He entered into the conspiracies for lack of will, and he always crept shamefully out of them because of lack of courage.' The Queen Mother was soon beyond even Richelieu's reach: she died in poverty at Cologne on 3 July, after being forced to sell her own furniture for food and fuel.

Despite his decisive measures against the plotters, Richelieu could barely move because of debilitating haemorrhoids,

abscesses and ulcers, and it was almost a floating cadaver that
travelled up the Rhone in late August 1642 to oversee the trial
of Cinq-Mars at Lyon. Cleopatra herself would not have felt
out of place on the cardinal's opulent barge, a sumptuously
equipped vessel dominated by a portable wooden chamber
with a framework outlined in gold, upholstered in scarlet velvet
decorated with crimson flowers. In one part was a desk and chair
for Richelieu's secretary and a couch to accommodate visitors;
beyond a screen the ailing cardinal lay on a pile of blood-red
cushions in a four-poster bed adorned with purple taffeta. No
extraneous noise was allowed to disturb His Eminence, who
from time to time eased himself upwards on his pillows and
dictated letters and memoranda. While Richelieu slept, only
the scratching of his secretary's quill pen as it crossed and
recrossed the paper interrupted the sound of the river lapping
gently against the prow. Outside, the cardinal's heavily armed
Guards, holding their breath, tiptoed nervously from bow to
stern.

Most evenings an elaborate gangway was set up from barge
to bank, to enable six strong men, wearing buff leather jackets
specially designed to help them support its weight, to carry
ashore the cardinal's wooden chamber on poles to the house
where he was to sleep. In all, five grand houses in succession
were commandeered at random, their terrified owners watching
helplessly as stonemasons knocked a hole in the front wall at
first-floor level, so large that at Avignon the entire setting sun
could be seen through it for an hour. Carpenters constructed an
ingenious ramp from the street to the improvised opening in
order that Richelieu could be carried directly inside the gutted
rooms, already prepared for his arrival. Here he was gently
transferred to another bed, decorated in rose and violet damask
and surrounded by his own exquisite furniture. Pikemen
protected the perimeter. Black morions on their heads, black
short breastplates over their long scarlet tunics, they scurried
about like giant ladybirds. The cardinal's Guards occupied every
part of each chosen house, including its roof and cellars, for fear

of assassination attempts or hidden explosive devices. Whatever the danger and discomfort, Richelieu was determined to reach Lyon.

The cardinal knew that without his physical presence, Cinq-Mars would be pardoned or given a token sentence and he was determined that should not happen. He arrived in Lyon on 5 September. The king had already returned gloomily to Paris. Fearing Cinq-Mars would incriminate him, Louis wrote a letter to Richelieu accusing his favourite of being an 'impostor and a calumniator', thereby uniquely becoming a witness in his own courts.

On 10 September Cinq-Mars fell for the interrogator's oldest trick of all: told, quite falsely, that all the others had talked, he made a full confession himself, thereby sealing his fate. Chancellor Séguier, who could always be relied upon to do Richelieu's bidding, presided over his trial and announced the inevitable sentence of death at 7 a.m. on 12 September. The scaffold, seven feet high, was already in place for the execution at noon. The regular executioner at Lyon, intimidated by sympathizers of the accused and by the cardinal's placemen alike, prudently absented himself, claiming to have broken his arm. His reluctant replacement, believed to be a builder's labourer, lacking any previous experience, botched the execution in the most gruesome fashion imaginable.

Cinq-Mars made a brave exit, bowing to the spectators in each direction from the scaffold and waving his plumed hat. 'What are you waiting for?' he then demanded of his uneasy executioner. The maladroit substitute was unnerved by the delay: his hands shook so much that his opening blow struck too high on Cinq-Mars' neck, cutting less than halfway through. Cinq-Mars rolled off the block on to his back, legs kicking, arms waving, screaming in agony. The executioner silenced him only by severing the vocal cords in his neck with a knife, and took three more attempts to cut off his head. The terrified headsman was later dragged off his platform by the angry crowd and beaten to death.

Cinq-Mars had clung to the hope of a last-minute intervention by the king, but having made the supreme effort to repudiate his favourite, Louis' mood was one of sadistic revenge. Already advised of the date and time of the execution, he sat in the Louvre playing checkers. Every so often, he consulted his pocket watch. At midday he said to no one in particular, 'I should like to see what kind of face Monsieur le Grand is making now.'

The cardinal, with his prodigious train, reached Paris on 13 October, still bent on pursuing Tréville with the same determination he had shown in condemning Cinq-Mars. At first, the king refused, saying to His Eminence's emissaries, 'it will damage my reputation, Tréville has served me well and faithfully'; until he was told bluntly, 'Sire, you must do this, you have no choice.' After Richelieu had threatened to arrest the captain of the Musketeers in the king's very presence, Louis gave in. On 20 November Tréville was dismissed and banished to his estates. He took his time leaving, so long in fact that Anne sent her captain of the guard, Guitaut, to force him to go. The queen was willing to sacrifice anyone to keep her children. On 1 December Tréville arrived at the abbey of Montier-en-Der in Champagne, on the river Voire, where his brother-in-law Antoine de Guillon was abbot.

By then, as Tréville must have hoped, Richelieu was fading fast. His charlatan doctors, who encouraged him to eat marinated sheep's excrement in a vain effort to keep him alive, probably accelerated his final illness. At 2 p.m. on 2 December Louis visited the Palais-Cardinal for a last audience and in an extravagant, hypocritical gesture, fed egg yolks to the dying Richelieu. The cardinal had only two days to live. Once out of the invalid's room, the king was seen to have a jaunty air and to spend time inspecting the rich tapestries in the palace. All the while the King's Musketeers, Athos and Aramis no doubt among them, were disarming Jussac and his men in the corridors and courtyards. Richelieu's Guards were made redundant even before the passing of their master and long before the cardinal had breathed his last, a Musketeer was stationed at every entrance. As he left what would shortly become the Palais-Royal, the king was heard to say to himself *sotto voce*, 'Never again will I have a minister with his own guards.'

4

DEATH OF A MUSKETEER

Exit the cardinal; enter the cardinal. After years of scheming and sycophancy in Rome, aided by Richelieu's strong diplomatic pressure, Mazarin had finally received his red hat, presented by Louis XIII at Valence, before Richelieu's last epic, vengeful voyage up the Rhone. With the old cardinal still lying in state at Paris in his great bed, waxen face and hands protruding from his crimson robes, Mazarin found himself at the eye of the storm as a host of eager suitors descended on Saint-Germain.

They took particular encouragement from Tréville's dramatic return. Once a candle held close to his lips confirmed that Richelieu had indeed breathed his last, Louis wasted no time in recalling Tréville and reinstating his ostensibly loyal captain of the Musketeers: he was not in a position to hold anyone to account for their part in the plot that had cost Cinq-Mars his head and he was almost certainly still unaware of Tréville's relationship with the queen. However, the king showed no intention of reinstating the lands, posts and favours lost by the other victims of Richelieu's regime. He left Mazarin, as the most recent appointee to the royal council, and Brienne, as the most disarming, to break the bad news to them. Tired of courtiers and tired of life, Louis took himself off to the solitude of Versailles, escorted by Tréville and his troop.

Despite distancing himself from the queen as often as he could, the king maintained his relentless enmity towards Anne. Louis saw Mazarin as firmly in his camp. His choice of Mazarin as godfather to the dauphin, as with his appointment of the marquise de Lansac as the boy's governess at Richelieu's behest, probably had no more complex motive than to spite the queen. On 21 April, the king, 'having always suspected her of a secret understanding with Spain', and believing his own death to be imminent, sought advice from his new cardinal on how best to use his will to exclude Anne from the future government of the kingdom. Mazarin disingenuously persuaded him that the queen could still be called regent but in name only; that the real power could be vested in a council of state.

On 14 May Louis XIII died at Saint-Germain. The queen, disregarding protocol, made no pretence at mourning his death. Instead, Anne immediately left for the Louvre with the boy king, Louis XIV, appointing a lowly courtier to oversee the obsequies. Procureur general Pierre Lenet, with heavy irony, described how the king's funeral was attended largely by people who had vanished from sight in his lifetime:

> All those who had been beyond the frontiers of the kingdom came back, one after the other, and at that poor Prince's funeral we beheld all the people who had been banished, hung, broken on the wheel, beheaded or thrown into prison!

The palace soon had a much more jovial air. Within three days, amidst much rejoicing, Anne recalled her most faithful servants, Marie de Hautefort from Le Mans and Pierre La Porte from Saumur; and, with more misgivings and less alacrity, permitted the duchesse de Chevreuse to return to Paris.

La Porte was made *premier valet de chambre* to the young king. He encouraged the queen's suspicions of Mazarin, whom she saw at first as a devious opportunist, his services forced upon her by her late husband. Mazarin won Anne over by adroitly using the principal legislative body, the Paris Parlement, to set aside Louis' testament and appoint her sole regent. In return Anne confirmed Mazarin as first minister, and if Tréville hoped for preferment from the queen by the exercise of her new sovereign power, he was quickly disappointed. Anne retained

Guitaut as the captain of her guard and the King's Musketeers, deprived of their responsibility for royal security by the death of Louis, found themselves on regular military duty. There were enough dissident voices in the kingdom without Anne fuelling suspicions about the legitimacy of Louis XIV. This may explain why even outside the campaigning season Tréville, with a growing family of his own, two sons born in 1639 and 1641, remained at his Paris headquarters and was rarely seen at court. The queen gave him only a modest reward for his discretion. In October the little *seigneurie* of Troisvilles became a *comté* and Tréville a count.

Anne's new confidant, Mazarin, had an entirely different personality to that of the old cardinal. Where Richelieu obsessively disguised his multiple ailments, Mazarin regularly pleaded sickness as a convenient excuse; where Richelieu angrily confronted, Mazarin disarmingly cajoled; and where Richelieu struck terror into the heart of even the mightiest subject, Mazarin insidiously flattered and seduced to achieve the same ends. When he turned his talents to Anne as a woman, rather than as the Queen Regent, she began to respond. By the autumn of 1643 they had probably become lovers. The most persuasive circumstantial evidence was a little incident recounted by the duchesse de Chevreuse and witnessed by La Porte. When the queen retired after supper, Marie Chevreuse usually remained within her apartments for some time in case Anne needed her. One evening a serving maid approached her and said, 'Madame, you must leave now.' On hearing Marie's imperious reply that the queen's instructions never applied to her, the maid said gleefully, 'I've been told by the queen that there are to be no exceptions tonight.' Not long afterwards, after overhearing tittle-tattle about her relationship with Mazarin, Anne remarked 'he did not like women, he comes from a country where they have inclinations of another kind.'

Even with Tréville's benign protection, d'Artagnan and the Three Musketeers remained at risk of assassination every time their regiments returned to Paris. In making a list of unfinished business on his deathbed, it would not have taken Richelieu long to decide that d'Artagnan's own captain and co-conspirator, Essarts, had trusted the young guardsman, so long the thorn in Richelieu's side, to carry messages about the plot to and from Tréville. As for Tréville's hand-picked men chosen to kill him, Richelieu had suspected they included the trio who got the better of his Guards in 1640: Athos, Aramis and Porthos. Despite Richelieu's death, all four friends were marked men. Richelieu had left his agents with secret, unaccountable funds to finish the job and the Cardinal's Guards, out of work, ensured a ready supply of hard-up, disillusioned, professional killers.

Realizing his protégé was in particular danger, for much of 1643 Tréville kept d'Artagnan out of harm's way by arranging for him to be part of a diplomatic mission to England, led by the comte d'Harcourt, whose instructions from Mazarin were to assess the likely outcome of the civil war between Charles I and Parliament without alienating either side. D'Artagnan was an incongruous appointment for such a task. He was certainly no diplomat, he did not speak a word of English and, because Bernes was his native tongue, he scarcely spoke French. On arrival in London, d'Artagnan nonetheless proved unexpectedly useful to Harcourt, helping to forage for furniture to enable his party to stay in Queen Henrietta Maria's former palace of Somerset House, which had been ransacked by the Parliamentarians. Some of it was said to have come from the bored wives of wealthy burghers, who gave d'Artagnan the choicest items in their houses in the hope that he would return for more. The Gascon apart, the whole delegation was relieved to bid farewell to the hostile atmosphere of the capital and pass through the lightly held Parliamentary lines in the direction of Charles I's headquarters at Oxford.

D'Artagnan was soon restless. His mood was not helped by the news that in his absence France had broken the Spanish army at Rocroi, depriving him of a chance of glory and promotion from the ranks. Unwilling to kick his heels for long in an Oxford college quadrangle, where many royalist troops were billeted, he took himself off to Exeter, hoping to join Prince Rupert's cavalry. His impromptu departure went down badly with Henrietta Maria, who was jealous of Rupert's influence over her husband and the elitist sentiments of his force. D'Artagnan was 'requested' to return to Oxford and enlist in the newly arrived regiment of French volunteers, raised by the queen on the Continent. Henrietta had been particularly successful in persuading young French noblemen with a thirst for adventure to join her standard, and d'Artagnan would have felt entirely at home in their company. However, when these undisciplined chevaliers had their first taste of action, they proved more of a hindrance than a help to the Royalist cause.

The queen's regiment took part in the first Battle of Newbury, which began at 7 a.m. on 20 September 1643 between two evenly matched armies. As the day wore on, the Royalists' clear superiority in cavalry counted for little in a fight up and down narrow lanes bordered by trees and hedgerows. Seeing this, d'Artagnan dismounted and used his horse only to change position; he fought as he had been trained at Arras, on foot with a musket. Had there been many more musketeers like d'Artagnan, the king might have won, but in driving rain the Gascon probably ran out of ammunition at the same time as the rest, unable to prevent the battered Parliamentary forces from making an orderly withdrawal towards Reading and eventually to London. Their escape was the turning point in the English Civil War and although Charles I did not appreciate it at the time, his last chance for victory.

With winter approaching, the season's campaigning was over. Having committed himself openly to the Royalist side, d'Artagnan was no longer welcome in any part of England under the control of Parliament, and Harcourt warned him not to return to London because there he faced certain arrest. Instead, d'Artagnan resourcefully passed himself off as the servant of the Roundhead sympathizer Lord Pembroke, crossed the Channel without incident, and made his way back to Paris.

Rosnay, the late cardinal's henchman, was waiting for

him. He bribed four of Richelieu's former Guards to murder d'Artagnan on his way to the theatre, but an informer betrayed their plans. Disguised somewhat incongruously as removal men, thirty *hoquetons* from the yeoman police force ambushed Rosnay's gang as they waited to strike. D'Artagnan's would-be assailants were quickly overpowered and Tréville made sure that they were sent to the galleys. There was no direct evidence of Rosnay's involvement, but Tréville had him arrested on a false charge of spying for Spain. Rosnay was sent to the Bastille, where he would remain for six years. Tréville believed he had caught the most dangerous of Richelieu's agents, but he was mistaken: the deadliest now took Rosnay's place. In *The Three Musketeers* she appears as the fictitious Lady de Winter, Baroness of Sheffield, but this mysterious woman, known by her fellow agents only as Milédi, was in fact the closest confidante of the Queen of England, and the wife of a peer of the realm. Her name was Lucy Percy, 'my lady' the Duchess of Carlisle, and she had been Richelieu's most resourceful spy for eighteen years.

Across the centuries the Percys had regularly heard the final swish of the executioner's axe. Betrayal was in their blood and Lucy was no exception, especially when she herself felt betrayed. In her teens she was regarded as the most attractive woman of quality in England, the 'youngest and most beautiful daughter' of Henry Percy, the seventh Earl of Northumberland, imprisoned in the Tower of London on suspicion of being involved in the Gunpowder Plot. In 1617 Lucy, wilful and obstinate, fell for Baron James Hay and scandalously moved into his apartments in Whitehall. Northumberland regarded Hay, although made an English peer by James I, as 'A beggarly Scot' and it took all Hay's powers of persuasion, going down on his knees in the Tower, to win round his prospective father-in-law. When Hay became the British ambassador to France, Lucy accompanied him to Paris and because her husband spoke indifferent French with a heavy Scots accent, acted as intermediary with the embassy's host of paid informers.

Upon their return to England, Lucy found the much younger

and exciting Duke of Buckingham more to her taste and in
1622 became his mistress. Buckingham, probably in return for
Hay's acquiescence, helped to elevate him to Earl of Carlisle.
This arrangement suited all three parties until 1625, when
Buckingham went to Paris and seduced the French queen.
According to La Rochefoucauld and Brienne, before the duke
left France Anne courted disaster by giving him, as a love token,
several studs from a diamond necklace presented to her by the
king. Buckingham was certainly brash enough to ask for them
and Anne foolish enough to agree.

Lucy was unwilling to play second fiddle to the Queen
of France and, motivated by extreme jealousy, she became
Richelieu's spy in the Buckingham household. La Rochefoucauld
said,

> Lady Carlisle, who had many opportunities to observe him,
> noticed that he was ostentatiously wearing a set of diamond
> studs that she had never seen before. To make certain that they
> were a gift from the Queen of France, she waited for a chance
> to be alone with Buckingham at a ball in London. She managed
> to cut two of the studs from his coat unobserved, intending to
> deliver them to the Cardinal.

The same evening Buckingham discovered the theft and
knew at once that only Lady Carlisle could have taken the
diamonds. He ordered the main ports on the south coast of
England closed, preventing Lucy from leaving for France. Two
replacement studs were made in frantic haste, as close a match
as possible to the originals. Buckingham returned the full set to
Anne by messenger, warning her to expect Louis to ask to see
the necklace, which he did, according to Antoine de Loménie.
Another French historian, Antoine-Marie Roederer, claimed
that Richelieu, with his usual panache, presented the stolen
studs to the queen; Dumas drew upon Roederer's account as his
inspiration for the main plot of *The Three Musketeers*.

Whatever her original motives, Lucy loved the excitement
of her secret role. She manoeuvred skilfully around the seat

of power, exercising huge influence over the greatest men in England, who found her fascinating and irresistible. After Buckingham was assassinated, she became the mistress of Thomas Wentworth, the future Earl of Strafford. When Strafford schemed to turn Charles I into an absolute monarch, which did not suit Richelieu's ends, Lucy abandoned him and in 1641, suddenly expendable, Strafford found himself on the execution block. Lucy transferred her sexual affections to the man who had done the most to put him there, a well-to-do landowner, Thomas Pym, leader of the House of Commons.

On 4 January 1642 Charles I, tiring of Parliament's relentless attempts to reduce his authority, planned to seize Pym and his four closest supporters at the House of Commons. An hour before the king left the palace at the head of his guards, Henrietta Maria made the mistake of confiding in Lucy Percy and, as a consequence, Pym not only knew that the king was coming; thanks to Lucy, he also knew exactly how long to bait the trap but still avoid arrest. The king had cut off his own line of retreat and had started the chain of events that led to the English Civil War.

Quite apart from the frisson it gave her, Lucy Percy remained Richelieu's spy for so long because she needed money. Her husband was famous for his extravagance and invented the 'double banquet', whereby all the courses would be put on display as the guests arrived, then replaced by identical hot dishes when they went in for dinner. By his death he had run through a staggering £400,000 and what remained of his land and property, including the future Leicester Square in London, had to be sold to meet his enormous debts. Lucy was forced to live in borrowed mansions, such as Berkshire House in London, and when even these proved too expensive to maintain, in the far less fashionable Drury Lane. Promised by Rosnay that she would receive more of the late cardinal's gold for one last mission, Milédi Carlisle had no option in 1643 but to follow d'Artagnan to Paris.

At first Lucy had a rival. Although d'Artagnan had

abandoned the Gaillard Bois for superior lodgings in the rue de Vieux Colombier in the district of Saint-Germain, his former innkeeper's wife wanted to leave her husband and live with him. D'Artagnan was unenthusiastic: 'This did not suit me at all, for although very willing to have a mistress, I did not thus wish to have her on my hands for many a long year.' D'Artagnan wanted a less demanding lover, one such as Porthos had, 'that is to say, a mistress who was young, pretty, well made, and who, besides, gave him money'. Porthos had just been awarded his Musketeer's tabard and always had a string of pretty girls in tow.

Many of the women pursuing the Musketeers had titles, rich, often absent husbands, a host of servants, a generous allowance and endless time to perfect their appearance. They scented their hair with *poudre d'Espagne*, a Spanish powder said to have the attributes of an aphrodisiac, and added a final touch to their make-up with a provocative *mouche* or beauty spot known as the 'assassin'. Thus armed for the kill, they attended respectable soirées in apparel that was anything but respectable. At formal occasions after dark, illuminated by soft candlelight, their breasts were often fully exposed, pushed up and supported by a boned corset worn under what remained of the dress to ensure a more enticing appearance. Coupling between willing parties frequently occurred, especially in the grand hôtels and at court, in dark corners rather than beds.

Milédi moved in such circles and had no hesitation in using her considerable sexual experience to achieve her ends. She was forty-three years of age but could pass for a great deal younger. Lucy was good-looking, voluptuous and witty, and d'Artagnan, whose weakness for older women was notorious, fell passionately in love with her, unaware of her true motivation. According to his biographer Courtilz, d'Artagnan, whose love-making evidently had its limitations, was only reassured when Milédi, 'who had enjoyed the first meeting she had accorded me, was not so much disgusted with the second not to ask for yet a third.'

Lucy used all her charms to try to persuade d'Artagnan to

accompany her to England, where he would have been at her mercy, but he had set his sights on becoming a Musketeer and refused. Piqued by this failure, she complained to d'Artagnan's gullible commanding officer, Essarts, that he had dishonoured her. Essarts feared a diplomatic incident and, despite his indignant protests, sent the hapless d'Artagnan to prison for two months, albeit subject to the lenient regime of the former Abbey Saint-Germain. Lucy Percy now had the ideal opportunity to make the necessary preparations to carry out the late cardinal's final commission.

When d'Artagnan was released in mid-December 1643, the Christmas Fair staged each year at Saint-Germain, close to his lodgings, was in full swing. The entire district was in turmoil, even by the standards of the capital, as the fair attracted huge numbers from every social class. Every means of transport imaginable seemed to be heading for a single spot. Well-heeled citizens fought over *fiacres*, the equivalent of the modern taxi, while the cream of the nobility came in private conveyances, with running footmen and trotting stallions. Newfangled glass windows in their coaches protected elegantly dressed ladies from the ribaldry of onlookers, who had plenty of time to gape, as progress was painfully slow. Wagons loaded with wine-barrels and huge cuts of meat, destined for the fair, blocked the already narrow approaches, and impatient carters whipped up their horses, scattering pedestrians. Those unfamiliar with the pitfalls of Paris were drawn irresistibly to a fake fight staged on a street corner as the local riffraff set up a cry of *'Tue, tue'*, 'Kill, kill'. In the crush, straining for a good view, the innocents would soon discover their purses had proved easy prey for *coup-bourses* and *tire-laines*, working hand-in-glove with the pseudo-combatants.

D'Artagnan's purse, alas, was not worth lifting. He sat despondently with the Three Musketeers in a *traiteur* near the gate to the Fair, confessing that he had been duped and acknowledging that he 'possessed a very dangerous enemy in the person of Milédi'. Poor company for his companions, d'Artagnan left to return home. Almost at once, at the congested entrance to the rue des Mauvais Garçons, the appropriately named Bad Boys' Street, complete strangers rudely jostled him: once, twice, three times. Normally a single such encounter would have been sufficient for d'Artagnan to force an apology at the point of his sword, but instinct told him to keep his notorious temper in check.

When d'Artagnan refused to be provoked, the third man blocked his way with a drawn sword and challenged d'Artagnan to unsheathe his own. His two menacing companions joined him. These were all hardened professionals, who knew how to kill expertly and quickly. D'Artagnan, outnumbered three to one, blocked almost simultaneous thrusts, his sword darting first one way and then another. However, even he could not survive unharmed for long. After suffering two minor flesh wounds to the body, he retreated with his back to a cul-de-sac and desperately shouted for help: '*A moi Mousquetaires!*' Athos, Porthos and Aramis were within easy earshot and soon came to d'Artagnan's aid. Milédi had anticipated this in her plan and within moments the number of would-be assassins had increased to at least seven. Their target was not just d'Artagnan but also the Three Musketeers. D'Artagnan had been the cheese in the mousetrap.

In the desperate struggle that followed, Athos received a severe sword-thrust in his side. Two other Musketeers, both Bretons, who had seen what was happening and bravely intervened, were quickly killed. Suddenly five or six more Musketeers, alerted by the cries of their colleagues, poured out of the gate to the Fair. As the odds dramatically moved in their favour, d'Artagnan ran through his closest opponent and two others also fell dead. The remainder, several carrying wounds, made good their escape down a honeycomb of alleys. The Musketeers made no serious attempt at pursuit because both d'Artagnan and Athos needed urgent medical attention. Athos was in a particularly bad way, having lost a great deal of blood. He was helped the short distance to a convent in

Saint-Germain, where they were used to treating wounded combatants who had duelled in the nearby Pré-aux-Clercs.

A 'commissaire who came up with a troop of archers' took the dead assailants to La Morgue, so called because *morguer* meant to scrutinize any person for identification. The morgue at the Châtelet prison used two adjoining rooms for its gruesome task. Attendants washed the bodies and removed most of their internal organs in the first room, which had its own well to swill away the blood. In the second they salted the cadavers and stuffed them with straw to prevent a stench, before putting them on display. No one claimed the three corpses, but this was hardly surprising. The contents of their pockets included various letters written in English, strengthening d'Artagnan's strong suspicion that some of the attackers had crossed the Channel and that Milédi was their paymaster. She was nowhere to be found. Fearing arrest, Lucy Percy had returned hastily to England. She was never brought to account as Richelieu's master spy, but six years later her plotting against the English Parliament would cost her several disagreeable months in the Tower.

At first Athos seemed on the mend, but soon the surgeons began to despair of his life. His wound had become infected and he grew steadily weaker, dying on 21 December 1643. Anticipating the worst, his friends had already made preparations for his funeral and Athos was buried the same evening. The register of the Church of Saint-Sulpice in Paris records the burial procession, interment and service for Athos and observes that he was 'taken [from this world] near the hall of the Pré aux-Clercs'. Ironically, Athos had died slowly in his bed within sight of where many duellists died instantly at dawn. Huddled in their cloaks against the cold at Athos' graveside, as the priest made the last sign of the cross, Aramis, Porthos and d'Artagnan must have wondered who would be next. Athos had been killed in his prime, aged no more than twenty-eight. Richelieu, who had died just over a year earlier, had reached out from the grave to murder him. Revenge, runs the old proverb, is a dish best served cold but rarely can its chef have been so much colder.

5

NOTHING BUT A SWORD

ୡ ঌ

At the end of May 1644, the new Palais-Royal was still in chaos, and the troops supposed to be guarding the gates gave up trying to weed out undesirables among its endless stream of visitors. A year after the death of Louis XIII, the Queen Regent had finally completed her move from the gloomy, run-down Louvre to Richelieu's former palace with her sons, five-year-old Louis and two-year-old Philippe. Where Anne went, ambitious courtiers soon had no choice but to follow and while servants waiting for instructions lounged about outside, protecting carts piled high with furniture, their noble masters were still manoeuvring frantically inside to obtain rooms in this smarter but much smaller residence. What the Queen Regent grudgingly granted them came with just the bare walls, so even dukes and duchesses could be seen arriving at the palace with tarnished candlesticks and cracked chamber pots bearing their coat of arms, anything of limited value that could be left prominently in their personal accommodation to reinforce title to their claim.

D'Artagnan paid little attention to these comings and goings because he was waiting for an audience with the young king. It never occurred to him that Louis XIV was one of the group of grubby children marching in unison on the terrace before his very eyes, miniature muskets sloped backwards at exactly the right angle, like troops on parade; they were led by the new, rather plump, drill sergeant-cum-governess Mademoiselle de Lasalle, wearing a man's plumed hat with black feathers, sporting a sword in her belt and carrying a rusty pike. Louis, the shabbily dressed child at the back, kept the beat, hammering furiously on a huge drum that bent him under its weight as he disappeared from view.

From where d'Artagnan was standing, shrill voices were clearly audible in the queen's private apartments. The richest heiress in Europe, seventeen-year-old Anne-Marie-Louise d'Orléans, Gaston's daughter and little Louis' first cousin, was vigorously defending her position in the royal pecking order and did not care who knew it. Mazarin had already supplanted her once when rooms were handed out and the aquiline, wilful Mademoiselle de Montpensier, known as 'La Grande Mademoiselle', was determined it would not happen again. The Queen Regent said she was an 'insolent girl' but, unwilling to give fresh momentum to the mutterings against Mazarin, reluctantly gave in.

For the moment, Mazarin had to make do with the sumptuous neighbouring Hôtel Duret, but every time he walked through the palace gardens to 'confer' with the queen behind closed doors for several hours at a time, it scandalized the court; Anne even found anonymous notes rebuking her conduct pinned to her pillow. Before long, builders would be instructed to create a new suite with a private connecting staircase so that Mazarin might live unobserved in the Palais-Royal itself and 'proceed commodiously' to the royal apartments. Later, when the council of state was asked to endorse this considerable expenditure retrospectively, Mazarin looked innocently out of the window and Anne 'blushed to the whites of her eyes'.

Mazarin had learned from his late patron that someone who purported to act in the name of the king could acquire huge wealth and power. If Richelieu had been forced to choose between them, he would have preferred power to wealth, an option that never occurred to Mazarin at all. In due course Mazarin would demonstrate that in the kind of kingdom he had helped to create, wealth was power, albeit power at a much less majestic level than that exercised by Richelieu, and power without proper recognition – still less respect. By systematically draining the state's coffers, Mazarin amassed a staggering fortune of almost 40 million livres, twice the legacy of his mentor, keeping at least one-third in realizable assets, gold bullion, coin and precious stones, hoarded up and down France.

As Mazarin grew wealthier he could extend his patronage, the institutionalized corruption that made almost everyone and everything in France for sale to the highest bidder. Anne took her cue from Mazarin in always receiving a cut to gratify the aspirations of her courtiers, however outrageous and impracticable: one of the court ladies purchased from the queen the right to tax all the Masses said in Paris.

These mercenary considerations did not augur well for the success of d'Artagnan's visit, given the Gascon's acute lack of funds. Despite all his exploits, d'Artagnan was still not a Musketeer and he needed the boy king's blessing to become one. In the past, Tréville had been his own recruiting officer, but with Mazarin in the queen's bed in his place, his influence had waned. Prospective Musketeers now could not join the company until they had appeared personally before the monarch, a ruling of the regent made at Mazarin's behest.

Finally ushered into the royal presence, d'Artagnan, hat in hand, produced his most obsequious bow. Much to his annoyance, if the Queen Regent were at all curious to see the Gascon who had caused so much discomfort to her late but unlamented enemy Richelieu, she showed no sign of it. Anne continued to converse in a low voice with Mazarin in her native Castilian. Brought up close to the Spanish frontier, d'Artagnan understood enough of the language to realize that the first minister was giving the queen instructions, cleverly disguised as advice. The king, all radiant good looks and flowing curls, was immaculately dressed and no longer looked like the little drummer in the ragamuffin army. He sat impassively on his throne, gazing intently at d'Artagnan.

At last Mazarin spoke. After whispering with the king, he said:

'His Majesty considers you too young to join his Musketeers. You must carry a musket in the guards for at least another two or three years.' It was all d'Artagnan, already notorious for speaking first and thinking second, could do to contain his fiery Gascon temper. A place had been found for Porthos to return to the Musketeers without all this rigmarole, and even the unloved Sergeant Besmaux was among their latest recruits. D'Artagnan made his way out of the audience chamber, fuming to think that he was still an obscure trooper in the household guards.

Aramis and Porthos were left in no doubt of d'Artagnan's displeasure. 'Here's a regular farce,' he complained to them bitterly:

> His Majesty is as yet only five and a half years old. It would have been much better to have brought him a battledore and shuttlecock to amuse himself with, than to ask his opinion on a matter that was so far beyond his understanding.

Obliged to remain in one of the household regiments, barely two weeks later d'Artagnan found himself on the march and soon engaged in yet another siege. Gravelines, a coastal town in the Spanish Netherlands, was defended by the formidable Fort Saint-Philippe, whose garrison stubbornly repelled every attack, helped by a shortage of powder for the French artillery. When one day at dusk the fort's guns unexpectedly fell silent, the lieutenant leading d'Artagnan's troop suspected a trap and told his men to keep their heads down. D'Artagnan, never noted for his patience, volunteered to find a way into the fort. Mainville, another cadet, accompanied him, but as the fort's walls loomed up ahead he decided the reconnaissance was far too risky, abandoned d'Artagnan to his fate and went back to his own lines. Pressed for an explanation, Mainville foolishly reported that d'Artagnan had fallen into the hands of the Spaniards, who, he claimed, had killed him without mercy. D'Artagnan meanwhile climbed the walls, feeling his way silently in pitch darkness, aware that the slightest noise might bring a volley of fire down on his head at any moment. He slithered gingerly over the parapet and came face to face with a corpse. It was soon obvious to him that no one remained alive in the fort: the defenders, sprawled over their guns, had been killed to the last man. D'Artagnan's apparent return from the dead, a feat he would repeat more than once, delighted all but Mainville, who deserted that same night and was never seen again.

Almost a year passed and d'Artagnan had begun to despair of ever achieving his ambition of becoming a Musketeer when, for once, his amorous activities worked in his favour. Both d'Artagnan and his commanding officer Essarts were pursuing the same woman, a former convent nun, in Paris. Essarts wanted d'Artagnan out of the way and had him transferred to the Musketeers as part of the bodyguard of Gaston, duc d'Orléans, who was leaving to take command of the campaign in Flanders.

Determined to make a name for himself, d'Artagnan did not devote much time to ensuring the infamous duke's safety or indeed his own. When the siege of Bourbourg, a small town on the river Aa near Dunkerque, began in July 1645 d'Artagnan led an impulsive attack that caught the Spanish by surprise and drove them out of their forward defensive earthworks, back towards the gates of the town. However, as soon as the defenders realized that they were faced by just a handful of Musketeers, they turned and counter-attacked fiercely from all sides. Caught in crossfire, four Musketeers fell, riddled with bullets. D'Artagnan, with more lives than a cat, escaped with a bullet hole through the brim of his hat and three more through his tunic. His triumphant return was greeted with wild cheers, and Bourbourg fell a few days later.

D'Artagnan took part in another six sieges that summer before returning to Paris uninjured. However, just as his fame was spreading, his career as a Musketeer came to an abrupt halt. Mazarin was determined to rid himself of Tréville for good. He let it be known that he wanted Tréville's post of captain for one of his nephews, Paul Mancini, even though this was palpably absurd, for Mancini was still a boy. The first minister made the command of the Musketeers an issue of fundamental importance with the Queen Regent and, perhaps aware that it was more than mere rumour that linked Anne to Tréville, even threatened to return to Italy. 'Your confidence in me must be very slight indeed', he complained to his mistress, 'if it comes second to the cunning of a Béarnais!'

Anne finally succumbed to Mazarin's pressure, only to find that she could not dismiss Tréville, who asserted that his appointment as captain of the Musketeers was for life and flatly refused to resign. Even several months spent as a prisoner in the Bastille in 1645 failed to change his mind. An impasse remained until, on 26 January 1646, prompted by Mazarin, the Queen Regent neatly sidestepped this obstacle by disbanding the Musketeers on the grounds of economy. Tréville suspected correctly that this was an expedient and grandly refused Anne's offer of compensation, preferring to keep the bargaining chip for another day. 'So long as it may please the King to do without the Musketeers,' he said self-effacingly:

> I shall remain at court without employment, but if His Majesty is ever pleased to set them on foot again, I trust he will have the justice to return this company to me, which I do not believe I have lost for having failed in my duty.

By such fine words and simply staying in Paris, Tréville also ensured that he could continue to collect personally the huge salary that went with his post.

In a mood of grim resignation, the Musketeers handed in their swords, muskets and blue mantles at the armoury of the Palais-Royal. D'Artagnan was unwilling to give up his dreams of glory but Porthos and Aramis, fearing that without the support of their fellow Musketeers on the streets of Paris they would suffer the same fate as Athos, decided to return to their native province of Béarn. Unlike d'Artagnan, Porthos and Aramis had become hard-bitten veterans, with a keen sense of self-preservation. They had been willing to take their chances as members of the elite royal bodyguard or even in the regular army but, once that protection had disappeared, they feared receiving a dagger-thrust in the dark.

Back in Béarn, for a while Aramis was quite content with the life of a country gentleman, especially when his reputation in the Musketeers helped him to marry into money. On 16 February 1650 his wedding took place at Oloron-Sainte-Marie with a host of lords and ladies in attendance, the bride a local young heiress, Jeanne de Béarn-Bonasse. Jeanne duly gave birth to two sons and a daughter, but Aramis was not cut out for fatherhood. Even though his wife was expecting their fourth child, he resolved to return to Paris, probably intending to rejoin d'Artagnan, as his will – made on 22 April 1654 – anticipated danger, even death. But as Jean Dufaur, notary of Barétous, records in his preamble to the will, Aramis was suddenly taken ill and died shortly after settling his affairs.

The third and last of the Three Musketeers, Porthos, had an elder brother, Jean de Portau, the governor of Navarrenx, an ancient hilltop citadel dominating the junction of two rivers west of Pau; Jean also held the posts of war commissioner and controller of artillery for the province of Béarn. For a lawyer with such good connections, the dangerous role he eventually found for Porthos, putting him in charge of munitions at Navarrenx, does not suggest that the brothers were particularly close. However, in 1658, through Tréville's persistence, Porthos was given the *seigneurie* of Lanne-de-Barétous by the queen, as a reward for services rendered. The little manor's tax-free income was sufficient for Porthos, aged forty or forty-one, to propose marriage to a local lady considerably younger. Their first son became a curé and the second went into the navy, both no doubt a disappointment to their father.

In late 1669 Porthos' brother died and d'Artagnan's eldest brother, Paul de Batz-Castelmore, a former Musketeer who had retired from the army as a result of injuries received during the 1640 siege of Turin, took over as governor at Navarrenx. Paul de Batz was already aged sixty, so other aspirants kept a close eye on his lucrative governorship in case it should suddenly fall vacant. At court nobles gambled a small fortune on his longevity, but bet after bet was lost and twice his death was prematurely announced in the *Gazette*.

Paul would finally expire at Château Castlemore on 23 May 1704. By then he had convinced everyone he was 100 years old but, although his mother had conceived him some months before her wedding and the exact date of his delivery was kept quiet, his birth late in 1608 made him ninety-five. Porthos, meanwhile, was still going strong. Born in Pau on 30 January 1617, he too would reach ninety-five, dying from an apoplectic stroke on 13 July 1712, back at his birthplace. Evidently most of those Musketeers who did not fall victim to the cannonball, the bullet or the blade had the constitution of an ox.

When the King's Musketeers were abruptly dissolved in 1646, and d'Artagnan was left alone contemplating penury in Paris, Tréville had been able to secure him a special favour. Rather provocatively, considering the circumstances, Mazarin had asked Tréville for the names of 'two Musketeers who were gentlemen and possessed but "cloak and sword", [so] as to be under obligations to him for their welfare'. Tréville knew which of his Musketeers were the poorest: he nominated d'Artagnan and his implacable enemy, Besmaux. They were also the pair whom Tréville could most rely upon to be his eyes and ears.

The two ex-Musketeers were jubilant, convinced their fortunes were assured by this surprising turn of events. As a popular French saying went at the time, 'Quails were about to fall into their mouths, fully roasted.' Both quickly discovered, however, that the wily Mazarin parted with money only in the context of various missions and expected it to cover their travelling expenses. As d'Artagnan remarked, they soon had to trim their aspirations, for 'if you buy fine stockings you cannot afford shoes.' The minister also anonymously sponsored a gambling den where it was essential to lose in order to stand a chance of promotion. As d'Artagnan and Besmaux found to their cost, those who had the temerity to win had great difficulty afterwards in collecting their salaries.

For d'Artagnan in particular, serving the Italian was the start of many weary nights in the saddle, using relays of mounts and sometimes sleeping rough in the undergrowth to avoid hostile patrols. His first task in 1646 was to carry orders from Mazarin to one of his generals, instructing him to move his troops into Provence. By June he was riding hard in the opposite direction, to the besieged city of Courtrai on France's northern frontier. The official *Gazette de France* – the former *Gazette* had changed its title and given up all pretence of being independent – recorded:

> On the 28th, the Sieur d'Artagnan, one of the *gentilshommes* of His Eminence, has returned from the army in Flanders and reports that the fortress of Courtrai is so beset that there is every hope that His Royal Highness [the duc d'Orléans] will capture it in four or five days.

The duke did capture the fortress.

In September the French army moved on to Dunkerque, a siege that took several weeks. Ordered by Mazarin to report on the besiegers' progress, d'Artagnan had a typically narrow escape when the comte de Laval, standing alongside and engaging him in conversation, was hit by splinters from a stray shell. Laval fell to the ground, apparently dead; but after a few moments staggered to his feet suffering from only minor cuts and bruises and coolly asked for pen and ink, having forgotten, he said, to write to his wife. For once, even d'Artagnan had been upstaged.

The following year, 1647, Mazarin sent d'Artagnan to England with dispatches for Oliver Cromwell, second-in-command of Parliament's New Model Army. He instructed him to take an extremely circuitous route by way of Germany so that no one would guess his final destination. These elaborate precautions suggest that, without the knowledge and approval of the two Roman Catholic queens resident in Paris, Anne and Henrietta Maria, Mazarin was quite prepared to abandon Charles I and to leave him to make what terms he could with the Puritan opposition to keep his throne. For a while Mazarin had hedged his bets just in case Henrietta, an empoverished political refugee who had been given charitable lodgings in the Louvre, succeeded against the odds in snaring the unimaginably rich Grande Mademoiselle for a daughter-in-law. Alas for Henrietta's hopes, her rebellious sixteen-year-old son, the future Charles II, thought the girl far too plain and instead of plighting his troth, angered the haughty heiress by pretending he did not speak French.

Mazarin's main motive, it turned out, had little to do with the divine right of kings or the strategic advantage of backing the right horse. He was hoping to place one of his nieces on the English throne, and unsure whether to negotiate a marriage with Charles or with Richard Cromwell, the future protector's son. Mazarin's instincts were to follow the money, which resided in Whitehall, not the Louvre. D'Artagnan made good progress with the Cromwells and, most untypically of Mazarin, he received a large recompense for his trouble on his return.

Besmaux, meanwhile, was less successful in his efforts to impress his master. On 15 June 1648, during fighting at Cremona in the Italian campaign, he imprudently led French troops from the front in hot pursuit of the enemy. A musket ball pierced his lower jaw, leaving him scarred for life. Thereafter he wore a mask over part of his face, the beginning of an obsession with masks that later would take on great significance.

For all his success in England, d'Artagnan's fortunes were inextricably linked to those of Mazarin, and Mazarin was about to find his own position in peril. The Paris Parlement, in direct defiance of the regent, refused to register a royal edict raising new taxes to pay for the war with Spain. Anne had to pawn some of her jewels to meet urgent debts and the royal cooks, fed up with working without pay, went on strike. On 26 August, in an ominous echo of Charles I's ill-fated attempt six years previously to arrest five members of Parliament, egged on by Anne, Mazarin tried to seize three *parlementaires*, including the elderly Pierre Broussel, the incorruptible idol of Paris.

A guards lieutenant, the comte de Comminges, was dispatched to seize Broussel. Historian Armand Praviel, from his study of contemporary pamphlets, concluded that Mazarin, not trusting Comminges to have the nerve to carry out the order, sent one of his *gentilshommes*, almost certainly d'Artagnan, with him. This shows how little Mazarin understood d'Artagnan's acute sense of fair play; it is likely that d'Artagnan was the one with doubts, the one who refused point-blank to arrest a sick old man stuck on his privy after taking a purgative. It was left to Comminges to force the half-dressed, diarrhoea-stricken Broussel to leave his house. The street was too narrow to take the count's coach, which had to wait on the corner; and Comminges would probably not have escaped with his life but for the courage of d'Artagnan in holding back an angry mob with his sword. Comminges' troubles were far from over, however. His coach lost a wheel on the deliberately circuitous route taken to the palace of Saint-Germain, where Broussel was to be held in secret. An alert bystander recognized Broussel as he was bundled into another carriage bearing a royal crest and realized what was happening; once the news got out the whole of Paris dissolved in uproar.

Back at the Palais-Royal, the apprehensive Mazarin sent d'Artagnan to judge the mood of the mob. Dressed as an artisan in the dirtiest clothes he could find, completely unarmed, d'Artagnan entered into the spirit of his task with customary zeal. He left the palace by a back entrance, befriended a group of rioters and settled down inside the hollow space behind their large improvised barricade, 'hobnobbing with the riffraff and consuming 'several bottles of wine with cold meat upon a barrel'. Here he met, perhaps even mischievously encouraged, several revolutionaries intent upon killing the first minister. He led their leader into an ambush but the mob released him the same day. Mazarin found d'Artagnan's wickedly blood-curdling report so alarming that with undignified haste he changed into anonymous grey, donned riding cap and boots, and ordered him to saddle his fastest horse. Mazarin 'was easily overcome by fright' and never willing to risk his skin. Anne took her lover's heavy hint. Her face deathly white from the humiliation, she ordered Broussel's release.

This unexpected victory over the established order on what became known as the Day of the Barricades prompted Parisians to take to the streets regularly, the start of a period of anarchy called the Fronde. The word meant catapult or sling, the favourite weapon of local hooligans, and the royalists also began to adopt it as a term of abuse. As the civil war continued, it became the symbol of resistance, and those opposed to Mazarin and the Queen Regent wore emblems of the Fronde on their sashes. The Fronde embroiled almost every interest group in French society: princes of the blood, great nobles, minor nobles, office holders, members of the Paris and provincial Parlements, clergy, townsfolk, thieves, vagabonds and peasants. Rebellion was in the air, prompting Mazarin and Anne to plan secretly to leave Paris while they could, for the safer royal palace at Saint-Germain, some ten miles away.

In the early hours of 6 January 1649, the court abandoned the Palais-Royal. Their clandestine departure in a fleet of coaches with muffled wheels had all the signs of d'Artagnan's involvement, for they achieved complete surprise, passing checkpoints at the city gates manned by rebels lying beside their dying braziers in a drunken stupor. Unfortunately nothing had been done by d'Artagnan or anyone else to prepare Saint-Germain for the king's arrival. It was empty and freezing, in a particularly severe winter: the Seine was frozen solid to a depth of fifteen centimetres. Morale at the palace, where for weeks most courtiers had to sleep on nothing but straw, was not improved by the news from England that Cromwell had cut off King Charles I's head on 30 January.

In failing to help make Saint-Germain habitable, d'Artagnan may have been distracted by a flurry of orders to save Mazarin's furniture and library, which proved impossible. The Italian's priceless effects were gleefully sold piecemeal at knock-down prices on the streets of Paris. When he heard the news, Mazarin was in no mood to grant favours, but d'Artagnan, with that impeccable sense of mistiming destined to blight his career, decided this was the moment to ask for a commission in the Guards. Inevitably Mazarin dissembled with all the skill for which he was famous: 'Monsieur d'Artagnan, I always considered you an eagle, but I find that instead you are only a common garden bird . . . A governorship is the least one of my servants should expect; think of the difference between a lieutenant's post in the Guards and a governorship.'

D'Artagnan naively withdrew his request in the confident expectation of higher advancement to come but of course received nothing.

In August, with d'Artagnan close by their side, Mazarin and the Queen Regent felt safe to return to the capital. However, the Fronde was far from finished and on 9 February 1651 Anne of Austria had to allow the Paris mob into the Palais-Royal to see the young king asleep in his bed or – given the racket, pretending to be – to dispel rumours that the royal family was again about to flee. Seeing the way the wind was blowing, Mazarin promptly departed for Germany, taking the crown jewels of France with him as an insurance policy.

At this juncture, any man with a sense of self-preservation would have abandoned the grand larcener and ingratiated himself with Mazarin's enemies. Instead, d'Artagnan arranged for four identically dressed impersonators of his master to leave Paris by different gates at the same time to confuse pursuit and then unhesitatingly accompanied the real Mazarin into exile.

His immediate task was to negotiate for him a safe haven. 'I have sent d'Artagnan to Bonne', wrote Mazarin to Anne, 'to pay my compliments to M. l'Electeur and to request him to give me some chateau for my retreat.' D'Artagnan was successful, securing the loan of the elector's baroque summer residence, Schloss Augustusburg, at Bruehl. Mazarin showed his appreciation by arranging for Anne to grant d'Artagnan a commission as a lieutenant in the Household Guards. As usual, however, the reward had strings attached: d'Artagnan first had to promise to remain in the Italian's personal service.

To protect his vast fortune hidden back in France, where it was held under assumed names, Mazarin turned to Jean-Baptiste Colbert. The son of a merchant, the methodical Colbert succeeded in protecting most of Mazarin's ill-gotten gains. Indeed, he managed to increase Mazarin's wealth in his absence by a mixture of speculation, embezzlement of state funds and the illegal sale of patents. Mazarin issued his instructions to Colbert through d'Artagnan, nearly always in writing. This put the Gascon in acute danger because Mazarin had a huge price on his head, 150,000 livres dead or alive, and other messengers sent by him discovered to be carrying his correspondence were killed without mercy. D'Artagnan possessed a rare combination of blind loyalty and infinite resourcefulness that kept him going, usually just one step ahead of his pursuers. Even Mazarin acknowledged that d'Artagnan's trips to Paris on his behalf were becoming increasingly perilous. He wrote to the Abbé Basile Fouquet, 'I beg you to tell d'Artagnan that he must return to me, and that he must take every precaution, less any misfortune befall him.'

Never one, though, to dwell on the risks taken by others on his behalf or to put all his eggs in a single basket, Mazarin also made use of the creative accounting of the abbé's younger brother, Nicolas Fouquet, who had made a name for himself as a precocious nineteen-year-old in the Parlement of Metz. Soon Fouquet could afford to buy the powerful office of procureur-general in the Paris Parlement, displaying an eloquent grasp of the law to complement his charm and good looks. It amused and comforted Mazarin to discover that despite their equally humble backgrounds, the dazzling Fouquet and the dour Colbert hated one another from the start, each making sure that the other could not get away with dipping his hand into the first minister's pocket.

Even in the midst of the crisis of his prolonged exile, Mazarin still remained focused on the removal of Tréville from court, perhaps fearing that the former captain of the Musketeers might take advantage of his absence to regain Anne's favour. One of Mazarin's last acts before his departure for Germany had been to raise again with Anne, in the presence of the young king, his proposal to revive the Musketeers under the command of his nephew, Paul Mancini, although he was still barely fifteen years of age. In July 1651, in an encoded dispatch sent via the Spanish Netherlands, he responded to 'certain passages' in a letter from the queen, since lost but possibly containing a reference to his rival. Mazarin said his scheme 'could be put into effect inside two months and by then I may have the means to pay off Tréville'. It would all come to nothing, however, because a year later, as the civil war spluttered on, Mancini would be killed in battle.

After his usual chronic indecision, Louis XIV's wicked uncle Gaston had backed the rebel princes against the young king. His tomboy daughter, the Grand Mademoiselle, was determined to return to Gaston's capital, Orléans, which had been invested by the royal army and with its liege lord absent, seemed likely to fall. She sneaked through the royalists' lines and climbed a wobbly ladder to reach a small hole at the top of the city's postern gate. Her exceedingly plump posterior had to be given a hefty shove before she was able to squeeze through the gap but, despite this highly undignified arrival, the citizens greeted their heroine as though she were a second Joan of Arc and thereafter the city remained defiant.

Soon afterwards, during the battle that cost Mancini his life, when the Prince of Condé's rebel troops, cornered by Turenne's pincer movement, were fighting for their lives in the Sainte-Antoine suburb outside the gates of Paris, Mademoiselle got carried away with her new heroic role. She instructed the governor of the Bastille to turn his guns so they were pointing outwards from the city walls instead of inwards in their usual fashion to intimidate its unruly citizens. On her orders, the governor fired several salvoes at the advancing royal cavalry, mowing down the leading formations and giving Condé and his rebels the breathing space they needed to retreat into Paris. To say the least, Mademoiselle's intervention was ill conceived; she was hoping to marry cousin Louis and because of her immense wealth, hitherto she had seemed a serious contender. Mazarin observed cryptically, *'Elle a tué son mari!'*, 'She has killed her husband!' In the figurative sense he was correct: she had indeed killed off her chance of marrying the king. Louis XIV never forgot a bad turn, as Mademoiselle would discover many years afterwards, embroiling d'Artagnan in her misfortune.

Mazarin 'resumed his political harness as though he had never divested himself of it'. With Gaston and Mademoiselle disqualified from their self-appointed role of moulding the monarch, Mazarin filled the vacuum himself. The seat of government moved with the royal forces, and by June the Queen Regent, the cardinal and the king were based at Melun, south-west of the capital. The printers of Paris did a roaring trade in pamphlets espousing the cause of the *Frondeurs*, and were unrestrained in their attacks on Mazarin, known as the Mazarinades; but by 1652 their polemic tone had reached a new level of intensity and momentum.

According to Jeffery Merrick in his detailed study of the Mazarinades, the pamphleteers identified Mazarin's habitual offence as:

> anal intercourse – first in the passive role, during his youth, and then in the active role, by the time he relocated to France . . . insisting that he had anal, not vaginal, sex with Anne of Austria.

They also 'charged the cardinal with sexual deviance as frequently as they did because they considered the accusation both plausible and effective'. Its plausibility was reinforced by an incident on the night of the festival of John the Baptist, Le Jour de Saint Jean, 24 June. Three Masses were usually celebrated on this holy day, with a good deal of food and drink consumed in the intervals between them. Louis XIV was thirteen, having officially come of age on his birthday in the previous September. He was handsome, well built, but probably not yet sexually active with any partner, although perhaps not for lack of curiosity, having once already attempted to join the Queen Regent in her bath. La Porte had remained suspicious of Mazarin, and unsuccessfully tried to implant an early distrust of the cardinal in the young king's mind. That day Louis dined at 1 p.m., which was customary, but alone with Mazarin in his rooms, which was not. Towards 7 p.m. the king sent word to La Porte that he wished to have a bath. He arrived in a state of distress and when he undressed La Porte was able to see visible signs that he had been forcibly sodomised.

La Porte wrestled with his conscience for five days, then wrote to the queen and told her what had happened. He kept a copy of the letter, which identified two further eyewitnesses to Louis' condition: his servants Bontemps and Moreau. Anne thanked La Porte for telling her but otherwise did nothing, or at least, nothing that saw the light of day. The queen needed Mazarin, politically and emotionally. In any event, Louis may not have corroborated La Porte's account, particularly if his rape had been preceded by other homosexual activity with Mazarin throughout the afternoon that he had enjoyed or at any rate tolerated. Mazarin probably brazened it out: he was known to have amused himself by collecting as many of the Mazarinades as he could lay his hands on.

Despite the Mazarinades, this incident made it even less likely that Mazarin was Louis' father. If they were not related, and the story came out, it was a survivable scandal. But if he were found guilty of homosexual incest with a reigning monarch, the death penalty would be inevitable for such an outrageous crime against the state. Not long afterwards Mazarin succeeded in removing La Porte from Anne's service, but in 1666 the king would make a point of inviting his old valet back to Saint-Germain and receiving him generously. Louis' sexual preferences became clear when, aged sixteen, he caught gonorrhea from Madame de Beauvais, Anne's first lady of the bedchamber. However, when he began to reign on his own account, the emergence of the king's strong personal antipathy to homosexuality, rife among his courtiers, could be much more easily explained by his own painful experience at the hands of the cardinal.

In February 1653 Mazarin returned to Paris and before long he made d'Artagnan a captain, but it was the spurious title of *capitaine et concierge* of La Volière, a small house in the Tuileries gardens within the gift of the king. Of course, Mazarin did not believe in gifts: d'Artagnan had to pledge 4,000 livres he did not possess for the privilege, loaned to him by the Italian at a usurious rate of interest.

The first minister continued to use d'Artagnan for clandestine enterprises and d'Artagnan appeared in various disguises to avoid detection: for added authenticity, he grew a substantial beard, which did not please his young mistress of the time. On one occasion Mazarin wrote to the superintendant of finances, hinting that d'Artagnan was to be found in monastic attire when it suited his master's purpose:

> The Englishman whom I have introduced to you through the Père d'Artagnan, Jesuit, will doubtless reveal to you great and important secrets; for I am aware, from other sources, what is being hatched between Cromwell, the Spaniards in Flanders, and the Prince of Condé.

After his experience at Cremona, Besmaux avoided military service as much as possible. Above his mask he wore an eye patch, suggesting his injuries were more extensive than those published in the *Gazette*, but d'Artagnan provocatively claimed that it concealed a perfectly sound eye underneath. Besmaux went on diplomatic missions for Mazarin in the Spanish Netherlands and elsewhere, but for much of the time remained in the relative comfort and security of Paris, where he fed the exiled minister scraps of information about the *Frondeurs*. When the rebellion faded away and Mazarin was no longer in serious danger, with impeccable timing, Besmaux volunteered to join his personal bodyguard. Mazarin used him to conduct negotiations with the recalcitrant Henri de Lorraine, who was threatening to hand over Brisach, a strategic fortress overlooking the Rhine, to the Imperial Habsburgs rather than submit to the French king. Besmaux bungled the task hopelessly and in February 1654 Mazarin wrote to him savagely, 'You are incapable of following orders and in a word, someone like that is not worth employing in any capacity.' D'Artagnan would have enjoyed delivering this particular letter.

When Mazarin showed signs of actually dismissing Besmaux from his service, however, d'Artagnan ceased his *Schadenfreude* and rallied support for his enemy. Given a breathing space by Mazarin, three months later Besmaux tried again, offering a bribe to the garrison of Brisach to go over to the king. Some of the suspicious old veterans voiced doubts that they would ever see the money, so the desperate Besmaux promised, 'If it's one *denier* short, throw Besmaux in the Rhine.' Within days Brisach was French and Besmaux's nightmare was over, but he always refused to acknowledge d'Artagnan's part in his political survival.

Besmaux made a habit of falling on his feet. In October he married the marquise Marguerite de Peyroz, granddaughter of the celebrated equestrian, the late Antoine de Pluvinel. The buxom Marguerite was just fourteen but well endowed in every sense: a considerable dowry came with her, the fruits of Pluvinel's inspired conversion of his loss-making riding school into a lucrative finishing academy for young gentlemen, with Richelieu among its former pupils. The age difference between bride and groom was thirty-five years, but Marguerite's step-mother wanted the wilful girl off her hands, caring little that Besmaux's face was marked for life and he was already forty-nine; she was also completely unaware that he had no resources of his own.

That autumn d'Artagnan's regiment left for the investment of Stenay, the Prince of Condé's fortress not far from Verdun. Shortly afterwards Mazarin informed his war minister Le Tellier that a captain and seven officers, including d'Artagnan, had been hurt in the opening attack on a fortified escarpment between two bastions. D'Artagnan predictably suffered just superficial cuts and bruises and was fit enough to take part in the relief of Arras a few days later; but three of his fellow officers died of their wounds.

The following year d'Artagnan put to the test Mazarin's earlier disingenuous suggestion that he was worth a governorship, by asking the cardinal to make him governor of the newly captured town of Landrecies. Mazarin declined on the grounds that d'Artagnan, then aged about thirty-two, was too young. D'Artagnan may have thought this a churlish response because he had offered himself as a hostage while the terms of the town's capitulation were under discussion. At the siege of Ardres d'Artagnan took further risks, reconnoitring the town's defences in disguise, pretending first to be a tobacco seller and later masquerading as the Prince of Condé's inebriated valet. D'Artagnan was exposed by someone who knew his true identity, a man destined to play a critical role in his life: Benigné d'Auvergne or, Saint-Mars, his *nom de guerre*.

Many soldiers fought under assumed names to hide their past and Benigné's father Louis, an infantry captain, was probably the first to call himself Saint-Mars. Benigné and his sister were born at Blainvilliers, a hamlet on the outskirts of the Rambouillet forest, south-west of Versailles. His parents both died when he was a small child and Saint-Mars was reluctantly brought up by an uncle, who in 1638 enrolled him in the Musketeers as a boy runner, an *enfant de troupe*, at the age of twelve. When the Musketeers were disbanded, Saint-Mars joined his father's old regiment, fighting under the colours of the Prince of Condé. No one was more surprised than Saint-Mars to come across the hero of the royal army in the heart of the rebel headquarters, pretending to be rolling drunk, and d'Artagnan must have thought his number was up. However, trying to keep a foot in both camps, Condé's *maréchal de camp*, Roye, allowed the Gascon to go free, even providing him with a horse. As d'Artagnan prepared to ride away, Roye dryly commented on the perils of espionage: 'I profess to be a good servant of the King, but my zeal for the interests of His Majesty has never extended to risk-ing a hanging in his service.' To which d'Artagnan replied: 'I believe you completely, for you are rich and a grand seigneur. An officer without means has no other way but to keep risking his skin.'

Early in 1656 a chevalier put his captaincy in the Royal Guards on the open market for 84,000 livres, three times the going rate. D'Artagnan was desperate enough for promotion to pay the asking price and raised 80,000 livres by the sale of the Tuileries house and his own lieutenancy. With Mazarin's approval, Col-bert loaned d'Artagnan the remaining 4,000 livres, a sum he was never able to repay.

With the rebels in retreat, in April Besmaux was sent to prepare the ground for Mazarin's final showdown with Tréville. When the chaotic state of royal finances left the titular head of the disbanded Musketeers without his salary, Tréville had retired angrily to his estates in south-west France. Mazarin sent Besmaux to give him the unpalatable news that the Musketeers would be revived, not with Tréville as their captain but instead under another of Mazarin's nephews, Philippe-Julien Mancini, just seventeen. If ever there was a moment for Tréville to whisper in what he saw as a sympathetic ear about the Queen Regent's ingratitude, and to be more and more indiscreet about his former relationship with Anne, then this was it. Besmaux probably took the road to Paris stunned by his secret knowledge of the royal parentage that for him would prove literally worth a fortune.

He also returned with the news that Mazarin had been waiting for, that Tréville would voluntarily surrender his post without compensation, leading Mazarin to assure Anne that the king could now safely sign the commission in favour of his nephew. Tréville, however, had said no such thing and sent an indignant letter of protest. When Mazarin ignored it and confirmed Mancini in the post shortly after his eighteenth birthday, Tréville returned to Paris. He summoned a notary to his crumbling hôtel in the rue de Tournon and signed and sealed a long document protesting against his dismissal, Mancini's appointment and Mazarin's falsehoods, declaring that he had been forced to promise his resignation in the face of the Italian's threats to ruin him. The queen invited Tréville to Saint-Germain and tried to exercise her charms, but found him in no mood for compromise. Anne had to undertake to pay Tréville 50,000 livres, grant him the governorship of Foix, appoint his elder son abbot of Montier-en-Der for life and make his younger son an ensign in the reformed Musketeers before he would finally relinquish his lifelong appointment.

Much to d'Artagnan's indignation, Mazarin rewarded Besmaux with a double promotion, first to lieutenant, then almost immediately to captain. Friction between the rivals continued unabated despite the peacemaking efforts of a mutual friend, Champfleuri, another captain of Mazarin's bodyguard. Champfleuri invited both d'Artagnan and Besmaux to dinner, without revealing to either that the other was coming, but the occasion was not a success. During the meal d'Artagnan mentioned in passing the serious illness of the governor of the Bastille, Bachellerie, suggesting to Besmaux with heavy irony that he apply for the post. Little did d'Artagnan realize that the germ of an idea was all Besmaux needed when serious money was at stake.

In March 1657, soon after the strained evening with d'Artagnan, Besmaux deliberately sought out Bachellerie, who was convalescing in the country, on the pretext of taking his wife to inspect a manor house for sale in nearby Sens. Bachellerie made the mistake of treating Besmaux as his disinterested equal and complained wittily that he was not just on sick leave but also sick of his job, because he had been waiting for years to be reimbursed by the state for the money he had spent in feeding his prisoners.

Besmaux hurried back to Paris, cynically repeated word for word what Bachellerie had said and Mazarin ordered Bachellerie to dispose of his governorship. When Bachellerie angrily objected, Mazarin replied that 'the king did not like to be served by people who complained their employment was putting them in the workhouse.' Bachellerie returned to the Bastille, ostensibly to remove his effects from the governor's lodgings, but was found by one of his officers the next morning, stone cold in his bed.

Biding his time, Besmaux waited almost a year before he asked Mazarin for the vacant post of governor. This was, for Besmaux, a pivotal moment. Having handed over his written request personally at the Palais-Royal and left Mazarin's suite, he took the risk of spying through a keyhole on the first minister, to see what he did with his petition. Besmaux had good reason to fear that Mazarin might not support him for such an important post, but his secret knowledge – gleaned from Tréville – must have made him indispensable to his master, and clinched his advancement. Nothing less would explain why Mazarin went to such huge trouble to persuade Bachellerie's family to accept half the official price of the late governor's office but instead of pocketing the difference, passed on the saving to Besmaux himself. On 10 April 1658, for 40,000 livres, Besmaux secured a job for life that would make him one of the richest men in the kingdom.

Despite having paid twice this sum for his captaincy in the guards, d'Artagnan could not resist rejoining the Musketeers when the chance came along. The spoiled and lazy young Mancini quickly showed that his only desire was to return to his palatial villa in Rome, leaving the running of the royal troop in the hands of his second in command, Isaac de Baas. Not long afterwards, Mazarin sent Baas to take charge of a regiment serving in Catalonia, thereby creating a vacancy in the Musketeers. On 26 May Mazarin decided at long last to repay the debt he owed d'Artagnan, appointing him sous-lieutenant and effective commander.

The following month, a guest for dinner at the Bastille, where Besmaux was already living in style and eager to display his affluence to the new head of the Musketeers, d'Artagnan made a favourable impression on the governor's young wife.

This was scarcely surprising, given that d'Artagnan was thirty-five and reputedly handsome, while Besmaux was fifty-eight and disfigured. Marguerite's dress showed her considerable assets to advantage, and d'Artagnan could not take his eyes off her. He was not invited again.

After years of romancing other men's wives, d'Artagan finally embarked on a serious relationship. In November the Musketeers escorted the young king and the regent to Lyon, where Louis was to meet Princess Marguerite of Savoy, to be appraised as a prospective bride. The negotiations came to nothing and Louis would soon marry the Spanish Infanta Maria-Theresa, but for d'Artagnan, the journey proved more productive. On the way to Lyon the royal party stopped at Chalon-sur-Saône, whose military governor held a lavish reception for the king. During the course of the evening d'Artagnan was introduced to the governor's step-daughter, Anne-Charlotte-Chrestienne de Chanlecy.

Anne-Charlotte was about thirty-four and a widow whose husband had died defending Arras against the Spanish. A description of Anne-Charlotte discovered in a contemporary prayer book said that 'her suffering was etched on her face, her dark eyes clouded with tears; her beauty was in her bearing rather than her figure,' a tactful way perhaps of hinting she was past her prime. Nonetheless the Chanlecys were part of the old nobility of the sword and Anne-Charlotte possessed a barony in her own right. An annual income of 60,000 livres from her late husband's possessions and another 18,000 livres from her own estates around the chateaux of Sainte-Croix in Bresse and Champlecy in Charolais made her an extremely good catch for a soldier hugely in debt. Unlike the great majority of officers in Louis' army, d'Artagnan had no other means but his pay.

D'Artagnan turned on all his charm for Anne-Charlotte, playing the daring captain of the Musketeers and holding out the prospect of an exciting life in Paris. After the swiftest of courtships, they were married just over three months later in the chapel of the Louvre itself, on the authority and in the presence of 'the very powerful monarch Louis de Bourbon, King of France and Navarre and of the most illustrious and eminent Monseigneur, Jules, Cardinal Mazarin'. Besmaux, governor of the Bastille, was among the witnesses, showing that he, too, had arrived among the good and the great.

The couple set up home in the capital, lavishly refurbishing d'Artagnan's rented hôtel on the corner of the rue du Bac and the quai Malaquais, overlooking the Seine. At first they spent a lot of time together in the principal bedroom, with its splendid views of the river, its Oudenarde tapestries and a four-poster bed whose canopy was covered in rich red damask. Although her first marriage of twelve years had been childless, in her second Anne-Charlotte conceived almost immediately. In light of the pitiful medical knowledge of the time she was at an advanced age for a first pregnancy, but she gave birth to a healthy boy early in 1660.

The arrival of a son and heir should have encouraged d'Artagnan to settle down to family life but it did not. Something in his psychological make-up compelled him to put most of his spare time and energy into the relentless seduction of women. While each successive move might be played out by d'Artagnan with style and panache, this served only to disguise a shameless sexual predator moving from conquest to conquest. D'Artagnan looked on every attractive female he met with sensual eyes, making cuckolds out of best friend and worst enemy alike. He said he preferred married women as they had fewer long-term expectations. D'Artagnan's reputation as a deadly swordsman ensured that their husbands rarely dared to call him out.

Anne-Charlotte was no fool and soon came to suspect her new spouse was unfaithful. D'Artagnan described her as 'a very jealous woman . . . who set a thousand spies at my heels'. His wife's paid informants returned with tales of d'Artagnan's regular visits to the fashionable salons of the Marais district. 'I was not the man to put up with the lectures she tried to give me,' confessed d'Artagnan. By the time Anne-Charlotte became pregnant a second time, the marriage was already in trouble; in July 1661 their second son was born not in Paris but on her estates at Chalon, to where she had angrily retired.

Anne-Charlotte was equally mistrustful of d'Artagnan where money was concerned. She refused to take responsibility for his growing debts, kept her income and possessions separate and made sure that whatever fate befell her, only her children and not her husband, would be well provided for. D'Artagnan was once again alone.

6

THE FALL OF FOUQUET

ॐ ॐ

On Wednesday, 17 August 1661, Nicolas Fouquet, the *surintendant des finances*, the French chancellor of the Exchequer, hosted the party of the century. He promised a unique, unsurpassed spectacle that no one – not the king, not the court, not the 6,000 guests – would ever forget. It lived up to its billing. As the afternoon shadows lengthened, in perfect weather Louis XIV and his courtiers made the three-hour journey north from Fontainebleau, their coaches escorted by d'Artagnan and his Musketeers. At 6 p.m. Fouquet received a smiling Louis at the gates of his new chateau, Vaux-le-Vicomte. As the visitors entered the gardens of Vaux a thousand fountains began to play, including 100 tree-high jets, creating an avenue of water that shimmered in the sunlight. Courtiers gasped at the chateau's magnificence, its marble and gold, its crystal chandeliers, its priceless collections of pictures, including works by Poussin and Veronese, its antique statues and its rare Chinese furniture. The famous chef, François Vatel, produced a memorable banquet for the more important visitors, consisting of pheasants, quails, partridges, ortolans, bisques and ragouts, served on 900 gold and silver plates, washed down with vintage wines, to the accompaniment of twenty-four violins. After supper, a ballet set to music by Jean-Baptiste Lulli was the prelude to a brand new comedy, *Les Facheux*, in high-society language *The Bores*, written and presented by Molière himself. As darkness fell, thousands of little lights picked out the contours of the chateau. From its dome a volley of rockets, sounding like cannon fire, launched an extraordinary firework display by the Italian Jacopo Torelli, signalling the start of a grand ball, with carriages at 3 a.m. For one night, Fouquet, not Louis, was the King of France.

At Vaux-le-Vicomte, the *surintendant* had brought together architect Louis Le Vau, landscape designer André Le Nôtre and artist-decorator Charles Le Brun to create the forerunner of Versailles. Money was, quite literally, no object. A labour force of 18,000 worked on the project; water for the fountains flowed through mile after mile of lead piping imported from England; huge, transplanted trees arrived and were dropped into the ground where gardeners with a normal budget would have sown acorns. When Le Brun despaired of finding enough suitable tapestries for the walls of the chateau, a factory, the forerunner of the Gobelins, was established in a nearby village to make 150 to his specific designs.

Fouquet could afford such expense because of the financial system he had inherited and scandalously exploited, although Colbert, Mazarin's unofficial financial steward, knew perfectly well what was going on because Mazarin had been guilty of the same malpractices on an even more spectacular scale. By 1661, according to Colbert's calculation, the crown had mortgaged future tax revenues to the hilt and owed 451 million livres. Every sou to keep the wheels of France turning had to be secured from financiers. Interest rates above 6 per cent were illegal but Fouquet kept the money coming in by offering as much as 20 per cent. He concealed the true rate by writing down the capital as much larger that it actually was and, to correct the balance, introduced fictitious expenses into the Treasury register. Many of the loans came surreptitiously from Fouquet himself, using money he had already borrowed at a much lower rate. He also negotiated discounts on outstanding bills but presented the full account for payment by the Treasury and pocketed the difference. After 1654, Treasury officials were not required to keep registers, so there was no check on what Fouquet was doing. His own money and that of the state became in effect one and the same. In 1659 he signed cash expenses without any supporting receipts amounting to more than 88 million livres.

Colbert knew that so long as Mazarin presided over the government, Fouquet had little to fear. Mazarin had taken too large a slice of crown revenue himself to risk an investigation into how one of his superintendants had acquired his wealth. But nonetheless Colbert laid down a marker that would be seen and noted by the young Louis XIV, come of age but not yet to power. In October 1659 Colbert wrote twice to Mazarin informing him of the abuses committed by the *surintendant des finances*. He said that Fouquet administered the accounts with an unparalleled extravagance and 'used the money to buy everyone'. Many government officials were indeed completely in Fouquet's pocket. Colbert's letters to Mazarin were intercepted by the *surintendant général des postes*, Arnould de Nouveau, who made sure that copies were on Fouquet's desk within a week.

Among the individuals to come into an otherwise inexplicably large sum of money at this time was Tréville. The source was certainly not the parsimonious Colbert, who with Queen Anne's typically ruthless and short-sighted agreement had paid out only 10,000 of the 50,000 livres promised to Tréville for relinquishing the captaincy of the Musketeers. At the very moment that Tréville should have been seriously short of funds, instead, thanks almost certainly to Fouquet, he began spending lavishly. He refurbished the former Parisian headquarters of the Musketeers in the rue de Tournon and commissioned a full-length portrait of himself by one of his neighbours, the court painter Mathieu Le Nain; then engaged the royal architect, François Mansart, to design a magnificent chateau in his comté of Troisvilles, where work began in 1660. Tréville, now in his sixties, could have been of little value to Fouquet apart from the knowledge he possessed about the circumstances of Louis XIV's birth, knowledge that at the very least promised to be a formidable bargaining chip for Fouquet.

More than a year before Mazarin's death in 1661, brought together by the realization they had in Fouquet a common, deadly foe, Louis and Colbert forged a clandestine alliance. Whenever the superintendant presented to the royal council his summary of the government finances, exaggerating the expenditure, understating the income, Colbert, the shadow behind the throne, would sit in secret with the king and, burning the midnight oil, unravel for Louis' benefit the evidence of financial wrongdoing, pulling deftly at each thread until the entire fabric of concealment collapsed. 'It was necessary,' said Colbert later,

> to disentangle a system which the cleverest men in the kingdom, who had been elaborating it for forty years, had snarled up so as to make of finance a science that they alone knew and which would render them indispensable.

He omitted of course to mention that he himself, on Mazarin's behalf, had previously done much of the snarling.

Mazarin's last advice, given shortly before his death, was that Louis should rule without a first minister, without his mother, without the princes of the blood, without Fouquet; he should rely on Colbert. The king had probably decided as much for himself. On 9 March 1661, once Mazarin had breathed his last, Louis sent for Fouquet. At a private meeting, held late that night, he assured the superintendant his job was safe but instructed him to begin to 'make use' of Colbert, thereby placing a viper in Fouquet's bosom. When the royal council assembled at 7 o'clock the following morning, the king announced,

> It is now time that I should manage my own affairs. You will assist me with your advice when I request it . . . I forbid you to sign anything, even so much as a safe conduct or passport, without orders from me.

Once Colbert had access to Fouquet's department, Louis had the superintendant directly in his sights. 'The finances were entirely exhausted', the king later recalled in his political testament, but 'the politicians seemed very well off, on the one hand concealing their corrupt administration with all manner of artifices and, on the other, displaying them in brazen, audacious luxury.' Fouquet was indeed brazen. During that summer of 1661 he sent his long-suffering mistress, Suzanne, marquise de Plessis-Bellière, to make overtures on his behalf to a young lady who had caught his fancy, Louise de La Vallière. Fouquet had come across Louise as the shy, demur maid of honour to Henrietta Stuart, the king's sister-in-law, and may not have realized she was already secretly meeting Louis in the Fontainebleau woods. Suzanne went to her with a lavish gift from Fouquet, 20,000 pistoles; but Louise turned it down, saying that even had the sum been 200,000, she would not commit such an indiscretion. She also told Louis, whose anger could easily be imagined: as historian Vincent Cronin put it, Fouquet was 'plotting to buy the girl the King loved with money embezzled from the King!'

The plot hatched by Fouquet went far further than attempting to compromise the king's future mistress. In 1658 the family of the discredited Cardinal de Retz had relinquished Belle Isle, an island lying off the south Normandy coast, near the entrance to Quiberon Bay. Fouquet acquired Belle Isle for himself and turned it into an impregnable domain, a second La Rochelle, fortifying and extending the harbour, creating a state within a state. It gave Fouquet a false sense of security; celebrating the completion of his chateau of Vaux-le-Comte in a style fit for a king became a dangerous obsession for several months, blinding him to the fact that Colbert was unleashed.

On 10 August 1661, a week before the date set for the festivities at Vaux, Fouquet received the first of many warnings, indirectly, and perhaps consciously, from Anne herself. A marquis told him that the king's mother had been heard to say loudly at court: 'The King would like to be rich and does not love those who are richer than he . . . he has no doubt that their great wealth has been stolen from him.' However, Fouquet's second high office of state, *procureur-général*, entitled him to be tried by his peers in the Paris Parlement and this made him almost untouchable, because its members would never convict one of their own. His enemies had to exploit his hubris, his overweening arrogance that made it impossible for him to believe he was in serious danger. Two days later, receiving a broad hint from Colbert that he would be made chancellor, the most senior ministerial post, if only he could only rid himself of any conflicting interest, Fouquet took the bait, sold the office of *procureur-général* and ostentatiously gave the money from the sale to the crown. 'He is digging his own grave,' said a delighted Louis to Colbert.

Vaux was superior to any of the royal palaces and its foundations had been built on fraud. It was also exceptionally provocative, because the king as a private individual was not wealthy: his personal estates yielded scarcely 80,000 livres a year. The breeding ground of resentment was as fertile in France as it had once been in England, when Cardinal Wolsey made the mistake of overshadowing Henry VIII by building Hampton Court Palace. Louis left the great ball of Vaux early. He was heard to mutter to his mother during supper, 'We shall make these people regurgitate what they have taken.' Fouquet's friend, Jean Hérauld de Gourville, warned him that at one point Louis had even decided to arrest his host in his own chateau at his own party and had sent for d'Artagnan. Anne, perhaps fearing Fouquet would take his revenge on her whatever the outcome, dissuaded the king, whispering fiercely, 'Think of your honour; not at an entertainment he is giving for you.'
Instead, Louis and Colbert took the gamble of their lives, deciding to seize Fouquet in his own backyard, the western provinces where Fouquet's writ ran strongest. On Louis' behalf, Colbert innocently suggested that the whole government should attend the meeting in Nantes of the provincial assembly, the Estates of Brittany, an unruly body thought to be deserving of some stern words from their king. Fouquet apparently did not suspect that he was being set up, but many others did. The Abbé de Choisy said, 'Courtiers were saying quite openly that the visit would be fatal either to Fouquet or to Colbert.'

On 24 August, in the dust and heat of summer, the king's

ministers left Fontainebleau by coach for Orléans, where they boarded two *grandes cabanes* – a kind of royal barge equipped with a large canopy to keep off the sun – each with fourteen oarsmen to propel it on the more congenial waters of the river Loire. Fouquet and his acolyte, Hughes de Lionne, acting secretary of state for foreign affairs, took the first barge; Michel Le Tellier, the war minister, and Colbert the second. Watching from the bank was the comte de Brienne's son, the young courtier Louis-Henri de Loménie, and a messenger in the royal postal service who told him, 'One of those *cabanes* must come to grief at Nantes,' but would not elaborate. On the same day, two of Colbert's clerks, drinking heavily outside a wine shop in Paris, boasted publicly that their master would be the next superintendant of finances because Fouquet's fall was imminent. The civil service knew what Fouquet did not.

Louis' own journey to Nantes on horseback, escorted by d'Artagnan and his Musketeers, seemed a bad augury for the confrontation to come. On 30 August, in heavy rain, he was persuaded to relinquish his mount in favour of a coach. But after leaving Angers, the coach became bogged down in the mud and the king had to get back on his horse. Drenched to the skin, Louis spent the night at Ancenis in an insalubrious auberge known as La Croix de Lorraine.

Finally, on 1 September, closeted in the old chateau of Nantes, the rain still falling heavily, Louis and Colbert were ready to strike. At the last moment they reluctantly decided that they could not rely upon the marquis de Gesvres, the duty captain of the king's bodyguard and an intimate of Fouquet, to carry out the arrest. Instead, against Colbert's better judgement, Louis summoned d'Artagnan, whom Colbert thought unreliable and yesterday's man, 'a creature of the late Cardinal'. His poor opinion of the Gascon seemed to be vindicated because d'Artagnan did not appear but sent a message begging to be excused; he claimed to be ill in bed with a fever. The king insisted on seeing him but when d'Artagnan arrived, sweating profusely and apparently barely able to stand, Louis relaxed;

without mentioning Fouquet's name, the king told him to return to bed and get well quickly, so that he could carry out an important mission.

Colbert, however, was far less sympathetic and almost gave the game away, asking d'Artagnan point-blank if he were 'a pensioner of the superintendant like so many others'. D'Artagnan indignantly denied this accusation but must have half expected it would be made. Back in 1657 Fouquet had offered him a purse of 500 louis d'or, which d'Artagnan could ill afford to decline as he was seriously behind with the instalments due on his lease. Had it not been for someone else at that moment lending d'Artagnan 200 pistoles, he said, 'I should not have known where to lay my head.' Fouquet also told d'Artagnan that he could rely on him for a loan of 100,000 livres to buy his captain's post. Despite the huge temptation, d'Artagnan never took up the offers, but Colbert knew of them and became extremely suspicious of such overtures.

As Mazarin's former agent, d'Artagnan understood better than most the extent to which Mazarin, aided and abetted by Colbert, had also used the state's money as though it were his own. He probably believed Fouquet was no guiltier than either of them and wanted nothing to do with the hypocrisy of his arrest. But if d'Artagnan hoped by pleading illness he could encourage the king to look elsewhere for help, his strategy was doomed to fail; Louis had no one else he could trust. Consequently various court officials were prompted to pay a courtesy call at d'Artagnan's lodgings in Nantes in quick succession, to see whether his fever had subsided.

At noon on 4 September d'Artagnan returned to duty but conspicuously failed to report to the king. Louis had to search him out and found him in a gallery in the chateau, surrounded by admirers. The king took him into his private apartments, under the pretence that he wanted news of his Musketeers. Louis instructed d'Artagnan to arrest Fouquet the next morning, the king's twenty-third birthday. D'Artagnan, to say the least, was still reluctant to become involved, and impudently asked for a written order. The king must have anticipated that d'Artagnan would not act without one; Le Tellier already had it in his possession. The minister, who was waiting for d'Artagnan to emerge, took the Musketeer into his own rooms and gave him the order signed by the king:

> His Majesty having determined for very good reasons to assure himself of the person of the sieur Fouquet, superintendant of his finances, has ordered and orders the sieur d'Artagnan, sous-lieutenant of the company of his mounted musketeers, to arrest the said sieur Fouquet, and to conduct him under secure guard to the place mentioned in the memorandum . . . making certain that the said sieur Fouquet has no contact with anyone on the journey either by word of mouth or in writing.

D'Artagnan's self-possession then for once completely deserted him. Even with the king's signed order and a mandate for 1,000 gold louis for 'incidental expenses', he was so overawed by the prospect of arresting Fouquet, the most powerful man in the kingdom, that he had to sit down; he asked Le Tellier for a glass of red wine to help pull himself together. When he had recovered, Le Tellier took him through a much longer set of instructions, stipulating the number of Musketeers d'Artagnan should have with him, how the arrest should be carried out, to where Fouquet was to be taken, the route and the overnight staging posts.

Fouquet and Lionne were staying in Nantes at the Hôtel de Rougé, which belonged to the family of the marquise de Plessis-Bellière. Fouquet, too, was said to be unwell; his fever was unquestionably genuine and prevented him from receiving many more warnings of the plan. Apart from Gourville, only Loménie was allowed to see him and, finding Fouquet in bed, supported by a mound of green cushions, his young supporter told him bluntly that he was facing arrest. Fouquet chose not to believe Loménie and also refused to go along with Gourville's suggestion that the following morning he should send an empty carriage with curtains drawn to the chateau at the time scheduled for the start of the king's council, to see if any move were made against him. This ploy would not have revealed anything, though, because Colbert's plan was to arrest Fouquet on the way out, not the way in.

The council meeting was early and brief, the king having expressed a desire to go hunting, which conveniently explained away the presence around the chateau of several detachments of mounted Musketeers. Colbert had worked out the arrest of Fouquet to almost the last detail. His memorandum said: '[On] the chosen day, on the pretext of a hunt, orders must be given to the musketeers to be mounted and the carriages ready.'

At 7 a.m., Louis shabbily wrung a last payment order out of Fouquet, 31,000 livres for the navy. He then encouraged the other ministers to leave, keeping Fouquet back while he pretended to search for some papers. Only when the king could see d'Artagnan from his window, impatiently standing beneath the trees beyond the castle courtyard, did he let Fouquet depart.

Even so, the arrest was nearly a fiasco. D'Artagnan had been told to wait until Fouquet passed the last sentry, the king suspecting that he could not rely upon the loyalty of his palace guard. When the other ministers emerged but Fouquet did not, d'Artagnan, catching sight of Le Tellier, hurried over to him and asked whether his instructions had been changed. Le Tellier, who had just ordered Fouquet's lodgings to be sealed, said they had not. At that very moment, while d'Artagnan, perhaps deliberately, perhaps subconsciously, had his back to the chateau, Fouquet emerged and summoned his sedan chair. He was swallowed up in a crowd of supplicants and was soon nowhere to be seen.

D'Artagnan sent a message to the king that the plan had gone wrong. Louis came down the outside staircase of the chateau several steps at a time, in a violent rage. D'Artagnan, finally realizing that he had no alternative, ordered fifteen of his Musketeers to follow him and dashed down the street in search of his would-be prisoner. Fortunately for him, Fouquet's sedan chair, delayed by various supplicants, had got no further than the place de la Cathédrale. D'Artagnan pushed his way through the crowd, saying he had an urgent message to deliver. 'Monsieur,' he told Fouquet, sweeping off his hat so low that onlookers remembered that the feathers touched the ground, 'I arrest you by order of the King.' Fouquet seemed astonished. 'I thought I stood higher with the King than any man in France,' he replied. Louis' capacity to dissemble, even as a young man, was already formidable.

Fouquet had been completely deceived but took the chance to cover his tracks in the chaos and confusion that followed. Among those trying to catch his attention in the square had been Jean Cordure, a seigneur in Anne's service, perhaps carrying a warning from the Queen Mother. As he was pushed into a coach packed with Musketeers, Fouquet whispered to Cordure, 'Quickly: to Saint-Mandé!' a reference to Fouquet's grand house beside the park at Vincennes on the outskirts of Paris. Cordure passed the message to Fouquet's most trusted servant, La Forêt, who left Nantes immediately and rode day and night to Paris on a relay of post horses established by Fouquet for just such an emergency. However, La Forêt's prodigious effort to reach Saint-Mandé in order to remove any incriminating documents proved in vain, because on Le Telier's instructions, the house had already been sealed and was surrounded by royal troops.

Fouquet's brother, the Abbé Basile Fouquet, and his mistress the marquise de Plessis-Bellière seriously discussed setting fire to Saint-Mandé to destroy its contents. Their reason for considering so desperate an undertaking soon became clear. Ironically, Fouquet had foreseen the possibility that one day he might be seized without warning. His detailed contingency plan, the *projet de Saint-Mandé*, as it came to be known, was to be activated by the marquise, 'to whom', wrote Fouquet, 'I entrust myself completely'. The plan's most damaging reference was to his purchase and fortification of Belle Isle. Years before, Fouquet had intended to destroy the document. He even went so far as to send a valet at Saint-Mandé to fetch a tinderbox. At the very moment he was about to light it, however, Fouquet received an unexpected visitor. As a temporary safeguard against prying eyes, he hid the plan behind a mirror, and neglected to retrieve it. Within a day of his arrest the document had been found, and at Oudon, en route to Angers, d'Artagnan received instructions to make Fouquet write a letter to the sieur de La Haye des Noyers, the governor of Belle Isle, commanding him to hand over the island to the forces of the king.

Cordure's risky involvement in the efforts to pre-empt the search of Saint-Mandé was an indication of Anne's fear that Fouquet had acquired evidence of her relationship with Tréville. If anything about the Queen Mother was discovered at Saint-Mandé, it was given to Louis and suppressed; others at court with guilty secrets were not so fortunate. In an infamous series of wooden caskets found at the house, the names of everyone in hock to Fouquet emerged: ministers, courtiers, financiers and ladies with a hitherto unblemished reputation. Some unsigned love letters also prompted malicious speculation as to the identity of the authors, for which Fouquet in due course was to pay a further penalty.

When Cordure's role came to light, nothing concrete could be proved against him, but he was sent to the Bastille for having arranged 'for the news of Fouquet's arrest to be carried to Paris ahead of the royal couriers', a neat twist of the truth that had the hallmark of Colbert. After almost five months Cordure would be released on condition that he went to live far from Paris, in the swamp-infested port of Aigues Mortes. But Cordure was a minnow among many big fish in the net. While Fouquet was still on his way to the chateau of Angers, escorted by d'Artagnan and 100 Musketeers, the repercussions of his fall began to be felt everywhere, like the after-shocks of an earthquake.

Louis' revenge proved relentless. The marquis de Gesvres indignantly swore he would have arrested his own mother if asked, but Louis did not believe him and he lost his lucrative position as a captain of the guard. The marquise du Plessis-

Bellière was imprisoned, bravely refusing to betray her lover. Two secretaries of state, Guénégaud and Pomponne, were accused; Guénégaud was arrested but Pomponne escaped to Germany. A third minister, Lionne, avoided imprisonment only by prostrating himself in abject humiliation in front of the king. Gourville went on the run and was condemned to death in his absence for embezzling public funds. Complaining that it looked nothing like him, he audaciously removed his effigy, symbolically hanged outside the Paris Parlement, before fleeing abroad. The writer Paul Pellison, Fouquet's most outspoken supporter, was sent to the Bastille for four years. Marie-Madeleine de Castille, Madame Fouquet, was refused permission to share her husband's prison and was exiled to Limoges. Louis would not allow their children to follow her and it took Anne to persuade him to let them to go to their grandmother, who was already seventy-two. The Queen Mother, however, could no longer protect her most faithful supporter. Brienne was dismissed from the council, on the bogus charge of losing some important papers. Almost his last act, on Louis' malign instructions, was to write to his own son, Louis-Henri de Loménie, and tell him that the price of his overt support for Fouquet was banishment forthwith from court.

Tréville, too, would soon leave Paris permanently for his provincial estates. Just as decorators had downed tools instantly at Vaux at the news of Fouquet's fall, craftsmen in Troisvilles stopped work on Tréville's chateau as the story of what had happened to his patron swept across France like wildfire. Tréville quickly had to find another source of revenue to pay them and tried to introduce a punitive tax on his Basque subjects in the valley of the Soule. This harsh terrain at the foot of the Pyrenees could barely sustain life, still less produce 150,000 livres, the target for Tréville's pitiless tax collectors. The Basques staged a violent revolt under a local priest, and when this was put down many fled across the mountains to Spain for fear of further reprisals. The local parliament, the Estates of the Soule, complained to Louis, who summoned Tréville to Paris to explain his conduct. The meeting went badly because Tréville did not show the deference due to his king and thereafter he was no longer welcome at court.

As for Fouquet himself, he was far from comfortable at the chateau of Angers, which had not been used to hold prisoners for some time. D'Artagnan reported to Colbert that although he 'understood nothing' about buildings, he could see that the roof leaked, the outer fortifications were crumbling and the chapel was on the point of collapse. He was also unable to find a bed for Fouquet suitable for someone of his rank and asked for permission to purchase one. In the heat of the moment d'Artagnan had omitted to collect the promised 1,000 gold louis for expenses and therefore as usual was seriously short of funds.

Fouquet was forbidden pen and ink or to receive letters, even from his family. In the tense atmosphere, Le Tellier issued a stern rebuke to d'Artagnan for his failure to keep him regularly informed about what his prisoner was doing. After d'Artagnan protested that there was nothing new to report, Le Tellier responded, 'Your employment is sufficiently important for you to write every day, even if you have no news to communicate.'

When d'Artagnan did write, it was usually to ask for money. The cost of keeping Fouquet under lock and key ran at about 1,000 livres a month in the provinces, rising to 4,000 livres a month when he was moved to Paris. D'Artagnan had to protest several times before Le Tellier passed on his expense claims to Colbert, and even then Colbert delayed approving the payment orders put in front of him by the treasurer-general. The ministers were unhappy with the way d'Artagnan was carrying out his duties, feeling that he was showing far too much concern for the welfare of his prisoner.

By making a fuss, d'Artagnan undoubtedly hoped he would be relieved of his duties as a jailer. On 21 November 1661 he seemed to have got his wish because Le Tellier ordered Fouquet to be transferred to the Château of Amboise and into the care of its governor, sending a coach with bars on the windows for this purpose from Paris. The bars proved of more use to keep the crowd out than Fouquet in, as there were demonstrations against the fallen minister on the route. Pellison, whom d'Artagnan was taking on to Paris and the Bastille, was forced to ride behind the coach on a horse, where he received several direct hits from rubbish hurled inaccurately at Fouquet.

At Tours the onlookers proved so hostile that d'Artagnan decided to depart at 3 a.m. the next morning to avoid further trouble. Fouquet was strictly forbidden to talk to anyone they passed, but managed to outwit d'Artagnan during the short journey east to Amboise. One of Fouquet's valets had found employment as a temporary cook at an inn called La Chapelle Blanche. He took Fouquet out to the privy and gave him the wherewithal to scribble and hand over several brief letters, including one to his wife, leaving d'Artagnan none the wiser.

Louis may have shared his ministers' reservations about d'Artagnan's performance but, unsure whom else he could trust, he resolved to put Fouquet back in his charge. On the last day of December, Fouquet was transferred from Amboise to the Château of Vincennes and allocated the first floor of its donjon, the inner keep. At 4 a.m. on 4 January 1662 the chateau's governor gave d'Artagnan the keys, the start of an unwanted vigil over his famous prisoner that was to last for three more years.

The strain of imprisonment soon told on Fouquet; by March 1663 his brown hair had turned almost completely white. But whatever its effect on his health, Fouquet fought an outstanding tactical battle against the representatives of the king. He challenged the competence of the judicial tribunal and demanded to be tried by the Parlement; when predictably this was declined, he refused to answer the prosecutors' questions. Instead, Fouquet wrote a reply to the charges that ran to fifteen volumes. He characterized the *project de Saint-Mandé* as an act of self-preservation not a blueprint for rebellion, claiming it had been prepared solely to protect himself from Mazarin and Colbert.

The trial was set for the Arsenal in Paris and on 20 June d'Artagnan, accompanied by 300 Musketeers, escorted Fouquet to his new prison, the Bastille. When d'Artagnan arrived, Besmaux at first refused to open the gate and it was only after d'Artagnan showed the governor his written orders from Le Tellier that he reluctantly let him pass. Besmaux resented the prospect of d'Artagnan having authority within his prison and bringing with him a troop of Musketeers, all eager 'to heartily caress Madame Besmaux, were she willing'.

Besmaux's wife, Marguerite de Peyroz, had blossomed into a famous beauty. The forty-five Musketeers that d'Artagnan selected to remain at the Bastille as Fouquet's permanent guard, most aged nineteen or twenty, had spent the entire journey to the prison eagerly speculating about her charms. Marguerite usually had a good deal of contact with the prison staff and the prisoners, making huge cauldrons of her home-made soup, Besmaux's miserly way of saving on the cost of their meals. The governor, however, had no intention of putting temptation in the path of the Musketeers and he was also well aware of d'Artagnan's relentless pursuit of married women and previous interest in his wife. Unable to lock Marguerite in a chastity belt, Besmaux's first outrageous solution, instead 'He bought one of the biggest masks in Paris with one of the biggest chin pieces and obliged her to wear it over her face all the time.'

Marguerite was not allowed to leave the governor's quarters without a mask, and two soldiers from the Bastille's regular garrison accompanied her everywhere, even to Sunday Mass at the nearby Church of the Sisters of Mary. This of course simply added to Marguerite's fascination and the Musketeers' avid interest. Certainly no mask was proof against d'Artagnan's sexual appetite in particular. It would have been contrary to his reputation and instincts if the Musketeer did not attempt to seduce Marguerite, who at twenty-three may have been tiring of her elderly and disfigured husband. D'Artagnan's advances towards Marguerite were sure to enrage Besmaux, whose obsession with masks would later take a much more sinister turn.

The governor also saw d'Artagnan's presence at the Bastille as a personal slight and complained to the king. Louis promptly reminded him that the letters found in Fouquet's caskets from corrupt government officials included one from himself. What saved Besmaux was that his letter asked Fouquet for a favour without disclosing what the governor proposed to do in return. Following this royal reproof, Besmaux's relationship with d'Artagnan grew even worse. One of the prosecutors, dining regularly in the prison after interviewing Fouquet, recalled he could eat with either the governor or the jailer but that they resolutely refused to sit down with him together.

Fouquet was lodged in the Chapel Tower, in a large room with windows on both sides. He had his own privy and a tiny ante-room taken up almost entirely by a highly unusual and expensive feature, six mechanical birds singing in a large gilded cage. Besmaux had gone out of his way to find and purchase this symbol of Fouquet's plight, confirming that the governor had a spiteful, malicious streak.

When the proceedings began, the prosecutor-general listed the charges of embezzlement and high treason, asking that Fouquet be sentenced to be 'hanged and strangled until death ensues on a gallows to be erected for that purpose in the courtyard of the Palais de Justice'. Not content with making his own uncle a judge in the trial, Colbert packed the bench with sycophants known or suspected to be hostile to Fouquet, and when he ran out of these, he chose men he believed would readily acquiesce in a guilty verdict. Colbert thought Olivier Lefèvre d'Ormesson, a *maître de réquêtes*, a minor but permanent post in the Parlement, was ideal because he had 'no imagination', was 'ponderous' and 'not up to dealing with such an important matter'. Colbert failed to appreciate that Ormesson was an honest man who would never compromise his integrity, however intense the pressure. Ormesson was even made one of the judge advocates, with the task of summing up.

Colbert equally miscalculated in appointing Chancellor Séguier president of the court. Séguier had disliked Fouquet intensely from the moment they became joint superintendants of finance because Fouquet always outshone him. As the trial continued, Séguier accused Fouquet of committing a crime against the state. In his response, Fouquet put forward a highly persuasive definition of such a crime: when the occupant of one of the principal government posts goes over to the enemy, persuades his relatives to do the same and uses his son-in-law to facilitate a foreign army to enter the country. Unfortunately for Séguier, it described exactly what he himself had done during the Fronde, and the other judges laughed heartily at this ironic masterpiece. One of them wrote of Fouquet in glowing terms to his friend, Madame de Sévigné: 'I must admit that this man is incomparable; he never spoke as well as this in the Parlement; he is more composed than ever.'

Fouquet argued it was Mazarin who had established the procedure whereby what belonged to the Treasury and what were his own private funds had no clear distinction. What was more, Mazarin had done it with the complicity of Colbert. Fouquet added that the Fronde and the war with Spain had made financial reforms impossible. Ormesson noted in his journal that 'the replies of M. Fouquet were made with much presence of mind and [were] as well expressed as they could have been.'

Although more than 16,000 documents had been seized from Fouquet and his supporters, something vital, believed to exist, had not been found. Fouquet's home at Saint-Mandé was practically taken apart in fresh but vain attempts to find it. Then on 28 May 1664 Le Tellier sent d'Artagnan a memorandum from the king, since lost or, more likely, destroyed. The surviving cover sheet from Le Tellier refers to d'Artagnan's 'secondment' and a 'journey' he was to keep '*très-secret*'. A letter written around this time by d'Artagnan's elder sister, the widowed Claude de Sarriac, still residing at Château Castelmore, refers excitedly to his visit. If d'Artagnan passed through Gascony on a secret mission so important that he had to leave his subordinates in charge of Fouquet, his most likely destination would have been a short distance further to the south-west, the new chateau at Troisvilles. Perhaps Tréville still possessed the papers that Fouquet had evidently believed worth a fortune, papers that undermined the legitimacy of the sovereign, which Louis could not afford to fall into the wrong hands. If d'Artagnan accepted them from Tréville for safe keeping himself, this was the point where he crossed the line, no longer convinced of the divine right of his king.

On 20 June 1664, soon after d'Artagnan's return to Paris, to all intents and purposes empty-handed, exactly a year after Fouquet had been taken to the Bastille, Le Tellier instructed the reluctant jailer to move his prisoner again, to the fortress of Moret-sur-Loing, on the edge of Fontainebleau forest, south-east of the palace. The tribunal would also sit in this new location. Louis, spending the summer at Fontainebleau as usual, wanted both the tribunal and Fouquet close by. Colbert was still working hard to influence the judges, but Fouquet had spent huge sums in bribing many of them and the king already may have feared the outcome of the trial.

So Louis turned the screw. Fouquet's two lawyers henceforth were allowed to see their client for two hours only on Tuesdays and Fridays, with d'Artagnan remaining in the room and the conversation kept loud enough for him to hear. The lawyers protested furiously to the tribunal and Ormesson suggested a compromise, whereby they would have time alone with Fouquet after each 'official' meeting. On 11 July the judges ruled against the compromise, by seventeen votes to five. President Séguier then ordered d'Artagnan to report what was said, but, after consulting Ormesson, d'Artagnan bravely refused to do so, except where it did not relate to the trial. On 8 November Fouquet disclosed to d'Artagnan that he did not propose to introduce any further evidence unless the prosecutor-general made fresh allegations against him. 'Do you want me to keep that a secret or tell the king?' asked d'Artagnan. After almost three years closeted together as prisoner and jailer, the two men had formed a close relationship, too close for d'Artagnan's own good. After his secret mission, d'Artagnan interpreted his instructions in a manner favourable to Fouquet wherever possible, seemingly indifferent to royal displeasure.

On 14 August, the tribunal was switched to the Arsenal in Paris and d'Artagnan returned with Fouquet to the Bastille. At Charenton, noticing Madame Fouquet and her youngest son standing by the roadside, d'Artagnan, although forbidden to stop, ordered the coachman to slow to a walking pace. The escort of Musketeers reined in their mounts and Fouquet, leaning out of the window, was able to embrace his wife and child. He had not seen them for three years.

The trial continued slowly. Séguier was old and tired and frequently dozed off during the hearings, which became progressively shorter, sometimes lasting only forty-five minutes a day. Fouquet protested vigorously through d'Artagnan to the king, and d'Artagnan told Louis that, unless something was done, he had no doubt that Fouquet would ridicule Séguier publicly in court. The king forced Séguier to hold two sessions of three hours each day to speed up the trial. D'Artagnan's intervention was bitterly resented by the court's president. Séguier was so angry at the way things were going that one morning he tore up, stamped on and threw into the fire the remains of 172 judgments in other lawsuits brought to him for his signature.

For each appearance at the Arsenal, Fouquet was escorted personally on foot by d'Artagnan, some fifty Musketeers following to the rear. On 20 November, returning from the court, they passed some workmen constructing a fountain. It was finished but no water was coming out and Fouquet stopped to give them some advice. Seeing d'Artagnan's quizzical expression, Fouquet laughed and said: 'Don't you marvel at my range of knowledge? I was once quite expert in this sort of thing.' He was recalling his wonderful fountains at Vaux-le-Vicomte.

A week later, as a small gesture of support, some ladies among the nobility, led by Madame de Sévigné, waited at a window overlooking the Arsenal to see Fouquet leave at the end of the day's proceedings to walk back to the Bastille. Fearing the king's wrath, each was masked and Fouquet, deep in thought, would have missed them altogether had not d'Artagnan tugged on his sleeve and pointed upwards. The ladies waved; Fouquet smiled and saluted them with a deep bow.

In the early hours of 17 December 1664, with the result of the trial imminent, a comet appeared over Paris. At three o'clock in the morning d'Artagnan went to wake Fouquet and together they clambered on to the roof of the Chapel Tower to see it, startling the Musketeers on sentry duty. Fouquet thought the comet was a good omen. The following day, Ormesson began his summing up. As he did so, he knew that Colbert had just visited his father, to say that if the younger Ormesson neglected the interests of France, then the king would no longer want him as the intendant of Picardy. Ormesson ignored the threat to his income and concluded that Fouquet had not committed any treasonable crime. Ormesson even rejected the charge of peculation – embezzlement – putting the blame on Mazarin and by implication on Colbert.

The judges retired to consider their verdict but only Ormesson was prepared to defy the king to the extent of finding Fouquet innocent of all charges. On 20 December a vote was taken on whether Fouquet was guilty of treason or only of '*abus et malversions . . . des finances*', 'abuse and misappropriation . . . of public money'. Nine judges voted him guilty of treason, which meant death, thirteen of only peculation. This carried a punishment of perpetual banishment, with all Fouquet's assets forfeit to the crown.

Ormesson was overwhelmed by a crowd of *parlementaires* who had come to congratulate him on the fairness of the verdict. He hastily retired to his office and locked the door. When the fuss had died down Ormesson went to collect various papers from the Bastille, where d'Artagnan, unwisely in front of so many witnesses, flung his arms around him and shouted he was an *illustre*, someone renowned for their bravery. Each of the thirteen judges who had voted against the death sentence paid in various ways for their independence, suffering loss of other offices, expulsion from court, even exile. D'Ormesson, as shrewd as he was brave, had sold his own offices before the verdict. He retired to his little chateau in the fertile Brie Française region of the Ile-de-France, not far from the empty edifice of Vaux. His home soon became a favourite weekend retreat for Fouquet's friends, including the indefatigable letter writer, Madame de Sévigné.

The king was making love to his mistress Louise de La Vallière when he was disturbed by a terrified valet bringing news of the judges' vote: it would be difficult to imagine a more precarious example of *coitus interruptus*. Any lingering doubt that he would have been merciful to Fouquet was dispelled when the servant heard the king say to Louise: 'If he had been condemned to death, I would have let him die.' Le Tellier, his son François-Michel Louvois, the newest member of the council, and Colbert met hurriedly with their sovereign. They felt allowing Fouquet to go abroad was unthinkable. Louis issued a new *lettre de cachet* – the royal instrument condemning a man to indefinite imprisonment without trial – re-imprisoning Fouquet for 'the good of the state'.

One of the king's advisers, probably Louvois, suggested that Fouquet should be sent to Pignerol, the most remote fortress in the kingdom. Pignerol commanded the entrance to three Alpine valleys and pointed like a dagger towards the heart of Italy. The entire town had been enclosed by battlements and bastions, with the indigenous Savoyard population employed to fulfil the needs of the French garrison, whether it be for pencils or prostitutes. Its citadel on the northern flank dwarfed houses and lower fortifications alike, a multi-tiered colossus of Italian masonry. At its highest point stood a grim keep, Norman in origin and design, which was to become Fouquet's home for much of the rest of his life.

D'Artagnan would have been among the first to know that Louis had arbitrarily overturned the verdict, as he was to command the escort of 100 Musketeers to take Fouquet to Pignerol, an arduous and perilous journey in winter. Ormesson said that d'Artagnan showed 'suppressed anger at being ordered to travel to Pignerol and would have got out of it if he could'.

It seems likely that d'Artagnan also told Fouquet what was happening, for when the chief clerk of the court, Foucault, arrived at the Bastille on 22 December, expecting to enjoy finding Fouquet on tenterhooks, the former superintendant was already embittered by the news and produced one last gesture of defiance. Foucault was shown into the room above the chapel, which had a long refectory table; he sat in the middle seat on the far side, flanked by a line of subservient court officials. Fouquet declined to sit and remained standing in front of the table, hat in hand. Foucault asked for his name. 'You know my name already,' replied Fouquet. 'We have to follow procedure,' said Foucault. 'In that case,' responded Fouquet, 'you should start the trial again, with all the *parlementaires* as my judges.' Foucault asked a third time and Fouquet repeated that he did not recognize the court. After an uneasy pause, Foucault realized that he could not leave without delivering the verdict. He began to read it quickly in a high-pitched, unintelligible voice. Fouquet did not wait for him to finish but turned his back and walked to the window. He saw Ormesson arriving in the courtyard below, waved to attract his attention, and shouted that he was a brave and honest judge.

Feelings in Paris were running high, so d'Artagnan was ordered to leave for Pignerol immediately. Fouquet had no opportunity to say goodbye to his wife. He was bundled into a coach, a Musketeer on either side, and two more sitting opposite. D'Artagnan rode alongside on horseback, with fifty Musketeers in front and as many behind. The people who had thrown rubbish at Fouquet on his arrival in Paris now cheered him and took off their hats as he passed through the Porte Sainte-Antoine for the last time. Ormesson observed tartly that Fouquet,

whom the whole of Paris could not wait to see executed after his trial had begun, had become the subject of public concern and consideration through the hatred that everyone has in their hearts against the present government.

D'Artagnan was afraid that he might be expected to remain indefinitely at Pignerol, but while the king believed he could be relied upon to escort Fouquet to the Alpine fortress, he no longer trusted him as Fouquet's jailer. Louis expected his instructions to be carried out competently without a fuss, which d'Artagnan had singularly failed to do in bungling Fouquet's arrest. He had also seriously compromised his position by his subsequent sympathy for Fouquet and his display of admiration for Ormesson. In d'Artagnan's place, the king had chosen one of his subordinates, Saint-Mars, to take charge of the Pignerol donjon.

Returning to the King's Musketeers as a corporal in 1660, Saint-Mars had made himself indispensable to d'Artagnan as his *maréchal des logis* or quartermaster, with the rank of sergeant. At a time when foraging for supplies assumed a huge importance because little or nothing was provided by the war department, Saint-Mars turned this into a fine art. For him, no request was too difficult if it resulted in personal profit. Saint-Mars, however, had few conversational skills and little humour. He hid his natural cunning behind a veneer of total subservience, which commended him to his superiors.

As d'Artagnan was never asked to recommend someone to be Fouquet's jailer, exactly how Saint-Mars came to be given the job is uncertain. Throughout the years of Fouquet's arrest and trial, Saint-Mars appeared on the political stage as a bit player, always at the centre of events, but never in a central role. He had been sent to the king with the papers found in Fouquet's pockets and may have registered in Louis' mind as the one unflustered individual among his Musketeers who seemed to know what he was doing. Then, when Pellison had to be brought from Nantes to join Fouquet in Angers prison, Saint-Mars headed a troop of sixteen Musketeers sent to fetch him.

Saint-Mars was also at the Bastille with d'Artagnan. On 24 December 1664 the king and Le Tellier signed the instruction to Saint-Mars that changed his life. He was to guard Fouquet in the citadel of Pignerol until he received 'fresh orders from His Majesty'.

Saint-Mars' master and tormentor would be Louvois, who later became minister of war. According to his biographer, Louis André, Louvois, when he joined the king's council in 1661 aged only twenty, was 'still of no consequence, because he was too young and knew too little. Two years later, he knew . . . [how] to get things done in the military administration: he . . . [was] ready to become someone.' Although it was not until October 1665 that Louvois formally took over the war ministry, he had already assumed day-to-day responsibility for Pignerol, Fouquet and Saint-Mars. On that Christmas Eve of 1664, he issued his first recorded order on the subject, to the *commissaire de guerre* at Pignerol, Louis Damorezan:

> Monsieur, you will receive these orders from the hands of the sieur Saint-Mars himself, who has been charged with guarding, in the donjon of Pignerol, the person of M. Fouquet, and to this end he has been given command of an infantry company which he has ordered to set out [for Pignerol] . . . you will not have to supply anything for Saint-Mars' company.

At that moment, Saint-Mars' 'free company', which was to be on the direct payroll of the war ministry, existed only on paper. Saint-Mars, appointed its commander, still held the rank of sergeant and would not be promoted to second lieutenant for another ten years. Saint-Mars left Paris two days after d'Artagnan and arrived in Pignerol on 10 January 1665, six days ahead of him, so his journey must have been on horseback, with practically no rest, in wind and rain and snow. Louvois allowed him to carry his orders for Damorezan personally, knowing that no courier could reach Pignerol faster. Saint-Mars may also have brought instructions for the governor-general of Pignerol, the marquis de Pienne; but as he was 'almost never there . . . on one pretext or another', perhaps Louvois did not bother.

The journey to Pignerol began badly for d'Artagnan. Just as Saint-Mars was setting out from Paris, d'Artagnan had to write an apologetic note to Colbert from his own overnight halt at Fontainebleau, for leaving the capital without his last-minute instructions. Fouquet's coach continued relentlessly southwards throughout Christmas Day, even though the prisoner was unmistakably ill. D'Artagnan sent a messenger back to Le Tellier, asking what he should do. Continue no matter what, was the reply. Should he give Fouquet a letter written to him by his wife? On no account, came the response, this time directly from the king. South again, via Dijon and Lyon, where d'Artagnan collected 6,000 livres for expenses on Louvois' mandate, then on to Grenoble. Here the French consul pompously blocked their entry into the town because d'Artagnan did not possess a pass affording him safe conduct. D'Artagnan's force heavily outnumbered the local troops on duty, so he disarmed them and put the consul behind bars overnight for his impudence.

Saint-Mars meanwhile had passed d'Artagnan's column unseen during the hours of darkness. On the afternoon of 11 January 1665, the day after Saint-Mars arrived at Pignerol, d'Artagnan had got no further than Gap. Here at least the consuls were much more welcoming: they offered lodging for the Musketeers, medicine for Fouquet and six bottles of wine for d'Artagnan. Fouquet had no suitable clothes for the trip across the mountains to Pignerol and suffered badly from the cold, so d'Artagnan found him some furs. According to Madame Sévigné, d'Artagnan, 'his only consolation on this terrible journey', did his best to keep up Fouquet's morale.

The quiet life of Monsieur Levé, the ageing architect at Pignerol, suddenly became a nightmare: at six days' notice he was ordered to prepare suitable accommodation for the best-known prisoner in France. Fouquet was to be lodged on the third floor of the donjon's Angle Tower but, despite workmen labouring day and night in freezing temperatures, plastering the walls by candlelight, when d'Artagnan arrived on 16 January the work was unfinished.

Fouquet had a sitting room measuring twenty-six paces by twelve, and a bedroom twelve paces by ten, with a privy set in the outer wall of the fortress. A third room, twenty-four paces by twenty-two, would be added as soon as possible, Levé assured Colbert. By any normal seventeenth-century prison standards this was exceptionally pleasant accommodation, complete with a magnificent view of the mountains. For Fouquet, however, it was a virtual coffin compared with his chateau at Vaux. Over the next fifteen years, he would come to know every inch of those three chambers.

When d'Artagnan learned of Saint-Mars' unorthodox elevation to jailer, he may have viewed his appointment with relief or irritation, probably a mixture of both. Saint-Mars always assumed that d'Artagnan had put in a good word on his behalf and d'Artagnan did nothing to disabuse him.

The local population feted Saint-Mars' former superior as Pignerol's most famous visitor. They dispatched someone to Turin to buy 'partridges, woodcock, hares and, if possible, some tender pheasants, the better to do him honour'. D'Artagnan soon discovered that he was less honoured in Paris, for on the very day of his arrival at Pignerol, Le Tellier wrote to inform him that the king had created a second company of Musketeers, with Colbert de Maulévrier, a captain of the guards, in command.

Even d'Artagnan could scarcely fail to read between the lines. Edouard François Colbert, marquis de Maulévrier, was the twenty-year-old brother of Jean-Baptiste Colbert, the new power at court. Maulévrier, given the rank of commandant, also outranked d'Artagnan, a mere *sous-lieutenant*. Worse, Maulévrier's installation as commanding officer had already been carried out with due ceremony in the courtyard of the Louvre and, in d'Artagnan's absence, Maulévrier had marched past the king at the head of both companies of Musketeers, merged for the occasion as one. Louis might hesitate to remove d'Artagnan altogether in case Fouquet had shared his secrets with him, but he had many ingenious ways of showing his disapproval. Despite delivering Fouquet into the hands of Saint-Mars without any more mishaps, d'Artagnan had overstepped the mark and would have to work very hard indeed if he was to have any chance of getting back into the king's good books.

7

THE THREE QUEENS

    ⌒ ⌒

Free at last from the role of jailer he hated, d'Artagnan did not linger at Pignerol, and by dusk on 25 January 1665 he was back at Gap. Its consuls were even more hospitable on his return visit, entertaining d'Artagnan lavishly in the courtyard of the Petit Paris inn, beneath flaming torches. This time they gave him a dozen bottles of their best wine. The innkeeper's wife kept seven of them, perhaps in return for d'Artagnan's board and lodging, but perhaps too, for providing him with personal services.

Chalon-sur-Saône, where Madame d'Artagnan sulkily resided, lay directly on her estranged husband's route to Paris. It was an ideal occasion for d'Artagnan to persuade his wife to pay his most pressing debts. Being d'Artagnan, he may also have seen it as an opportune moment to reassert his marital rights. Whatever passed between them, it had the opposite effect to what d'Artagnan had hoped. A few weeks later Anne-Charlotte d'Artagnan formally ended in the courts the communality of her own and her husband's possessions, a clear signal to any would-be creditors that she had no intention of meeting d'Artagnan's debts out of her own resources. On 16 April Anne-Charlotte renounced the marriage altogether and entered the convent of Sainte-Croix in Bourgogne, putting her body beyond his reach as well. D'Artagnan made only a token effort to change his wife's mind, since the prospect of separation 'pleased her so much'. They would never meet again.

After an absence of almost three and a half years, d'Artagnan returned eagerly to his regular duties but found the court changed beyond all recognition. Fouquet's creative team of Le Vau, Le Nôtre and Le Brun had been busily redeployed in the royal palaces. They refurbished the Louvre and smartened Saint-Germain-en-Laye before starting work on Versailles, still only a modest country retreat. Everywhere d'Artagnan could identify various furnishings and scores of *objets d'art* that Fouquet had purchased for Vaux-le-Vicomte, but for once he prudently held his tongue. Louis XIV had stripped the detested chateau of tapestries, silverware, crockery and carpets; even its orange trees were dug up and replanted at Versailles. The king was guilty of the same peculation as Fouquet and on an even grander scale, although Louis simply regarded it as the recovery of possessions that were his by right.

With Colbert – angered by his support for Fouquet – systematically undermining him at court, d'Artagnan found that his relations with the king remained as capricious as ever. In late 1665 Louis wrote to d'Artagnan, following complaints about the conduct of some of his Musketeers, demanding to know what punishment he had given the miscreants. 'As you are aware, I have not always been satisfied with your own conduct, either,' added the king, ominously.

D'Artagnan had become resigned to the fact that while he was captain in all but name, his lack of capital meant that even if Louis mellowed, he would never be formally appointed captain of the Musketeers. It would cost him 200,000 livres to buy the post, which might just as well have been 2 million for all d'Artagnan's ability to raise such a sum. This insurmountable obstacle vanished overnight, however, when Louvois, energetically pushing ahead with reforms in the war department, persuaded the king to abolish the sale of key military offices to improve the standard of leadership in the army. It almost certainly did not occur to either Louvois or Louis at the time that this change of policy would greatly improve d'Artagnan's particular prospects of advancement, for it still took an unlikely event to bring him in from the cold.

For many years now, Mazarin's Mancini nieces, Olympe, Marie, Hortense and Marianne, had provoked much interest at court. Not only did they receive the lion's share of his fortune, but these heiresses with an aptitude for French and Italian literature also covertly set new records in indiscriminate and casual sexual relationships, as they sought ennobled husbands suitable for their new station.

After Mazarin died, Hortense had received 28 million livres and most of the first minister's property and wonderful art collection, which under French law her husband Armand, marquis de la Meilleraye, could enjoy and dispose of in any way he pleased. This infuriated d'Artagnan's absentee commanding officer, Philippe-Julien Mancini, duc de Nevers, Hortense's brother, who thought he should have been Mazarin's sole heir. He made the mistake of saying as much to the richest of all heiresses, the Grande Mademoiselle, who deliberately repeated his remarks in the decidedly unsympathetic hearing of her cousin, the king. Armand was a prude, even removing the genitalia from many of Mazarin's priceless statues, while Hortense was instinctively promiscuous, so the couple had furious rows, making it all too easy for Philippe to fan the flames of discontent. He encouraged Hortense to enter a suit in the Parlement for separation of her goods, hoping that through his pliable sister he might gain indirect control of much of Mazarin's fortune.

When this seemed likely to fail, Philippe tried a different tack. At his suggestion, Hortense made it harder for her husband to get his hands on her money by entering the convent of Chelles. Philippe then incited Armand to take the law into his own hands and seize his wife by force, even lending him sixty of d'Artagnan's Musketeers for the task. The abbess, Armand's aunt, locked the convent's huge iron gate against the bungling attackers and gave the keys to Hortense, who defiantly jingled them just out of reach and refused to admit her husband. Louis, fed up with this increasingly acrimonious quarrel about assets that were far in excess of his own and angered by the misuse of his Musketeers, impulsively decided to make an example of Philippe. Early in 1667 the king forced him to relinquish his company of Musketeers in favour of d'Artagnan, even though in doing so he was giving d'Artagnan a promotion Louis did not feel he deserved. Colbert was outraged by his perverse decision and d'Artagnan's friends were astonished. With something of an understatement, Ormesson wrote in his journal, 'M de Colbert does not like d'Artagnan . . . the king's decision in this respect is surprising, he knows d'Artagnan is a friend of Fouquet and Colbert's enemy.'

Colbert was powerless to remove d'Artagnan from his post but with his hands firmly upon the state's purse strings, he could still make it as difficult as possible for the new captain to turn out his men in the appropriate style. The income d'Artagnan received from the French Treasury for day-to-day expenses was nowhere near sufficient to dress his company to the same standard as that of Maulévrier's rival Musketeers. Colbert deliberately gave his brother extra funds to spend in order to embarrass d'Artagnan, who felt obliged to borrow more and more money to purchase increasingly grand cosmetic items, including straps and hat plumes, to avoid his own troop looking shabby by comparison.

D'Artagnan had to find other means of increasing his income and in desperation he became a trader in valuable horses. Surviving bills of sale show that he disposed of three such animals, probably three of many, for thirty pistoles, twenty-five gold louis and 2,000 livres, but not whether he made a profit. D'Artagnan also received several monetary gifts from his latest unnamed wealthy mistress, whom he was convinced would have willingly become his wife, had he not remained married in the eyes of the Church.

As d'Artagnan had begun to learn, the court was a hotbed of political, dynastic and sexual rivalry. In three years it had grown in numbers by a factor of five, and many of the newer arrivals among the 600 courtiers paid large sums for almost meaningless posts on the ladder of royal etiquette, with its tiny steps of nuances and nonsense that no one had the nerve to challenge. Louis XIV exploited this precise social calibration ruthlessly to reinforce his power and to create a sense of mystique and divine authority. His other less salubrious motive was to further his systematic seduction of women at court.

An apologist for the king's conduct would no doubt point out that very few women he approached were unwilling: a young, vigorous, good-looking monarch who happened to possess the power of life and death over his subjects did not need to force his attentions on those that took his fancy. It was also true that in 1660 Mazarin had manipulated Louis into a political marriage with a queen he did not love, the Spanish Infanta Maria-Theresa, whose physical and mental attributes were little incentive for him to remain faithful. One lady-in-waiting unkindly said Maria-Theresa 'was too short, her lips were too thick and her breasts were too big'. Even in the company of nobles and courtiers who were in most instances far from clever, she always looked conspicuously stupid. 'A seat at the Queen's card table was as good as an extra pension; the simplest gambling games . . . were beyond . . . [her] comprehension.'

Finding it easy to deceive the queen, Louis chose to flout the existing conventions of propriety, morality and chastity if they became obstacles in his path. He had liaisons in quick succession with three of the Manzini sisters, Olympe, Marie and Hortense and made Olympe, who played hardest to get, superintendant of the unsuspecting queen's household.

When opportunistic courtiers told Maria-Theresa what was happening, at first she refused to believe it, then allegedly sought comfort in the arms of a sturdy black page called 'Nabo', who disappeared one day 'very suddenly' when the foolish queen discovered she was pregnant. Try as they might, apparently the royal physicians could find no way of obfuscating in their confidential notes that Maria-Theresa gave birth to 'a small girl, black as ink, from head to toe'. The child was said conveniently to have died soon afterwards but instead may have been spirited away from the palace and brought up discreetly by Benedictine nuns at Moret-sur-Loing, near Fontainebleau.

Officially, Louis was told that the child was stillborn and his wife had nearly died in childbirth. If he was aware of the rumour given currency at court, the king was in no position to criticize his wife's unfortunate lapse. Louis' wandering eye had even alighted on his own sister-in-law, Henrietta Stuart, the sister of Charles II of England. The Restoration of 1660 meant that Henrietta, after years of humiliation in France as a penniless refugee, the daughter of a beheaded monarch, the sister of a king in exile suddenly had become a highly eligible asset in the royal marriage market. Her union with Louis' homosexual brother Philippe d'Orléans, although clearly one of convenience, gave her the title 'Madame' and placed her at the very centre of power. Henrietta had blue eyes, chestnut hair, and one shoulder slightly higher than the other but, although she lacked the raw beauty of the Mancini sisters, her strong sexual magnetism attracted the French king.

Henrietta flirted outrageously with Louis at Saint-Germain and accepted his familiar ploy of invitations to midnight walks in the woods; each time they returned to the palace circuitously by coach in the early hours of the morning. Its blinds were always fully drawn, providing a heady, secluded environment in which it is hard to imagine either Henrietta or Louis exercising restraint.

When his scandalized mother prevailed upon the king to end his near-incestuous relationship, Henrietta devised a cunning plan to divert her attention. The smokescreen in question was to be sixteen-year-old Louise de La Vallière, the daughter of a foolhardy cavalry major. Brought up mainly at Blois, Louise was a country girl who knew and cared nothing for the political intrigues of court, although her widowed mother had secret ambitions for her, borrowing heavily to buy her daughter a suitable wardrobe. For Louise, simply to be Henrietta's lady-in-waiting was the fairy tale, never mind the coming of her prince, and Louis was supposed to be only pretending to be interested in her.

Within a fortnight, however, Louise's looks, her blonde hair, brown eyes and demure smile had captivated the king. Jealous court ladies exchanged asides criticizing her lack of conversation and intellect, and bitched about her small bosom, long nose, bad teeth and slight limp; but her lameness had forced Louise to ride rather than walk from an early age and she had acquired a level of equestrian expertise rarely seen outside a circus. In the gardens of the Tuileries she brilliantly took an unsaddled and untamed Arab stallion through its paces, circling the track standing upright on its back, 'with only a silk cord in its mouth as a bridle'. Louis, the passionate huntsman, was hooked but careful to keep the court guessing. Soon Louise lay naked in his bed in the afternoons, but Henrietta was given the coveted place in the gaming room of the Queen Mother.

Anne's influence over her son, however, was in decline, and so was her health. In April 1663 she had a violent fever and in October the following year showed the early symptoms of breast cancer that obliged her to stay for a day or two at the convent of Val-de-Grace. By May 1665 she had the first signs of gangrene and was taken to the Louvre to be closer to her doctors, a dubious benefit, as they arrived each morning and evening to cut out the pus and rotting flesh around her arms and breasts with razors. In those last days, perhaps on her final night, when the king stayed in her room, slumped against a solid silver table, Anne made her confession to her almoner, the bishop of Auch, and in all probability told Louis the name of his real father: not Mazarin, but Tréville. Before 5 a.m. on 20 January she was dead. The following day, to general consternation, Louis showed that his mistress mattered more than his late mother, seating Louise de La Vallière next to Queen Maria Theresa at a special Mass in Anne's memory held in the chapel of Saint-Germain.

Henrietta Stuart, who had been suspected having of sexual intercourse with Louis and had been snubbed by the queen, found herself moved from centre stage, leaving Louise, her own lady-in-waiting, as the *maitresse en titre*. Both, however, alternately still occupied the king's bed when the mood took him and already a new rival had swept serenely into view. Unlike Louise, Françoise Athénaïs de Rochechouart de Montespan came from one of the leading families of France. In 1663, aged twenty-two, she had unexpectedly married the marquis de Montespan, an impoverished yet possessive husband, by whom she produced a girl and a boy. Never a doting mother, she was quite content to abandon her young children for the glamour of Parisian society.

When, after sparkling at court, Athénaïs was made a lady-in-waiting to the queen, the lonely Maria-Theresa welcomed the companionship of someone she naively believed to be the marquis' faithful wife. Louise, just as unsophisticated, thought Athénaïs enchanting and outside the royal bedchamber the two became inseparable. As a result, the king had endless opportunities to make unfavourable comparisons between his current mistress, the anodyne, quiet, sweet and conscience-stricken Louise, and the aspiring candidate, the vivacious, witty, scheming and amorally seductive Athénaïs. Apart from her prominent nose, a trait of the upper nobility through eons of inbreeding, Athénaïs was almost physically perfect. Athénaïs was a brunette – in due course she dyed her hair blonde to please Louis – with azure-blue eyes, medium height and a well-proportioned body.

These potential changes in the pecking order meant that in d'Artagnan's official, higher-profile role as the new captain of the Musketeers – 'the best job in the land' said Colbert disingenuously, having done his damnedest to prevent him from acquiring it – he immediately had delicate matters of precedence and protocol to consider. Louis had decided that the whole court should go to war. His invasion in May 1667 of the Spanish Netherlands, sweeping aside the uneasy peace that had followed his marriage, lacked the element of surprise because every foreign ambassador in France had already known for months where Louis was going and why. He was taking the show on the road: the Bourbon Theatre Company was making a grand tour of the provinces, allowing the humblest citizens in northern France and some unsuspecting Spanish subjects to see the Sun King live on stage for free. Wagons rolled in the direction of the frontier, heavily burdened with domestic paraphernalia. The king's bed was the size of a small house; the Grande Mademoiselle's included a bed head so tall that whole floors had to be dismantled at the overnight stops in order to accommodate it. Louis' generals pored over the logistical details of the royal advance and only if they had time and energy to spare, tried to solve the problems of manoeuvring and supplying their armies as well.

Fortunately for the French, most of the Spanish garrisons besieged in the borders were outgunned and outnumbered, with low morale and little prospect of reinforcements or fresh supplies. Their fortified towns such as Armentières, Charleroi and Coutrai fell like rotten apples from a tree, often without firing a shot. The king could watch his troops counter-marching up to the enemy's gates, almost as though part of a military parade. So long as they were more of a ballet than a battle, Louis particularly loved sieges. They gave him an opportunity for two or three hours each morning to pretend to be a real soldier in the rear approach trenches, although their counterparts in the First World War would have scoffed at the French monarch's concept of danger and discomfort as he retired for luncheon in silken tents. Lacking an appreciative audience for his exploits, he called for the queen to come right up to the front, or rather for Maria-Theresa and her retinue, which just happened to include Athénaïs de Montespan.

Louis intended his current mistress, Louise, who was six months pregnant, to make herself scarce in one of the almost empty royal palaces until after the birth. To general astonishment, however, she defied convention and arrived under her own steam at the last overnight stop before the trenches, like some unwanted outsider at a wedding, humiliated and ostracized at every turn.

Even the stupid Maria-Theresa had heard whispers of whose

baby Louise might be expecting. She told d'Artagnan, whose Musketeers were responsible for her military escort, that no one – and especially not Louise – should be allowed the following morning to set out ahead of her coach on the last lap of their journey, so that the queen could be sure she would be the first to congratulate the king. Unfortunately, as they approached their destination d'Artagnan had not bargained on Louise, placed well back towards the rear, bribing her coachman to pull sharply out of the trundling procession of coaches and wagons on the road and to drive pell-mell over the hill and directly across the fields to where Louis stood waiting with his officers. This action was the catalyst for a unique set of emotions: d'Artagnan embarrassed, the king hugely discomfited, the queen beside herself with fury and the mistress scarcely able to credit herself with such decisiveness.

Before being sent back to Paris in disgrace, Louise received a small reward for her initiative. With the king's unspoken acquiescence, the next day she rode in the queen's crowded coach to Mass, the escort of curious Musketeers riding as close as they could to catch a glimpse of her swollen belly. Maria-Theresa was forced to make room for Louise, while Athénaïs sat opposite them, privately hoping for her turn at adulterous musical chairs.

Most of the court stayed at Avesnes on the Dutch border out of cannon range in lavish tentage. Athénaïs was lodged in a house some distance from Maria-Theresa, not at all convenient accommodation for her to carry out her normal duties and wait upon the queen. It was, however, but a step or two from the king's apartments on the first floor, and d'Artagnan was told to move a Musketeer on sentry duty there to another position downstairs, so that Louis could cross the upstairs corridor unobserved to the room where Athénaïs just happened to be taking a bath. Louis disguised himself in the uniform of a Swiss Guard, but whether his attire was designed to stimulate Athénaïs' desires or to put Maria-Theresa off the scent, remains uncertain.

Louis' successful attack on Athénaïs' flimsy defences left only one formidable military obstacle, Lille. When the Musketeers faltered during a night assault on the city, d'Artagnan intervened personally where the fighting was fiercest, even though he was completely unarmed. Relishing a chance to return to action, he rallied his men, suffering only a 'light contusion' from a hail of bullets. Louis admonished d'Artagnan for being so reckless, and forty-eight hours later Lille surrendered, perhaps realizing further resistance was hopeless in the presence of a latter-day Achilles.

His campaigning season over in every sense, Louis' new love interest reinforced the general consensus back at Saint-Germain that Louise de La Vallière was not wearing well: the clandestine births, the latest of her illegitimate children discreetly smuggled away by Colbert to foster parents, were taking their toll. Louise was made a duchess, a sure indication that she was yesterday's mistress; but she clung on obstinately at court. Soon, humiliatingly, she was required to join Athénaïs' suite and to sit and watch helplessly as Louis passed by each afternoon to make love to his new flame. A story did the rounds, possibly apocryphal but consistent with the more ruthless side of the king's character, that one day in exasperation he threw his favourite spaniel into Louise's arms as he passed, with the words, 'This is all you need for company!'

Louise of course was not the only humiliated woman at court. For the first twenty years or so of Louis' personal reign, the queen was obliged to put up with a succession of mistresses, but the most durable were undoubtedly the triple act of Henrietta Stuart, Louise de La Vallière and Athénaïs de Montespan. On one extraordinary occasion, when the travelling circus was literally bogged down in Flanders in atrocious weather, the innocent and the guilty had to spend the night together side by side on a row of mattresses in a peasant's cottage near Landrecies: the queen, then, in order, Henrietta, the king, the Grand Mademoiselle, Louise and Athénaïs. 'What's the harm in everyone being on mattresses, fully dressed?' asked Louis, feigning innocence, having slept with almost all of them naked. Henrietta's indiscretions remained in the confines of the court, but the rest was common knowledge. Parisians, as always ready with malicious wit, called Louise, Athénaïs and Maria-Theresa 'The Three Queens', because they knew from courtiers' wagging tongues that even after Louise's ostensible fall from favour sometimes the insatiable king often had sexual relations with all three of them in the same palace on the same day.

To the consternation of the inner circle of courtiers, Athénaïs' wildly unpredictable Gascon husband returned to Paris in August 1668. The marquis de Montespan, a distant cousin of the Grande Mademoiselle, commanded a troop of irregular cavalry in the Pyrenees, who were more of a menace to the local population than to their Spanish opponents. Unwilling to abandon his marital property without a fight, the marquis arrived at Saint-Germain in a hearse with the stag's horns of a cuckold lashed to the roof, and denounced the king as an adulterer. He broke down the door of Athénaïs' bedroom and struck her with a stick. Athénaïs' servants dragged him away, kicking and screaming, and d'Artagnan's Musketeers escorted his hearse several miles from the palace.

The marquis did not give up that easily. Rumours began to circulate that Montespan, with the help of another eccentric Gascon, the comte de Lauzun, was plotting to abduct his wife from court. Lauzun, a captain of the king's bodyguards, was ideally placed to turn rumour into fact because his tour of duty had just commenced. When the king heard what was supposed to be planned, and that his bodyguard might be compromised, he could only turn to d'Artagnan to arrange a permanent escort of Musketeers for Athénaïs whenever she left the palace.

Louis showed no obvious sign of displeasure towards Lauzun but he did entrust to him a task that might have been thought poetic justice: spiriting of Athénaïs' second illegitimate child by the king out of the palace. Just before midnight on 31 March 1669, Athénaïs gave birth at Saint-Germain to a boy. In the haste to remove him from court undetected, he was wrapped in a sheet; there was no time to put him properly into swaddling clothes. Lauzun hid him under his cloak and tiptoed through Maria-Theresa's bedroom, terrified that the child would start screaming and wake the queen. The count handed him over at the remotest palace gate to the new governess and foster mother, waiting in a darkened carriage. This job had gone to a certain Françoise Scarron, who was on the outer fringes of the court: she had received an invitation to the first great party at the new palace of Versailles during the previous July. So far, few courtiers had showed more than a passing interest in the future royal mistress who would become Madame de Maintenon. D'Artagnan, however, knew more about her than it was prudent to know.

She was born Françoise d'Aubigné on 28 November 1635 in a jail, the scandalous offspring of a forty-three-year-old inmate and the sixteen-year-old daughter of the prison governor of Niort, near La Rochelle. Françoise was brought up in poverty in Martinique – where after his release her father unsuccessfully looked for work – and later in France by successive aunts; she seemed destined to life in a convent. Then, in January 1652, newly arrived in Paris, she attracted the attention of the talented court poet Paul Scarron and saw in him a means of escape.

The age differential of sixteen and forty-two was almost as large as that of her parents at her unwanted birth, but Scarron's marriage to Françoise on 4 April had to overcome a much more serious impediment. The poet was so seriously crippled by chronic rheumatoid arthritis that the registrar asked him bluntly at the wedding ceremony whether the union could be fully consummated. The straight answer the registrar never received was that it could not. Anne of Austria, who could always be relied upon on to produce an injudicious bon mot, remarked that if there were ever a superfluous piece of furniture in her poet's house, then it was a wife.

As a very pretty young woman, Françoise had smooth beautiful skin, light chestnut hair, large dark eyes, full lips and a winning smile. Such physical charms no doubt explained the enthusiasm with which young men attended the literary circle held at the Scarron household in the rue Neuve Saint-Louis in the Marais district of Paris. Here Françoise was a 'witty young hostess' who recited for the benefit of their guests some of the bawdier verses of her fading husband with an enthusiasm hard to reconcile with the prim decorum of her later life. Scarron acknowledged that his wife lacked sexual fulfilment and used his final testament to encourage Françoise to see the 'fast' of her marriage as an incentive 'to whet the appetite' for the physical pleasure he had been unable to give her.

After Paul Scarron's death in 1660, Françoise became a regular visitor to the salons at the Hôtel d'Albret and the Hôtel de Richelieu, presided over by some of the leading ladies of the day, and she soon worshipped at the shrine of good taste and manners itself, the Hôtel de Rambouillet.

Improbable as it may seem, d'Artagnan attended the same salons and had much in common with the leading hostess, Madame de Rambouillet. They had both peremptorily declined Richelieu's patronage; they both instinctively disliked the double-dealing and dual standards of court, where their integrity was scorned rather than admired; and they both had a penchant for practical jokes. Of course, d'Artagnan could no more contribute to a serious literary discussion than fly in the air, but his frequent exposure to the upper echelons of society had smoothed some of his soldier's rough edges. On the guest list a man of action made a nice contrast to a man of letters and d'Artagnan had learned, at least in love, how to play a long game. If the prize looked promising enough, he could make small talk with the best of them in Madame de Rambouillet's Chambre Bleue, with its high windows from floor to ceiling hung with blue velvet and opening on to an exquisitely manicured garden.

D'Artagnan was an admirer of Marie de Rabutin-Chantal, Madame de Sévigné, whose captivating letters full of court gossip drew heavily on what she was told by other well-informed members of the Rambouillet society. D'Artagnan's penchant for married women and duels ensured that he would know exactly how to empathize with Madame de Sévigné upon the violent death of her adulterous husband when she was just twenty-five. He might, though, have had the mental reservation that her late spouse should have been a better swordsman, considering that he had been rash enough to call out a rival for his mistress' bed.

The tone of the betrayed widow's letters indicates a long-term friendship with d'Artagnan, three years her senior. Madame de Sévigné was a kindred spirit who had an earthy candour about sexual matters and a surprisingly ribald sense of humour that she revealed only among those she could trust. It seems possible that d'Artagnan was amongst her handful of lovers because the Gascon, for all his boasting about his amorous exploits, realized that titled ladies were more inclined to make themselves available if he gained a reputation of never identifying in public the women who went to bed with him.

Encouraged by Marie de Sévigné, Madame Rambouillet enthusiastically added Françoise Scarron to her illustrious circle, which also included the elite courtesan Ninon de l'Enclos. Ninon introduced Françoise to the marquis de Villarceaux, a gentleman of the king's household. He fell passionately in love with Françoise and 'very often' Ninon lent them the Chambre Jaune, her love nest in the hôtel. As one historian commented dryly, 'one does not lend a room to a couple in order that they should say their prayers in it together.' The Italian nobleman and court observer Giovanni-Battista Primi Visconti described how a pageboy saw them in bed together at the marquis' country house, where Villarceaux painted a portrait of a beautiful young woman whose features bore an uncanny resemblance to those of Françoise, emerging naked from her bath. The picture later disappeared and was only rediscovered after Françoise's death, hidden behind oak panelling at the chateau. Françoise maintained her friendship with Ninon de l'Enclos even after she became all-powerful at Versailles because Ninon knew the secrets of her youth.

Françoise was no ingénue: her art of dissembling had been well honed long before she arrived at court. In August 1660, perched on the front of one of the hôtel balconies, she watched Louis XIV's colourful procession through Paris with his Spanish bride and wrote a vivid description of the occasion in a letter of breathtaking hypocrisy to the marquise de Villarceaux, her lover's wife. Françoise rather fancied the king, beginning her letter with more than a hint of ambiguity, 'Last night the queen must have gone to bed well satisfied by the husband of her choice.' She was also much taken by their escort of d'Artagnan and his Musketeers, wearing their best hats 'with their different plumes; the first were white, the second yellow black and white, the third blue white and black, the fourth green and white'. What happened when she subsequently met d'Artagnan at the salons in the flesh is mere conjecture, but if the Musketeer did not make a pass at her it would only have been because Françoise was nearly penniless and, as always, d'Artagnan was in grim financial straits.

It was Madame de Sévigné who introduced the widow Scarron to Athénaïs de Montespan, who took 'poor little Françoise' under her wing. Athénaïs found her various housekeeping jobs among the nobility and soon she was 'more or less running' the household of a duchess. When Athénaïs needed someone discreet and dependable to look after her illegitimate offspring, Françoise seemed the obvious choice. However, it did not take long for Françoise to exercise that disingenuousness for which she would become notorious. She employed her favourite weapon, piety, as a means of elevating her status, refusing to commit the sin of caring for Athénaïs' royal bastards unless Louis required it of her personally. This delicate negotiation brought Françoise to the attention of the king, who early in 1669 reluctantly gave her an audience and made the formal request. As a consequence he did not immediately take to Françoise, for Louis, as he had told Louise de La Vallière on the battlefield, disliked having his hand forced.

What the king did admire, however, was Françoise's dedication and efficiency. Louis set her up with a nursery in a large house with a high-walled garden outside Paris. Françoise was careful to keep callers to a minimum and would not permit anyone to enter the property. She climbed ladders and put up curtains herself, rather than employ curious contractors. All the while she was continuing to attend the salons and to act as a kind of housekeeper-consultant to titled ladies. This demonstrated both Françoise's stamina and her remarkable ability to dissemble, because none of her friends and acquaintances had the slightest idea about her demanding new role as a foster mother for the king.

After running the gauntlet of the queen's apartments, bearing the latest fruits of Louis' illicit union with Athénaïs, Lauzun hoped for further preferment in the summer of 1669. The king duly promised him the post of grand master of artillery, but Louvois, seeing him as an implacable opponent to his army reforms, and knowing him to be Colbert's ally, persuaded the king to renege on his decision.

Lauzun did not give up but secured Athénaïs' promise to intercede with the king on his behalf. He was unaware that Athénaïs had already begun to use Françoise as a sounding board, albeit in this instance after the event, and that Françoise had raised serious doubts about the wisdom of Athénaïs giving him her support. Nevertheless, after a week had gone by and nothing had come of Athénaïs' assurances, Lauzun grew suspicious and resolved to test her sincerity in the rashest possible manner.

The sexual encounters of Louis and Athénaïs de Montespan were carefully scheduled, like everything else in the king's day. Lauzun bribed her *femme de chambre* to hide him under the bed in the room where the lovers were to meet. It was adorned with large mirrors from floor to ceiling, increasing the risk that Lauzun would be discovered. 'The story makes one gasp and shudder at the same time,' said Saint-Simon. After the protagonists had doubtless also gasped and shuddered to perfection, they settled down for a post-coital conversation on the bed. Far from pleading Lauzun's cause, however, Athénaïs made the king laugh by telling him how she had duped Lauzun into believing she was his ally, when in fact she concurred entirely with Louvois' vehement objections to his promotion. 'Lauzun will not have the Artillery', agreed Louis. According to Saint-Simon, 'after the King and Madame de Montespan had left the room, the anxious *femme de chambre* dragged Lauzun out from under the bed,' where he was transfixed by a mixture of cramp and fury.

Later that evening, Lauzun returned to Athénaïs' apartments, waited patiently for her to emerge on the way to a dance and offered to escort her to the ballroom. He listened with what seemed like infinite patience while Athénaïs, gently taking his hand, recited an imaginary account of all the efforts she had made with the king on his behalf, unfortunately, she said, without success.

Lauzun then repeated to her in a whisper every word of her intimate conversation with Louis, holding her powerless in an iron grip as they walked along corridor after corridor and finally, putting his mouth to her ear, murmured, 'liar, bitch, whore'. All the other courtiers could see was a smiling Lauzun completing his gallant task as escort to the favourite, as Athénaïs tottered a few further steps on her own into the ballroom and fainted clean away. Later she informed the king what Lauzun had done and, perplexed how he knew the truth, said the Devil himself must have been his source. Louis lectured Lauzun on his bad manners but forced the warring parties to embrace in his presence. In due course, some courtier with good connections below stairs would discover, amidst giggles, what had really taken place and it would reach the ears of the king.

Although she had frustrated Lauzun's ambitions for advancement, it was beyond even Athénaïs' wiles, however, to make her royal lover faithful, let alone monogamous. Louis' voracious appetite often meant that he was servicing, as he no doubt dispassionately viewed it, his wife after dawn, having been randomly engaged elsewhere for hours. Sometimes he could be seen clambering over the palace rooftops in the dark to complete the conquest of one of the queen's maids-of-honour, until the prudish duchess responsible for their welfare ordered bars put over their windows at Saint-Germain.

Overlapping royal paramours had become the norm in the bizarre atmosphere of court, a kind of surreal theatre where the curtain never came down on the audience. Each performance of the star with his all-female supporting cast served to stimulate the ambition of the hopeful, the anxiety of the threatened and the anger of the deprived. No measure was too ruthless or too cynical to secure Louis' affections. Try as he might, d'Artagnan would not be able to escape from the consequences of the perpetual conflict between the candidates. By taking no one's side, he became everyone's enemy.

8

THE DOUBLE AGENT

D espite his triumphs of seduction among the ladies of quality in the Paris salons, d'Arragnan possessed perilously few influential allies at court. Louis XIV was at best ambivalent and his three principal ministers, Colbert, Le Tellier and Louvois, were all hostile. If d'Artagnan had ever stopped to consider the reasons for his predicament, he might have realized that the aid and comfort he had innocently given to Fouquet was something to do with it: Fouquet wanted revenge on his persecutors and was plotting to kill them all.

Fouquet's ministerial rivals had hoped for his execution. When Fouquet avoided the death penalty, one of Colbert's civil servants said of his master:

> He fears Fouquet's return, but he is not the only one afraid. Chancellor Le Tellier and his son Louvois fear it also and it seems that the house of Le Tellier and the house of Colbert, who are never in agreement, are united only in fear.

They had good reason to be concerned that Fouquet intended to use poison to dispose of his enemies. Before his arrest, Fouquet had sent Christophe Glaser, a Swiss chemist living in Paris, to Florence and Venice for many months at his expense, to learn how to make 'the finest and most subtle poisons'. In Italy murder by poison had become an industry in itself. The Republic of Venice openly employed a full-time poisoner, with a price list for assassinations, based upon the prestige of the intended victim and the level of security surrounding him.

Italian poisons had a reputation for deadly efficiency and were said to be 'the surest . . . aids to . . . vengeance'.

In fact, it was the skill with which poisons such as antimoniate and arsenic trioxide were applied, rather than the formula, that made them almost undetectable. Antimoniate was an acid that could be easily converted to salt, making the common salt cellar a lethal weapon. Clothes were impregnated with arsenic trioxide, sometimes called white arsenic, where the victim often died if he or she unwittingly transferred the poison from hand to mouth; even when it caused only milder symptoms, they resembled those of syphilis, thereby discrediting the victim. Both poisons were sometimes administered in the form of enemas, which were a popular method of supplementing the bowel movements of the nobility.

Fouquet's choice of Glaser was deliberate because he had arranged for the chemist to gain access to the king's inner circle. A royal physician in Fouquet's pocket used his influence to obtain for Glaser the title of apothecary-in-ordinary to Louis XIV and his brother Philippe. This meant that Glaser sometimes mixed medicines ordered by the court doctors. Perhaps fortunately for Louis, Glaser was never sufficiently certain for whom a particular remedy was intended to take the chance of poisoning it.

Fouquet then tried a different approach, enlisting a long-standing associate with many different identities. In time, this elusive figure would become known as 'Eustache Dauger', the prime candidate for many historians as the Man in the Iron Mask. Dauger's previous name, his role and the reasons for his imprisonment hitherto have been shrouded in mystery. How he acquired a position of influence remains uncertain but by 1661 he called himself Étienne Martin and was employed as a *greffier* or chief clerk in the Paris Parlement, where he performed an invaluable service as Fouquet's main 'fixer'.

In France the Parlement was wholly judicial, with, as had been the catalyst for the Broussel affair, the power to hold up legislation but not to create or defeat it. The Parlement's counsellors, most of whom were hereditary office holders, concentrated on making money, and the six *greffier*s were not slow to follow their example. Prospective litigants were obliged to deposit a substantial sum at the chamber of the *greffier*, in order for their case to be listed. As the gatekeeper to the magistrates, a *greffier* could delay a suit indefinitely. He received the signed depositions of litigants and their witnesses, and sometimes one party bribed him to supply them with an advance copy of their opponent's version of events, in order to improve their own before the deadline for submissions.

Colbert and Le Tellier were aware of Martin's importance as the *greffier* who handled Fouquet's affairs, and after Fouquet's fall they believed he might lead them to the minister's ill-gotten gains. Their list of those to be seized had Martin almost at the top and on 10 October 1661 he was arrested and taken to the Bastille. The procurer-general wanted to interrogate Martin immediately, but the president of the Parlement refused permission and he had to give way. Instead, one of the president's staff interviewed Martin at the Bastille. Despite intense pressure from Colbert and Le Tellier for evidence to be obtained quickly to back up the charges against Fouquet, the president did not receive a report of what Martin had said until 14 December, fully two months later. Le Tellier wanted him re-interviewed but discovered that Besmaux had released Martin from the Bastille, although the *ordre de sortie* on which the governor relied was undated and unsigned. Martin had been told to return to what was thought to be his home province of Brittany, but if Musketeers looking for the many associates of Fouquet still wanted for questioning ever arrived at Pierres, the small village south-west of Caen from which Martin professed to come, they would have found an elderly artisan christened Étienne Martin who could not read or write and who had never been to Paris in his life.

Consequently, the *greffier* known as Martin never gave evidence against Fouquet, despite the detailed knowledge he must have possessed of the superintendant's affairs. He had friends in high places, anxious to keep him out of the clutches of Fouquet's prosecutors. One counsellor provided Martin with a safe house on his country estate until the hue and cry died away. Another, the treasurer at Montauban, found Martin a job in the town for a while as a humble tax collector.

Using funds supplied by Fouquet, Martin established links with a ring of Parisian poisoners, and was probably behind the ambitious attempt to sabotage the royal kitchens just before they were due to provide a feast at Fontainebleau for the king's council. A Burgundian poultry farmer with past links to Fouquet's chateau at Vaux-le-Vicomte was accused of supplying the cooks with fresh ducks and chickens heavily impregnated with toxins. Although this plan might conceivably have succeeded in poisoning his ministers, in reality it had little chance of ensnaring the king. Louis was protected by an elaborate food-tasting ritual: his *écuyer* sampled every dish and checked each utensil by rubbing across it a small piece of bread, which he then proceeded to eat before his monarch sat down to dine.

However, if Fouquet had hoped that this might be the prelude to a more determined attempt on the life of the king, he was to be disappointed. The fallen minister soon found it difficult to maintain contact with the poisoners of Paris. It was one thing for him to smuggle messages in and out of Angers, a ramshackle fortress badly in need of repair, where his jailer, d'Artagnan, had complained to Colbert that he had insufficient Musketeers to mount a proper guard. It was quite another to communicate from the Alpine fortress of Pignerol under Saint-Mars' relentless supervision. On 18 June 1665, six months after Fouquet's arrival, a huge bolt of lightning struck the powder magazine at Pignerol; it blew up and brought down part of the Angle Tower in which Fouquet resided. Fouquet was fortunate to survive, but, hidden in the back of an upholstered chair, part of his fine furniture left wrecked in the rubble, Saint-Mars discovered pens shaped from chicken bones, ink ingeniously created out of water and soot, and white linen strips cut from shirts, covered in notes and messages. Thereafter Fouquet's shirts and ribbons were changed from white to black, making writing upon them almost impossible.

Meanwhile, as a result of the discovery of the deadly ducks, security around the king was significantly increased. After his return to court, d'Artagnan encouraged Louis, though without conspicuous success, to hunt for live game only inside his walled estates. He left nothing to chance when the king insisted on leaving his palaces for open woodland, by posting Musketeers along the long perimeter wherever Louis chose to hunt and refusing access to locals. Henri d'Aloigny, the marquis de Rochefort, a captain of the royal bodyguard who disliked d'Artagnan, ridiculed these precautions and undermined them as often as he could, annoying his apprehensive monarch by saying that his only bad subjects were those who gave him such unfounded fears.

The king entrusted the task of discovering the truth to Gabriel Nicolas de La Reynie, appointed on 15 March 1667 the first ever *lieutenant de police* for Paris, a job he would hold for thirty years. La Reynie inherited a filthy, lawless city, no safer than it had been on d'Artagnan's arrival back in 1640; for example, two decades afterwards fourteen murders occurred in a single night, and 372 in a year. To tackle the problem, he created a uniformed force of 400 officers to patrol the streets. La Reynie also pioneered the separation of justice and policing but eventually would face intense pressure from the establishment to sweep its most spectacular transgressions under the carpet.

By 1668 Fouquet had all but exhausted his resources and could no longer bankroll spies and assassins. Fouquet's brother Louis, the bishop of Agde, asked Martin to find a professional killer to assassinate Louvois but became increasingly vague about where the money to pay him could be found. As funds from the Fouquets began to dry up, Martin looked elsewhere for employment, pragmatically transforming Louvois from target to patron. Martin may have seen the minister as the most promising sponsor of his unusual services, in view of Louvois' deteriorating relationship with Colbert.

In late 1666, when Louvois was put in de facto charge of the war department, Colbert had described him as 'a young man . . . of very quick temper who . . . wants to ruin [the country] . . . because I want to save it!' The following year Savoy's ambassador in Paris reported back to Turin that Colbert had 'powerful enemies', then in 1668 that Louvois and Colbert were 'at daggers drawn'. The ambassador ventured the opinion that 'something unpleasant was bound to happen to one or the other.'

In July 1668 Colbert was bed-ridden, suffering from gout. His ailments showed no sign of easing so, to cheer him up, three months later the king paid him a visit in his own home, accompanied by d'Artagnan and his Musketeers, wearing their best uniforms and carrying drawn ceremonial swords. Colbert had been accused of misappropriating state funds and the king's gesture of support, an exceptional honour that went down badly with Louvois, may have provoked the attempt on Colbert's life under the very nose of d'Artagnan. For Louis, thinking he might help Colbert, also brought with him his official apothecary, who was none other than Glaser, expert in Italian poisons.

After he had taken Glaser's remedies, Colbert's health not surprisingly grew worse rather than better and in November he had dysentery. The following month Colbert complained of severe stomach pains after taking a 'royal' physic. According to historian Pierre Clément, police chief La Reynie said that one of Colbert's valets had been accused of adding poison to the medicine and had promptly disappeared. Much later La Reynie would speculate that Martin and his associates had attempted to murder Colbert, but for the moment they escaped detection by scurrying across the English Channel.

Whether or not Étienne Martin had been the temporary valet under suspicion of poisoning his master in the Colbert household in Paris, he certainly slipped convincingly into this domestic role in London, in the service of a notorious French Huguenot plotter, Claude Marcilly de Roux. Although Roux could not have known Martin was a double agent in Louvois' pay, the tasks he asked his servant to perform showed that he realized he was no ordinary valet. Martin regularly collected at the office of the Committee of Foreign Affairs confidential correspondence sent to Roux from the British embassy in Paris and even persuaded ministers to give Roux immunity from his many British creditors.

In April 1668 Roux had installed himself in Chandos Street at a small hotel run by a Swiss wine merchant. Ironically, the hotel was called The Loyal Subject. Roux was anything but loyal to Louis XIV as his mission was to embroil England in an uprising of Huguenot provinces against Louis, supported by an alliance of Holland, Spain and, if possible, several of the Swiss cantons, whose participation depended on the extent of English involvement. His task was made more difficult, however, by the parallel, and incompatible, objectives being pursued from London. Official British foreign policy was to contain France, but Charles II privately intended to use French money and military strength to return England to the Roman Catholic faith, if needs be by force, and to rule independently of Parliament.

Charles would have hated such a stark summary of his policy. He never adhered to it in an obvious straight line from start to finish but embarked on a meandering course designed both to put pursuers off the scent and to give him a chance to draw back from the brink, if he looked over the political precipice and disliked what he saw. Until he reached that defining moment, if he ever did, Charles saw no harm in constructing an alliance against France that included the Swiss cantons, in order to raise the ante and thereby induce Louis XIV to make him a better offer.

With even Charles willing to sell his own strategy short, Martin had a splendid opportunity to make money by playing one side off against the other. He excelled himself by arranging for a French agent to sit behind a curtain in Roux's rooms and take notes as Roux outlined his plans to a British government representative, while Martin served them dinner.

France accordingly knew from the start that Roux's letter of introduction to the Swiss, which Roux later unavailingly produced to claim diplomatic immunity, was written 'as if from Charles II himself'. Fortunately for Charles, his officials had found an undetectable way to open and reseal French dispatches, giving him time to take the initiative and spin a cock-and-bull story to explain everything away. 'You will see how little credit he had here,' Charles glibly said of Roux in a letter to his sister, Henrietta Stuart, who was passionate in the Catholic cause.

Charles easily persuaded Henrietta that he had no intention of double-crossing Louis, but she was worried that his plans to reconvert his kingdom to Roman Catholicism would be leaked. At the turn of the year Charles wrote to her, saying, 'I assure you that nobody does, nor shall, know anything of it here but my self, and that one person more, till it be fitte to be publique.' Charles had already given a strong hint that 'that one person more' was 'he that came last, and delivered me your letter of 9 December'. Charles added, 'He has given me a full account of what he was charged with, and I am very well pleased with what he tells me.' If so, the one other person in the secret was a French emissary from outside the normal diplomatic circles, Abbé Guiseppe Prignani.

Born in Naples, Prignani was an habitué of various European courts, where he collected intelligence for Louis XIV, who had granted him an absentee living at Beaubec in Normandy, not far from Dieppe. In the summer of 1668 Prignani had been urgently recalled from the Bavarian court to Paris, where he used his skills at astrological forecasts to entertain Charles' illegitimate son, the Duke of Monmouth, who was visiting Henrietta. Prignani soon became an obvious choice to take sensitive letters between Henrietta and Charles, and as a Catholic priest he was someone in whom she could comfortably confide. There is strong circumstantial evidence that he brought a letter from her for Charles in January 1669 and carried a vital one, containing a new cipher code, to Henrietta in return. 'I received yours by the Italian . . . in a passage, where it was so darke, as I do not know his face againe if I see him,' reported Charles, accepting that Prignani wished to remain incognito.

It was soon time, however, for the abbé to come out into the open and arrange for himself, through Monmouth, a public invitation to England. From Louis' perspective, Prignani was perfectly placed to give the French king an informed assessment of whether Charles' professed intentions to convert to Roman Catholicism were genuine.

The abbé was also an ideal conduit to the king. Martin had an offer in his pocket from Fouquet's brother Louis, of 60,000 livres to anyone who could set Fouquet at liberty, provided that England also offered him a safe haven. The money had been scraped together by Fouquet's family and there was very little that Charles would not do for such a considerable sum, but, however tempted he was, eventually the king must have realized that springing the most important state prisoner in France and offering him asylum would prove a provocation too far.

When Prignani returned to London on 26 February, 8 March in the Continental calendar England had still to adopt, he took rooms next to Martin and Roux in Covent Garden, and Martin allowed him to use Roux's clandestine postbox for overseas communications. Letters were to be left with a surgeon in Bedford Street whose lodger, a French importer from Metz who had been a resident in London for twenty years, received wine by the barrel from his brother in Paris. The barrels contained a secret compartment and dispatches inside them went back and forth across the Channel with no one the wiser. This gave Martin an opportunity to intercept and read the abbé's reports to the French king and, rather more significant, many of the letters sent between Henrietta and Charles II. The king had been told by successive ambassadors in Paris that Louis knew the contents of mail bags, including, perhaps especially, letters to and from his sister, before they reached the British embassy. The wine-barrel stratagem, once disclosed by the garrulous Prignani, offered a much safer route to the French capital.

Prignani shared with the king of England a passion for

chemistry, a convenient and innocuous way of explaining his regular visits to court. If Charles felt in need of spiritual sustenance, by celebrating Mass for him the abbé represented a much smaller risk than if he had involved an English priest.

Prignani's reputation as an astrologer was immediately enhanced when he declined an invitation from Charles to travel in the royal coach to Newmarket racecourse and the coach promptly overturned in the dark at the King's Gate in Holborn, precipitating its occupants into the mud. Prignani made his way independently to Newmarket but may have begun to believe his own propaganda, as he attempted in vain to forecast the winner of the first three races, on which Monmouth and his cronies foolishly wagered and lost heavily. In a letter to Henrietta, Charles suggested it was all a pretence, that Prignani 'was only trying new tricks . . . and gave as little credit to them as we did', to keep the abbé from being taken too seriously. If so, the ploy worked rather too well, as news of Prignani's apparent discomfiture reached the French foreign ministry, and their ambassador in London had to work hard to keep him in England.

Martin had ample opportunity to ingratiate himself with Prignani because his employer, Roux, was frequently abroad on his mission to undermine the French state. However, in March 1669 Roux decided to move his base from London to Geneva and to take Martin and another valet with him. A wine merchant met both servants at Dover, 'one blond, a German, and a brown-haired man of English nationality'; he was evidently convinced by Martin's fluent English that he must be an Englishman. At the last minute, however, Martin refused to board the boat with the others, amidst angry exchanges. Despite this, Martin continued to release false information from London about Roux's whereabouts, each time sending news of his location anonymously to the French authorities at the very moment he knew Roux would be moving on.

The longer the hue and cry continued, the easier it was for Martin to pursue his own objectives from the comparative security of England, especially the lucrative scheme to free Fouquet. In May, however, Roux was kidnapped in Switzerland by French troops and taken to the Bastille. Much to Martin's dismay, Roux's arrest brought him a flurry of unwanted attention. Although Martin had English papers and even an English wife, foreign minister Lionne was convinced he was a Frenchman by birth. At Lionne's instigation, efforts were made to persuade Martin to travel to France to testify against Roux 'as a good subject of his sovereign'. Lionne observed that while Martin was clearly implicated in Roux's designs, it was sometimes necessary to allow some crimes to remain unpunished 'in order to have a sufficient number of witnesses'. Martin had already been bribed to steal some of Roux's papers and Lionne suggested some further 'recompense' might persuade him to return to France.

Martin, of course, had no intention of putting his head in the lion's den. On 12 June, 22 June in the Continental calender, the French ambassador, unaware that Roux had just been executed in Paris, reported that Martin had refused all inducements to cross the Channel, saying that the valet had expressed fears he would not be allowed to return to his family. The ambassador wanted permission to ask Charles II personally to have Martin arrested and taken to Calais.

The prospect of Martin being forcibly repatriated to France and placed in the care of Lionne and Colbert, then perhaps revealing who had paid him to poison Colbert, did not appeal to Louvois. Towards the end of May he went to Dunkerque to see Captain Alexandre de Vauroy, the local garrison commander, who had risen through the ranks. Vauroy had undertaken regular assignments for Louvois since 1665. His superiors were often requested to grant Vauroy leave to attend to urgent business and knew better than to ask awkward questions. Louvois was taking steps to ensure that, if Martin were to be apprehended, it would be by men whom the minister could trust.

For his part, Martin realized he must act quickly or the English would deliver him to Lionne and Colbert, but he did not intend to put himself in Louvois' hands willingly. He turned for help to the Protestant network to which Roux had belonged and that regarded Martin, his trusted associate, as one of its own.

According to Roux, four French towns possessed secret stocks of arms and were ready to rise up against Louis XIV if his conspiracy, run by a 'Committee of Ten', had gathered pace: Aigues-Mortes, Montpellier, Narbonne and Pont-Saint-Esprit. Roux's plans had relied on the fact that these Huguenot pastors enjoyed huge influence in their communities. Some were already exhorting their flocks to 'Leave Babylon!' and large numbers of skilled and industrious Protestants were quietly disappearing into England and Holland.

Montpellier's local cleric, David Eustache, was strongly suspected of belonging to Roux's Committee of Ten but motivated more by potential profit than by religious conviction. Martin knew the names of all the conspirators and their weaknesses. What better solution than to become one of them, especially to masquerade as a greedy Huguenot pastor from a remote part of France who was prepared to take money for the use of his identity for a while and go to ground. Martin ran little risk of being exposed unless he was unfortunate enough to come across someone who actually knew him or the man he was impersonating.

Martin may have disclosed his decision to leave England to Prignani, who departed from Dover himself on 7/17 July. Prignani took with him a communication from the French ambassador, which the disgruntled Lionne received at the French foreign ministry more than a week late, probably because in the intervening period the unfortunate abbé was in the clutches of Louvois' men. Within a day or two Louvois had been informed when to expect Martin and no doubt wanted to know everything that Prignani knew before sending him on his way. Shaken by his experience, the abbé soon returned to Italy where, six years later, he would die in Rome defrocked and in disgrace, suffering from venereal disease.

Prignani was also carrying a letter from Charles to Henrietta dated 4/14 July but neither this nor any other letter afterwards written by the English king to his sister has survived, and many of hers to him are also missing. Their earlier correspondence, containing intimate details of health and sexual matters, shows that they had a distinctly unorthodox relationship, more akin to that of lovers than siblings. If, as seems likely, Henrietta told Charles about her marital problems, it would have made uncomfortable reading. From the start Henrietta's husband, Philippe d'Orléans, was undeniably homosexual, unable or unwilling to satisfy his wife. In July 1669 she was nearly eight months pregnant, still the king's occasional lover, and the father of her child was more than likely to be Louis himself. Henrietta may have hoped that Louis would give the unborn infant the status at court of some of his other bastards, but if she approached her brother-in-law before the birth, then she should have known better. The British ambassador, Ralph Montagu, noticed a certain *froideur* between them and in July reported as much to Lord Arlington in London. If Martin, through Prignani, was aware of the reason for this, it was dangerous knowledge indeed.

On 9/19 July, Louvois wrote from Paris to Saint-Mars about Martin. It came as an unwelcome surprise for Saint-Mars, who was on his honeymoon, albeit, because he was forbidden to leave his post, a honeymoon spent in his own jail. Louvois' letter warned the jailer to prepare a secure dungeon at Pignerol for an unnamed prisoner 'of lowly birth' not yet in custody. Saint-Mars could economize on furniture for his cell because, said Louvois, he was 'only a valet'. The space for the name of the prisoner was left blank. Louvois was not yet senior enough to issue a warrant on his own authority, so he deliberately kept from Colbert and Lionne his plans to arrest Martin by persuading his father Le Tellier to countersign the blank warrant on which the king's signature already appeared – and he conspicuously failed to record the warrant in the Register of Orders of the King.

It was Prignani, however, who inadvertently set a hare running that for many years continued to circle the track despite the efforts of the fleetest historian to catch it, by informing Louvois' interrogators on his arrival in France of the identity that Martin would be using. As a naturalized Englishman, or at any rate someone with convincing forged papers describing him as English, Martin was able to obtain a passport in London. Travel papers, then brief informal parchments, were invariably written in French, the international language of the time. The usual style of Martin's permission to travel as pastor David Eustache would have been to enter the surname with an initial, 'Eustache, D.', followed by *anglais*, indicating his nationality. Even official documents were often in almost illegible handwriting and it would have been easy for Prignani to misread an entry on Martin's passport shown as 'Eustache D. anglais', thereby arriving accidentally at the mysterious 'Eustache Danger', whose name has hitherto baffled historians in pursuit of the identity of the Man in the Iron Mask.

The name erroneously supplied by Prignani was entered on Louvois' warrant as 'Eustache Danger', and not 'Eustache Dauger', as was originally thought. Historian Bernard Caire proved this by a meticulous study of the original documents. He discovered several other words in the warrant, for example, *comandé* [sic] and *manière*, where the letter 'n' had been written in an identically careless manner and just as easily could have been a 'u', had not the context made that impossible.

Although another historian, Andrew Lang, was among the many mistaken on this important detail, his main conclusion had an irresistible logic to it. Lang said that when at the highest political level there were proposals to take Martin, one valet, under arrest from England to Calais and a few weeks later 'Dauger', another valet, was arrested there or thereabouts on a warrant signed by Louis XIV, 'it is hardly conceivable . . . that . . . the two valets should be different men. Martin must be Dauger'.

By the warrant dated 18/28 July, Vauroy was ordered to arrest 'Eustache Danger' on sight and to escort him to Pignerol. Louvois' instructions arrived not a moment too soon, because

Martin was almost certainly already on his way to France. Passengers leaving England for the Continent had to depart at dawn on a small bark, parsimoniously hired by the English Post Office in place of a proper packet-boat, which 'attempted the passage twice a week but did not always effect it'. Unless the winds were particularly favourable, it often took twelve hours to cross, usually following the currents to Dunkerque and stopping at Calais on the way back.

In his new disguise, Martin would have preferred to disembark at Calais, whose mainly Huguenot population of 3,000 souls existed in a region with 15,000 Catholics, an imbalance explained by a regular influx of Protestant refugees at Calais from the Spanish Netherlands. Vauroy, who had received an advance on his expenses of 3,000 livres to cover the cost of four men, including Vauroy himself, travelling from Dunkerque to Calais; and of five men from Calais to Pignerol, evidently also expected to find his prisoner there. Warned too late that Martin was at sea, Vauroy might have missed the valet altogether had the boat made better time on the dogleg to Calais. After sunset, however, huge chains were stretched across the entrance to Calais harbour, forcing late arrivals to drop anchor in the roads and land their passengers laboriously up the coast by a small 'cock-boat'. This entailed a night at the austere Petit Saint-Jean inn, the only hostelry that lay outside the Calais town gates, which were shut at dusk. This was probably where Vauroy caught up with Martin, taking him to nearby Fort Nieulet.

The contrast between the security arrangements for the earlier transportation of Fouquet and those for Martin could not have been greater. When Fouquet was escorted by d'Artagnan from Paris to Pignerol, d'Artagnan had with him 100 Musketeers. Vauroy's expenses show that he was accompanied on the journey of more than 600 miles by just three 'archers' or constables, hired help of some kind, not even soldiers from the Dunkerque garrison; they all travelled together in the mail coach with its endless stops to change horses, and they slept at ordinary inns on the way.

Given Louvois' anxiety to ensure Martin's arrest and incarceration, at first sight it seems strange that he took so few precautions on the route to Pignerol and eschewed the opportunity of having Martin interrogated in Paris. The most likely explanation is that the last thing Louvois wanted was for Martin to become a high-profile prisoner and to tell the usual authorities what he knew, because his diverse knowledge both incriminated Louvois himself and, suitably edited, gave Louvois a useful future bargaining chip with the king.

In his original dispatch to Saint-Mars, Louvois was not concerned to conceal Martin's face, but he went to great lengths to deprive Martin of any opportunity to talk. When the prisoner arrived at Pignerol on 21 August his new cell, much to Louvois' annoyance, was not ready, but this was scarcely surprising in view of the special arrangements demanded by the minister. Louvois had ordered that the cell's windows should overlook only inaccessible ground and the cell should be reached via three doors that could be opened and closed separately, 'one after the other, so your sentinels cannot hear anything'. Saint-Mars was warned 'never to listen to him' and told to threaten to kill Martin 'if he opens his mouth to speak to you about anything except the bare necessities'. The jailer followed this instruction with his customary unquestioning zeal. 'I spoke to him in Monsieur de Vauroy's presence' he reported to Louvois on 24 August, 'and told him that if he tried to speak to me or anyone else of something other than his personal needs, I would put my sword in his belly.' Three days later one of those subjects never to pass Martin's lips, Henrietta Stuart, gave birth at Saint-Cloud to a baby girl, Anne-Marie. Barely acknowledged by the king as his brother's child, still less as his own, Anne-Marie would later marry the Duke of Savoy.

As Louis was almost certainly unaware of Martin's existence, his signature on the warrant obtained when it was still blank, it was Louvois, and Louvois alone, who wanted Martin under lock and key. If Martin possessed knowledge so dangerous to the war minister, it prompts the question of why Louvois had not simply disposed of him quietly in London, where alley-lurking villains were two a penny. Indeed, Louvois' instructions to Saint-Mars show that he was prepared to have Martin summarily eliminated if he did not keep silent. However, Martin had access to a ring of highly skilled and ruthless poisoners; as Fouquet's former *greffier*, he was still suspected of knowing where Fouquet had hidden his ill-gotten gains; and probably he had been told a good deal by the Abbé Prignani about the detail of Charles II's scheme to reconvert England to Roman Catholicism. Add to this his knowledge of the intimate confessions of Henrietta to her brother, and Martin was a lot more useful to Louvois alive than dead.

Louvois left the marquis de Pienne, as governor of the citadel, in no doubt that he was to give Saint-Mars 'all help and assistance' with his new prisoner; that Saint-Mars and not Pienne was master of the donjon. The marquis could not stomach this continued loss of face and lack of authority over someone many levels beneath him in society and within a few months found a way to resign his post. His decision proved fortuitously well timed because Louvois was soon looking for scapegoats after La Forêt, one of Fouquet's servants, made an attempt in December 1669 to arrange his master's escape from Pignerol.

La Forêt and one of Fouquet's oldest friends, André de Valcroissant, obtained menial jobs inside the fortress and, 'well furnished with pistoles', set about bribing several of the guards. Loose talk led to the plot being betrayed, however, and although La Forêt and Valcroissant escaped across the Italian frontier, the Savoyan authorities – in contrast to the Swiss – had no intention of harbouring the enemies of the French state and promptly sent them back to Pignerol.

Valcroissant, found to be carrying a letter from Fouquet to his wife, was sentenced to five years in the galleys, but Madame de Sévigné and d'Artagnan successfully intervened on his behalf, and Louvois, with a rare flash of humour, turned the harmless old man into an inspector of prison security. A much grimmer fate awaited La Forêt. Saint-Mars had no compunction in summarily executing him on a gallows erected in the courtyard and suspending his rotting corpse over the dormer window of Fouquet's apartment, in full sight of the former minister. La Forêt had condemned himself by contacting Martin inside Pignerol and asking 'if he had anything of consequence to tell him'. As a result, Louvois instructed Saint-Mars to modify still further Martin's cell 'in such a manner that the prisoner will not see or be seen by anyone, will not speak with anyone whatsoever, and will not hear those who want to tell him something'.

Quite apart from what he might have to say about Louvois, the knowledge Martin possessed of the plan to reconvert England to Roman Catholicism had become pivotal. In May 1670, after eighteen months of negotiations between the kings of England and France in which Charles' sister had played a key role as intermediary, she crossed the Channel herself to finalize what became known as the Secret Treaty of Dover. By the treaty, signed on 22 May/1 June, Charles made a commitment 'to reconcile himself with the Church of Rome as soon as the welfare of his kingdom will permit'. This could mean whatever Charles wanted it to mean but if, as Louis and Henrietta believed, it meant the conversion of England by force, then 6,000 French troops would be supplied to make the scheme feasible.

For Charles, despite his sister's influence, the treaty seems a commitment entirely out of character, the biggest risk of his reign. He went to great lengths on all other occasions to avoid such hostages to fortune. One of his ministers, in vain seeking a signed order from the king to intercept foreign mail, 'to justify myself . . . in case of [the king] forgetting', received the curt response from Charles that 'he would remember it well enough'.

Years later, on 7 January 1674, Charles would deny the existence of the secret treaty, disguised by the signing of a public version without the damning clauses, during a speech to both Houses of Parliament. 'I assure you,' he told lords and commoners, 'there is no other Treaty with France, either before or since, not already printed, which shall not be made known to a committee of this House.' It was so brazen a lie, that even Charles 'seemed nervous and fumbled with his notes'.

If the secret treaty had been discovered after such a speech, no matter his true intentions, the King of England might well have suffered the same fate as his father. Instead, it left Charles II for the rest of his reign at the mercy of the King of France, and of other men in the shadows on both sides of the Channel who, by accident or design, were privy to the deception. Part of the explanation for such recklessness may be that, deep down, Charles was more fervent a Roman Catholic in life than was ever acknowledged or apparent from his alleged deathbed conversion by a Benedictine monk.

As for Louvois, he used the attempt to free Fouquet as an excuse to visit Pignerol personally and arranged for his protégé, the great military engineer Sébastien de Prestre de Vauban, to travel with him to advise on structural alterations. Vauban was ordered to look at the defences from a new perspective; for like every key frontier fortress, Pignerol's fortifications had been planned not to keep people in, but to keep people out.

On 9 July 1670 Louvois notified the seigneur de Loyauté, his new *commissaire de guerre* at Pignerol, of his intention to pay a two- or three-day visit. He was due to travel in the week beginning 15 September but something must have made it more urgent – perhaps his fear that the fortress was less secure than it looked – because Louvois suddenly told Vauban to be ready to leave on 15 August. Then on 27 July Louvois brought the date forward again, to 2 August, a Saturday. It has been suggested that Louvois kept changing his departure date to avoid his absence being noticed at court, but there was nothing surreptitious about Louvois' visit, only a good deal of scepticism about its true purpose.

On 25 July the Savoy ambassador reported,

They say M de Louvois is going to Pignerol to see what has to be done to improve the fortifications . . . I hardly think he would undertake such a long journey in the summer heat or that he would separate himself from the King for such a long time just for these supposed fortifications.

Speculation that there was more to the trip than met the eye was reinforced by Louvois' decision to take with him his troubleshooter, Nallot.

Typically of Louvois, the journey was undertaken at a furious pace. The postmaster at Lyon was ordered to install in the post chaise three fully reclining chairs made of padded velvet, so the travellers could sleep on the next leg to Besançon. They arrived at Pignerol in the evening of 7 August and stayed not with the governor but in the town with an old friend of Louvois' father. This deliberate snub caused tension among the garrison, as Louvois no doubt intended. He kept the Pignerol authorities waiting still longer for the start of his formal inspection and on 10 August visited Turin, paying his respects to the Duke of Savoy and dining with the French ambassador. From 11 August, however, Louvois gave his undivided attention to Pignerol and his secret prisoner. He remained at Pignerol for more than a week, as he did not return to Paris until 26 August.

Louvois ordered his eyes and ears at the fortress, commissioner Loyauté, to send him a report on what had really been going on behind the scenes. Louvois' immediate acknowledgement confirms that Loyauté had a lot to say 'about the tales circulating there', but the commissioner's report is missing, presumably destroyed. It almost certainly pointed to widespread corruption at Pignerol, part of a plan to release Fouquet. On 27 August Louvois tipped off Loyauté that four senior officers were to be dismissed. In the end, the entire garrison of the main fortress was changed and only Saint-Mars and his group of turnkeys survived unscathed. No doubt even the irreplaceable jailer had breathed a huge sigh of relief when Louvois' post chaise left Pignerol and disappeared from view.

9

RETURN TO PIGNEROL

       ❧   ❧

Henrietta Stuart believed her life to be at risk, not because of the secret clauses in the Treaty of Dover, but because of her husband's jealousy of his own brother. On 26 June 1670 Philippe d'Orléans surprised Henrietta and Louis in what was discreetly described as a 'confidential conversation' and forced her immediately to return with him to their palace at Saint-Cloud. Philippe was certainly not above encouraging his paramour, the exiled chevalier de Lorraine, to find the means to poison his wife in a fit of revenge because of her affair with the king, especially if he knew her child could not be his own. It remains just as likely that she was already suffering from a fatal illness but the royal physician, Vallot, chose a clever double entendre when he later observed it was nothing short of a miracle that she had lived as long as she did.

When, four days later, in the early hours of 30 June, barely six weeks after her diplomatic triumph across the Channel, Henrietta died aged only twenty-six, Louis showed the cold-blooded side of his character. That very day at lunch, Louis summoned his maturing and unmarried cousin, the Grande Mademoiselle, and offered her 'the vacancy': marriage to the newly widowed Philippe. Louis was already planning to embrace the assets of the richest heiress in Christendom within the family, rather more enthusiastically than the Grande Mademoiselle could expect to embrace his homosexual brother.

The Grande Mademoiselle rejected Philippe as a potential suitor with almost indecent haste. Instead, she was to come to an extraordinary, controversial decision, one that all but paralysed the French court, to marry the comte de Lauzun, whose chequered career had survived his part in the marquis de Montespan's madcap plan to kidnap Athénaïs. 'It is you,' wrote the Grande Mademoiselle to Lauzun, in a billet-doux explaining her choice, like some impulsive, adolescent girl.

Born Antoine Nompar de Caumant, marquis de Puyguilhem, Lauzun was raised in the Paris household of his father's cousin, the duc de Gramont. As a second son with no assured inheritance, he was considered a poor match for his first love, the duke's daughter, Charlotte Catherine de Gramont, who was married instead in 1660, against her will, to the Prince of Monaco. Lauzun's chance of advancement was not improved by his physical appearance and characteristics. Madame de Choisy summed him up as 'little, dirty and ugly'. He must have been extremely small in an age of short people, because his sardonic cousin, Bussy-Rabutin, described him as 'one of the smallest men the good Lord ever created'. He possessed 'the eyes of a lynx and the ears of a hare' and, said Bussy-Rabutin, pursuing the feline analogy, the features of a 'skinned cat'. The irascible marquis de La Fare thought Lauzun 'the most impudent little man who has existed for a century'. Saint-Simon, who as his brother-in-law was biased but knew him better than most, said that Lauzun 'was always pursuing some intrigue', he was 'envious, spiteful, bold and audacious in every way', and when it came to women, he was 'impertinent in the last degree . . . loving very few'.

But how they loved him. Even Madame de Choisy, who pretended to be above such base considerations, acknowledged that 'his wit, vivacity, *gasconnades* [made him] an enormous success with ladies.' *Gasconnades* told for the purpose of seducing a woman were a speciality of all Gascons, so in this respect d'Artagnan and Lauzun were one of a kind.

When it came to his daring relations with the king, however, Lauzun brooked no rival. Louis, surrounded by fawning sycophants, found his breathtaking cheek amusing. After Lauzun had distinguished himself in some heroic charges at the sieges of Lille and Coutrai, Louis appointed him colonel of a regiment of dragoons and in due course gave him almost unrivalled right of *entrée* into his private apartments. It appeared that Lauzun could get away with anything, until he made the mistake of interfering with the king's sexual pursuits.

Lauzun's passion continued unabated for the unhappy Princess of Monaco, who had returned to court, and they again became lovers. When Louis noticed her considerable attributes, he ignored her relationship with Lauzun and arranged a tryst with the princess, leaving the key to the door to his private apartments where it could easily be found. Lauzun, knowing the time and the place of the rendezvous, removed the key and with it still in his hand, hid in a small adjoining closet. He was able to watch in secret through a crack in the panelling, relishing every moment, as the king's valet, Bontemps, smuggled the eager princess up the back staircase and the anticipated physical liaison was frustrated in every sense when, try as they might, the princess and Louis were unable to force open the locked door that barred their union.

Lauzun was unable to resist both upbraiding his lover for her intended betrayal and rejoicing in the detail of his triumph; the princess complained to the king and Louis decided it was high time to order his colonel of dragoons to rejoin his regiment, which was campaigning against brigands in Béarn. Lauzun, in a rage, refused to go and said he would rather resign his commission. Drawing his sword, he broke it over his knee and swore he would never carry a weapon again in the service of a king who could behave as shabbily as Louis had done. The king by then was equally furious but, turning away, threw his cane out of the open window, saying, 'for fear that I should have to reproach myself for striking a gentleman', and left the room.

Lauzun did not escape that easily. The following day, he was arrested and imprisoned in the Bastille, whose governor, Besmaux, received orders from Louvois that the king wished him kept in solitary confinement without the services of a valet. Lauzun remained in the Bastille for five months and after his release took revenge on the Princess of Monaco in brutal fashion, treading, with feigned innocence, on Catherine's hand as she lay on the grass at Versailles.

However, the taste of life in the Bastille made Lauzun a little more cautious. In his pursuit of the Grande Mademoiselle; for once the impoverished count did not make all the running. On the contrary, said his biographer Mary Sandars:

> though Lauzun used his utmost art as a professional lady-killer to subjugate the Princess, he was for a long time extremely doubtful of the possibility of the King allowing any marriage between them, and was in a state of nervous tension at Mademoiselle's impetuous determination about the matter.

In the rigid French class structure of the period, it was by any standards a huge mismatch. Mademoiselle brought with her a vast dowry of ducal titles, grand houses with retinues of servants, extensive lands and liquid assets, whereas Lauzun had almost nothing. Mademoiselle had been short-listed as a suitable bride for the monarchs of England, France, Spain and Portugal and for the Holy Roman Emperor, while Lauzun was a minor noble of no consequence. However, Mademoiselle, never an attractive woman, realized that at forty-three, six years older than Lauzun, this was her last chance of a respectable relationship. She wanted Lauzun desperately and had convinced herself that he wanted her.

Lauzun could aspire, just, to the hand of the richest heiress in Europe, to a princess of the blood, if he were very, very careful. But he was not about to take such a reckless step into the unknown: first Mademoiselle had to sound out cousin Louis. In the early hours of Monday, 15 December 1670 she plucked up enough courage to do so, after waiting up until two o'clock in the morning for the king to finish a game of cards. Louis kept the Grande Mademoiselle standing in a narrow passage between his apartments, a sign of his irritation at her breach of protocol. The king did not give the match a ringing endorsement but finally he promised not to stand in her way.

The news that Lauzun was to wed the Grande Mademoiselle went around Paris society as a tempest might whip up a forest fire. Madame de Sévigné almost ran out of adjectives in writing excitedly to her daughter about 'the most astonishing thing, the most surprising . . . marvellous . . . miraculous . . . unheard of . . . singular . . . extraordinary . . . incredible . . . a thing which makes everyone cry out in amazement'.

Lauzun, in a brief triumph of hope over experience, obtained the support of Athénaïs de Montespan, and in writing. Perhaps Athénaïs thought that if Louis would allow such a dramatic departure from tradition she could aspire to greater things herself, even to becoming queen, should, God forbid of course, Maria-Theresa die young. On 20 December, in a letter tied with rose-coloured silk and bearing two seals, Athénaïs wrote to 'Monsieur de Losun' in her usual phonetic French. 'Nothing is forgotten that might be of use to you,' she assured him, adding however, 'I hope a certain person will not come to Versailles, for I have already seen [him] provoking retractions on similar occasions.' Lauzun knew all about that 'certain person'. It was Louvois, who had scuppered his chances of becoming grand master of artillery despite the king's promise. Yet Lauzun dithered uncharacteristically and one of Mademoiselle's few allies at court, the duc de Montausier, demanded of him angrily to know whether he 'wanted to start a painter's shop instead of getting married, as there was no time to be lost'.

As Montausier believed, the king's tentative approval of the match cried out for a rapid ceremony before the opposition could recover; but Mademoiselle wanted a grand wedding with all the trimmings and Lauzun did nothing to dissuade her. He may have decided already that without the king's unmistakable endorsement – manifested in his physical presence at the ceremony planned to take place just after midnight on 22 December at the Queen's Chapel in the Tuileries – it would all end in tears.

In this, Lauzun was probably correct. To say that this upstart would not receive a warm welcome from the serried ranks of the Bourbon family was putting it mildly. Even the deferential queen plucked up enough courage to speak bitterly to Louis, who turned on her angrily, whereupon she remained awake all night, crying. The king's spurned brother Philippe said that Mademoiselle should be put into a lunatic asylum and Lauzun thrown out of a window. The prince de Condé threatened to shoot Lauzun directly after the wedding ceremony. 'Louvois . . . was almost beside himself with rage.' With the exception of Colbert, who hoped to use Lauzun to curb Louvois' power, and Athénaïs de Montespan, 'all the Royal House, the Ministers and the court, raised their voices clamorously against the marriage'.

Oblivious to the uproar and the gathering of the Furies, Mademoiselle ordered her horrified lawyer to draw up papers that would transfer almost all her property to Lauzun, including the jewel in the crown, the *comté* d'Eu, the first peerage in France, and the duchies of Chatellerault, Montpensier and Saint-Fargeau.

Mademoiselle's lawyer procrastinated and prevaricated in his efforts to keep his client's assets out of Lauzun's hands. However, the papers at last were ready to be signed and all the protests about the marriage seemed to have come to nothing when Françoise Scarron quietly intervened. Her influence had been immensely strengthened by the behaviour of Athénaïs' husband. The marquis de Montespan was given permission to claim his father's estates in south-west France strictly on condition that he did not stand in the way of a formal separation from his wife. On 11 July 1670 the Châtelet court in Paris had heard the opening legal submissions in a petition on behalf of Athénaïs de Montespan to live separately from her spouse and to recover her dowry, on grounds of cruelty and unreasonable behaviour. The marquis was not supposed to defend Montespan *versus* Montespan, but with her dowry at stake he would do so doggedly, dragging out the litigation for almost four years. During that time it was more important than ever for the lovers to conceal the whereabouts of Athénaïs' illegitimate children, whom Françoise looked after with such discretion, because under French law the marquis could claim them as his own.

When Athénaïs turned to Françoise Scarron for advice on whether to continue to support Lauzun's intended marriage to Mademoiselle, Françoise told her bluntly that 'in time even the king would reproach her with the results of her handiwork,' and the die was cast. Louis discovered, rather to his surprise, that Athénaïs had changed tack.

It seems probable that Louis also asked Françoise directly for her views. He was beginning to notice and appreciate the attractive new addition to the inner circles of court. Françoise had a calming influence on Athénaïs and was playing a pivotal role in caring for their secluded offspring. Just before his second, fateful meeting with the Grande Mademoiselle, Louis received a secret visitor who was still with him as Mademoiselle arrived outside his apartments and whom the duty captain of the royal bodyguard, Rochefort, was under strict orders not to allow her to see. It is difficult to think of anyone else whose presence, because of their lowly status, would have created a potential embarrassment for the king if Mademoiselle had known them to be there.

Barely four hours before the ceremony was due to take place, Louis told his cousin that she could no longer marry Lauzun. He was even tactless enough to blame the Grande Mademoiselle for lingering and giving everyone time for reflection. However, there were other, more disreputable reasons lurking in the dark recesses of the king's mind. Marriage would remove his cousin's wealth forever from his clutches and Louis, personally, was still poor. He had a growing number of children, legitimate and illegitimate, in need of legacies. And, long ago, Mademoiselle was the blood relative who had turned the guns of the Bastille on his army; Louis made a point of never forgiving a bad turn.

Once she had left the royal presence, Mademoiselle's reaction to the king's change of mind was one of grief and fury, which continued unchecked on her return journey from the Palais-Royal to the Luxembourg Palace. She smashed every window in her carriage, in a fit of hysterics.

Lauzun, who might have been expected to show equal signs of outrage, did nothing of the kind. For him, he humbly told the king – who must have been apprehensive about what might happen when he summoned Lauzun – it was a chance 'of giving the greatest mark possible of my submission to the will of Your Majesty'. Louis confirmed as much in issuing, through his foreign minister, Hughes de Lionne, what in modern times would be called a press statement, for dissemination by his ambassadors abroad, an indication of the furore the episode had caused. He said that Lauzun had received the disappointing news 'with all the . . . submission that I could possibly desire'.

However, the leopard had not changed its spots. Lauzun had simply learned the lesson that a frontal attack was likely to result in a bloody nose, the Bastille again, or worse. Lauzun decided on an outflanking movement designed to weaken the influence of at least one enemy who had the king's ear. Athénaïs de Montespan had betrayed him once too often.

In February 1671, Lauzun sowed the seed of the idea in the uncomplicated mind of Louise de La Vallière, the supplanted mistress, that she had suffered humiliation enough and, rather than be subjected to any further insults from Athénaïs, she should do what she had threatened for some time and enter St Mary's Convent at Chaillot on the Paris outskirts. Louise departed from court very early on Ash Wednesday in a plain linen dress, leaving all her worldly goods behind but also a letter designed to pluck at the heart strings of the king; the note was reputedly penned in Lauzun's unmistakable style, long on hyperbole and short on good grammar.

The letter achieved its desired effect. The following day, Lauzun travelled to Chaillot, where he was seen in animated conversation with Louise, sitting next to her under a tree in the convent garden, presumably urging her to play hard to get. In the end, the great Colbert himself had to go personally to plead with Louise, armed with a royal warrant signed by the repentant king. By midnight, a triumphant Louise de La Vallière was back in the palace and back in the king's bed.

Lauzun's timing was perfect; Athénaïs was in the last stages of pregnancy and in no state to be making unbridled love to Louis.

Buoyed up by his success, Lauzun took the gamble of his life and persuaded the lovesick Grande Mademoiselle to marry him in secret. At least, a number of influential people were convinced that he did: the anonymous editor of the court gossip sheet, *La France Galante*; the Abbé Melani, Mademoiselle's confidant; and the writer Angliviel de La Beaumelle. They all believed that a simple ceremony consisting of a 'nuptial benediction' by a priest had taken place in Mademoiselle's rooms at court, while Melani went further, hinting that the king had quietly given his consent. This seems unlikely, for Louis had already been ridiculed in the foreign press for the original fiasco. He even tried to shut down some Dutch scandal sheets, with predictable lack of success.

In her memoirs, Mademoiselle went close to confirming her clandestine marriage to Lauzun:

> People continued to say we were married. Neither he nor I said anything, not daring to speak about it to our intimate friends
> . . . I went back and forth to Paris very frequently

Back and forth, that is, by water in her private barge from her palace to the Hôtel Lauzun, an exceptional mansion built in 1657 by Fouquet on the quai d'Orsay. Mademoiselle acquired the house after Fouquet's disgrace and presented it to Lauzun, adding gold leaf everywhere but especially in the principal bedroom. In 1906 a subsequent owner would stumble across a secret passage leading from the wine cellar to the Seine, where Mademoiselle had been able to tie up her barge and visit her alleged husband unseen.

In his new position as a man of property, perhaps married into the Bourbon family, someone who had helped restore Louise de La Vallière to favour, Lauzun's arrogance knew no bounds. He even turned down the king's offer to make him a *maréchal de France*, saying he preferred to wait until his prowess in battle had earned it. In pointedly taking the position he did, Lauzun was aware that Louis paraded many such 'unearned' military titles of his own. Not content with putting the king on the defensive, Lauzun treated Athénaïs with complete contempt and as the months went by might have continued to do so with impunity but for the one factor he always overlooked: the growing influence of Françoise Scarron.

In the summer of 1671, the drama was played out a second time, with Françoise casting another crucial vote against Lauzun, in the guise of giving Athénaïs some more sound advice. 'Was it right', she asked deferentially, 'for Madame de Montespan to leave at large near the king one who was her deadly enemy, and who could scarcely open his mouth without vindictively abusing her?'

The Hôtel Lauzun, as it had become known, was also doing Françoise's work for her. Married or not, there was little to stop Mademoiselle giving away not just the hôtel to the count but everything else as well. Mademoiselle's lawyer, who had worked hard once already to keep her assets out of Lauzun's clutches, regarded the transfer of the Paris house to him in 1671 as the thin end of the wedge and warned the king. With Louis receptive to the message, an unholy alliance of minister and mistress closed in for the kill. Both Louvois and Athénaïs complained to the king about Lauzun's 'odious epithets' and accused him of insolence and ingratitude. This reference to ingrates struck a chord with Louis, who a little later was to remark that Lauzun had never even 'deigned' to thank him for giving him an income from the titular post of governor of Berry. The king added what evidently vexed him still more, that Lauzun 'had not paid the bill' for it.

La France Galante reported that 'most of the court were now earnestly wishing for his long-deferred disgrace, as he behaved with such arrogance,' but Lauzun inconveniently declined to provide a credible pretext. Françoise Scarron referred afterwards to 'the constant rages of little Lauzun' but, however scathing he might be towards Athénaïs in person and about her to others in private, Lauzun, the consummate courtier, kept himself in check in front of the king.

The marquis de la Fare, hearing Lauzun speak of Athénaïs 'with so much indignation and contempt', believed nonetheless that Louis would take severe action against him. He warned one of Lauzun's intimates that if the count did not rein back, he 'is a lost man; he will not remain six months longer at court'. On the advice of the genial comte de Guitry, in the summer of 1671 Lauzun made a half-hearted attempt at reconciliation with Athénaïs, 'hanging five or six little pictures by the best masters' in her rooms at Saint-Germain, which she grudgingly accepted.

Louis still wanted to act against Lauzun but discovered it was not easy to do so. To begin with, Lauzun was a captain of the royal bodyguard, whose men respected his authority. For three months from 1 July, he was even the duty captain and could scarcely be expected to arrest himself.

As the second company of the King's Musketeers was in the hands of Colbert's son and Colbert was seen as a supporter of Lauzun, to make the arrest Louis once again turned to d'Artagnan, who was thought to dislike Lauzun intensely. A year previously, in August 1670, the two Gascons had crossed swords, almost literally, before the siege of Hesdin, a bitter quarrel that left them barely on speaking terms. Despite that, and despite the king's wishes, d'Artagnan procrastinated; throughout the summer and autumn of 1671 Lauzun remained at large. Seizing a minor noble whose principal crime was to have ideas above his station did not reconcile easily with d'Artagnan's strongly held concepts of honour, procedure and justice.

The search for someone else willing to see Lauzun behind bars began in mid September, when Nallot, one of Louvois' most trusted officials, was sent to Pignerol with a secret dispatch. The recipient was not Saint-Mars, probably thought too close to his former commander, d'Artagnan, but Rissan, the newly appointed king's lieutenant at the citadel. In his reply, dated 6

October 1671, which Nallot, 'having just arrived' presumably took back himself, Rissan referred specifically to 'receiving M. de Lauzun . . . in order to hand him over to M. Saint-Mars'. Like the careful bureaucrat he was, Rissan added pointedly that he 'would then receive orders from the king on this subject', implying he would do nothing without proper written instructions. This was not an enterprise to be involved in unless it were sanctioned right from the very top.

According to a dispatch from the papal nuncio to France, Lauzan showed no sign of softening his approach. He had another heated exchange with Athénaïs de Montespan on 19 November and Louis ordered him to apologize, giving him five days to comply. On Wednesday 25 November, after Lauzun had failed to meet the deadline, he was placed under arrest. Louis had deliberately waited for a changing of the guard, for the tour of duty of Rochefort, the veteran palace plotter, and d'Artagnan's enemy. Rochefort was particularly adept at taking d'Artagnan's frequently imprudent remarks out of context and making them sound like open rebellion. Seven years earlier, when Fouquet was to be taken into custody, d'Artagnan was almost the first to know and the palace guards were deliberately left in the dark; but when they arrested Lauzun, d'Artagnan was no longer trusted to obey orders and he and his Musketeers were almost the last to be informed.

On the fateful day, Lauzun, who thought himself an expert in jewellery, travelled to Paris at the request of Athénaïs de Montespan, to buy precious stones on her behalf, further evidence that so far as Lauzun was concerned, no irretrievable breakdown had occurred in their relationship. Athénaïs probably knew exactly what was happening and sent Lauzun into the city to keep him out of the way whilst preparations were made.

At about 6 p.m., bearing an order signed by Louis and Chancellor Le Tellier, Rochefort arrested Lauzun upon his return to Saint-Germain, just as he was about to enter his apartment, and demanded his sword. Lauzun, surprised and horrified, flung his weapon onto the marble floor, the sound resonating along the empty corridor. The count was frogmarched across the courtyard, surrounded on all sides by guards carrying blazing torches, watched by little groups of courtiers who could scarcely believe their eyes. In vain Lauzun demanded to speak to the king or to Athénaïs de Montespan, whom he clearly thought capable of exerting influence on his behalf: after all, he had Athénaïs' diamonds in his pocket. He asked for pen and paper to write a note to the king but, on Louis' explicit orders, this too was refused. Lauzun was taken to the Bastille, where he sat slumped in front of the fire in his room in one of its towers, not saying a word, brusquely refusing Besmaux's offer of supper and a comfortable bed in the governor's quarters.

Lauzun's friend and former subaltern, Henri de Barrail, bravely asked Louvois if he could write a letter to the prisoner asking for his instructions on what should be done with his property. Louvois agreed: property rights were to be respected, human rights were not. According to the code of ancient France, the individual counted for nothing, but the inheritance one day due to his family remained sacred. The king could lock up a prisoner forever with complete impunity but when it came to his personal assets he dared not touch a single penny, without the sanction of a judge.

D'Artagnan became aware of Lauzun's arrest only when the Musketeers received orders that same evening to search Lauzun's hôtel for a large casket. Naturally d'Artagnan would have had to make sure that they had found what the authorities were looking for, by opening the casket, with or without a key. According to Athénaïs, it contained the portraits of more than sixty women whom Lauzun had the habit of 'fluttering', some intimate descriptive notes and 'correspondence to match'. Many had sat naked for the artist in sexually provocative poses, including one whose head was subsequently removed from the portrait, prompting speculation that it might be Athénaïs herself, and another whose eyes had been pierced with a sharp point, probably by Lauzun in a moment of fury, this a likeness of his unfaithful first love, the Princess of Monaco.

Although the king issued strict instructions that the names of these ladies should be kept secret, d'Artagnan, whose lips were sealed when it came to the identity of the women who featured prominently in his own romantic affairs, seems to have been somewhat less discreet about the seedy contents of Lauzun's casket. Most of the ladies' names became public property including, much to Louvois' discomfiture, that of his own sister, whose compromising portrait and letter showed her, too, to be one of Lauzun's passing conquests.

Louis had another role for d'Artagnan. He might be captain of the First Musketeers but he could suffer for his recalcitrance, by personally taking the long road to Pignerol a second time, again in nearly impossible conditions, in the heart of winter. There is no record of d'Artagnan's reaction. He may have been too busy with preparations to make any public comment or, seeing that one of the king's favourites could be arrested for no good reason and that he would be escorting him to the most feared prison in the kingdom, he may have felt it prudent for once to keep his own counsel, to avoid joining Lauzun in a cell at Pignerol himself.

The following morning, however, d'Artagnan sat on his horse in the outer courtyard of the Bastille, 100 of his Musketeers milling about to the front and rear, guarding for the moment an empty coach. D'Artagnan would not begin his journey to Pignerol without written instructions nor allow the fuming Besmaux to hand over his prisoner.

After a long delay, one of Louvois' lackeys arrived with a dispatch signed by the minister stipulating Lauzun's destination. It ended, 'His Majesty desires that you inform him in every detail of everything you can learn from your prisoner.' On the journey to the Alps, d'Artagnan was expected to be interrogator as well as escort. Hour after hour, league after league, he sat with Lauzun in their carriage and, after a day of silence and depression, Lauzun began to respond. D'Artagnan was taking his orders seriously, or so it seemed. He was also beginning to appreciate that even Lauzun's cautious answers hugely increased his own knowledge of what had happened in the past behind the scenes at court.

The cortege moved slowly. Each morning, d'Artagnan allowed Lauzun to decide when he was ready to travel. After two days, a courier caught them up with an inventory of Lauzun's possessions, drawn up assiduously by Barrail on Louvois' instructions. D'Artagnan was told to provide Lauzun with pen and ink so he could mark the document, indicating his wishes for each item. Lauzun peremptorily refused and d'Artagnan sent the messenger back with an unapologetic note.

Nallot passed the column, carrying instructions for Saint-Mars that d'Artagnan was not permitted to see. When the procession reached the Lyon state prison, Pierre-en-Scise, Lauzun began the farewell speech to d'Artagnan that good manners oddly required, expecting this to be his final destination. Learning for the first time from d'Artagnan, who had kept the bad news from him for as long as possible, that he was to be imprisoned not in Lyon but at Pignerol, Lauzun sighed, 'I am lost.'

The further they travelled, the heavier became the snowfalls and the thicker the crowds, who turned out in every town and village to see the fallen favourite and the dashing d'Artagnan – not quite so dashing, in point of fact, then two years short of fifty. On 14 December they arrived at Gap, where d'Artagnan commandeered a horse to replace the injured mount of one of his Musketeers; and recruited two guides, one for the main party, the other for the luckless assistant to the quartermaster sergeant, who was sent on ahead to scout for avalanches.

Two days later the column wound its way into Besançon, where almost the entire population was waiting patiently in the place d'Armes to see 'le comte d'Oison'. For all their indifferent spelling, the town consuls had anticipated d'Artagnan's needs: true to tradition, they gave him four bottles of the best local wine.

On 19 December, still hampered by bad weather, which forced them to detour south to the Turin Gate, d'Artagnan and his party reached Pignerol just before 5 p.m., in gathering gloom and freezing temperatures. Lauzun looked up at the grim towers of the fortress and, raising his voice, uttered a few words of Latin, '*in saecula saeculorum*', as a priest might chant them at the end of a creed, meaning 'forever and ever'.

Lauzun was given rooms below Fouquet, but overlooking mainly the blank walls of an interior courtyard. The grilles and the grime on the small windows left Lauzun in an environment of almost perpetual twilight. Louvois, said the marquis de la Fare, was Lauzun's 'mortal enemy, who made his imprisonment the most cruel that can be imagined'. The marquis perhaps had a rosy view of the conditions experienced by most inmates of the prisons and galleys or floating concentration camps of Louis XIV, for Lauzun's physical confinement was lenient by comparison; his conclusion was nonetheless correct. Louvois, with Louis' blessing, was trying to bring about Lauzun's mental collapse in a harsh regime of virtual silence.

From the first, Lauzun was denied all news of and communication with the outside world, especially from the Grande Mademoiselle, all books and writing materials, any exercise or visitors – except d'Artagnan. The captain of the First Musketeers sent his men home but unexpectedly remained at Pignerol, a miserable place in winter, for a further five days. Saint-Mars was powerless to prevent d'Artagnan from visiting Lauzun several times before his departure because, after all, had not Louvois himself instructed the Musketeer to try again to persuade Lauzun to arrange his affairs? However, Lauzun had no more intention of cooperating with Louvois than d'Artagnan had thoughts of helping him to notarize an inventory. They both may have sensed the importance of what Lauzun had to say.

In his dingy prison, Lauzun was at his most desperate, convinced that, like Fouquet – now starting his second decade in detention – he might never leave Pignerol alive. So Lauzun enlisted d'Artagnan's support by giving him a glimpse of the hidden levers the count had once pulled so effectively at court, as Mary Sandars put it, 'strong enough to set the most powerful machinery in motion'. For Lauzun had access to almost all the royal skeletons, the catalogue of lust and lies that made up the character of the Bourbons, the pieces of the jigsaw that made sense of Tréville's relationship with the queen. Whereas d'Artagnan had never been privy to 'the ceaseless plotting which went on', Sandars concluded that 'Lauzun – indefatigable at strategy, adroit, and secret – was in the midst of it all, and was possessed . . . of peculiar powers of gaining information.' Louis and Louvois could never have imagined that their order, which turned d'Artagnan inquisitor, would encourage Lauzun in his anger and despair to tell him everything and complete the picture of an unscrupulous king with no right to rule.

It left d'Artagnan acutely disillusioned; the principles he held so dearly were shown to rest upon foundations of sand. Returning slowly to Paris, he spent Saint Nicholas' Eve and New Year's Eve at inns in the company of strangers, in no frame of mind to seek out friends and acquaintances.

A few months earlier, overshadowed by Lauzun's spectacular effort to self-destruct, one of Louvois' deadliest enemies had died in sinister circumstances. For a long time Lionne had been a thorn in his flesh. Despite barely surviving the fall of Fouquet because of his close friendship with the superintendent of finances, Lionne had flourished as Louis' foreign minister. Agile, resourceful, with a flair for languages that Louvois neither understood nor cared to acquire, Lionne consistently outmanoeuvred his rival at court. In 1668 Louis had supported Lionne's proposal to give back a key Spanish territory won in battle, Franche Comté, as part of a wider settlement, against Louvois' fierce opposition. Then in 1670 the king backed Lionne's policy of arming the German principalities and including them in an offensive alliance against the Dutch, which Louvois regarded as a waste of time and money. In the meantime, Lionne had been breathing down Louvois' neck in the hunt for Étienne Martin, whom Louvois spirited away to Pignerol at the last possible moment.

Louvois' visit to Pignerol in the summer of 1670 was a

diversion that baffled his biographers, and makes sense only because Louvois felt a pressing need to have a face-to-face meeting with Étienne Martin. It may have taken Louvois a week to persuade Martin to leave the sanctuary of the Alpine fortress and return to Paris on a new and dangerous mission; it may then have taken Martin many months to penetrate Lionne's security, using his tried and trusted method: becoming a valet in his household. In this he was probably helped by the pressures on the minister's domestic staff that arose from Lionne's personal foibles: a predilection for all-night gambling and frequent assignations with ladies of the court. The conduct of Lionne's estranged wife was rather more scandalous, so much so that in August 1671 Lionne had her incarcerated in the convent of Saint Marie. The charge was gross immorality, unusual grounds for separation in these amoral times. When Lionne almost immediately became a victim of poison, falling into a mysterious coma and dying on 1 September, suspicion at once fell on his wife. She was found to own a house in a seedy district of Paris, and a search of it turned up a sinister skull and the decomposing body of a black cat. In due course, based on the testimony of someone destined to become France's most notorious poisoner of the age, the marquise de Brinvilliers, Lionne's wife would be accused of purchasing the poison from the marquise's lover, Gaudin de Sainte-Croix. This left Gaudin's closest associate, Martin, conveniently in the clear. Louvois, however, must have considered him a liability if he remained in Paris and ensured that Martin returned to seclusion at Pignerol.

Although Saint-Mars later would have in his care other prisoners who in fact were not prisoners at all, notably General Catinat, closeted in a cell at Pignerol to disguise French plans to attack the nearby pocket state of Casale, only Martin occupied the twilight zone where he was closely guarded one moment and set at liberty the next. For someone with Saint-Mars' blinkered logic, this must have been a highly irritating state of affairs, especially since he had been told by Louvois from the start that Martin was 'only a valet': as it happened, a commodity at Pignerol in the shortest of supply. Protocol demanded that prisoners of Fouquet and Lauzun's rank should have two valets apiece, whereas in fact each had only one. So on 20 February 1672 Saint-Mars wrote to Louvois and disingenuously suggested that Danger would make a 'fine valet' for Lauzun. As Saint-Mars probably half expected, Louvois wasted no time in dismissing the suggestion out of hand.

At court, meanwhile, everyone acted as if Lauzun were dead. The Grand Mademoiselle recalled:

> at supper, there was discussion about a horse. The king said, 'I remember, it belonged to . . .' and without finishing his sentence, looked at me, blushed and stopped short.

The situation did not improve when d'Artagnan finally returned to Saint-Germain, following a conspicuous delay. Instead of reporting post-haste to the king after delivering Lauzun to Pignerol, as protocol demanded, he sent his young cousin, Pierre d'Artagnan, in his place. Pierre did not even go directly to court but spent his first day at the Luxembourg Palace repeating every detail of the journey to the lovesick Grande Mademoiselle. Having slept in the same room as Lauzun throughout the passage to Pignerol, Pierre was able to assure her of Lauzun's undying love and that d'Artagnan had made every effort to meet his prisoner's needs and requests. The apprentice Musketeer brought letters for Mademoiselle from Lauzun, which was certainly not Louis' intention and such communications were subsequently forbidden. In sanctioning his cousin's actions, d'Artagnan appears to have gone out of his way to be as provocative as possible to the king.

Oblivious to this, the Grande Mademoiselle persuaded the Gascon several times to intervene with Louis XIV on Lauzun's behalf. No record has survived of their conversations but it is unlikely that d'Artagnan, having heard from Lauzun every scrap of information detrimental to the king, approached this hazardous task with any degree of tact. His relations with the king were irretrievably damaged, but d'Artagnan did not seem to care.

After d'Artagnan's departure from Pignerol, Louvois had increased the strength of the Saint-Mars' company by an additional thirty former Musketeers. He warned the jailer to be

> much more on the alert in guarding this prisoner . . . because he is capable of doing very much more to escape by strength, or cleverness, or corrupting someone, than is Monsieur Fouquet.

Louvois was correct. One night early in March 1672, less than three months after his arrival, Lauzun shook himself out of his trauma and set about the beams of his floor with a lighted candle, intending to find a way into the space beneath. He burnt a hole sufficiently large to put his hand through and with astonishing strength, raised the damaged beam, even though it was clamped and nailed to the one adjoining. It would not go back into place, however, and Saint-Mars found it in the morning.

The jailer began to search the prisoner regularly and in July discovered a large nail in the lining of Lauzun's jacket. Saint-Mars interrogated his own men, one of whom eventually confessed to accepting a bribe to deliver a message to Lauzun, by wrapping a note around the nail and throwing it through the window. The trail led outside the prison to one of Lauzun's erstwhile valets, a Béarnais called Heurtaut, who committed suicide before he could be brought back and persuaded to talk.

Among Heurtaut's belongings Saint-Mars discovered a letter in code written by Lucie de la Motte d'Argencourt, former lady-in-waiting to the queen and briefly mistress of the king. Dumped by Louis, she had found solace in Lauzun's bed and the combination of love and revenge induced her to finance Lauzun's escape. In his concern to keep Lauzun secure, however, Saint-Mars sprang the trap too early and nothing could be proved against any of the conspirators.

Louvois was 'intensely anxious to discover the scope of the plot and also whether those engaged in it had managed to communicate with Lauzun'. The count knew something of vital importance to Louvois and the minister wanted to discover the full extent of that knowledge. Despite his instructions, d'Artagnan had declined to repeat what Lauzun had disclosed to him, so it was left to the luckless Saint-Mars, on Louvois' orders, to attempt to engage the count in conversation. Lauzun ran rings around him. Asked about the weather, Lauzun said he had been put in a place where he could see neither sun nor moon; asked about his health, Lauzun said he was better than he wished to be.

As the walls were too thick to make a hidden spy hole into Lauzun's accommodation, Saint-Mars had to resort to climbing a tree outside the count's windows to see what he was doing. The jailer was not the most athletic of men and this undignified surveillance, which smacked of desperation, produced nothing tangible to report to Paris. However, if Lauzun was leading Saint-Mars a merry dance, bombarding him with a daily litany of pleas, protests and complaints, in other ways the jailer's life was about to take a turn for the better. His ministerial master, Louvois, the scourge of the army and the court, the most ruthless schemer of his time, had met his match in Saint-Mars' wife Marie-Antoinette, soon to become his de facto sister-in-law from hell.

Marie-Antoinette and her sisters Françoise and Marie Collot were the daughters of a humble apothecary. Their mother died when Marie-Antoinette was 11 and she showed her resourcefulness by bringing up her younger sisters unaided before becoming housekeeper to Pignerol's *commissaire de guerre*, Louis Damorezan.

When Saint-Mars arrived at Pignerol to guard Fouquet, Damorezan was already courting Françoise Collot and later married her. Saint-Mars preferred the youngest sister, Marie, but she did not consider a diminutive sergeant, former Musketeer, stuck indefinitely in a prison, any sort of catch. Saint-Mars had to settle for the rather plain Marie-Antoinette. When they married he was thirty-eight and she thirty-nine, suggesting that Marie-Antoinette had never been inundated with suitors. Subsequently, Damorezan also found a prospective husband for

Marie in Louvois' principal secretary Élie Dufresnoy, who put Louvois' words on paper and dispatched the sensitive letters that were galloped from Paris to Pignerol for the pressing attention of Saint-Mars.

Marie jumped at the opportunity of marrying Dufresnoy, knowing this would put her on the fringes of Parisian high society. In December 1672, Marie made a sensational entrance on her first day at court, attracting *'une grande presse'*, 'a great crowd'. Marie had no great intellect but she possessed the kind of looks that stopped everyone in their tracks. The marquis de la Fare, ever one for the memorable put-down, observed that Marie responded to flattery with 'all the insolence that can be derived from beauty and prosperity, whenever it is combined with low birth and lower intelligence'. Madame de Sévigné nonetheless welcomed her with open arms. 'She's a nymph, she's divine,' she wrote, inviting Marie to supper in the hope she might fall for her son.

However, Marie had her eye on a much bigger catch, the minister for war himself. Louvois was already married to Anne de Souvré, daughter of the marquis de Courtenvaux. Anne had given Louvois seven children, was 'rich, virtuous and charitable', yet possessed 'all the charisma of a waste-paper basket'. The minister himself had not improved with age, becoming grossly fat, his hands and body constantly covered in a thick and odorous layer of sweat; but whether Marie Dufresnoy had a less developed sense of smell than most or simply lay back and thought of court, the beauty soon coupled with the beast. Louvois got Marie's new husband out of the way by sending him alone to Dunkerque as *lieutenant du roi*, then promoting him to *chef du troisième bureau du secretariat*, responsible for the lucrative administration of patents and building projects, which kept him at his desk in Paris until the early hours.

Marie 'treated Louvois like a little boy, and made him do stupid things'. Louvois did not object because he was 'absolutely besotted' with Marie and before long asked the king to make her *'une dame du lit de la reine'*, 'a lady of the queen's bed', with 'all the rights and privileges of ladies of the first order'. Louis, aware that his courtiers, in anticipation of the request, had already dubbed Madame Dufresnoy, *'une dame du lit de Louvois'*, responded: 'Do you really want everyone at court to make fun of you?' before eventually giving way.

However, Louvois quickly found that while he might have one Collot sister in his bed, he had another to contend with almost everywhere else. Marie-Antoinette regularly returned to Paris to visit her sister, and she encouraged Marie to withdraw her sexual favours whenever Louvois displeased either of them. Under her sister's tutelage, Marie tamed Louvois as one might break in an unruly horse. Marie-Antoinette also showed her how Louvois could be made to give way, simply by making a huge fuss in public. Marie was a quick learner and her outbursts, resembling something of the noise and violence of a medieval siege, were said to outdo by some measure even the spectacular tantrums of Athénaïs de Montespan.

10

THE RED CASKET

   ❧   ❧

In April 1672, having failed to budge Louis even a centimetre on behalf of Lauzun, d'Artagnan reluctantly left court, having been made governor of Lille. In his formative years d'Artagnan had been eager for a genuine governorship but not since he had become captain of the Musketeers. Most appointments given to high office holders such as d'Artagnan were sinecures and at first he had wrongly assumed that all he had to do was make one or two token visits to the city. The fact that the Gascon would actually be expected to reside in Lille and carry out his duties as governor on a daily basis was an unpleasant surprise for d'Artagnan and highly unusual. To create the vacancy, Marshal d'Humières was given a field posting under Marshal Turenne at very short notice and when he refused to go, was sent on leave. In theory d'Artagnan could have declined the job but, as always, he was short of money and the tempting governor's salary came on top of his regular pay. His former captain in the Musketeers, Tréville, the only man to whom d'Artagnan had ever listened, would almost certainly have advised him to remain at court; but the seventy-three-year-old lay seriously ill in Béarn and died not long afterwards at his chateau in Troisvilles, on 8 May, thereby removing the last serious impediment to sanctions against d'Artagnan himself.

It was Louvois' idea to make d'Artagnan a governor, all too readily accepted by the king, and it coincided with the start of a renewed French campaign against the United Provinces. The king accompanied his troops into the field, but d'Artagnan, usually more concerned than most with Louis' personal protection, was left kicking his heels in Lille's equivalent of city hall, the Hôtel de Santes. Effectively, this was a clever snub for d'Artagnan, a huge setback to his hopes of acquiring a field marshal's baton. France consumed the United Provinces piece by piece and the war might have been over altogether that summer had not the Dutch in sheer desperation opened their dykes, preferring to flood their own country than find French soldiers in the streets of Amsterdam.

As Louvois knew perfectly well, d'Artagnan's new appointment was also a poisoned chalice. Governors were weighed down with paperwork and d'Artagnan was barely literate. Governors were expected to be skilled at diplomacy and d'Artagnan could not remotely be called diplomatic. Louvois anticipated that sooner or later d'Artagnan would become embroiled in some dispute. It proved to be sooner.

In his role as governor of Lille, d'Artagnan was technically in command of the town's citadel. As with Pignerol and the distinction there between the fortress and the donjon, however, much depended upon whom the war minister and king supported in the event of disputes. What Louvois no doubt omitted to mention to d'Artagnan before he took up his appointment was that over the previous four years a team of Vauban's engineers had been reorganizing the city's defences and they did not operate in accordance with regular military discipline. Vauban was a favourite of the king and believed he had a free hand at the citadel, a pivotal point in the new fortifications under construction at Lille. Vauban's staff of engineers, his 'band of Archimedes', took their lead from him and frequently failed to keep d'Artagnan informed of their plans.

The governor was particularly angry when one of the engineers diverted part of the river running through the town and removed two sections of the old ramparts where d'Artagnan was accustomed to parade his garrison. He said these were:

things he certainly should not do without warning the man who commands in a place like this, since by doing so the people see the little respect paid to the man who commands here.

When the engineer tried to make amends by calling on the governor, he was snubbed for his pains and from that moment on, refused to acknowledge and salute d'Artagnan.

Louvois could have dealt with the quarrel himself but, knowing it would further disadvantage d'Artagnan, referred it to Louis. On 13 August, Louvois told d'Artagnan that the king 'does not approve of the way you have treated [the engineer] and wishes you to find a way of putting right what you have done'. D'Artagnan would have been wise to accept this criticism but instead wrote again to Louvois, saying,

> I am convinced, Monseigneur, that the King would be angry with me if I suffered a little engineer of two days to slight the character His Majesty has done me the honour to give me here.

In less than a fortnight d'Artagnan found himself involved in another dispute, this time with the king's lieutenant, the royal representative who commanded the citadel in Vauban's absence. D'Artagnan went on a tour of inspection of Lille's immediate surroundings and did not return until after 6 p.m. Because of the lateness of the hour, the king's lieutenant failed to make his customary report to the governor and went to the officers' mess to have dinner, much to d'Artagnan's annoyance.

When something similar happened the following day, d'Artagnan angrily ordered his carriage and drove to the citadel to confront the king's lieutenant, but found the gates locked. D'Artagnan flew into a rage and sent the officer on duty to the king's lieutenant with instructions to come and explain his conduct. Instead, a subaltern appeared with a note that blamed the duty officer for failing to report to the governor that day for orders. D'Artagnan sent him back for the king's lieutenant, threatening to have him arrested if he did not personally arrive at the gate. This time he did come himself but repeated his explanation face to face that the duty officer had been told to attend the governor in his stead.

D'Artagnan wrote in fury to Louvois, 'I demand justice from you . . . you cannot wish that I command here without having the authority that my commission gives me.'

Louvois again chose to refer the dispute to Louis, who decided that d'Artagnan was the one entirely to blame. This was Louvois' response:

> The King . . . found that it would have been much better [for you] to have waited until the following day to ascertain the reason for . . . [the king's lieutenant's] failure to come for orders, than to have gone yourself after the citadel gates had been closed, and that, when you determined yourself to go in the evening to ascertain the reason, you should have been content yourself with what . . . [they] came to tell you . . . without going at such an hour to threaten an officer who commands a citadel and make him come out at an inconvenient hour to tell you the same thing that he has already told you by two different people.

A more comprehensive rebuke would be difficult to imagine but d'Artagnan wrote again to Louvois on 10 September. His dispatch of interminable length, in execrable phonetic French, amounted to an assertion that everyone had failed to respect '*selluy quy coumende*', 'he who commands', namely d'Artagnan himself. The governor went over every incident ad nauseam and said, 'I am the only man to whom such things have ever happened and I am the more vexed because that makes me scorned by the garrison.'

Two weeks later Vauban returned to Lille and, when his engineers told him what had occurred, he protested to Louvois that his authority had been undermined. 'I cannot imagine that the King wants me to play here the role of Prince Trivellin,' he said, referring to the character of a court jester in an Italian comedy. Louvois urged him to be patient: 'Monsieur D'Artagnan's commission [as governor] ends in a month,' was his soothing, if inaccurate, reply.

Former governor Marshal d'Humières having retired to his estate, as Madame de Sévigné put it, to 'plant cabbages', his opportunist wife heard on the grapevine that Lille was in uproar. She asked Louvois, 'Doesn't the King think it advisable that the Maréchal should return as governor of Lille, where his presence would not be altogether useless in the circumstances and lack of intelligence going on there?' The king did. On 6 December d'Artagnan handed over to Humières, as glad to leave as the city was glad to see him go.

Returning to Paris, d'Artagnan found that his troubles were not over. The Musketeer entered into a relationship with a married lady in the capital, which did not escape the attention of the eagle-eyed Françoise Scarron, who was now making regular appearances at public events. She later recalled her conversation with Louis XIV at a military parade:

> I found myself on such terms with the King that I might speak to him frankly . . . I had the honour to be walking with him . . . When we were out of earshot, I stopped and said to him, Sire, you are very devoted to your musketeers . . . what would you do if Your Majesty were told that one of those musketeers whom you cherish so much had taken the wife of another man, and was actually living with her? I am sure that from that very evening he would be barred from the residence of the musketeers, and would no longer be allowed to sleep there, however late it might be.

By suggesting sanctions against an unnamed Musketeer, Françoise was trying to sow a seed in the king's mind that d'Artagnan should be dismissed from court. The opportunity to rid herself of a disagreeable connection with her less reputable past was too good to resist. The number of influential people who wanted d'Artagnan out of the way was growing.

The captain of the Musketeers remained oblivious to this threat, partly through his nature and partly because his attention was focused upon security issues. D'Artagnan did not know it, but he had good reason to be concerned. Some months earlier,

Martin had returned to the capital from Pignerol, initially on a damage-limitation exercise, prompted by the death of both the chemist, Glaser, his principal source of poisons; and of his fellow conspirator, Sainte-Croix, who was married to Martin's cousin, Madeleine de Breuil. Glaser, formerly bankrolled by Fouquet, may have died from natural causes but Sainte-Croix was held to have suffered a lingering demise through coming into contact with his own poisons. The story was given credence by a notorious sceptic, police chief La Reynie, who ordered his apprehensive subordinates to make a search of Sainte-Croix's laboratory, a room in the house of the widow Brunet in a cul-de-sac off place Maubert.

Sainte-Croix had many debts, so his rooms were sealed by an official from the court of the Châtelet. When they were opened for the benefit of creditors, Martin was among those allowed in the house, where he also lived; but he paid no attention to the proceedings, instead spending his time smashing small glass phials in the cellar. On a shelf in the smaller of Sainte-Croix's two rooms stood a red pigskin casket, about forty-five centimetres long and thirty centimetres high. This, too, contained phials, some with arsenic and other poisons, and some whose sinister contents could not be identified, even by the most expert apothecaries in Paris. It also contained damning evidence of a conspiracy between Sainte-Croix and the marquise de Brinvilliers to murder her father and her two brothers to secure the entire inheritance. A decree of arrest was issued, but the marquise, tipped off in advance, fled to London with a single maidservant. In late 1672 the French exerted enormous diplomatic pressure to have her extradited, including a letter from Colbert that according to those who had read it was more like an ultimatum than an appeal to a supposed ally. Charles II neatly deflected the problem by giving permission for the marquise's arrest but making it impossible to execute the warrant. Quite apart from the potential embarrassment of the marquise's link with Martin, and he with the British secret service, Charles probably sensed that the perfect storm would have reverberated around Parliament had La Reynie's agents been allowed free rein on British soil.

Louis took a personal interest in the affair when it emerged that the first person to be convicted and executed for his part in the murder of the Brinvillier brothers, a valet called Jean Hamelin or Amelin, had been a prospective new employee in the royal household just as the news broke of his arrest. Sainte-Croix had purchased for Hamelin a royal appointment as an 'officer of the goblet', which ominously entailed the care of the king's table linen, wine glasses, bread and fruit. In October 1672 Hamelin's nervous last-minute replacement at court dropped dead while on duty, having apparently poisoned himself in error, using a phial found half-empty in his pocket.

Fouquet, suspected of being behind this botched attempt on the life of the king, made a last effort from Pignerol to secure his liberty. On 21 January 1673 he persuaded Saint-Mars that he knew a secret of such importance that Louis would grant him his freedom in return for it. On hearing this, Louvois instructed Saint-Mars to give Fouquet five or six sheets of blank paper, and to forward to Paris whatever his prisoner wrote, sealed and unseen. Fouquet's letter left Pignerol on 15 March. Louvois' reply on 29 March was final and brutal: 'I have read with great care the handwritten sheets from Monsieur Fouquet and do not consider them important enough to show to the king.' If Fouquet had revealed his knowledge of Louis' true father, given to him by Tréville many years earlier, the secret reached Louvois, but went no further.

During that same month of March, Étienne Martin, calling himself Martin de Breuil – quite possibly his real name – turned up unexpectedly at the Châtelet criminal assizes to give an account of himself. The judges, unaware that they had in front of them probably the most wanted man in Europe, listened politely as Martin described himself as a gentleman in the king's service, scarcely an accurate description of his work for Fouquet and Louvois; and formerly as a tax collector at Montauban, which at least was true. Martin admitted to business dealings with Sainte-Croix but claimed he had never heard him speak of poisons.

With Paris rife with rumours of fresh poisonings, the King's Musketeers checked comings and goings at court, an almost impossible task, and manned the city gates. Unable to leave the capital, on 22 April Martin found himself summoned back to Le Châtelet, this time to give evidence on oath. The record of these proceedings is missing, probably destroyed afterwards on Louvois' orders; but a transcript survives of the next witness, Madame Gaussin, who happened to be the wife of the royal barber, for whom Hamelin sometimes worked as a *perruquier* in their shop in the rue de Grenelle. When Madame Gaussin said that Martin had brought the infamous red casket to their shop, he stood up in the court and accused her of lying. After the judges rose for a short break, Martin was overheard warning Madame Gaussin not to say another word about the casket.

Had d'Artagnan attended either hearing at Le Châtelet, the game would have been up, for d'Artagnan would have recognized Martin as a visitor to the Bastille in 1663 when Sainte-Croix, a fellow Gascon, was briefly an inmate. Instead, the Musketeers relaxed their grip on the capital and left with Louis for the front. It was not until 16 July that the judges issued a warrant for Martin's arrest and by then he was long gone, safely back behind Pignerol's walls.

The catalogue of d'Artagnan's increasingly dangerous knowledge had one final page to turn. Since Lauzun's arrest, a posse of guards had accompanied Athénaïs everywhere, short of her boudoir, but early in 1673 the king's mistress asked for her protection to be removed when she left the palace, saying it was no longer necessary. Athénaïs was unaware that d'Artagnan did not withdraw his Musketeers completely but instead kept them at a safe if undetectable distance, and it would quickly become apparent why she was anxious to avoid witnesses to her excursions from Saint-Germain.

At the time Louis' health, not the safety of his mistress, was causing the greater concern. The king was suffering from severe headaches, dizziness, acute tiredness at night and hair loss, which prompted him to start wearing a wig. His physicians were baffled; they did not realize that the symptoms were triggered by aphrodisiacs, or pseudo-aphrodisiacs, which Athénaïs administered in ever-increasing strength to heighten Louis' sexual satisfaction. While Louise de La Vallière still clung on at court, this was still not enough, however, to ensure Athénaïs' pre-eminence. In an attempt to achieve this, she took extraordinary risks and turned to someone who looked as horrific as the crimes he committed, Abbé Étienne Guiborg.

A man blind in one eye and with 'purple veins that seemed about to burst', Guiborg had been directly involved for twenty years in the traffic of infants and their live sacrifice on an unholy altar. He was the chaplain to the comte de Montgomery and was widely rumoured to be the illegitimate child of the count's late father, for he did more or less as he pleased. This included holding a Black Mass in March 1673 in the chapel of the Montgomery family's Château de Villebousin, a gloomy, moated, medieval fortress on the Orléans road, just south of Paris.

The lady in whose name the Mass was celebrated covered her face with a veil but otherwise lay completely naked, stretched out on the altar with her legs apart, a linen cloth folded on her stomach, a chalice resting on her groin. Into that chalice was poured the blood of a newborn infant, its throat pierced by Guiborg with a knife; and semen ejaculated during the ceremony by an unknown Englishman, rumoured in some quarters to be the second Duke of Buckingham. Part of the black exhortation recited by Guiborg was that the woman should 'have and keep the love of the King . . . and that the King's love for her shall wax and flourish . . . so that he shall abandon and no longer gaze upon the face of de La Vallière'. Shortly afterwards the Black Mass was repeated twice in other locations in Paris for maximum effect, each time performed on the body of the same female. That naked woman was almost certainly Athénaïs de Montespan.

If Athénaïs, not content with her blasphemous incantations, was inadvertently poisoning Louis with her potions, perhaps it was because others were tampering with their contents. In May, Olympe Mancini, comtesse de Soissons, having already sought murderous revenge on Henrietta and Louise de La Vallière after failing to keep the affections of the king, poisoned her own obnoxious husband, the autocratic comte de Soissons, in order to marry her lover. The widow then joined the court on the summer military campaign in the United Provinces, daring anyone to voice publicly the accusation made behind their hands in the royal rumour mill.

That same summer, one of the priests at Notre Dame, struggling with his conscience, left the Paris police chief La Reynie a note. It warned him of the large number of exalted sinners who, in the secrecy of the confessional, sought forgiveness for having committed murder by poison. La Reynie took this seriously. He had heard the burgeoning whispers about the activities of the comtesse de Soissons but he was confronted with a conspiracy of silence about Athénaïs' experimentation with black magic. The one exception was Primi Visconti, who claimed to belong to the highest nobility of Italy, although his detractors said he was the son of a tradesman in 'wool and worthless junk'. Whatever the truth of that, Visconti was the darling of the French court, where he made a living out of chiromancy, graphology, horoscopes, the interpretation of dreams and forecasting the future. There was very little that Visconti did not know about the courtiers' comings and goings. His reputation depended on his ability to ferret out private information about people that he could use to entertain and surprise as though it came from his divining skills.

Of the court diarists, only Visconti knew of, or dared to comment upon, Athénaïs' unsavoury activities. He discovered that the aphrodisiacs she gave to the king came from the sinister soothsayer and mass murderer, Catherine Montvoisin. Known as 'La Voisin', she lived in a disreputable part of Paris – Bonne-Nouvelle, a retrieved wasteland formerly part of the city walls –

and practised profitably as a witch from the rue Beauregard. She told fortunes, carried out abortions by the hundred, disposed of live illegitimate babies in ways too horrific to imagine, provided potions for everything from breast enlargement to murder; and had at her disposal a retinue of priests such as Guiborg, either defrocked or who should have been, willing to say perverted forms of Mass for material ends. Her lovers included a number of lesser nobles and the headsman of Paris, unaware that he was sleeping with someone he might have been burning at the stake.

'How well I knew the viper and her venom!' said Visconti of Athénaïs, adding that La Voisin 'boasted that it was by her art Madame de Montespan and Louvois kept themselves in favour'. Louvois had as much interest as Athénaïs in keeping the lid on the story if he was also a customer of La Voisin: they both might face imprisonment and disgrace should even half the truth emerge.

To Athénaïs' way of thinking, the Devil did what she asked, for within a year Louise de La Vallière would leave court for good. Still only thirty, she became a Carmelite nun. With Lauzun imprisoned in Pignerol, this time there was no one to write a touching farewell note and prompt a recall for Louise by the king.

For the time being, however, Louise dutifully took her place alongside Maria-Theresa and Athénaïs de Montespan. The war against the Dutch resumed on 1 May 1673 and Louis left Saint-Germain for the Flanders front, accompanied by d'Artagnan and his Musketeers, who at Templemars drank the auberge Rossignol dry, the last inn in France. The column was followed, yet again, by the three queens. Athénaïs, her condition disguised by flowing dresses, was eight months pregnant but Louis appeared callously indifferent to her condition. She and her imminent arrival would have to take their chances on the journey in a swaying coach over bumpy roads, covered in dust clouds raised by the movement of fifty-eight huge siege guns and 45,000 soldiers.

Athénaïs hung on as far as Tournai, where, hidden behind the walls of its citadel, she went into labour and gave birth to a healthy girl. Françoise Scarron, a reluctant member of her household, was in none too sympathetic attendance, cursing this 'boring fortress'. She could scarcely wait to add the child to the two royal bastards she was already looking after, to return to the large house near Vaurigard with its beautiful garden and its 'coach, servants and horses'. In his *Louis XIV*, Anthony Levi concludes that the governess was attracting the 'predatory attention' of the king long before Athénaïs realized it, and that a 'physical liaison' between Louis and Françoise might have begun 'as early as 1674'. However, subsequently Levi acknowledged that the key ingredients, motive and opportunity, were also present in this frenetic spring of 1673, when Athénaïs was heavily pregnant and Louise was irritating the king with her constant agonies concerning their relationship.

Louis had begun to visit his young children, who called Françoise '*maman*', in a delightful domestic scene played out on the edge of Paris. Given the king's insatiable sexual desire, it is hard to envisage him keeping his hands off the attractive governess, unless she firmly rejected his advances. The gossip at court was that Françoise was living in this remote retreat because she was pregnant by the king. A letter she wrote early in 1673 to a friend began with an ironic reference to this rumour: 'What a pleasure to be incarcerated for the reason you give!' And in response to those who could scarcely credit she might have replaced Athénaïs, 'Is it . . . difficult to believe that I have supplanted my friend?' Finally, referring to her master, the king, she said: 'That master sometimes comes to see me, in spite of myself, and leaves in despair, but without having been rejected.' Such circumstantial evidence of a physical relationship, considered in the context of the disreputable aspects of Françoise's past, undermines her later protestations of piety. It was much more likely that when faced with the king's sexual advances, Françoise allowed Louis to go so far, and no further. The proper parallel might be Henry VIII and Anne Boleyn, who for a long time allowed Henry intimacies that stopped just short of penetrative sex, until the king would agree to almost anything to achieve his goal. As the children went for their afternoon nap, leaving Louis and Françoise alone together for an hour or two, the royal escort of Musketeers waiting outside the high garden walls no doubt exchanged knowing glances and reported every speculative titbit to Captain d'Artagnan.

Françoise's favours might be unproven supposition but Athénaïs' child was undeniable fact. The delivery at Tournai on 1 June of the product of her adultery with the king was for Maria-Theresa the final straw. The queen decided she was ill, deliberately delaying the march for several days while baffled physicians fussed about her: she was fully aware this would upset Louis more than anything else.

The French objective was Maastricht, a strategic point on the left bank of the river Meuse, guarding the approach to the United Provinces from the east. A year previously France had been offered the great fortress without firing a shot, but Louvois had tried to impose such humiliating terms on the Dutch that they had rejected them, goaded beyond endurance. Louis set his generals, even the best, the vicomte de Turenne, the task of keeping Spanish and Imperial forces occupied in Germany. He wanted the glory of taking Maastricht for himself. Courtiers could scarcely stifle their yawns as the king spent hour after hour with Vauban discussing the details of its fortifications and how best to defeat them.

The siege of Maastricht gave Vauban, the supreme builder of fortresses, a chance to show that he also possessed the technical mastery to capture one of the most formidable in Europe. The Dutch had surrounded Maastricht with elaborate fortifications in the shape of a pointed star, providing overlapping arcs of artillery fire, which all but eliminated blind spots where an attacker could take shelter.

Against Maastricht's sophisticated defences, Vauban employed his own ingenious new counter-measures for the first time. He began by digging a main trench parallel to the fortress, just out of range of defending artillery, then a series of further trenches, pushed out towards the walls in short zigzags, known as 'saps', angled to prevent them from being raked by musket or cannon fire. The 'saps' all linked into another main trench parallel and closer to the fortifications. The whole sequence could be repeated indefinitely until the engineers came close enough to build a causeway across the moat and dig holes under the walls to accommodate the gunpowder mines that would be exploded beneath them.

Vauban's solution had the advantage of keeping casualties to a minimum because most troops did not need to be exposed to enemy fire until the final assault on what remained of the walls. A humanitarian at heart, Vauban was seriously concerned when on 24 June, after just one week of preparations, with the zigzag trenches still well short of their objective and the defences largely undamaged, Louis deliberately abandoned the agreed strategy. Instead, the king ordered his first company of Musketeers to take part in a night offensive against the defences protecting one of the key gates to the fortress, the Porte de Tongres. The precipitous use of the king's own bodyguard in such a perilous attack was most unusual, especially as Louis knew that d'Artagnan, unlike many of his commanders, would feel obliged to lead the Musketeers personally into battle as a matter of honour. In this period, prudent senior officers rarely led from the front because the odds on being killed were so high.

Maastricht was protected by 6,000 experienced Dutch troops, ironically under a French-born colonel, Jacques de Fariaux, one of the few soldiers who could say they had beaten Turenne in battle. As the Musketeers emerged from their trenches on the stroke of 10 p.m., the defenders poured down withering fire from the fortifications and threw large numbers of grenades, cast-iron balls about the size of a grapefruit, packed with gunpowder and small pieces of metal, with a temperamental fuse attached. The Musketeers had eighty-five men killed and fifty more severely wounded, a casualty rate of more than 40 per cent, but once again d'Artagnan defied the odds to come through unharmed. He was almost the first to gain a precarious foothold in the moat, forcing the defenders to retreat.

Soon after daybreak on 25 June, as the exchange of gunfire subsided, d'Artagnan had a furious row with Jean Louis de Montbrun, who, although d'Artagnan's equal in rank as commander of the second company of Musketeers, had been placed in overall charge of the attack. Unlike d'Artagnan, Montbrun had remained at the rear and arrived at the front at 8 a.m., immaculately dressed and looking askance at d'Artagnan's dishevelled appearance. Montbrun wanted to consolidate the position by constructing a wooden platform, complete with firing positions; but d'Artagnan thought this work would expose his remaining men to needless risk from enemy sharpshooters. After several angry exchanges, Montbrun, as technically the senior officer, insisted and got his way.

D'Artagnan, still smarting from his failure to overturn Montbrun's order, went for breakfast with the Duke of Monmouth, Charles II's illegitimate son, instead of returning to the Musketeers' camp. The duke had only a tiny British force under his command, fewer than fifty men, but he had been made officer of the day to bolster the Anglo-French alliance. D'Artagnan may have hoped to persuade Monmouth to intervene. He was also friendly with Monmouth's subordinate, Captain John Churchill, the future Duke of Marlborough, who did not suffer fools gladly and had already fallen out with Louvois. D'Artagnan was full of admiration for the way Churchill managed to be bankrolled by Charles II's mistress, the formidable Barbara Castlemain, which had caused the disapproving Louvois to say that the English officer was 'far too given over to his pleasure' to be a good soldier. In due course, Churchill would show the whole of Europe just how wrong he was.

After the night action no one present expected to fight again that morning, so the besiegers consumed a good deal of wine and spirits with their meal. However, at about 11 a.m.

their animated conversation was suddenly interrupted by the noise of an explosion: the Dutch had detonated a huge mine on the escarpment, killing about fifty French troops. Led by governor Fariaux himself, sword in hand, they had sallied out of the fortress and it looked as if all the night's gains, won at such great cost, would be lost, until Monmouth, Churchill and d'Artagnan launched 'the bravest and briskest action they had seen in their lives'.

As the Dutch were already back on the escarpment, there was no time for the attackers to go through the zigzags of the communication trenches. The duke, after an embarrassing little hiatus when his sword became stuck in his scabbard, started directly towards the Dutch position, together with several English gentleman, their loyal servants and a dozen Life Guards. Not to be outdone, d'Artagnan followed in support with the handful of Musketeers he could muster, in a mad sprint towards the enemy across open ground, as potentially suicidal a move as it is possible to imagine. Aged fifty, d'Artagnan could not keep up with Monmouth, who was particularly nimble; but this quickly did not matter as both were among the survivors, all huddled together, gasping for breath, sheltered by the barricade leading to the moat.

Churchill, who had already distinguished himself by boldly planting the French flag on the escarpment the previous night, received a flesh wound in the charge. The course of history might have changed forever had the future scourge of the French at Blenheim and Oudenarde not lived to fight another day. Seeing Churchill falter, Monmouth decided to press ahead himself through a small gap in the barricade. Realizing that the fire from a dozen Dutch muskets was concentrated on this particular spot, d'Artagnan tried to persuade him to stay where he was. When Monmouth stubbornly refused, d'Artagnan quickly pushed him through the opening and was struck in the neck by the bullet otherwise destined for the duke. His famous luck had run out at last.

11

THE MYSTERIOUS PRISONER

y the summer of 1673, Paris was rife with rumour about the identity of a mysterious prisoner recently incarcerated in the Bastille. Many believed him to be the playwright Molière, who had supposedly died in the French capital on 17 February, in curious circumstances. Molière was the stage name of Jean-Baptiste Poquelin, who first arrived in Paris from the provinces in 1658, sharing a theatre with Scaramouche. Louis XIV became Molière's patron, but the playwright made powerful enemies, ridiculing the hypocrisy and pretentiousness of both the Roman Catholic Church and the court through his comedies. In 1662 he had also been imprudent enough to marry Armande Grésinde Béjart, the daughter of his mistress, and later he was accused, perhaps correctly, of being the father of his own wife, a crime punishable in France by burning at the stake.

Ironically, on the night Molière allegedly died in Paris of consumption, just a few hours earlier he had played the role of Argan, the hypochondriac, in his own comedy *Le Malade Imaginaire*. There was no direct eyewitness to Molière's death, but an actor in his troop called Michel Baron realized how ill he was and took him home at the end of the performance. Baron, who was having an affair with Molière's wife, put the playwright to bed and went to find Armande; by the time they returned to the house with a doctor, Molière was said already to have expired.

Molière did not receive a proper funeral: no burial service took place and the entry in the church register remained unsigned; his body was taken directly to the cemetery of Saint-Joseph late at night. In 1792 his presumed grave would be exhumed and found to be empty. To add to the sense of mystery, most of Molière's original manuscripts disappeared at the same time. On the burial certificate he was described not as a playwright but as a royal valet and upholsterer to the king, the profession of his father, as though someone in authority was determined to belittle him to the last.

Whoever he might be, the Bastille was the natural choice to accommodate the prisoner who would become known to history as the Man in the Iron Mask. But at the approach of autumn, the impregnable prison was shown to be unassailable no longer. During the night of 15/16 September 1673, two men escaped: Baudouin, former controller of the royal household, and Charles-Amboise, chevalier de la Boissière. According to governor Besmaux, who the following day wrote a fearful letter of explanation to Louvois, they had a great deal of help from outside. Tools were smuggled into the Bastille to enable them to force *'doucement'* a door leading to one part of the roof terrace and to raise a plank to bridge the gap across to another part. From there, they signalled to friends waiting below, who used a catapult to fire a lead weight up to the terrace. A cord was attached to the weight, and a rope to the cord, which the prisoners secured and used to descend to the moat, a desperately dangerous feat that Besmaux described as 'almost impossible'. As Baudouin had just completed his fifth year in the Bastille, Besmaux feared the wrath of the king, but Louvois interceded on his behalf, noting tersely on the letter that Besmaux 'must learn from this incident to stop it happening again'. According to a gossip sheet, *Des Nouvelles à la main*, printed in Holland a month or two later, for a while the special prisoner was guarded day and night by four soldiers and Besmaux was so fearful that he, too, might escape that he slept in the same room.

It was not long, however, before the minister decided that the risk of keeping his most secret prisoner at the Bastille was too great. Steps were taken to remove the Mask to the donjon whose primary purpose was to hold prisoners of the highest importance to the state. So on 10 March 1674, Louvois sent Saint-Mars an order from Paris that he may have been half expecting for some time:

> For the good of his service, the King has seen fit to send to Pignerol a prisoner, who, although 'obscur', is however a man of consequence. His Majesty has sent him from here in the hands of the sieur Legrain, who will conduct him to the mail staging-post at Bron, where he will arrive on thirtieth of this month. You will take care to have a reception party waiting of ten reliable men from your company, commanded by one of your officers, to whom the sieur Legrain will pass on all the necessary instructions to ensure that the prisoner is well guarded. You will advise your officer to use as inconspicuous a route as possible, and to enter Pignerol quietly and [in] such a way that no one will realise he is escorting a prisoner to the donjon. You will treat him in the same way as the prisoner Monsieur Vauroy once brought you.

So at Pignerol the Mask was to be as anonymous as Eustache Danger, and no one would know he was there. According to the records unearthed by Théodore Iung, on 23 March Louvois ordered Legrain, the high constable of France, to bring the Mask to the remote staging-post of Brun on the road from Lyon to Chambéry, where his transfer could take place without attracting any attention. He was to be 'manacled at night' and 'kept from view' in such a way that he could neither 'shout out or write . . . who he was'. The chevalier de Saint-Martin, Saint-Mars' longest-serving and highest-ranking lieutenant, was to escort the Mask the rest of the way to Pignerol 'without delay . . . using only those roads than run through the territory of the King'.

Iung traced the arrival at each prison of every prisoner supervised by Saint-Mars. The new inmate was the only one without any reliable clue to his true identity; the only one whose very existence, even within the donjon itself, was a state secret.

Louvois, in his instructions to Saint-Mars to describe his new charge, used the word *obscur*, which had many different meanings but in particular signified someone 'unknown, hidden' or 'without renown or glory'. This bearer of 'considerable secrets' was to be 'treated very harshly; no fire shall be given him in his room unless it is bitterly cold or if an illness compels you to do so . . . you will give him no other food than bread, wine and water'.

Despite the severe conditions of his strict confinement, according to the historian Quirino Triverio, who made a special study of this period at Pignerol, within a matter of months the mysterious prisoner almost succeeded in eluding his jailers. Held in a first-floor cell in the Saint Donato Tower, the Mask discovered that due to a much earlier building fraud, his floor had no main beams and consisted almost entirely of flimsy ceiling joists. He broke through them easily and descended to the ground level on a rope made mostly from his own hair; he then lifted a flagstone and crawled through a sewer that issued beyond the fortress walls, before his absence was frantically noticed and he was seized by Saint-Mars' men as he emerged. Louvois' reaction, had the Mask got clean away, can easily be imagined but Saint-Mars evidently succeeded in keeping all knowledge of the incident within the confines of Pignerol itself. None of the garrison relished the thought of another visit from the war minister.

In similar circumstances at the Basille, governor Besmaux would have chained the Mask to a wall, but Saint-Mars simply moved him to a much more secure part of the prison halfway along the south-eastern wall of the keep. It was known as the Lower Tower, perhaps because its height was less than the other towers, but more probably because it had a grim basement with its share of sewers and rats. Above ground level a spiral staircase connected its three floors, each consisting of a single circular room. This tower overlooked only a blank wall of the citadel and its small windows just below ceiling level were little more than air vents, depriving its occupants of almost any natural light.

Saint-Mars probably locked the Mask in the top floor cell,

with its three separate doors barring any approach, moving Martin to the basement. This had the added advantage of putting the Mask on the same level as Saint-Mars' own apartment under the roof, consisting of a scullery, privy and two modest rooms that he occupied with his wife and son André, who would celebrate his second birthday in July. Fouquet and Lauzun enjoyed more substantial accommodation on the two floors immediately below the jailer, each of which opened out into the Angle Tower, with its views over the mountains and the main fortress town of Pignerol.

Lauzun took rather longer than the Mask to get beyond the donjon's walls, almost as if the manner of his escape mattered more to him than the escape itself. Pignerol had much in common with the Second World War prison, Colditz Castle, both supposedly escape-proof but in reality full of bricked up chambers and conduits long forgotten. Lauzun started digging upwards and downwards, and to disguise what he was doing he began to behave like a madman, declining to wash or shave, wearing a handkerchief twisted round his neck instead of a cravat, ensuring that his rooms were in total chaos, leaving them freezing all that winter and lighting a large fire during a heat wave the following summer.

Eventually, Lauzun breached the chimney stack that led up and past Fouquet's apartment above; one night, with Saint-Mars fast asleep in his own quarters, he emerged covered in soot in the fireplace of the astonished former superintendant. When Fouquet was at the height of his glory, Lauzun had been a minor noble at court. But what a tale Lauzun had to tell a man desperate for news: of how he had become the master of a magnificent house in Paris, almost grand master of artillery, almost (or actually) the husband of a princess of the blood, almost the owner of more duchies than the rest of the court put together. Oh, and he had also insulted the king and the king's favourite mistress for good measure. However, Fouquet, after eight years at the fortress, may have had something of interest to offer Lauzun in return: his knowledge of the existence of a mysterious third prisoner, Étienne Martin alias Eustache Danger, who, according to Pignerol's grapevine, was there one moment and missing the next. Lauzun eagerly devoured every scrap of information, however slight, that might help his ceaseless crusade to extract himself from this remote Alpine jail.

In February 1676, after three years of unrelenting effort, working almost entirely at night, Lauzun broke through into the empty rooms and cavities beneath his quarters; and from there, loosening the bars on a window, let himself down to the moat by a rope made of table napkins, 'so clever a contrivance that Saint-Mars sent a piece of it to be inspected by Louis XIV'. The Grande Mademoiselle, learning of the detail afterwards, said 'it was a miracle he did not break his neck'. The solid rock of the outer wall defeated even Lauzun, but instead he dug his way into the inner courtyard, where, as he broke through at dawn, he came face to face with a kitchen maid collecting wood for the stove. Lauzun, who had sequins of jewellery sewn in his clothes, offered her a king's ransom to help him escape but fear overcame greed: she called the guard and the game was up.

Lauzun embarked on several rather more hopeless schemes to break out of the fortress; once he set fire to the walnut beams of the room below with the help of his valet, who suffered severe burns to his legs. In the bizarre, contradictory world of Pignerol, both Fouquet and Lauzun, despite various attempts to escape, by right of rank were entitled to be looked after by servants. Their valets were confined to the precincts of the fortress and forbidden to communicate with the outside world. The longer Fouquet and Lauzun were locked up, the more difficult their servants became. Saint-Mars reported gloomily to Louvois that the valets gave him 'more trouble than all the rest put together, because they would not [were not willing to] spend their whole life in prison'. He found it particularly difficult to obtain servants for Lauzun. The duke's peremptory treatment of underlings was unhelpful enough, but the prospect of joining their new master in indefinite confinement made up their minds. Saint-Mars told Louvois, 'All my valets would not enter there for a million. They saw that those I put in Monsieur Fouquet's [rooms] never got out.'

Sure enough, on 8 September 1674, one of Fouquet's two valets died, whereupon Saint-Mars tried Louvois again on the subject of Martin as a valet, this time for Fouquet. Louvois probably would have refused, not wishing to put together two men who had conspired to murder one or more ministers of state. However, the king had an obsessive interest in Fouquet's security and circumstances, which led him to notice Saint-Mars' dispatch and think it a sensible proposal. Louis did not know Martin's real identity or his previous link with Fouquet and it was certainly not in Louvois' interest to enlighten him. For Martin, it was an ominous development: a sign that his incarceration at Pignerol had become permanent.

Unable to explain why Martin should be kept in seclusion, Louvois was forced to allow him to become an occasional valet for Fouquet. In January 1675 he began his response to Saint-Mars, '*Sa Majesté approuve*', not his usual style at all, implying that he, Louvois, was far from happy with the decision. Louvois also added a private postscript in his own handwriting before sealing the letter. In it he made sure that Saint-Mars understood that he could give Martin to Fouquet 'if his valet [the surviving valet, called La Rivière] is not available to him, but not otherwise'. Louvois no doubt reassured himself that whatever Fouquet learned from Martin, he would never be allowed out of prison to make use of it. However, Martin had to be kept away from Lauzun. When Saint-Mars asked again if Martin could also serve Lauzun, he was told firmly by Louvois that 'whatever the reason may be, you must not give him the prisoner that Monsieur de Vauroy brought you [Martin]; in case of necessity, he must serve only Monsieur Fouquet, as I instructed you.'

As Louvois must have feared, once Martin was in Fouquet's service, he started to be of significance to the king himself. Despite Louvois' reticence, Louis came to suspect that Martin had some previous connection with Fouquet and that Louvois had imprisoned him in Pignerol because he possessed a good deal of sensitive information. Louvois may have been forced to disclose the least damaging explanation for Martin's incarceration: his knowledge of the Secret Treaty of Dover. As a result, the king became concerned about what Fouquet's other valet had been told by Martin and took the extraordinary step of asking his own state prisoner directly. In November 1678, the king had Louvois send a letter to Fouquet for Saint-Mars to give him unopened, together with 'pen, ink, a seal and Spanish wax', so that Fouquet could also seal his reply. The incentive held out to Fouquet was 'considerable alleviations' in his prison regime. The letter to Fouquet that Saint-Mars was not allowed to see has survived:

> His Majesty wishes to be informed . . . whether the man called Eustache, who has been given to you to serve you, has not spoken in front of the other valet [La Rivière], of how he has been employed before being in Pignerol. His Majesty has commanded me to tell you that he expects you to inform me truthfully about this matter, without qualification, whatever his revelations [to La Rivière], so that he can take the appropriate measures regarding what he hears from you as to what Eustache might have said of his past life to his colleague. His Majesty's intention is that you answer this letter, in particular, without giving M. de Saint-Mars any opportunity to witness its contents.

Fouquet's response is missing but it must have satisfied the king because on 18 January 1679 his stringent regime was relaxed: Fouquet was allowed to meet Lauzun whenever he wished and both prisoners were permitted to exercise under supervision within the precincts of the citadel. Two days later, however, Saint-Mars received a separate dispatch from Louvois imposing severe restrictions on Martin's movements. Whenever Fouquet or Lauzun visited the other's rooms,

> M. de Saint-Mars will take care to withdraw the man called Eustache and to put him back into Monsieur Fouquet's room only when M. Fouquet and his old valet [La Rivière] are inside.

Likewise, when M. Fouquet takes a walk in the citadel, the said
Eustache should be made to stay in M. Fouquet's room and be
allowed to accompany him only when M. Fouquet goes with his
old valet to the place where for some time His Majesty has seen
fit to allow M. de Fouquet to take the air.

This opening and closing of cell doors and shuffling around of
Martin alias Eustache may have had the theatrical characteristics
of a bedroom farce, but a serious purpose lay behind it. By these
precautions Louvois intended to prevent Lauzun from seeing
Martin, let alone talking to him, and to avoid Martin and La
Rivière being left together unmonitored. Martin could 'take the
air' with Fouquet and La Rivière only in that part of the citadel
where they would not have contact with anyone else. Two days
later Louvois sent a separate note to Fouquet:

> You will learn from M. de Saint-Mars the precautions which
> the King wishes to be taken to prevent Eustache Danger from
> communicating with anyone except yourself. His Majesty
> expects you to give your closest attention to the matter because
> you know how important it is that no one [else] has knowledge
> of what he knows.

While the Mask languished in what had formerly been
Martin's impenetrable cell protected by three separate doors
at the top of Pignerol's Lower Tower, Lauzun made the most
of the easing of his imprisonment. He was allowed to exercise
four horses within the confines of the citadel, which he did
almost every day at breakneck speed, endangering the lives of
Saint-Mars' company as well as his own. Fouquet was regarded
as too elderly to attempt some athletic escape but whenever
Lauzun went for walks along the ramparts, Saint-Mars and
two of his lieutenants had to accompany him, together with
six of their men, muskets primed and loaded. Local dignitaries
eagerly accepted Lauzun's generous invitations to dinners in the
donjon held, of course, at Saint Mars' expense, with the glum
jailer forced to attend and listen to endlessly repetitive tales of
Lauzun's halcyon days at court.

The more relaxed conditions at Pignerol led Fouquet to believe that even he might eventually be released. In May 1679, after almost eighteen years in captivity, he was allowed a visit from his wife, his youngest son and his youngest daughter, Marie-Madeleine. Aged twenty-three, she was rather plump and plain but Lauzun, deprived of female company for the best part of a decade, put all his talents into seducing her. Madame Fouquet was obliged to go away on business so the coast was soon clear; and Saint-Mars obligingly had a new staircase constructed so that Madeleine could sleep at the donjon in a small room above her father, not realizing that Lauzun could access it via the gap he had made in the common chimney breast. These passionate, if somewhat sooty, sexual encounters continued undetected for some time, with Madeleine an eager partner. They began to take greater risks by also meeting during the day until inevitably Fouquet caught the couple *in flagrante delicto* and sent his wayward daughter back to Paris in disgrace.

Fouquet was not alone in finding that Lauzun was taking advantage of his newfound freedom. Saint-Mars had thought guarding Lauzun difficult enough while he was locked up in the Angle Tower. The 'arduousness of the task was multiplied a hundredfold' once Lauzun could roam about the prison. Lauzun pretended he knew the contents of the jailer's letters to Louvois, which logic told Saint-Mars was impossible but nonetheless he still suspected might be true. The jailer was tormented by so great a fear of Lauzun's 'almost superhuman powers of circumventing him' that he was ready to believe him capable of anything.

By August Lauzun had convinced Saint-Mars that he was in possession of Pignerol's great secret, the imprisonment of the Mask, leaving the jailer in agonies of indecision about what to do next. As he could not mention the unmentionable, he wrote to Louvois saying only that he had vital information to give him. Louvois responded on 18 August: 'Since you have something to let me know, that you cannot confide in a letter, you may send M. de Blainvilliers to report to me.' So Saint-

Mars sent his cousin Zachée de Blainvilliers, one of his officers, to Paris in September and what he had to say must have placed Louvois in a particular quandary, for more than three months elapsed before, in January 1680, Blainvilliers was allowed to return to Pignerol with his response. Finally Louvois decided to try to establish exactly what Lauzun knew and he was allowed to write to the minister. Lauzun wrote:

> My impatience to leave prison is no greater than my impatience to have you informed of what I have to tell you, but it must be by word of mouth and you alone should be informed . . . I ask only that I might inform you by someone in whom I have entire confidence . . . for this particular matter I need Barrail . . . He alone can do it properly . . . it is of importance to you above anything you could imagine.

The mysterious, almost threatening, message went as close as it dared to confirming Saint-Mars' worst nightmare, that despite all his precautions, Lauzun knew the identity of the Mask and realized this could be a formidable bargaining chip. Louvois had little choice. On 7 February Barrail, Lauzun's faithful friend, was given leave to visit Lauzun at Pignerol, provided that Saint-Mars remained present throughout.

At his first meeting with Barrail, Lauzun nonetheless succeeded in keeping the full extent of his knowledge from his jailer. Ingenious as ever, Lauzun hid a letter for Barrail, containing the key to a spoken code, in an ostensibly innocuous piece of linen that he had hung in front of the fireplace. 'You can see that imprisonment has affected his mind,' said Saint-Mars optimistically to Barrail, when at their next meeting Lauzun made a series of incomprehensible speeches to his visitor. In fact Lauzun was using the code to tell Barrail far more in conversation than Saint-Mars realized, including the name of his secret prisoner. Having failed to escape by conventional means, Lauzun now had to use his stealth and cunning to persuade Louvois that he would be less of a threat to the minister outside Pignerol's walls than within.

12

'POWDERS FOR DEATH, POWDERS FOR LOVE'

Louvois was noted for his skill in mastering complex military logistics but as the war minister surveyed the scene at the remote fortress of Pignerol from his frenetic office at Saint-Germain, even he must have occasionally wondered whether he was losing his touch.

Lauzun's new leverage was but one of Louvois' many difficulties. He had the Mask hidden away, unbeknown to anyone. In a nearby cell was the expert in 'indetectable' Italian poisons, Martin alias Danger, allowed to leave his cell from time to time to serve Fouquet and whose existence accordingly was known to the king but not his real identity. Then there was Fouquet himself, like the war minister, once the valet's employer; as Martin polished the silver in Fouquet's rooms, what damaging detail might he have let slip to the former superintendant about his work for Louvois?

An even more pressing problem for Louvois was the malignant character of Athénaïs, which again began to manifest itself when she in her turn became a royal mistress under pressure.

Like Louise de La Vallière previously, Athénaïs found that repeated pregnancies ravaged her appearance. Visconti, catching a good glimpse of her upper thighs as she alighted clumsily from her carriage, ungallantly said each was as broad as his waist. Athénaïs, nearly thirty-nine, complained to him that the young maids of honour fluttering about the palaces were a sexual hydra: no sooner had Athénaïs disposed of one, than another would be making eyes at the king.

The latest was eighteen-year-old Marie Angélique de Scoraille de Roussille, otherwise known as Mademoiselle de Fontanges. Her provincial parents had borrowed heavily to finance her debut at court, reported by the Palatine ambassador as that of 'an extraordinary blonde beauty, the like of which has not been seen at Versailles in many a year'. Athénaïs wrongly assessed her as too empty-headed to be a serious threat and during a hunt in November 1678 rashly presented Angélique, an expert horsewoman, to the king. She undid Angélique's costume and deliberately spilled out her breasts, saying 'See, Sire, what a beauty we have here!' Louis did see: Angélique was in his bed before the month was out.

According to evidence that would be in the hands of police chief La Reynie before long, the outraged Athénaïs did not hesitate to renew her connections with the gang of poisoners still at large in Paris, in particular Françoise Filastre and Magdelaine Chapelain, both up to their neck in black magic practices. In December, with their help Athénaïs planned to eliminate her new rival by means of a deadly gift, a pair of poisoned gloves, made of the finest leather from Grenoble. Angélique did not die but was ill for some time and began to suspect the worst. Said Madame de Sévigné, 'Mademoiselles de Fontanges . . . believes she has been poisoned, and she is now requesting bodyguards.'

When La Reynie, investigating this and other alleged poison plots, began to arrest and interrogate the usual suspects, they named some of the most illustrious members of society as their accomplices. La Reynie showed the list of those implicated to Louvois, who on 8 March 1679 persuaded Louis that a trial of the accused in open court would result in an enormous scandal. Instead, they established the Commission of the Arsenal, popularly known as the Chambre Ardente, reminiscent of the English court of the Star Chamber and a revival of a similar old French tribunal where the high and mighty had been brought before Richelieu in a dark, intimidating atmosphere, heightened by black drapes and burning torches.

La Voisin, the high priestess of poisoners, had been under suspicion for some time. Her arrest by La Reynie on 12 March, ironically as she was coming out of Sunday Mass, led to the incrimination of more members of the court by her and her accomplices. In September, Louis ordered La Reynie 'to make transcripts of these responses on separate folios, and keep these folios apart from the official records of the investigation', the first sign that he was becoming seriously alarmed by the potential political fallout.

On 23 January 1680 the Chambre Ardente issued arrest warrants for a duke, a marquis, a vicomtesse and, most sensationally of all, for Olympe, comtesse de Soissons, the superintendant of the queen's household, amidst strong rumours that further would follow. The court was amazed and astonished, fearfully watching the whirlpool of accusation and innuendo that threatened to engulf even the most exalted among them at any moment.

The king, having set up the Chambre Ardente, promptly undermined it. Aware of the acute embarrassment that Olympe's arrest would cause him, within hours Louis sent Olympe's brother-in-law, the duc de Bouillon, elderly husband of her youngest sister, Marianne, to the Hôtel de Soissons where Olympe and some friends were playing basset, an old Venetian card game. The message he brought was stark: Olympe had the choice of imprisonment in the Bastille, pending a trial on charges that La Voisin had mixed lethal poisons for her, or of permanent exile. As the king surely had counted on, Olympe was not sanguine about her prospects if she remained in Paris. 'Louvois is my mortal enemy because I refused my daughter's hand to his son,' she told the duke. 'He has been powerful enough to have me accused. He has false witnesses at his command.'

At three in the morning, the countess' coach with its eight horses was heard rattling over the cobblestones on the place de Carrousel, bound for Spanish Flanders, never to return. Olympe soon discovered, however, that Louvois had a long reach. In Brussels, one of his agents 'loosed a sack of black cats in a church where she was attending Mass . . . The people . . . took the cats for demons and the Comtesse de Soissons for a witch . . . and . . . forced her to . . . search for another refuge.'

Marianne was made of sterner stuff. The last of the Mancini sisters, with her cute little retroussé nose, had the street intellect and spirit to brazen it out in front of the Chambre Ardente. Accused of asking La Voisin 'for a small dose of the poison to kill an old tiresome husband . . . to marry a young man she was fond of', that is to say, her lover the duc de Vendôme, Marianne turned up at her trial on 29 January 1680 with both lover and husband, sitting on her left and right. Marianne's defence was that she had no need to murder her husband because 'The duc de Bouillon did not object to sharing his wife's favours with others . . . so long as she had enough to go round, for him as well as for them.' Asked by La Reynie whether the witches had raised the Devil on her behalf, she replied, 'I did see him, and he looked just like you!' Louis once again intervened, stopping the trial by *lettre de cachet* and sending Marianne for her sheer effrontery to the obscure settlement of Nérac in the foothills of the Pyrenees. Despite their good looks and their great wealth, all four of the surviving Mancini sisters suffered some form of exile.

Early in February 1680, La Voisin's house was searched with results that were a mixture of the hideous and the hilarious. A note accidentally left there, in the hand of the duchesse de la Foix, said, 'The more I rub, the more they grow.' This so intrigued the king that he pulled rank on La Reynie and questioned the duchess himself. She finally admitted that she had asked La Voisin for a cream to enlarge her breasts. There was nothing at all amusing, however, about the sacrificial residue of 2,500 'infants and embryos', by La Voisin's own admission, found in her garden at La Villeneuve-sur-Gravois, just beyond the Porte Saint-Denis.

La Voisin was resigned to her fate but had still not mentioned Athénaïs de Montespan. She did not identify Athénaïs under interrogation nor at her trial in Paris, possibly in return for a tacit understanding that she would not be tortured. On 22 February, though, La Voisin suffered agony enough, burned alive at the stake in the place de Grève, violently rejecting a last confessor and his crucifix.

The rest of the witches' coven showed no such inhibitions about naming names. They included Filastre, the old Abbé Guiborg who had probably performed Satanic rites upon Athénaïs' naked body, and La Voisin's own daughter, Marguerite Montvoisin. There was no collusion between them: they were kept in solitary confinement and interrogated, using the Question – the method of torture previously threatened to be used on La Porte. Soon the various accused gave corroborating testimony that implicated Athénaïs' former maid, Claude de Vin des Oeillets, said to have made more than fifty visits to the poisoners; and finally they named her former mistress, Athénaïs herself.

The most damning confession came from Madame Filastre, sentenced to the Question before burning at the stake. Under torture she screamed out:

> It was Madame Chapelain who commissioned me, and it was Madame de Montespan who commissioned Madame Chapelain . . . and the purpose was to procure poisons to kill off Madame de Fontanges, and love powders to restore Madame de Montespan to the king's good graces . . . powders for death, powders for love . . . all for Madame de Montespan!

Even Chapelain's arrest failed to disconcert Athénaïs, who clearly believed herself untouchable. For this Louis was partly to blame, as he had appointed her superintendant of the queen's household in succession to Olympe de Soissons. Athénaïs also had a secret ally, Louvois himself. He was pulling the strings behind the scenes, aware that if Athénaïs were interrogated, his own dealings with the poisoners would almost certainly come to light. The minister interviewed many of the underworld suspects himself and influenced their testimony. Louvois discouraged La Reynie from following certain lines of inquiry that might have brought suspicion on himself and interposed his department between the police chief and Louis, insisting upon seeing every transcript of every interview, and selectively summarizing them for the king.

What drove Louvois to take such extraordinary risks during the poisons scandal was his vaulting ambition to make Louis entirely dependent upon him, which meant engineering the downfall of Colbert. The common denominator of almost all the members of the nobility implicated in the 'Affair of the Poisons', including Athénaïs, was that they were either Colbert's friends or related to him by marriage. Even Fouquet could be used as a potential weapon against Colbert. Louvois was prepared to see Fouquet freed from prison and thereby to take the credit for persuading the king to end his captivity, because Colbert had always been first in Fouquet's sights and the former finance minister's release from Pignerol would increase those influential voices that could be raised against Louvois's rival.

With Louvois' tacit support, Fouquet's family were now encouraged to renew their efforts on his behalf and they soon found a new ally at court. The dauphin, Louis' only surviving legitimate son, had serious financial problems, which were delaying his marriage to Marie-Anne Christine Victoire, Princess of Bavaria. Marie-Anne lacked a substantial dowry and beyond question was the ugliest princess in Europe, with a huge nose and the rough hands of a ploughman; so she proved enormously grateful when an old friend of Fouquet extended the couple a long and indefinite line of credit, enabling the wedding to take place. One of Fouquet's six daughters, Marie, believing that Louis would be reluctant to refuse Marie-Anne's first request, easily persuaded her to intercede with the king and ask him to grant Fouquet an audience where he might plead for his own pardon. Early in February 1680 the court travelled to meet the new dauphine at Vitry and, according to Robert Challes,

Colbert's secretary, Louis was much taken by the princess, or at any rate by her newfound affluence; he heard in private what she had to say and agreed to see Fouquet.

As an initial step, Fouquet was informed that he could take the waters at Bourbon, still under house arrest, but a step closer to court. Within a month he was escorted to Lyon, where the governor had even better news for him: Louis XIV would allow him an audience. As Louvois no doubt gleefully anticipated, these developments caused consternation in Colbert's circle. Picon, Colbert's closest aide, discovered that members of Fouquet's family had also met the dauphin, with a much more ambitious objective than merely the former minister's release: they were plotting to remove Colbert and reinstate Fouquet in his old ministry. Picon was a formidable civil servant, widely believed to have written most of Colbert's erudite *Testament Politique,* and very little escaped him. However, at first Colbert found it hard to persuade his monarch that a palace revolution was in the offing on the basis of Picon's testimony. Louis XIV could never take Picon seriously because he had one glaring weakness: '*Il aime à boire,*' 'He likes to drink,' observed Challes, something of an understatement in respect of a man once sent by Colbert to the king to explain a complex matter of finance and who had turned up, in Louis' words, 'Drunk as a pig'.

Colbert then played a much cleverer card. In 1674 the king had given Françoise Scarron the money to buy the estate and title of Maintenon, not far from Versailles, but Madame de Maintenon, as she thereafter became known, remained of modest status, still governess to his illegitimate children. It was only in 1680, with the arrival of the new dauphine, that Louis dramatically elevated Madame de Maintenon to be her second *dame d'atour,* or lady of the bedchamber, bringing Françoise formally into the highest royal circle. This revived rumours that Françoise was simply the king's latest sexual conquest. As one court witticism put it, gleefully repeated by Madame de Sévigné, Françoise was Madame de *Maintenant* – '*maintenant*' meaning '[for] now'. When speculation was at its height,

Colbert disclosed to Louis he had received copies of certain letters that he suggested might be in much wider circulation, whose contents could seriously damage Françoise's reputation and therefore that of the king. The letters were unsigned but said to be in Françoise's handwriting and dating back to about 1660, when she was a young widow heavily in debt. In one letter she wrote to Fouquet:

> I have always of course fled from vice and sin, but I assure you that I hate poverty more. I have received your 10,000 écus, and if you wish to bring me 10,000 more in the next two days, I will see what I must do.

From the text of the next letter in the same hand, Fouquet's charms, as well as his cash, seemed to be working:

> The last meeting I had with you left me spellbound. I discovered in your conversation a thousand enchantments which I had not expected, indeed, if I ever see you alone, I do not know what will happen.

The unmistakable inference that at the time Françoise had been ready to sleep with Fouquet, an invitation he probably accepted with alacrity, would have rekindled Louis's hatred of him. Back in 1660 Fouquet had already attempted to seduce the king's mistress of the hour, Louise de La Vallière, and here he was again, caught slipping into the bed of another.

Louis had shown himself more than capable of dissembling in the past. He might have been expected to go through the motions of seeing Fouquet but afterwards keeping him under open arrest, away from court. The circumstances, however, were anything but normal. As February gave way to March with one dramatic event after another – La Voisin's execution, the sittings of the Chambre Ardente – Louis must have felt he was completely losing control, especially when La Reynie arrived to give the king his detailed report on 'that person to whom the use of poisons is not unknown, that person whom you consider it dangerous to allow to remain at court', which can only have been Athénaïs herself. The potential disgrace of one royal mistress was embarrassing enough, but three at once – Olympe, Athénaïs and, prompted by the discovery of her letters to Fouquet, Françoise de Maintenon – threatened to make the king a laughing stock.

So Louis simply changed his mind. He would not see Fouquet, whom, according to Challes, had arrived at Chalon. Fouquet would be returned to Pignerol. Louvois suggested that such an overt sign of bad faith would go down badly at court and abroad, but Louis was adamant, and Louvois quickly had to come up with a more diabolical solution to help his master. It would be announced that Fouquet had suddenly died; he was to follow the Mask into oblivion and the living death of imprisonment in secret.

Fouquet's purported demise must have been made public in Paris by 24 March because a day later the comte de Bussy was writing to a friend, as though she was already likely to be aware of it: 'You know, I expect, that Monsieur Fouquet has died from apoplexy, just when he had been given permission to visit the waters at Bourbon.' This made the contents of Louvois' letter to Saint-Mars on 8 April dubious in the extreme. 'From the letter you wrote to me on the twenty-third of last month, the King has learned of the death of M. Fouquet.' That alleged letter has never been traced and in all probability never existed. If Fouquet had died at Pignerol on the 22 or 23 March, as Louvois' response implied, Saint-Mars' report could not possibly have reached Paris in time to account for Bussy's comments.

Fouquet's family did not seek an inquest, but on 29 March his eldest surviving son, the comte de Vaux, asked to be allowed to remove his father's body from Pignerol, where they believed it to be. 'I have spoken to the King,' replied Louvois, 'Rest assured there will be no difficulty about that; His Majesty has given the necessary instructions.' However, it was not until 9 April that Louvois told Saint-Mars, 'His Majesty consents to your delivery of the body of the late Monsieur Fouquet to his widow, to be transported to wherever it may please her.' Louvois knew that by the time that permission had been conveyed to Fouquet's family, anyone wishing to examine Fouquet's supposed corpse would have found it unidentifiable.

Madame de Sévigné wrote: 'If I were advising Monsieur Fouquet's family, I would see that they did not send his poor body on a journey, as I hear they propose to do.' Whether or not they heard of her advice, the Fouquets seem to have changed their minds, for they made no attempt to acquire the remains until March 1681, when, following the death of his mother, Fouquet's body reportedly was taken to be buried alongside her in their private vault in the church of the convent of the Dames de la Visitation Saint-Marie, on grand rue Sainte-Antoine, in Paris. An entry in the *registres mortuaries* stated that Nicolas Fouquet was laid to rest in its chapel of Saint-François de Sales on 23 March 1681. The Fouquet vault would be closed in 1786 and the convent forcibly shut in 1790. In 1836, however, the cathedral of Bourges was anxious to reclaim the bones of its former archbishop, who had been buried at the convent. To help the search, a record was made of every coffin and inscription. The archbishop's skeleton turned up in the Fouquet vault but there was no sign of any coffin for Nicolas Fouquet. Its absence must have already been known to the family because in 1812 they paid a local resident of Pignerol to look for the body at Pignerol itself. He concentrated on the former monastery of Sainte-Claire, which had been turned into a workhouse for the poor. The coffins of former Pignerol prisoners used to be kept in its church whilst awaiting burial, which invariably took place in its adjoining common grave; but no trace could be found of Fouquet's remains.

This of course was not surprising because Fouquet had joined the Mask in the Lower Tower, imprisoned in secret and in far worse conditions than previously, deprived of his apartment and his valets. However, for one of them, Martin alias Danger, told that Fouquet had suddenly died, the fake report of his master's death would have come as a huge psychological blow, for the first time giving Martin the status of a real prisoner and one kept in complete isolation.

Still worse from Martin's perspective, in gathering together Fouquet's effects, Saint-Mars had discovered Lauzun's secret access to Fouquet's bedroom by means of the chimney. Although he had used the entrance mainly at night while Martin was locked in his own cell, Saint-Mars concluded that Lauzun could have seen, even spoken to Martin, and reluctantly reported this to Louvois. Lauzun had to be put off the scent. On 8 April Saint-Mars was instructed 'to persuade M. de Lauzun that both Eustache Danger and La Rivière have been freed, and that you say the same thing to all those who ask about them'. In reality, Martin and Fouquet's unfortunate valet were to be imprisoned in the remotest cells, probably in the basement of the Lower Tower, where Saint-Mars could 'assure his Majesty that they will communicate with no one whatsoever, either orally or in writing, and that M. de Lauzun will not see that they are locked up'. If Lauzun could be convinced that Martin had been released, he would be much more likely to believe him an ordinary valet, not a person of some importance he perhaps recognized from Paris, someone who possessed information of great value.

Cut off from all human contact, dependent on scraps from Saint-Mars' own table – he was no longer even an official mouth to feed – Martin probably saw his position as hopeless. In June 1680 he committed suicide with a poison draught of his own making. Although Saint-Mars' report to Louvois is missing, on 10 July Louvois added this postscript to a letter to Saint-Mars, his way of ensuring that neither his secretary, nor anyone reading the copy of the letter placed in the ministerial file, would see it:

> Let me know how it is possible how the one called Eustace did what you sent me, and [from] where he has taken the necessary drugs to make it, since I cannot believe you supplied them to him.

Saint-Mars had not exactly supplied Martin with poisons but the jailer's carelessness did help him to get hold of them. After the plot to free Lauzun by his former valet, Heurtaut, had been foiled seven years earlier, Heurtaut's accomplice left behind at a local inn a bag containing a variety of poisons, intended for use against Saint-Mars' prison officers. Saint-Mars reported this discovery to Louvois but kept the bag at the donjon, where it was soon forgotten. When Martin was allowed more freedom at Pignerol, he could have found and hidden some of the poisons for his own use, eventually calling on the skills he had learned from Glaser many years previously. And if Fouquet's family eventually did ask to see the former minister's decomposing body, the corpse of the late Étienne Martin would have served one last purpose. It could easily have been mistaken for that of Fouquet, as he was of a similar age and might well have been dressed in hand-me-down clothes from his temporary master.

Some French historians have interpreted Louvois' oblique words as meaning that Martin had poisoned Fouquet. This seems improbable, as the earlier amelioration of his conditions of imprisonment had depended entirely on the former superintendant. Martin had reason, too, to be grateful to Fouquet, who had enabled him to continue his visits by discounting suspicions that he might have revealed important information to Fouquet's other valet, La Rivière.

After 10 July 1680, the name of 'Eustace Danger' never appeared again in the dispatches between jailer and minister. His alter ego, Étienne Martin, had been many things: fixer, double agent, poisoner, but not the Iron Mask, the prisoner of legend. His knowledge, rather than his identity, was the dangerous secret. Martin could implicate Fouquet in attempts to kill the king, Louvois in the bungled poisoning of Colbert, and Charles II in the kind of treason that had cost his father his head. So long as Martin's whereabouts remained known only to Louvois, the minister could safely keep him in seclusion in case Martin, or what he knew, could be put to further use. Once the king discovered his presence at Pignerol, however, Martin's days were already numbered, even if he had not chosen to take his own life. The letters from Saint-Mars to Louvois reporting the events surrounding Martin's death and explaining how Martin had acquired the means to kill himself were almost certainly destroyed. Perhaps Louvois himself held them over a candle flame, until they blackened and burnt, with a quiet smile as one of the threats he saw to his growing prestige and power also crumpled to dust.

On Louvois' instructions, Saint-Mars now moved Lauzun into Fouquet's former rooms, reinforcing the impression that Fouquet had died. Lauzun took this deception at face value, seeing it as a further indication that he might soon be set free. Barrail was still at Pignerol and Louvois sent explicit orders to Saint-Mars that he was to be allowed as many tête-à-têtes as he wanted with Lauzun, provided that the jailer remained present. However, armed with their secret code, Lauzun and Barrail had no need to say anything about the Mask that was comprehensible to Saint-Mars. When Barrail returned to Paris, Louvois remained in the dark about how much either Lauzun or his loyal emissary really knew.

This cat-and-mouse game continued for many months, Barrail reasoning that the greater the cunning and subterfuge he displayed on Lauzun's behalf, insinuating this and hinting at that, the more likely it was that Louvois would conclude that Lauzun could be relied upon to keep silent and that releasing him was less of a risk than leaving him in Pignerol with nothing to lose. So in the end, Louvois gave in and on 22 April 1681 Barrail arrived back at Pignerol with the news Lauzun had been waiting for. He could exchange his dreary prison for Bourbon, the spa that Fouquet had never reached; Saint-Mars' lieutenant Maupertuis and twelve Musketeers would escort him there. Barrail, however, was under no illusions about the dangerous role he had been playing and at the earliest opportunity he retired permanently from court.

Bourbon was supposed to be but a stepping-stone back to the royal presence for Lauzun but Louis, increasingly disillusioned by the climate of suspicion around him, showed no inclination to receive such a conspicuously disloyal subject. Louvois sent Athénaïs to Bourbon to urge Lauzun to be patient.

That Athénaïs was now at his beck and call was an indication of how far her stock had fallen in the eyes of the king, not helped by her suspected contribution to the ill health of Angélique de Fontanges. Angélique experienced a miscarriage while carrying the king's child, sexual intercourse became painful for her, and in March 1681 she had been packed off, like so many previous mistresses, to a convent. Three months later she died at the abbey of Port-Royal in Paris, aged only twenty-one, shortly after the mysterious death of two of her female servants. Rumours abounded at court, fuelled by the king's opposition to an autopsy, that Angélique had also succumbed to the poisoner's skills. The ambassador from the duchy of Prussia reported that her death was 'attributed to a beverage given to her on Madame de Montespan's secret orders'.

What to do about Athénaïs was the subject of four meetings at the highest level held in the spring, sixteen hours of emotional discussions between Louis, Louvois, his father Le Tellier, Colbert and police chief La Reynie. The outcome was a triumph for Louvois: the ending of Athénaïs' influence but a restatement of her immunity, removing any risk that the trail might lead to his door. La Reynie, deprived by their premature execution of his key witnesses, La Voisin and La Filastre, and refused permission to interview Athénaïs, prudently decided not to reach a conclusion on her guilt or innocence. The trial of many of those charged could not continue, because Louis would not allow the judges to see any allegation or confession that mentioned his mistress. The Chambre Ardente, already suspended on the spurious grounds that to pursue the inquiry 'would denigrate the nation in the eyes of foreigners', was disbanded and Louis used *lettres de cachet* to condemn fourteen of the accused, including Marguerite Montvoisin and Abbé Guiborg, to perpetual imprisonment.

Athénaïs was left in limbo, no longer welcome in the king's bed but allowed to keep her lavish apartments at court. According to one of her confidantes, when Louis asked Athénaïs point-blank about her involvement in the poisonings, she haughtily reproached him, wept buckets, but never actually denied it. One last route back remained available to Athénaïs. Louis was anxious to obtain property for their illegitimate son, the duc de Maine, and asked Athénaïs to approach the Grande Mademoiselle. Athénaïs failed to persuade her to hand over immediately two of her finest duchies in return for a vague promise that Lauzun would be allowed to return to court and that the couple could eventually marry with the king's blessing. In the absence of concrete assurances, which of course were not forthcoming, Mademoiselle was prepared to make the duc de Maine her heir, but 'not to dismember her estates during her lifetime'. She willed the properties to Maine but stubbornly reserved their use and income for the remainder of her life.

When the carrot failed, Louvois brutally used the stick. He threatened Mademoiselle with imprisonment and made out that she had gone back on her word. Louvois sent her a blunt message: 'The king is not mocked: when you promise something, you do it.' Mademoiselle gave way. Next, Lauzun, languishing first at Bourbon, then at Amboise, was forced to relinquish his own claim to the duchies, in return for a promise by Louvois that he would be granted an audience with the king.

Louis duly received Lauzun in March 1682 but refused to restore him to a place of honour by his side, as a captain of the royal bodyguard. Although Lauzun could return to Paris, the two places where he most wanted to be, the palaces of Saint-Germain and Versailles, were henceforth to remain off limits. Louvois, fearing that Lauzun might gamble everything by revealing to Colbert what he had discovered at Pignerol, urgently summoned him to a midnight meeting. Lauzun would have been left in no doubt that if even the slightest whisper about the Mask reached Louvois' ears his fate would be sealed. A grant of 400,000 livres made the message a little more palatable to Lauzun than it would otherwise have been.

As ever failing to read the runes, before leaving court Lauzun did not bother to pay his respects to Françoise de Maintenon, who remarked with asperity that Louvois was no doubt more useful than she. Mademoiselle was astonished to hear that Lauzun had been closeted with Louvois and said as much to Athénaïs, who replied with unusual bitterness: 'What! Can you *still* be astonished? In these days one must be astonished at nothing!'

Mademoiselle and Lauzun also met, but the old spark had gone. She was shocked at his appearance because Lauzun, hoping to win the king's sympathy, had arrived at court 'wearing a dreadful wig and his old doublet all in holes' and, worst faux pas of all, 'twelve years out of fashion'. He for his part saw an elderly, raw-boned woman whose ruddy complexion, accentuated over the years, had assumed 'a hue of brick-dust red'. They would never become the contented married couple of Mademoiselle's dreams, accepted by the cream of society. There were no fairy-tale endings at the court of Louis XIV.

THE TWO *MERLES* OF MONSIEUR
SAINT-MARS

ven if Lauzun had thrown caution to the winds and revealed the real identity of the Mask, Louvois had already concocted a cover story to convince the rest of Europe that the mysterious extra prisoner at Pignerol was Ercole Mattioli, an Italian count.

Mattioli's imprisonment at Pignerol from May 1679 was genuine enough, the penalty for deceiving Louis XIV. The count had been a minister of the impoverished Ferdinand-Charles, Duke of Mantua and Monferrat, a pocket Italian state on the Lombard plain whose fortified capital Casale was coveted by all the major powers because of its strategic importance: it dominated the upper reaches of the river Po east of Turin and the road from Genoa to Milan.

Mattioli persuaded his master to sell Casale secretly to France. Using the French ambassador to Venice, Jean-François, Abbé d'Estrades, as a go-between; a grateful Louis received Mattioli at court and showered him with gifts, including a large diamond ring. France sent an infantry brigadier, Nicolas Catinat, to Pignerol, posing as one of Saint-Mars' prisoners, intending him to move his troops to Casale as soon as the deal was done. However, when Duke Ferdinand-Charles refused to ratify the agreement, fearing his irate neighbours' reactions, Mattioli's only source of further profit was in disclosing the plot to Spain and Savoy.

The enraged King of France ordered d'Estrades to go to any lengths to punish Mattioli, and even Saint-Mars was allowed to leave Pignerol to help the ambassador. Brigadier Catinat and Saint-Mars arranged a meeting with Mattioli in Casale itself. Mattioli predictably did not appear and both Frenchmen were arrested on suspicion of being foreign agents, but their false identity papers fooled the governor of Casale, who let them go.

D'Estrades told Mattioli he had nothing to fear from France and that Catinat intended to make him a further large payment in return for his continued assistance. Mattioli was greedy enough to take the risk of riding in the ambassador's coach to the rendezvous with Catinat at a remote house, which Mattioli believed to be on the Italian side of the frontier. After three days of rain, however, the fords were almost impassable and the coach became bogged down in the mud. D'Estrades' abduction scheme seemed destined to fail until Mattioli ensured his own downfall. He insisted on continuing on foot and even spent an hour dexterously repairing a broken bridge with wooden planks so that d'Estrades and he could cross a turbulent stream that, unknown to Mattioli, marked the French border. Once across, Mattioli was arrested by Saint-Mars and two of his lieutenants and taken directly to Pignerol, three miles away.

Mattioli, having betrayed France, proved far more useful in propaganda terms than he could ever have imagined. His punishment was always intended to provide a dreadful public warning of the consequences of treachery. As historian Rupert Furneaux dryly put it, 'His captivity would have lost its point if all Europe had *not* known the fate of the man who had attempted to double-cross the King of France.' With French connivance, in 1682 an account of his abduction and imprisonment was published in an Italian pamphlet printed at Cologne.

This made no reference to a mask, but five years later, as rumours of the existence of a masked prisoner began to surface, another pamphlet would provide both an invaluable distraction from his true identity and a false explanation for the mask itself. In August 1687 a Dutch printer at Leiden published the

French translation of an Italian letter that claimed Mattioli had been invited on a hunting trip and that not far from Turin he 'was surrounded by ten or twelve horsemen who seized him, disguised him and masked him, and conducted him to Pignerol'. Although alleging that Mattioli was forcibly masked by his captors to forestall any attempt to rescue him, the Leiden pamphlet also said that Mattioli sometimes wore a mask in jail itself because masking one's face on a voluntary basis, as a protection from the sun, was a common practice through Italy. This bizarre explanation continued to be given credence for almost two centuries.

Knowing nothing of the Mask's fate or the need to keep his identity secret from his guards, nineteenth-century historians could not devise a better explanation. Even the distinguished Marius Topin, whose reputation for careful research was previously impeccable, lamely declared that because Mattioli was Italian, a mask 'would certainly have formed part of his personal effects'. Théodore Iung challenged his conclusions and sardonically dismissed his rival's logic. 'It is as if one were to say, "Since this man is Spanish, he must be carrying castanets".'

Meanwhile, the relationship between Louvois and Saint-Mars had perceptibly changed. It might be an exaggeration to say that Louvois needed Saint-Mars as much as Saint-Mars needed Louvois, but the jailer was no longer a man expressing servile gratitude for his employment.

Saint-Mars already had substantial property to his name, having inherited the Château de Palteau from his uncle on 24 August 1669. The will had been disputed by other relatives and Saint-Mars could not afford a lawyer but the jailer soon discovered how useful it was to have powerful allies when, with a nudge from Louvois, the Paris Parlement unexpectedly found in his favour.

During the decade or so that followed, Saint-Mars had also grown seriously rich. Some of the largesse that came his way is on record, and there may have been considerably more. In 1677 Louvois sent Saint-Mars a huge bonus of 30,000 livres and, two years later, another 15,000 livres. In April 1680 Louvois allowed Saint-Mars to dispose of the choicest pieces of Fouquet's prison furniture, which brought him in a further 6,000 livres. Louvois also allowed Saint-Mars to keep the diamond ring given to Mattioli by Louis XIV, with which Mattioli in vain had tried to bribe his captors.

Historian Marcel Pagnol calculated that Saint-Mars made an annual profit of 5,000 livres a year on the Treasury grant intended to be spent on feeding his prisoners and that, in two and a half years to March 1680, he had a total income over expenditure in excess of 75,000 livres. The true seventeenth-century purchasing power of what Saint-Mars is known to have received can be put in even sharper perspective by comparing it with the wages of a skilled worker, which at that time amounted to just one livre per working day, about 300 livres a year. Saint-Mars' average annual net receipts, one hundred times larger, were truly remarkable for a junior officer who had almost allowed Lauzun to escape and who had failed to prevent Martin's suicide. It showed what Louvois felt was necessary to ensure his jailer's silence about his two secret captives, the Mask and Fouquet.

Louvois made the first surviving reference to both prisoners in his letter to Saint-Mars dated 10 July 1680. 'It will be sufficient', he wrote, 'to have *les habitans de la tour d'en bas* {'the inhabitants', that is to say, the prisoners, 'of the lower tower'} confess once a year.' This letter of 10 July was the very one where Louvois added his private postscript about 'Eustache' and the drugs, suggesting to some historians that the pseudo-valet, 'Eustache Danger', was one of the secret prisoners to whom Louvois referred in the same dispatch. There is no logic to such a hypothesis. Louvois did not mention either of the prisoners by name in the original version of the 10 July letter dictated to his clerical staff – without, that is, the paragraph in his own hand referring to 'Eustache' – because the true identity of the prisoners was seen as a threat to the security of the state. Yet this letter, with its afterthought allegedly revealing one of their names, had to be carried by royal couriers on a journey of several hundred miles, over Alpine terrain, and at risk throughout of being lost, stolen or intercepted, before it reached Saint-Mars. This was a serious prospect: one of Louvois' messengers was kidnapped by bandits a few miles from Pignerol, and never reached Saint-Mars at all. These regular communications from Paris were accordingly far from secure and it seems inconceivable Louvois would have recklessly disclosed in the fourth paragraph of a letter the identity of a secret prisoner that he was at such pains to conceal in the second.

Far from reprimanding Saint-Mars for his failure to prevent Martin's suicide, Louvois offered him command of the entire citadel of Pignerol; but the jailer replied saying, in extraordinary fashion, that he did not want the job. Saint-Mars knew that the governorship of the nearby fortress of Exilles had become vacant and that such an appointment at last could give him the status in society he craved. It was a considerable gamble. Even the high and mighty had been sent to the Bastille for less insubordination than the 'extreme repugnance', as Louvois described it, that Saint-Mars showed for the offer of promotion at Pignerol, to a job previously given to the nobility. However, Louvois and Louis, who had the gift of the Exilles post, immediately went along with his wishes.

The secret prisoners were to be installed in Saint-Mars' care at Exilles 'with as much security as in Pignerol'. He was told to visit the fortress immediately to decide what work needed to be done, leaving his lieutenants to look after the donjon. Louvois was insistent that while he was away, Saint-Mars would ensure that 'the prisoners . . . have no more communication with anyone than they have ever had since in your charge.'

In August 1680 an Italian engineer in the pay of the Spanish governor of Milan stole the plans of both the citadel and donjon at Pignerol. When their loss was discovered, Herleville, the new commander of the citadel, already at odds with Saint-Mars, launched an immediate investigation. Much to Herleville's glee, the engineer was found to have obtained the plans on the pretext

of explaining to one of Saint-Mars' nephews how security could
be improved. Louvois could not touch Saint-Mars, so instead he
vented his anger on Pignerol's citizens, ordering the expulsion of
every foreigner living within the walls, 'be they Pie[d]montais,
Savoyards or Italians . . . [because] they had no business in the
citadel, let alone the donjon'. Even then, Louvois was careful to
exempt from the order the three long-serving Italian domestics
employed by the formidable Madame Saint-Mars.

Most of Bénigne Saint-Mars' correspondence went to the
war minister, with whom, at least when it came to identifying
his prisoners, the jailer remained extremely circumspect. This
makes Saint-Mars' letter of 25 June 1681 to d'Estrades of
particular significance. D'Estrades was the closest Saint-Mars
had to a friend, the pair of them fresh from deeds of derring-do
directly involved in luring Mattioli across the French frontier and
in his subsequent capture. In this letter Saint-Mars apologized
for not letting d'Estrades know earlier what was happening, he
shared with him his relief that the advance of 2,000 livres on his
salary and expenses as governor of Exilles had finally arrived,
and bemoaned the fact that his family would have to stay
behind at Pignerol for several months until he had improved
their accommodation at the new fortress.

Saint-Mars would dearly have loved to share his prestigious
secret with d'Estrades and went as far in the letter as he
dared. He made it clear from the outset that Mattioli would
not be going with him, writing: 'Mattioli is to stay on here at
Pignerol.'

'I will keep my company of French soldiers and my two
lieutenants', continued Saint-Mars, 'and I shall have in my
custody two *merles*, who have no other names than the *messieurs*
of the lower tower.'

Messieurs meant 'gentlemen', even when referring to complete
strangers, so long as they were of quality. If the status-conscious
Saint-Mars, forever seeking promotion or ennoblement, thought
he had *messieurs* in his Lower Tower, not just the *habitans* of
Louvois' earlier letter, he gave them that respectful title by

virtue of their place in society. The literal meaning of *merle* was a blackbird, distinguished by its yellow beak, and very common in France. As for the colloquial meaning, by the 1660s it was already an abbreviation for '*un fin merle*', slang for someone particularly adroit, or '*un dénicheur des merles*', a jailbird skilled in identifying the weak points of a prison, who could not be left unguarded for a second. By referring to *merles*, Saint-Mars was giving d'Estrades a broad hint that both his prisoners were in a special category, who would stop at nothing to escape.

In the same month Saint-Mars received his formal letters of appointment as governor, together with instructions to transport 'the two prisoners of the lower tower . . . in a litter as soon as . . . Exilles . . . is ready to receive them'. The jailer estimated that it would take three months to complete the work needed to improve security at Exilles, but Louvois told him to slow down the job surreptitiously to ensure he was still in charge of the donjon at Pignerol in August, when Catinat, his regiment on full alert, posed as a prisoner there for a second time to disguise the impending, much-delayed French move on Casale. Catinat's fake incarceration, he wrote gaily to Louvois, was alleviated by 'a profusion of figs of an admirable plumpness and excellence'. The apparent lack of progress irritated Herleville, especially when Saint-Mars refused to enlighten him. Herleville complained to Louvois, who angrily replied that the commander of the citadel would be well advised not to show resentment of Saint-Mars' conduct because the jailer 'has orders from the king for which he is not accountable to anyone'.

With Casale finally in Catinat's hands, Saint-Mars made the transfer to Exilles during the first week of October 1681. The journey of twelve leagues, about sixteen miles, across mountainous terrain, took place under cover of darkness, a considerable risk to both men and horses on such a dangerous route. Saint-Mars' orders were to ensure that no one communicated with his prisoners and that as few people as possible even knew of his departure. He achieved this by using his staff to carry Fouquet and the Mask, hooded, gagged and pinioned, out of the donjon via the concealed postern gate on a closed litter suspended on wooden shafts. This avoided the civilian areas of the citadel and enabled them to link up unseen with the main escort waiting on the Briançon road.

The fortress at Exilles was later pulled down to make way for new fortifications and much of these, too, lie in ruins, so little trace of the buildings of Saint-Mars' day remain. Iung discovered an undated plan of the original fort in the war ministry archives, from which he deduced that the old Roman tower was chosen to accommodate the secret prisoners. Saint-Mars had additional walls constructed in the western end of the courtyard to make extensive accommodation for himself and his family, and to create a new access route to the tower, so that no one could enter it unobserved.

The tower had two circular cells, one on the first floor and another on the second, reached by way of a tight, stone spiral staircase. The upper cell was about six metres in diameter, much the larger of the two, with windows, each with a high sill, facing south, east and west; a double door, one opening inwards, the other outwards, closed off the cell immediately at the top of the staircase from the first floor. The lower cell was less than half the size of the upper due to the thicker walls at this level and the construction of a large landing with a chicane approach, where two doors, spaced several metres apart, made it impossible for the sentry positioned around the corner on the landing to catch even a glimpse of the prisoner. The upper cell was almost certainly reserved for Fouquet, the prisoner of higher rank, but the lower cell allocated to the Mask was the more impenetrable.

As with the accommodation originally constructed for Étienne Martin at Pignerol, visitors had to pass through three separate doors, including one at the entrance to the tower on the ground floor. The upper cell in the Roman tower had three windows, facing west, east and south, each with high sills and gratings. The lower cell had a southerly aspect and overlooked the grey, rocky valley, with the fast-flowing river Doria far below. The view was severely restricted by two gratings, one fixed in the windows themselves and the other set further back, preventing access to the large, rectangular window embrasure. What looks like a latrine is marked on the lower cell, and it is probable that both cells had a means of disposing waste direct into the bowels of the fort. There was no reason for either prisoner to leave their place of confinement in the Roman tower and, for added security, Saint-Mars installed one of his lieutenants, La Prade, in the storeroom above.

Having abruptly declined command of the citadel of Pignerol and moved to Exilles, Saint-Mars then proceeded to act even further out of character. Gone was the timid jailer who was chained to Pignerol as much as his illustrious captives. Saint-Mars became quite content regularly to leave the task of guarding his secret prisoners to his subordinates whilst he gallivanted about the countryside. Nor did he have to ask permission on every occasion: Louvois and the king gave him close to carte blanche. In December 1681, Louvois wrote to Saint-Mars, 'There is nothing to prevent you going to Casal[e] from time to time to see Monsieur de Catinat,' and, he told the jailer, 'His Majesty sees nothing wrong in your spending a night away from Exilles when you want to visit locally.'

Saint-Mars also made one highly irregular journey, smuggling his wife's brother-in-law, Damorezan, across the frontier to Turin after hiding him at Exilles. A warrant had been issued against Damorezan for siphoning off government funds, but Madame de Saint-Mars persuaded Louvois to delay it so that the embezzler could escape. As always, quite unable to refuse her, Louvois even incriminated himself in a letter. 'Tell him to leave France as quickly as possible,' he wrote, 'because if he stays where he is, I am certain he will be arrested.'

Saint-Mars became a regular visitor to Turin, where d'Estrades had been appointed ambassador. Louvois also gave him permission to take his wife 'for fifteen days or three weeks' to the waters at Aix, then part of Savoy. Saint-Mars later joined the governor of the Suze province in an agreeable hunting party.

Soon the two governors were hunting not game but Protestants, who were attempting to escape across the border following the revocation of their religious autonomy granted by Edict of Nantes. Saint-Mars went personally to set up a roadblock at Bardonneche to close the Huguenot trail to Savoy through the Rho Pass. Ettore Patria, archivist for the Suze valley, concluded that although from time to time Saint-Mars returned the Suze governor's hospitality at Exilles, his guest never had the slightest inkling that the Roman tower contained two secret prisoners, so relaxed was Saint-Mars in a fortress he regarded as virtually escape proof.

Back at court, the king, aware that Fouquet was at Exilles, and Louvois, who of course knew the true identity of the other inmate, did not quite share the jailer's confidence. Saint-Mars had to find a priest who was almost senile to confess the prisoners once a year, and he prevented any direct, face-to-face contact during the confessional by hanging a screen consisting of stretched drumskin between the double doors of each cell.

The king was still uneasy, and Louvois wrote again to Saint-Mars in February 1682:

> As it is important that the prisoners who are in Exilles, who at Pignerol were known as 'the prisoners of the lower tower' have no contact with anyone, the King has ordered me to command you to have them guarded so strictly and to take such precautions that you can promise His Majesty that they cannot speak to anyone, not only [with people] from outside but even from the garrison at Exilles; I beg you to keep me informed from time to time about them.

Saint-Mars, sensing the need quickly to reassure the king, wrote back to Louvois:

> The prisoners can hear people talking as they go by on the road below their tower, but even if they [the prisoners] want to, they cannot make themselves heard. They can see people on the mountainside opposite their windows but they themselves cannot be seen because of the gratings on the outside. Night

and day I keep two sentries of my company at a reasonable distance either side of the tower where they can see, obliquely, the prisoners' windows. They have orders to take care that no one speaks to them [the prisoners], that they do not shout through the windows, and that passers-by who linger on the road or on the mountain slopes are made to move on. Since my room is linked to the tower and overlooks only the road, I hear and see everything, including the sentries, which keeps them on the alert.

As for the interior of the tower . . . The servants who bring the food for the prisoners leave it on a table, from where my lieutenant takes it into them. No one talks to them apart from me and, but only in my presence, my officer; their confessor . . . and a physician who comes from Pragelas, six leagues away. As for their linen and other necessities, I take the same precautions as I did for my prisoners in the past.

The secret prisoners could communicate with each other by standing by the windows and shouting up and down, but this would have proved exhausting because of the distance between each floor. Fouquet, already in poor health, having sipped from the cup of freedom only to have it cruelly dashed from his lips, went into terminal decline. The Mask, more resilient, watched and waited. His isolation may not have been quite as complete as Louvois intended and Saint-Mars supposed. Madame Saint-Mars had a soft spot for the Mask and ordered him some fine linen shirts from Paris. During her husband's frequent absences, she was able to visit the Mask unseen, direct from the governor's quarters. While the cat was away, the mice may have been at play.

Louis XIV almost certainly believed that the second secret prisoner was Fouquet's valet, La Rivière, a black African slave from the Portuguese Cape Verde Islands. However, Saint-Mars probably released La Rivière in 1681 on the eve of his move to Exilles, disingenuously relying on long-standing instructions he had received from the king that had never been revoked. Many years previously Louis had agreed that Saint-Mars could always dispense with La Rivière's services, provided that he kept the valet behind bars for seven or eight months, so that 'any message he might be carrying from his master' would no longer have any value.

La Rivière was mentioned only once again by name, on 16 April 1684, in a letter Louvois wrote to Saint-Mars:

> It's been a long time since you talked to me about your prisoners. I must ask you to tell me how you are supervising them and how they are getting on. I command you also to send me what you know of the birth of the man named La Rivière and the circumstances in which he was placed in the service of the late M. Fouquet.

Louvois' correspondence showed his amazing capacity for entering into detail without losing sight of major issues. However, the sheer scale of his task of reforming the army and the volume of orders meant that he had many things on his mind at once, dictating at speed, sometimes returning to a letter after several interruptions. This explains why many paragraphs in Louvois' correspondence were so disconnected and why attempts by some historians to read something significant into an accidental juxtaposition were almost invariably misguided.

This was almost certainly true of this April 1684 dispatch. Louvois knew that any reference he made to Fouquet could be rendered harmless by adding the prefix 'late', so this had no particular significance. However, in view of the exceptional care that Louvois had previously taken not to identify the prisoners transferred from Pignerol to Exilles with Saint-Mars, it is most unlikely that any deliberate link between the first and second part of his letter was intended, and that a valet was actually Fouquet's companion at Exilles. In respect of La Rivière, Louvois used the phrase to Saint-Mars, '*Mandez-moi aussi,*' 'I command you also.' This suggests that Louvois was changing the subject and asking Saint-Mars what he knew of La Rivière. It may have been a report from some other source of La Rivière's death elsewhere that prompted Louvois to ask questions about the valet's background, perhaps recalling that he had once been a highly rated riding instructor in Paris who had shown himself capable of refining even those skills of the talented Louise de La Vallière.

The final piece of persuasive evidence lies in the Pignerol accounts. After ostensibly losing his master, Fouquet, La Rivière continued to be classified by the Treasury as a valet, worth just fifty livres a month to Saint-Mars – 600 livres a year – rather than as an official prisoner, whose minimum annual reckoning was 1,440 livres. On 9 June 1681 the Treasury established the jailer's future allowance for each of the two special category prisoners moving to Exilles at just over 180 livres per month, 2,190 livres a year, nearly four times the valets' rate. The inescapable conclusion is that La Rivière was not one of them.

At Exilles the cost of both prisoners' upkeep remained as large as ever. Security had increased from high to formidable, regardless of expense. Saint-Mars' personal troop consisted of forty-five men, a ratio of guards to prisoners of more than twenty to one, and the sentries themselves were watched as closely as the prisoners. Only Saint-Mars and La Prade, not even his other lieutenant, could visit the prisoners alone, and La Prade was forbidden to see them on his own except when Saint-Mars was away. Three separate doors barred access to the prisoners, who probably never left the Roman tower. To all intents and purposes, they had disappeared from the face of this earth. Louvois was determined to prevent the slightest hint of their identities reaching the outside world.

14

THE FIRE TONGS AFFAIR

ৎ ৩

Saint-Mars enjoyed his newfound freedom at Exilles, but his wife Marie-Antoinette, although she had sanctioned, possibly even sought, the move, did not like the change at all. Their new apartment, grafted at huge cost on to Exilles' medieval structure, soon lost its appeal. Marie-Antoinette had enjoyed her role as hostess to the great and the good at Pignerol when Fouquet and Lauzun began to be allowed visitors. Even after that halcyon time ended, Pignerol still had its cluster of counts in the service of the crown, grateful for an invitation from the Saint-Mars to dinner. In contrast, Exilles was a narrow, claustrophobic society. Monsieur and Madame Saint-Mars had become bigger fish, but only by swimming in a very small pond.

Geographically, too, they were completely isolated. Turin, with its markets and elegant shops, was no longer within easy reach. Madame Saint-Mars usually had to make do with Mont Genèvre, a small village in the Dauphiné, and occasionally with Briançon. To appease his wife, Saint-Mars gave her personal servants, a valet and a chauffeur, who had a carriage 'aveque sa beste', 'with its animal', probably a mule. Louvois paid the bills without demur, but the gesture was not enough.

Saint-Mars half-heartedly began to ask for a change of governorship. When Louvois did not respond quickly enough, Madame Saint-Mars took matters into her own hands. Towards the end of 1686, she travelled to Paris to see Louvois. What passed between them was not recorded but the minister would have been acutely aware that if anyone knew the identity of both the secret prisoners, other than himself and Saint-Mars, it was probably his wife. Soon afterwards, Louvois asked the king to transfer the jailer to a more agreeable location. On 8 January 1687, Saint-Mars was promoted to 'governor of the islands of Sainte Marguerite and Honorat', with an increase in his annual salary to 7,000 livres.

His orders from Louvois were:

> [to] visit the said islands to see what has to be done to put the installation in proper condition to safeguard the prisoners who are in your charge . . . You will send me a plan and a specification on which I may take His Majesty's instructions. You will then return to Exilles and await His Majesty's orders to take them [the prisoners] and your company. There is no need for me to recommend, while you travel to Sainte Marguerite and back again, that you take the necessary measures for the guarding of the said prisoners so as to avoid anything untoward happening to them, and their communicating with anyone.

The dispatch made it clear that Saint-Mars was to take both his prisoners to Sainte-Marguerite but, unknown to Louvois, one of them, Fouquet, had died just three days earlier. The doctor from Pragelas, who was not allowed to see the prisoners' faces, had warned Saint-Mars that Fouquet was suffering from dropsy, an accumulation of watery fluid on various parts of the body; back in October 1686 Saint-Mars had asked Louvois if the old priest could confess his ailing prisoner before the regular twelve-month interval was up. Louvois took his time replying, and then was typically laconic. Saint-Mars could let the prisoner confess 'when you see his death approaching', he said.

Having determined with some difficulty which of the prisoners had died, it being unwise to mention names, Louvois almost certainly allowed the king to think it was La Rivière. He needed Louis to believe that Fouquet was still alive, otherwise the king would not have sanctioned the cost of upgrading the jail on Sainte-Marguerite.

Louvois instructed the postmaster at Grenoble to forward a fresh dispatch to Saint-Mars at Exilles by special messenger. He added an uncharacteristically friendly note:

> I don't have to say anything about your desire for a change of governorship because you know by now that the King has granted you more than you wished for, something that suits you admirably. I am as delighted as you will be, and for the part I continue to play in everything that affects you.

He was making sure that Saint-Mars, and especially his wife, appreciated his own role in the transfer. Saint-Mars, replying a week later, assured Louvois that he would take great care of his surviving prisoner, both while he was visiting the islands on a reconnaissance trip and when he came to move him there:

> The orders I will give for the surveillance of my prisoner will be as strict as always, preventing any communication with my lieutenant, whom I have forbidden ever to speak to the prisoner. My lieutenant always obeys me to the letter, so I can answer to you for the prisoner's complete security. I feel that the most secure method of transporting him to the islands would be in a sedan chair covered with an oil cloth, so that the prisoner will have sufficient air without anyone being able to see him or speak to him during the journey, not even the soldiers I pick to be close to the chair. It will be less troublesome than a litter, which can often break down.

Louvois replied immediately, approving the use of a sedan chair.

Saint-Mars arrived at Sainte-Marguerite, a brief boat ride from Cannes, then a tiny fishing village, on 19 February. For all but five days of the next month he was sick and bedridden, but on 2 March he managed to send Louvois details of the building work required to ensure the security of his prisoner, at an estimated cost of 5,000 livres. A fortnight later Louvois approved the expenditure 'out of emergency funds' and attached the king's order for his jailer's departure from Exilles. Saint-

Mars was still awaiting this a further week later, when, perhaps fearing the wrath of his wife, waiting back at Exilles, he wrote again anxiously to Louvois:

> As soon as I am honoured with your orders, I shall set out with my prisoner whom I promise to bring here in total security, without anyone seeing him or being able to speak to him . . . Upon my honour, I vouch for the security of my prisoner.

Saint-Mars' reconnoitre of Sainte-Marguerite had already caused a buzz of excitement on the island, reported by a local abbé, referring to 'that unknown prisoner who is being transferred with great precautions' and who nonetheless 'has been made to understand that when he grows tired of living, he has only to speak his name out loud . . . to be given a pistol-shot in the head'.

Saint-Mars left Exilles for the last time on 18 April, taking the Embrun road via Briançon, Grasse, Mougins, Le Cannet and Cannes. With him were his wife, their two sons and all their worldly goods, travelling in a sprung coach pulled by thoroughbred horses, an extravagance specially sanctioned by Louvois. Accompanying them were Saint-Mars' prison officials, a large escort of soldiers and the Mask himself, carried in the sealed sedan chair by eight porters. The jailer had hired the chair and the porters in Turin, at a combined cost of 203 livres. Even for eight men, the journey from Exilles to Sainte-Marguerite of more than 200 miles was a back-breaking exercise. Saint-Mars made sure that the porters spoke only Italian, to make it almost impossible for the Mask to communicate with them.

As planned, Saint-Mars arrived at Briançon after dark, the front riders in his escort lighting the way through the sombre streets with huge torches. Saint-Mars and his senior officers lodged themselves and their prisoner on the first floor of the Maison du Roi in the Grande rue. The escort found billets in houses around the place des Halles, apart from an unlucky half a dozen soldiers sent to guard the three town gates. Saint Mars had expected to be received by the town's consul but he and his command were stuck in a deep snowdrift on the Lauteret Pass. The consul succeeded in reaching Briançon a day late without his men, but his dignity did not allow him to enter the town '*en catimini*', 'on the sly', so Saint-Mars had to delay his departure and turn out his own troop to salute him. The jailer forced a hard bargain with the consul for this extraneous service, charging him 362 rations for himself, his family, his staff, the prisoner, two lieutenants, two sergeants, forty-three soldiers and their horses. The size of Saint-Mars' escort caused a stir in the town, because single prisoners condemned to the galleys who had passed through Briançon in the preceding three months were each accompanied by two or three men at the most.

At Grasse the heat inside the Mask's oilskin-covered litter reached an intolerable level after midday and Saint-Mars was forced to remove it briefly to give his prisoner some air. Among the eyewitnesses was a local priest, who reported what he had seen to Bishop Louis Fouquet, brother of the disgraced, and now finally deceased, Nicolas Fouquet.

Louis Fouquet was a Jansenist, a supporter of the theology that increased the role of the clergy in French society to a level where it was seen as politically subversive. His clique of clerics met regularly in Paris at the Café Procope, the newly opened Italian coffee-shop in the rue des Fossés-Saint-Germain, where intellectuals in the arts, letters and politics gathered close to the embryonic Comédie-Française to exchange ideas. The bishop was behind *Les Nouvelles Ecclésiastiques*, a numbered newsletter that always appeared on paper with an identical watermark and measuring twenty-five by eighteen centimetres, so the recipients would know it was genuine. These handwritten newsletters were passed from parish to parish, eagerly awaited by priests throughout France, for, apart from advocating Jansenism, they often contained information and comment that authorized publications dared not print. It was here on 4 September 1687, three months after the Mask's arrival in the Mediterranean and only weeks after the Leiden letter had unwittingly downplayed the significance of a prisoner wearing a mask, that the story of the Man in the Iron Mask first sensationally appeared:

> By order of the king, Monsieur Cinq-Mars [sic] has transported a state prisoner from Pignerol to the islands of Saint[e]-Marguerite No one knows who he is. He is forbidden to speak his name and there is an order to kill him if he disobeys.
>
> No doubt other prisoners of that kind have been taken to Pignerol. There was one man there who killed himself.
>
> This prisoner was enclosed in a sedan chair with a steel mask on his face and all we were allowed to know by Cinq-Mars [sic] was that he was at Pignerol for many years and that all the people one believes to be dead are not.

The newsletter containing Saint-Mars's indiscreet remark, '*Tous les gens que l'on croit morts ne le sont pas,*' attracted great interest and several copies were made. Its ecclesiastical distributors were actively pursued by the authorities, and as a result the section on the Mask was excised in whole or part from most of them, including the one presently held by the Bibliothèque Nationale. Another Paris library, the Bibliothèque Saint-Geneviève, possesses the only known copy to survive intact.

The anxiety to destroy the newsletter was surely prompted by the vital clue it contained to the identity of the Mask. He was someone universally believed to have died some time previously and, it must follow, of sufficient prominence for his death to have been widely reported and of considerable public interest. One man, the only man to meet all the necessary criteria, is the captain of the King's Musketeers, d'Artagnan, thought to have been killed at the siege of Maastricht on 25 June 1673, almost fourteen years earlier.

Like many such bloody conflicts, the charge led that day by d'Artagnan and the Duke of Monmouth belonged to a scene of utter chaos. When they saw him hit in the neck by a bullet, his colleagues left d'Artagnan where he fell and clambered into the ditch to engage the enemy. Furious hand-to-hand fighting followed. The Life Guards threw away their carbines, which were useless at close range, and drew their swords. The ferocity of the counter-attack caught the Dutch by surprise but the situation was still critical until 500 French reinforcements arrived. More than 1,000 troops were killed or wounded on both sides before the attackers recovered what they had originally gained the previous night.

The British contingent was distracted by the cries of one of their own officers, who had been shot through both legs. Bodies lay everywhere, and d'Artagnan was forgotten in the confusion. He was probably unconscious and covered in blood and there were many seriously wounded casualties screaming in pain for the orderlies to deal with.

Three contemporary accounts exist of d'Artagnan's last skirmish but two can be immediately discounted. His fellow Musketeer, Pierre Quarré d'Aligny, was concussed by the exploding mine and did not see this part of the action at all. Louis Duras, a French Huguenot noble, also claimed to be an eyewitness but was so notorious a liar that he became a laughing stock. The third account came in a letter from Lord Alington, an undistinguished Irish peer from County Killard, who had a reputation for profligacy in both wine and women. Everyone who took part in the counter-attack had not expected to fight that day and was the worse for drink; but Alington was almost certainly drunker than most. He suffered badly from gout and it is doubtful whether he arrived at the defences until most of the action had taken place, instead relying for his information mainly on what he gleaned afterwards from Monmouth, Churchill and the other British officers.

Alington was told that the struggle had been particularly bloody and the casualties particularly high. 'Some lacked a leg, some arms. Here there was a soldier whose guts were pouring from his body and over there lay a soldier with half his face shot away.' But in reporting that d'Artagnan had been killed, rather than injured, by a shot to the head, Alington relied upon second- or third-hand information, which was contradicted by the circumstantial evidence.

As senior officers were not included in the Musketeers' roll call, many hours elapsed before d'Artagnan was missed. By then he was completely anonymous, one of the hundreds of wounded eventually recovered from the battlefield and cared for in the new French field hospitals introduced, with what proved to be ironic timing, by Louvois that summer. For soldiers accustomed at best to rudimentary surgery where they lay, this was a startling improvement. One officer wrote home from Holland to say, 'I could not be better off if I were in my mother's house.'

It may have been the lack of any initial treatment, however, that saved d'Artagnan, lying unnoticed in a muddy field for much of the day with a serious wound to the neck or throat. If the blood had clotted, this would have avoided the septicaemia that occurred with the majority of treated wounds and invariably proved fatal.

The injury may have affected d'Artagnan's ability to speak, delaying his proper identification but sooner or later he was bound to be recognized by one of his own men receiving treatment. Few of the Musketeers injured that day reappeared in subsequent military rolls, prompting speculation that those who saw d'Artagnan in a field hospital and realized who he was, did not live to tell the tale.

The story of d'Artagnan's Musketeers risking life and limb under withering fire in order to recover the body of their fallen commander was an afterthought never reported at the time. There would have been no need for such heroics, because frequent truces were declared so that dead and injured combatants could be removed from the battlefield under a white flag. The Dutch defenders, who surrendered the city a week later, had been exemplary in following the conventions of 'civilized' warfare and were allowed to march away with full honours. The source of the legend of the fanatically loyal Musketeers was the Grand Provost of France, the marquis de Sourches, who ran the royal household and was frequently bullied by Louvois. He asserted that more than eighty Musketeers died in this valiant cause of recovering the 'dead' d'Artagnan and, despite the inherent improbability of the claim, it would subsequently be reported as fact by his son, a diarist of Louis XIV's court. In 1674 *le Mercure Galante*, a periodical usually devoted to the theatre and the arts, incongruously ran a different version of the story. It said that just four Musketeers had been killed attempting to retrieve d'Artagnan's corpse ahead of any truce and that they had failed. For straying from the official line, *le Mercure Galante* was promptly shut down by the authorities and its editor imprisoned.

Meanwhile, as the siege ended and awkward questions began to be asked about the circumstances of d'Artagnan's death, Adrien Malais, sieur de Saint-Léger, the Musketeers' quartermaster, stepped forward to say that he had seen and recovered his body. Prompted by Louvois, Louis XIV rewarded him with a gift of more than 30,000 livres, an extraordinary sum. However, despite the intense efforts of a group of Dutch historians, who in the 1960s would succeed in establishing the spot where d'Artagnan fell, no grave for him at Maastricht has ever been found. Nor is there any reliable evidence of his corpse having been returned to France. Château d'Olhain, north-west of Arras, claims that d'Artagnan was buried in its medieval chapel, but no trace of a gravestone exists.

Louvois knew what Louis did not: that d'Artagnan had avoided the glorious death arranged for him. Louvois was present from the first day of the siege until the last. Every train of munitions, each man, musket and meal, were part of Louvois' grand logistical plan. It was said that not a blade of grass quivered in the breeze unless Louvois had personally commanded it. Nothing escaped the war minister at Maastricht, certainly not d'Artagnan's disappearance on the battlefield.

It may have been Saint-Léger who eventually brought the disagreeable news to Louvois that d'Artagnan, although badly wounded, had inconveniently refused to die. Reports of d'Artagnan's supposed demise had spread like wildfire throughout the army and many eulogies were written about him. Louis, asked to contribute, chose his words carefully. In a message lightly tinged with malice, he described d'Artagnan as almost 'the only man who found the means to make himself loved by people while doing things not altogether obliging to them.' Most people assumed that the king was simply referring to d'Artagnan's reluctant role as Fouquet's jailer, unaware that d'Artagnan had been extremely unobliging to his monarch for most of that period.

On 28 June, three days after d'Artagnan's supposed demise, before returning to Saint-Germain Louvois wrote personally to Besmaux at the Bastille, a letter carried by his troubleshooter, Nallot. To authorize the incarceration of an unnamed prisoner, Besmaux was evidently expecting a more formal document, a *lit blanc*, a catch-all judicial order that flowed from the *lits de justice*, a legal process by which the crown avoided discussion of contentious legislation in the Parlement. It offered a particular advantage over a *lettre de cachet* in that it did not need to be signed by the king. On 4 July Besmaux referred to the absence of this order in his reply, and pointedly said that without it he 'would be unable to do everything' Louvois had ordered but would 'do as much as he could'.

This did not satisfy the war minister, who evidently wanted to avoid putting too much in writing. Saint-Mars, who previously had been unable to obtain permission to leave Pignerol for more than one night at a time, who had the two most important state prisoners, Fouquet and Lauzun, locked up in his donjon, was suddenly dispatched by Louvois to Maastricht. From there, on 20 July 1673, he sent the war minister a very strange message indeed. It began, quite abruptly:

> Monsieur, if the wound I have received here is not serious enough to stop me finishing the campaign, the same infliction that latterly kept me at Metz for some time makes it impossible for me to continue. That's why, Monseigneur, I ask you humbly to have the goodness to grant me leave.

In 1872 Théodore Iung, who as a staff officer at the French War Office had unfettered access to the War Department archives, would unearth this letter in the course of his research into the identity of the Man in the Iron Mask. However, Iung was completely baffled by its contents, speculating that Saint-Mars might have had a brother, then in the same breath rejecting his own hypothesis because no brother was mentioned in the jailer's will. Saint-Mars had only one sibling, a sister. Iung also noticed that the letter was signed 'Sainct-Mars', which, if anything, reinforced the view that the jailer had signed it, because he regularly misspelled even his own name. Only Saint-Mars and his immediate family ever used this *nom de guerre*. His father was long dead and the elder of Saint-Mars' two sons was aged just thirteen months at the time.

Iung did not realize that the letter, filed at the Dépôt de la Guerre with most of the surviving exchanges between Saint-Mars and Louvois, received a reply on 4 August that specifically acknowledged the original dispatch, making it certain that the two correspondents concerned were the minister and the jailer. Louvois wanted to know whether Saint-Mars' 'request for leave' meant that he intended 'to retire entirely from the service of the King . . . or whether it was only to receive treatment'. It is inconceivable that Saint-Mars had been allowed leave from Pignerol to take part in a hazardous siege and had been wounded during the action. The only credible explanation is that the letters were coded exchanges about the state of health of a third party, one so important that Saint-Mars himself and some of his men had been sent from Pignerol to Maastricht to guard him. Saint-Mars, of course, was one of the few people whom the injured d'Artagnan would trust implicitly and whom his fellow Musketeers in the field hospital would allow to remove their commander from Maastricht without concern.

Their mission was noticed by Guiseppe Caluzio, the son of a native of Pignerol, and a spy for Savoy. He had wormed his way into the confidence of Loyauté, Louvois' *commissaire de guerre*, and had even been appointed *greffier* to the Pignerol governor. Many confidential papers passed across his desk, but in trying to find out exactly what Saint-Mars was up to, Caluzio came under suspicion. He fled to Paris where, hunted by Nallot, he went into hiding. Before long, however, Caluzio abandoned the comfortable anonymity of the backstreets of Paris and made his way to Maastricht, perhaps because he hoped to find there a bargaining chip that would induce Louvois to call off his pursuers. His plan failed because on 20 July (the exact date Saint-Mars wrote to Louvois from Maastricht) his wife Francesca and Franco, their manservant, were arrested back in Pignerol and sent to the donjon; Caluzio himself fell into Louvois' hands four days later. Louvois had him taken directly to the Pierre-Cize prison in Lyon, issuing the order in his own handwriting, thereby preventing it from being seen by his clerical staff.

Caluzio may have reached Maastricht too late; Saint-Mars' dispatch also suggested that the mysterious invalid was being moved secretly to Metz, the capital of Lorraine and a bishopric on the safest route from Maastricht to Paris. The fortress at Metz was usually garrisoned with foreign mercenaries because of the political sensitivity of its position as a French possession illegally seized from the Holy Roman Empire. As such, they would have been unlikely to recognize the heavily bandaged patient as the most famous of all the Musketeers. Having previously shown little interest in Lorraine, Louvois suddenly moved the administration of the bishopric into his own department and paid it an unscheduled visit. If this were not sufficiently mysterious, after calling off the hunt for Caluzio in Paris, Nallot died suddenly on 16 July, just four days before Saint-Mars sent his letter. Louvois was most concerned because Nallot had in his possession, in a locked casket, a *lit blanc*, no doubt the particular *lit blanc* Besmaux wanted as authority to accept an unnamed prisoner. The casket was found in Nallot's effects by his sister, who opened it but wisely knew 'how to remain silent' about its contents. On 28 July Louvois ordered two of his staff to retrieve the casket 'before it does us harm'.

Although Besmaux wanted written authorization to protect himself, once d'Artagnan was moved from Metz to Paris, Louvois could count on the full cooperation of the governor of the Bastille. D'Artagnan had ridiculed Besmaux when the governor hid his wife Marguerite's fine features behind the biggest mask in Paris. Not long afterwards, in April 1667, Marguerite had died suddenly at the Bastille, aged only twenty-seven, leaving Besmaux a lonely, embittered, unbalanced figure. Besmaux suspected that d'Artagnan had slept with his wife and also hated him for his heroics in the Musketeers, the prestige of his post as their commander, the affection his men showed for him, and finally for the humiliation he had inflicted long ago on his fellow Gascon because of his inferior belt.

Louvois no doubt emphasized the need to ensure that no one would recognize d'Artagnan and that the prisoner's identity had to be kept from his guards. In wanting the Musketeer masked and silenced, Louvois did not envisage the Iron Mask, but unwittingly gave Besmaux an opportunity that he had never imagined would come his way, even in his wildest dreams. The governor of the Bastille seized the chance to take his revenge on d'Artagnan in the cruellest manner possible and at the same time to indulge his obsession with masks, to create one in metal, with all the ingredients of a story from the genre of Gothic horror.

The Bastille possessed its own forge and employed a smith, but Besmaux would have needed a craftsman with exceptional skills and tools for such an unusual task. It would have taken someone of outstanding ability to make a lockable steel mask that fully enclosed the head and d'Artagnan would have been forced to endure an agonizing fitting before the metal was properly cooled, so that it could still be hammered into its final shape.

Soon d'Artagnan, officially dead, was imprisoned in one of the worst cells in the Bastille, where no outsider could hear him or see his mask. These cold and damp octagonal vaults lay partly underground, their bare walls grey with mould, the ceiling a groined arch of brick from whose crumbling intersection dropped a perpetual shower of dust. The only furniture was a bench, a bed of straw and a bucket serving as a toilet that remained unemptied until it was full to overflowing. A vent, opening on to the moat, allowed in a feeble shaft of daylight. Whenever the Seine flooded, water gushed through the vent, eventually reaching the height of the palliasse but at least dispersing the rats.

If Besmaux visited his prisoner, it would have been only to inform him that all his worldly possessions were to be sold and predict that d'Artagnan himself would soon be but a faded memory. The erstwhile captain of Musketeers had no way of knowing that his servants, taking advantage of the rigorous French laws on property, had refused to cooperate with the commissioner sent by Louvois in search of sensitive papers kept at his rented house on the quai Malaquais. D'Artagnan had possessed many such documents, including some signed by ministers and the king, perhaps the evidence of his parentage supplied by Tréville, dating back to the arrest of Nicholas Fouquet in 1661. When a Paris notary finally gained access to his house on 22 December 1673, almost six months after d'Artagnan's alleged death at Maastricht, the civil lieutenant of Paris, Le Camus, glanced at the handwriting on several bundles of papers hidden in a closet. He could see from a few words on the outside wrappings that they related to Fouquet. On New Year's Eve Le Camus, having weighed up where his best interests lay, sent them unopened, not to Louvois but to his arch-enemy, Colbert.

Apart from these significant papers, d'Artagnan had little to show for a military career that stretched across more than thirty years. The inventory of his possessions valued them at barely 4,500 livres, which eloquently confirmed that d'Artagnan had never been for hire in an age when the whole world seemed for hire. D'Artagnan owned only a few pieces of furniture, some clothes in a chest, his precious Musketeer's mantle and two swords, one with a guard made of unpolished gold and a brass hilt, the other a menacing blade consisting entirely of black steel. In the courtyard stood his two elderly carriages — the larger with stylish windows, green damask curtains and plush green upholstery, the smaller with a single red damask seat behind a front panel of Venetian glass – sad souvenirs of his heady days living with a rich wife in the grand manner.

Madame d'Artagnan returned to Paris just long enough to decide to renounce any claim to her husband's goods and chattels, observing their title to be 'more onerous than profitable', which was certainly the case, as d'Artagnan predictably also had large debts. His elder brother Paul, who had made the long journey from Navarrenx to the capital to help settle d'Artagnan's affairs, was appointed honorary tutor to the Musketeer's two sons, aged thirteen and twelve; like Madame d'Artagnan, they had not seen their father for eight years. Three months later their long-postponed baptisms would take place, with the king and queen as godparents to the elder, the dauphin and the Grande Mademoiselle to the younger. Content that she had exploited d'Artagnan's fame just once, to give their offspring a helping hand in life, Madame d'Artagnan returned to her solitude at Chalon-sur-Saône, oblivious to her husband's true fate.

D'Artagnan slowly recovered from his injuries but might have remained locked in his mask until madness eventually consumed him. Besmaux wanted only to prolong his agony and would not kill his prisoner without a direct written order, which Louvois had no intention of providing. What saved d'Artagnan from this indefinite mental and physical torture was the successful escape of two men from the Bastille. This proved enough to persuade the nervous Louvois that d'Artagnan should be removed from Besmaux and handed over to Saint-Mars, in the belief that his secret would be safer in the remote surroundings of Pignerol.

Once out of Besmaux's clutches, despite Louvois' uncompromising orders, at Pignerol d'Artagnan could expect much better treatment from his former subordinate. Saint-Mars would have released the padlocks on his steel mask and removed it when he was safely in his cell. However, he could not dispense with the mask altogether: Saint-Mars knew that many of his troop were former Musketeers who would have recognized their former captain and might have been tempted to help him escape. Whenever d'Artagnan was allowed exercise, moved from place to place or had to be seen by outsiders, such as a doctor, he was made to wear the mask again.

Saint-Mars arrived at Cannes on the evening of 30 April 1687 and was rowed across to Sainte-Marguerite. D'Artagnan was ill, complaining that he had been all but suffocated underneath the oilskin covering his sedan chair. His health was not improved by his temporary accommodation on the island, a small cell previously occupied by a young chevalier, imprisoned for trying to rob his own father at the point of a pistol. Later, the Mask may have been taken by Saint-Mars to the notorious Château d'If, off Marseilles, a short sea journey along the coast, until his new prison was ready. Its most secure cell, with a suitable ante-chamber, is attributed to him. The Mask was known simply as 'La Tour', a codename derived from his original abode at Pignerol in the lower tower, *la tour d'en bas*.

At Sainte-Marguerite it took eight months to complete the new cell block. In January 1688, Saint-Mars could tell Louvois that the cells were:

> large, handsome and well lit, and as for their quality, I do not believe there could be any stronger and more secure in Europe. This is especially the case with regard to the risk of prisoners communicating orally with someone nearby or far off.

The jailer followed the pattern established at Exilles. Access was possible only via Saint Mars' private apartments and no fewer than four doors. The passageway was barred by an elaborate timber framework; reinforced with iron, it housed two separate doors, each with bolts and padlocks. D'Artagnan's cell itself had a double door, one opening outwards, the other inwards, consisting of thick hardwood, studded with iron, with provision on each for two bolts. The floor was paved in brick to prevent tunnelling. The inner walls were three feet thick, the outer six feet thick, pierced only by a single, large window, whose bottom edge was four feet from the ground. Three separate sets of uneven iron bars restricted the view to the distant shore; below the window was an unseen, sheer drop to rocks and the sea 100 feet below. Against the outer wall, a fireplace was provided on one side for colder days, and on the other, a privy. The cell measured twenty feet by fifteen feet, the equivalent today of a luxury hotel room across the water on the Croisette. Not quite Fouquet's grand apartment at Pignerol, perhaps, but by contemporary prison accommodation standards still remarkable.

D'Artagnan had no resources of his own, and Saint-Mars was obliged to buy new furniture for him at Sainte-Marguerite. The miserly jailer told Louvois:

> The prisoner's bed was so old and dilapidated, as was everything he possessed, the table linen as well as the furniture, that it was not worth the trouble of bringing it here . . . I received only thirteen écus for the lot.

In these more secure surroundings, however, Saint-Mars could allow d'Artagnan to take exercise, at first in the governor's secluded garden behind the cell block and his quarters, and later elsewhere. 'With relatively few precautions,' he suggested tentatively to Louvois on 8 January 1688, 'You can even have prisoners taking walks around the island without fear they might escape or give or receive any news.' Louvois did not object. The 'precautions' almost certainly included a steel mask, which had three functions: to hide the prisoner's identity, to make him almost inaudible if he spoke to someone whilst wearing it and to deter him from jumping into the sea.

Saint-Mars' officer, Blainvilliers, said that the prisoner

> often took walks and always with a mask on his face . . . he only wore this mask when he went out to take the air or when he had to appear in front of some stranger.

The king's lieutenant on the islands, Charles de Lamotte-Guérin, said that when the prisoner 'was ill or had need of a physician or surgeon, he was obliged on pain of death not to appear in their presence except in his mask of iron'. However, evidently the mask was easily removed, because when the prisoner 'was alone he could amuse himself by pulling out the hairs of his beard with tweezers of brightly polished steel'. According to Blainvilliers, the Mask was given the respect his military rank required:

> The governor and his officers remained standing in his presence until he [the prisoner] allowed them to put their hats on and sit down . . . they often kept him company and took their meals with him.

For almost two years, Saint-Mars and his men, about fifty-five in all, guarded their solitary prisoner. Soon, however, the jailer was asked to increase the capacity of his prison and in March 1689, Louvois sent the first of seven recalcitrant Protestant clergy to Sainte-Marguerite. These new arrivals apart, dispatches from Louvois grew more mundane, largely concerned with approving Saint-Mars' lavish expenses.

The minister had more pressing problems. Most unwisely, Louvois had strongly opposed the king in his wish to make public his marriage to Françoise Scarron, Madame de Maintenon. She had been secretly married to Louis since October 1683, following the death of the Queen. If Louis should persist, Louvois insisted, 'Remove me from my posts, put me in prison, rather than I see such an indignity.' His father, Chancellor Le Tellier, often the calming influence on both minister and king, had died in 1685, leaving Louvois isolated in the council. Despite Louvois' notorious outbursts, as long as the war went well, he remained almost untouchable; but France was no longer sweeping all before her on the battlefield. By concentrating on the pocket German states of the Rhineland, fearing interference from the emperor following the defeat of the Turks, Louis XIV had given William of Orange a precious breathing space. In 1688 William unexpectedly sailed from the United Provinces to England, catching the French fleet off balance in the Mediterranean, and seized the throne from the discredited Catholic, James II. Together, Dutch and English trading wealth could support a great military coalition and, for the first time, Louis found himself facing an army that matched his own. He continued to besiege Dutch and German cities but his resources were stretched almost to breaking point. In the same year, France created a militia, a tacit admission that the reservoir of full-time, professional soldiers was exhausted.

As the war began to go badly, Louis and Louvois fell out over everything. Louvois, by then also responsible for building works, quarrelled with the king over the quality of workmanship at Versailles. They squabbled over troop movements, the king sending the cavalry in one direction, Louvois bringing it back. Louis called him, sarcastically, that 'great man of war', and they had angry exchanges in the council, culminating in Louis' accusation that Louvois had issued orders without his authority. Louvois stormed out, saying, 'I no longer wish to concern myself with your affairs.'

For the minister to lose his temper was a daily event; for the king, it was extremely rare, and the idea that he might resort to actual violence was almost unthinkable. In the winter of 1688–9, the unthinkable happened. Inside Madame de Maintenon's apartments, where many affairs of state were conducted, Louis XIV seized a pair of glowing fire tongs from the grate and tried to attack Louvois. He would have succeeded had not Françoise interposed herself between them.

Saint-Simon suggested the incident was ignited by the burning of Trier without Louis' approval, but he admitted subsequently in his diary that the minister had still to transmit the order by that date. Something else quite extraordinary must have caused Louis to lose control, because Saint-Simon's explanations did not ring true. Trier's fortifications had been dismantled stone by stone five years previously, and it was one of many occupied places where atrocities were sanctioned on specific instructions from Versailles, of which Louis was fully aware. The wanton destruction of Trier was not of any special significance and could not explain such a spectacular quarrel.

Much more likely was that Louvois, sensing his days in

power were numbered, in a desperate effort to save himself, finally revealed that d'Artagnan was the secret prisoner on Sainte-Marguerite and that he knew Tréville was the king's real father. The ramifications of such a sensational story becoming public knowledge would have appalled Louis and could have provoked his violent reaction against Louvois. After the minister left Madame de Maintenon's apartments, it is easy to imagine the direction of the conversation between the monarch and his closest confidante. Their inevitable conclusion was that everyone would believe the king had personally given the order for the cruel imprisonment of his captain of Musketeers and, if d'Artagnan were released, he might wreak retribution by revealing everything he knew. To make public Françoise's unseemly early life and the naked participation in a black Mass of Athénaïs de Montespan, the mother of Louis' favourite children, would be bad enough; but should d'Artagnan assert that Tréville, not Louis XIII, was Louis's father, it would call into question the very legitimacy of the Sun King's rule. In Levi's view, the 'near certainty' that Louis XIV knew the truth and was forced into 'unremitting dissimulation' to keep it hidden, made him paranoid about his parentage. Even if d'Artagnan could be bribed with honours and stopped short of this ultimate disclosure, not a promising hypothesis, Louis and Françoise were afraid that the ensuing scandal would still bring down derision and scorn upon the king's head.

Louis must have been sorely tempted to dispose of d'Artagnan and eliminate the risk. However, in an age when hellfire was still taken literally as a punishment for the damned, the king may have shrunk from the idea of arranging his murder. He may equally have suspected that Saint-Mars would refuse to carry out any such order, both because of his past relationship with d'Artagnan and because the jailer knew that his livelihood depended upon his prisoner and his secret. Saint-Mars had no intention of killing the goose that laid the golden eggs.

So, by playing his strongest card in the king's presence and threatening to reveal the identity of the Iron Mask, Louvois saved himself for the time being; but he had simply postponed the inevitable. Servility and dependence were the only means of pleasing Louis and as Saint-Simon observed, 'Once a man had left that path there was no return for him.' As time passed, Louis probably came to realize that Louvois had as much to lose as he did by any disclosure: such an overbearing minister could scarcely claim he was just obeying orders. Rumours of his impending disgrace gathered momentum. Louvois took an unprecedented afternoon off but, heavily preoccupied, drove a coach and pair straight into Le Nôtre's ornamental lake at his palace of Meudon. He told Beringhem, the king's valet, he did not know whether Louis would be content with 'relieving me of my offices or whether he will put me in prison'. When Beringhem observed that the king had made similar empty threats to Louvois twenty times in ten years, Louvois responded, 'This time it's different, his mind is made up.'

On the morning of 16 July 1691, Louvois dictated and signed twenty-three letters. In the afternoon he worked with the king, who sent Louvois home at 4 p.m. because his minister complained of feeling unwell. Within a few hours Louvois was dead. His wife was convinced that Louvois had been poisoned, because the bottle of fresh water always kept by his desk was missing. At her request, the king reluctantly ordered an autopsy. It took place the following day, in the presence of five royal physicians, who concluded that Louvois had died of 'pulmonary apoplexy'. The doctors knew, however, that Louis XIV did not want to hear that persons unknown had poisoned a minister said by many to be on the point of public disgrace.

Saint-Simon watched the king closely after news of Louvois' demise reached him, and observed that he had 'a new lightness of step, as though a weight had been lifted from his shoulders'. Louis was overheard by one of his courtiers to observe it was no great loss, saying: 'If Monsieur de Louvois had not died promptly, you would have seen him lodged in the Bastille before two days were up.'

The war ministry went to Louvois' third son, the marquis de Barbezieux. This undoubtedly suited Louis, for Barbezieux was only twenty-three, younger even than his father when he took on the post, much more pliable and spectacularly idle. He was also accident prone. The following May, Barbezieux's courier would be given the wrong result of the naval battle of La Hogue, leaving Barbezieux to announce to the court a French victory over the combined English and Dutch fleets, when in fact it had ended in disaster, with most of the French warships set alight. Not long afterwards, fed up with Barbezieux's frequent excursions into Paris, the king would appoint seven new marshals of France without consulting his absentee war minister. 'Barbezieux', said Louis, 'will hear of these promotions on his rambles.'

Barbezieux almost certainly did not know the identity of the Mask in 1691. His father had no warning of his illness, if illness it was, and would not have shared the secret with him prematurely. Saint-Mars wrote to the war ministry on 26 July, immediately after learning of the death of Louvois. His letter is missing but we have Barbezieux's reply of 13 August:

> Whenever you have something to tell me about the prisoner who has been in your charge for twenty years, I ask you to use the same precautions that you used when you wrote to Monsieur de Louvois.

There is no record of Saint-Mars receiving any prisoner in 1671 who could have become, in due course, the Iron Mask, suggesting that Barbezieux did not possess precise information about how long he had been in captivity, but was relying on the limited knowledge of his officials. Nor, in any dignified fashion, could Barbezieux ask Saint-Mars in an official dispatch who this most secret of prisoners was. If he did not know d'Artagnan was the Mask, then the jailer was unlikely to tell him. Barbezieux would need to ask the king and the king had good reason, at least for the moment, to consider his young minister less than reliable.

Barbezieux had one advantage over his father: he did not have to contend with the formidable Madame Saint-Mars. Marie-Antoinette had died suddenly on 9 April 1691 and was buried in the garden of the monastery on Saint-Honorat, the other island in the jailer's tiny domain. Two years later Saint-Mars suffered a further bitter loss, when his elder son André was killed in action. In September 1693, Barbezieux wrote to Saint-Mars to say the king wanted to do something for him 'on the occasion of the loss of your son'. Not long afterwards, possibly in December, Barbezieux invited Saint-Mars to Paris. It would have been extraordinary if the minister did not try to discover the identity of the Mask during his jailer's visit, and the king may finally have decided to let Barbezieux into the secret.

Soon afterwards, Saint-Mars wanted to know what measures he could take whenever d'Artagnan misbehaved, hinting at a possible recent attempt to escape. On 8 January 1694, Barbezieux replied that he could use the same means that 'you brought to my attention when you and I spoke here'. This might have included subjecting d'Artagnan, as a punishment, to wearing his steel mask for prolonged periods. Barbezieux and Saint-Mars arranged a series of coded phrases concerning d'Artagnan, of which only they would know the meaning. Saint-Mars put something about them on paper on 21 January 1694, a dispatch subsequently destroyed. In his reply Barbezieux assured Saint-Mars that no one apart from him would see the jailer's letters.

In March 1694, Barbezieux issued an order to transfer to Sainte-Marguerite three prisoners, including Mattioli, from Pignerol, which was under increasing threat of attack by Savoy. Barbezieux wrote to Saint-Mars at the same time, suggesting that the jailer move some of his existing prisoners to different cells, so that the new arrivals could be given the most secure accommodation. He wrote: *'Comme vous savez qu'ils sont de plus de conséquence, au moins un, que ceux qui sont présentement aux iles.'* In the past this has been translated, 'As you know they are of more consequence, at least one of them, than those at present on the islands,' suggesting that the secret prisoner was less important than Mattioli. However it made much more sense if Barbezieux's dictation had been slightly misrecorded, and he in fact said '*à moins d'un*', that is, 'barring one' [the Mask], as in, '*à moins d'accidents*', 'barring accidents'.

In December 1695 Barbezieux wrote to Saint-Mars, asking what arrangements he had made for the prisoners if he were sick or absent, so that 'the king can issue corresponding orders for such an eventuality'. Louis was now obsessively concerned with d'Artagnan's security, as Saint-Mars must have appreciated, for his response on 6 January 1696 was long and detailed:

> You ask me to tell you what arrangements are made when I am away or sick with regard to the daily visits and the precautions regarding the prisoners in my custody. My two lieutenants serve meals at fixed times in the way they have seen me do so and as I very often still do when I am feeling well. Here is how, Monseigneur. My senior lieutenant takes the keys to the cell of my *ensien prisonnier* with whom he begins. He opens the three doors and enters the room of the prisoner, who duly hands him the dishes and plates, which he has piled one on top of the other. My lieutenant has only to pass two doors to hand them to one of my sergeants who puts them on a table two steps away, where my second lieutenant, who inspects everything going in and out of the prison, makes certain there is nothing written on any of the dishes. After he [the prisoner] has been given all that he needs, they proceed by checking in and under the bed, then the bars of the window . . . and the privy. They make a complete search of the cell and very often a body-search as well.

In the same long dispatch intended for the king, Saint-Mars reported that one of 'the prisoners of consequence', almost certainly d'Artagnan, had 'attempted to bribe the washerwomen'. However, said Saint-Mars with some satisfaction, 'they were unable to do what was asked of them' because he had the linen soaked and the whole laundry process closely supervised. Twice a week the prisoners were 'made to change the table linen as well as the shirts and body linen they use'. The clean linen was given to them, the old linen 'taken back and counted after it has all been checked'. Warming to his theme, Saint-Mars continued:

> One must be on one's guard about the candles, too . . . I found some in which the wick had been replaced with paper . . . I used to send for some to Turin, to shops which were not suspect . . . Ribbons leaving the prisoners' cells are also dangerous, because they write on them as they do on their linen, without any one noticing it.

The first part of the second page of Saint-Mars' original letter may have held some clue to the identity of the Iron Mask because it was subsequently burnt, leaving only a few letters visible:

en
l'hon
quy
l y a
quy a leurs

The letter ended:

> As a final precaution, surprise visits are paid to the prisoners, at irregular hours of the day or night, and it is frequently discovered that they have written messages on their dirty laundry. No one else is given an opportunity to read what they write, however, as you know from the pieces I have sent you.

Saint-Mars painted a picture of a battle of wits between himself and his prisoners, who made many attempts to communicate with the outside world. According to stories handed down to descendants of the garrison's officers, d'Artagnan twice almost succeeded.

A barber attached to Saint-Mars' company was looking for shellfish by the shore when in the distance he saw a white bundle floating in the water under the window of d'Artagnan's cell. The barber managed to retrieve it from the sea and discovered the object was a fine linen shirt, covered in line after line of writing. He took the shirt to Saint-Mars, who was extremely agitated, and asked the barber if he had read what it said. The barber hastily said he had not, but two days later he was mysteriously found dead in his room in the barracks.

On another occasion, d'Artagnan used a knife to scratch a message on one of his dishes and threw it out of his window into the sea; it was picked up by a solitary fisherman, who, instead of returning to Cannes, took the dish to the governor. Saint-Mars asked him who had seen the plate and whether he had read what was written on it. 'No one else has seen it,' replied the fisherman, who, unlike the barber, proved to be illiterate. Saint-Mars sent him on his way, saying, 'Count yourself fortunate that you cannot read.' As the three sets of bars in the Mask's cell were fixed at different levels, it looks almost impossible to penetrate all of them with a silver dish, however small, from whatever angle it might be thrown; but d'Artagnan, a determined man with endless time on his hands, apparently succeeded, against all the odds.

15

THE BIOGRAPHER'S TALE

O n 18 December 1698, Besmaux, governor of the Bastille for almost forty years, died after a long illness, leaving his estates and 600,000 livres in cash to his daughter, who could inherit his fortune but not his post. The governorship, the pinnacle of a jailer's profession, immediately became the subject of intense interest at court, for it was both prestigious and highly lucrative. The governor's annual salary was 21,608 livres, but his profit came in supplying food and furnishings on a fixed daily tariff according to each prisoner's rank: fifty livres for a prince, thirty-six for a marshal of France, fifteen for a councillor in the Parlement, ten for a priest, all the way down to three livres for valet. Besmaux had milked the system for all it was worth, realizing that his knowledge of d'Artagnan's grotesque imprisonment and the true identity of the king's father made him irremovable. The odds were immense against the vacancy created by his death going to someone of common stock in charge of an obscure island prison at the outer extremities of the kingdom, with no visible influence at court; but as always, Saint-Mars held the trump card, the Man in the Iron Mask.

Ironically, the jailer did not really want the job. He was seventy-two years old, set in his ways, and had lost both his wife and his elder son, the apple of his eye. The dead hand of Madame Saint-Mars continued to exert its influence, however. A few years earlier Marie-Antoinette had sent their younger son, Bénigne, to visit her sister Marie in Paris, and whilst there he fell in love with the daughter of Desgranges, secretary to the comte de Pontchartrain, financial controller at the treasury. Desgranges was responsible for ensuring the cavalry had enough feed for their horses, a task that took him from time to time to the Bastille, where in wartime large stocks were kept. He heard for himself the rumour and counter-rumour of who might follow Besmaux as governor and realized that Bénigne's wealthy father, Saint-Mars, could be a potential candidate.

Pontchartrain and Barbezieux belonged to rival dynasties of ministers and public servants. They were engaged in a fierce power struggle at court, and the tremors could be felt even at the distance of Sainte-Marguerite, where Pontchartrain asserted responsibility for the imprisoned Protestant pastors and Barbezieux for the rest. A year earlier, in a pointed dispatch, Barbezieux had ordered Saint-Mars not to answer a query from Pontchartrain about the Mask. 'You have only to watch over the security of your prisoners', he said, 'without ever explaining to anyone what it is your long standing prisoner did.'

Meanwhile Marie's husband, Dufresnoy, Madame Saint-Mars' brother-in-law, who had risen high up the war ministry, was urging Saint-Mars to put his hat in the ring for the governorship of the Bastille. Saint-Mars accordingly had an advocate in both camps and was probably the only candidate on whom Barbezieux and Pontchartrain could agree.

Even then, on 1 May 1698 Barbezieux felt compelled to write an obsequious letter to Saint-Mars, begging him to take the post. He pointed out that the new governor would make a 'considerable' profit from his prisoners and 'would have the pleasure of being in Paris, gathered there with his family and friends, instead of being stuck at the end of the kingdom'. Barbezieux added, 'You know your own best interests, and the King won't make you accept the post if it doesn't suit you.' Saint-Mars could read between the lines. Realizing it did not pay to cross the king, he accepted the offer.

Louis took his time confirming Saint-Mars' appointment. He might have been piqued by the jailer's earlier vacillation but, much more likely, he was busy planning the war game to end all war games. In July almost 60,000 troops, including fifty battalions of foot, fifty-two squadrons of cavalry and forty artillery pieces, began to assemble near Compiègne for a mock siege of the chateau.

'I have been a long time in replying to the letter you took the trouble to write to me on the eighth of last month,' explained Barbezieux to Saint-Mars,

> because the King did not explain to me his intentions sooner. His Majesty saw with pleasure that you had decided to come to the Bastille as its governor. You can make your preparations to be ready to leave as soon as I instruct you to do so, and to bring with you your longstanding prisoner, with all possible security.

Some historians have seen in the grammatical construction of this last sentence, '*Vous pourrez disposer*', the suggestion that Saint-Mars had the option not to bring his secret prisoner with him, downgrading the Mask's significance. However, Barbezieux often used a deferential tone to Saint-Mars and in reality was no more giving the jailer a choice of when to make preparations to depart than he was of allowing Saint-Mars to choose whether or not to take d'Artagnan with him to the Bastille. If the king had no need of the Mask, he had no need of Saint-Mars either.

On 19 July 1698, Saint-Mars received the king's command to transfer his prisoner, taking precautions 'to prevent him being seen or revealing his identity to anyone'. In August Barbezieux added:

> His Majesty has not judged it necessary to send the order you requested to arrange lodgings along your route to Paris, and it will be sufficient for you [to] find and pay for the most convenient and secure accommodation in the places you decide to stay.

Saint-Mars' prisoner remained as important as ever, but the royal coffers were empty, forcing economies everywhere. The strain of keeping huge armies on four different fronts was enormous: 80,000 in Flanders, 40,000 in the Rhineland, another 40,000 in Italy and 20,000 in Catalonia. France was ravaged by famine, her people starving and exhausted, her soldiers' wages far in arrears. When the king said the new governor of the Bastille should 'find and pay' for accommodation for his men and his prisoner on the way to Paris, he meant it literally.

On 1 September Saint-Mars left Sainte-Marguerite for the last time. He had learned the lesson of the glimpse given of the masked d'Artagnan at Grasse and ordered the villagers of Riez, at a key junction in Provence, to turn their backs as his cortege passed. True to character, with his expenses unpaid, the jailer planned to spend at least two nights on the road in accommodation that would not cost him anything. The first was at the Pierre-Cize prison in Lyon, the second near Villeneuve-sur-Yonne at his own estate of Palteau, which Saint-Mars almost certainly had never previously visited.

At Palteau, the peasants lined up in awe to greet their *seigneur*, who arrived in the second of two litters, accompanied by several men on horseback. The first litter contained the man in the mask, made apparently of black velvet, not steel, which d'Artagnan wore whenever he crossed the courtyard of the chateau. The peasants could see only that he was tall and had a shock of white hair; just his teeth and lips were visible beneath his mask. He positioned himself with his back to the window for supper with Saint-Mars, who sat with two loaded pistols on his side of the table; even at seventy-five years of age, d'Artagnan was still considered a threat. Saint-Mars' nervous cook carried each course to an ante-chamber, from where the jailer went to collect it, always closing the door to the dining room behind him. Jailer and prisoner spent the night in the room at the top of the chateau's solitary tower, Saint-Mars sleeping in a cot placed alongside d'Artagnan's bed.

The source of this description of the Mask's brief visit to Palteau was Saint-Mars' great nephew, who inherited the chateau. It was not of course a first-hand account, but the estate workers had told him the story when he was a boy, recollecting in detail what was probably the most memorable happening in their otherwise uneventful lives.

Saint-Mars wrote ahead to Étienne Du Junca, the king's lieutenant at the Bastille, ordering him to prepare the third room in the Bertaudière Tower for his prisoner. Du Junca was second in command of the Bastille from October 1690 to August 1706. Originally a 'soldier of fortune' from Bordeaux, who knew at first hand how a *lettre de cachet* could consign a prisoner to perpetual captivity at the stroke of a pen, Du Junca covered himself by keeping a meticulous journal of everything that happened at the Bastille, dating each entry. In one he recorded the arrival at the Bastille in 1698 of Saint-Mars and his special prisoner:

> On Thursday 18 September, at 3 o'clock in the afternoon, M. de Saint-Mars, governor of the Bastille, arrived from the islands of Sainte-Marguerite and Honorat to take up his appointment, bringing with him in his litter a long term prisoner he had with him in Pignerol, and whose name must never be spoken; the prisoner, always kept masked, was placed in the first room of the Basinière Tower until nightfall, then at 9 p.m. I moved him to the third room of the Bertaudière Tower that I had furnished before his arrival, in accordance with instructions received from M. de Saint-Mars . . . I was accompanied by the sieur Rosargues, whom M. de Saint-Mars brought with him and who will serve and look after the prisoner. The governor will be responsible for his upkeep.

Two drawbridges and three gates barred entry into the main courtyard of the Bastille, enclosed by six of the towers. Du Junca may not have seen the new arrivals until after they had left the governor's residence, which was located outside the great keep. He mentioned only one litter, whereas Saint-Mars had started out with two, and would have had no reason to make the final leg of his journey more uncomfortable by discarding it. Nor did Du Junca record whether the prisoner's mask was made of steel or black velvet, although he was to refer to a velvet mask five years later. In the streets of Paris, Saint-Mars probably used the steel mask until his prisoner was safely locked in a cell, then substituted the velvet mask.

D'Artagnan was allowed to visit the chapel. Six weeks later, Pontchartrain, who had evidently won the battle with Barbezieux for control of the prisoner, informed Saint-Mars that the king agrees that 'your prisoner from Provence makes his confession and takes communion whenever you judge proper.' A Bastille chaplain who spoke to contemporaries said the prisoner was made to wear a mask 'only when he crossed the courtyard of the Bastille to go to mass, so that he was not recognized by the guards'.

In his cell, except when he had outside visitors, d'Artagnan remained unmasked. An English surgeon, a patron of Procope, left his fellow coffee-drinkers an enduring anecdote of the day when he was sent to bleed a prisoner in the Bastille. The governor, Saint-Mars, took him to see a man whose face, and quite possibly his steel mask, was completely hidden by a huge towel knotted behind his head. The prisoner complained of a severe headache. The surgeon thought the man spoke French with an English accent, but it could just as easily have been someone with a provincial dialect, such as d'Artagnan's first language, Bernes.

Using the registers of the Bastille held in the national archives, Iung made a careful analysis of d'Artagnan's fellow inmates at the beginning of 1699. Nineteen could be easily accounted for, seven women, mainly prostitutes, and twelve men. Iung also found evidence of *un inconnu*, an unknown, whom Iung believed to be a Protestant galley captain accused of betraying naval secrets, but according to Du Junca's meticulous journal, this captain had been released in October 1697. The real anonymous twentieth prisoner of the Bastille was far more fascinating: he was Gatien de Courtilz, sieur de Sandras, the author of the *Mémoires de Monsieur d'Artagnan*.

Courtilz went to such lengths to conceal his identity that the authorities were unsure of his real name. His family, originally from Liège, had both money and titles. Courtilz was born in Paris in rue de l'Université, probably about 1644, although, according to Du Junca, in 1702 Courtilz gave his age as fifty-five, which would have placed his birth in 1646 or 1647. He started out as a common private in the regiment of Champagne, eventually becoming its captain; in the early 1670s he commanded the French rearguard in an action inside Spanish territory on the Col de Bagnols. In 1678, when Courtilz married for the second time, he gave his occupation as captain of the Beaupré regiment. However, a year later he was dismissed from the army in disgrace and fell heavily into debt; he avoided prison in 1682 only because his wife, Louise Pannetier, bound herself to repay his creditors.

It was then that Courtilz embarked on his second career as a writer of pamphlets, political tracts and biographies, more than one hundred works in all, largely printed outside France to escape censorship. Embittered by the way he had been treated, he attacked Louis XIV in four different publications, calling him 'Le Grand Alcandre', a reference to Corneille's comedy of 1636, *L'Illusion Comique*, in which the old sorcerer, Alcandre, lives in a cave with his deaf and dumb servants. The Sun King would not have liked the analogy.

Courtilz also began to write a series of political testaments, supposedly the work of prominent statesmen, including Mazarin, Colbert and Louvois. They were not, as Courtilz claimed, their own memoirs and it remains uncertain how much of their contents were reliable attributions. They proved nonetheless highly popular and were reprinted many times, mainly in Amsterdam and The Hague, Courtilz's main base. Courtilz might have remained safely in Holland had he not also written a commentary on the Franco-Dutch war that cast his hosts in unfavourable light. Believing it prudent to return to France until the fuss had died down, for some time Courtilz stayed comfortably ahead of all his pursuers. In 1693, however, two booksellers were arrested for possessing copies of his anonymous banned books and the French police stumbled across an unfinished letter written by one of them, thanking Courtilz for his services; it included his address in Paris. Courtilz was renting a room in the rue de Berry and was on the point of returning to Holland when police chief La Reynie ordered his arrest. The warrant described Courtilz as 'a dangerous manufacturer of libels, full of atrocious calumnies against France, its government and its ministers', and on 22 April he was taken to the Bastille. Governor Besmaux was told that 'a close watch should be kept on him,' and upon hearing the news of Courtilz's arrest, Pontchartrain scrawled a single word on the report: '*bon*'.

Courtilz's wife Louise obtained permission to see her husband 'only once, with a guard present'. However, Madame Courtilz had considerable influence through her father, the secretary of a prominent government official, and within a year she was allowed to see her husband two or three times a week to talk about domestic matters. In June 1696, Courtilz obtained '*la liberté de la cour*', freedom to go more or less where he liked within the Bastille's walls, and twice in 1697 Madame Courtilz asked permission from Besmaux to give her husband 'family documents' for his comments. Besmaux referred the second request to La Reynie, but in such terms that it was almost certainly granted. After that, Courtilz was probably allowed to pass any amount of papers he wished back and forth.

Courtilz used his time profitably to start a series of works based almost entirely on information supplied by fellow inmates, the memoirs of J.B. La Fontaine, the duc de Tirconnel and the marquis de Montbrun, a highly significant *modus operandi* that established the precedent for the memoirs of d'Artagnan.

Jean-Baptiste La Fontaine, a minor French nobleman, held the rank of brigadier in a French expeditionary force sent to Ireland but his ship was intercepted by a British frigate. In return for his freedom he was persuaded to become a spy, only to be betrayed by his lover, the mistress of another enemy agent. Using the name Fontenay, he was arrested on Louvois' orders on 27 December 1689 and taken to the Bastille. The warrant described him as 'slightly built, with a sabre scar on his cheek'. La Fontaine's memoirs portray him as 'small . . . carrying the scar of a wound above the eye', close enough – given that the police description was of a man not yet under arrest – to confirm that La Fontaine and Fontenay were one and the same person. Courtilz's account of La Fontaine's adventures, including those as an accomplished duellist, tallies with all known facts about him. It ends in 1697 with La Fontaine lying, half-crippled from rheumatism, in a damp, dark cell. According to Du Junca's journal, he was released from the Bastille on 31 December that year. As Courtilz's book was published in 1698, it must have been smuggled out of the Bastille by his wife Louise, for Courtilz himself was not released for another twelve months.

La Fontaine was also one of two sources for Courtilz's memoirs of the Duke of Tirconnel, his commanding officer in Ireland. The other was the duke's natural son, Richard Talbot, held at the Bastille between March 1696 and December 1697, and to whom Courtilz specifically refers in his 1701 work, *Les Annales de la Cour*. A notice of intended publication placed in another example of Courtilz's prolific output from prison, *Elite des Nouvelles*, which appeared in 1698, showed that the Tirconnel memoirs were almost complete.

According to Courtilz's biographer, Benjamin Woodbridge, both La Fontaine and Talbot may also have provided him with some leads for a third memoir, that of Pierre, marquis de Montbrun. The illegitimate son of the duc de Bellegarde and a pretty Parisian pattissière in the rue Saint-André des Arts known to be free with her favours, Pierre went to seek his fortune in England. He made a great deal of money by betting on himself to beat all comers at real tennis, winning consistently by a combination of skill and gamesmanship. His impecunious father was more than happy to legitimize Pierre in return for a payment of 50,000 livres. Taking the title of Montbrun on his marriage to Anne de Rogers, Pierre soon found that his wife had been unfaithful with the marquis de Villandry. He forced the marquis into a duel in the place Royale by slapping his face

during a service at Notre Dame, and was sent to the Bastille
not for duelling but for blasphemy.

However, the most significant elements of Montbrun's life
are repeated in the memoirs of d'Artagnan, who would have
known a great deal more than La Fontaine and Talbot about
the marquis, his contemporary in Paris when Montbrun and
Cavoie held the valuable concession for sedan chairs. And if
d'Artagnan was Courtilz's primary source for the memoirs of
Montbrun, he must also have been his primary source for the
Gascon's own memoirs.

Twenty-five years had elapsed since d'Artagnan's last military
campaign, the siege of Maastricht, and outside the senior ranks
of the armed forces he was long since forgotten. There is no
evidence that Courtilz had met d'Artagnan during his military
career and Courtilz was never a Musketeer. Courtilz showed
no signs of husbanding information on potential subjects for
future use, let alone a quarter of a century after the event.
Nor was there any obvious reason why Courtilz should choose
d'Artagnan as a subject in 1698 or at all, unless, as with La
Fontaine, he had an immediate and readily accessible source of
information. It could not have existed in documentary form.
Almost all libraries remained in private hands; no one had
previously attempted a biography of d'Artagnan; and in any
case, Courtilz was locked up in the Bastille.

The dictionary compiler, Pierre Bayle, indignantly said that
d'Artagnan had not written a single word of his memoirs. This
was true enough, but prompted the question of where their
contents had come from. Some historians claimed that Courtilz
created the work entirely from his own imagination but this
would have been a formidable task, in view of the extent to
which d'Artagnan's experiences were interwoven with real
events and people. Arthur de Boislisle, editor of Saint-Simon's
diaries; Jules Lair, author of the definitive biography on Fouquet;
and Charles Samaran, who undertook a great deal of original
research on the Three Musketeers, all rejected the cynical view
that the memoirs were pure fiction. Samaran concluded that,

'not only on general events, but on the deeds and actions of individuals, there are amazingly accurate details.'

In the memoirs Courtilz made the first known reference to Athos, Aramis and Porthos, whom everyone wrongly claimed to be fictional characters. Dumas, despite finding the Three Musketeers in Courtilz's book, brazenly asserted them to be 'bastards of my imagination'. Their opponents in the famous duel with the Cardinal's Guards were also shown to have existed. The only credible explanation is that Courtilz, as with his memoirs of La Fontaine, Tirconnel and Montbrun, had a prime source of information among the prisoners in the Bastille; but none of his nineteen fellow inmates listed in the prison register had the remotest connection with d'Artagnan. That left the sole prisoner not accounted for, the Man in the Iron Mask, confirming, given the wealth of detail he supplied, that he could only be d'Artagnan himself.

Courtilz and d'Artagnan were prisoners in the Bastille for a period of nearly five and a half months from September 1698 to March 1699. Courtilz's cell was the 'first room' in the chapel tower, probably on the ground floor, where he would have seen d'Artagnan close at hand on his way to the chapel. As Courtilz had a good deal of freedom within the prison, he could soon have found a means whereby the two men could regularly communicate, using one of the many holes in the walls, floors and ceilings made by earlier prisoners or, more likely, a common chimney.

His memoirs of Tirconnel, although almost complete, were abandoned; those of Montbrun were left unfinished. Once Courtilz decided to write d'Artagnan's memoirs he had no time to lose, because Courtilz was also trying to obtain his own release. He possessed powerful friends in high places, amongst them a baron who presented incoming ambassadors to Louis XIV at Versailles. On 18 January 1699, an unsigned letter, believed to have been written by Pontchartrain, ordered the Paris police to interview Courtilz, to see where he would reside if released, and what assurances he would give concerning his loyalty to the king. Courtilz evidently provided all the right answers because on 28 February the new governor, Saint-Mars, received an order for his release. The signature is missing but the letter probably came from Pontchartrain. It was subject to two conditions: Courtilz had to leave Paris '*incessement*', 'almost immediately', and could not approach within twenty leagues of the city.

Courtilz was freed on 2 March, probably without any prior warning. His conversations with d'Artagnan might have remained incomplete, or he might have found the ageing Musketeer rambling and incoherent, which would explain why his memoirs contain almost nothing about d'Artagnan's early life, whereas those of La Fontaine and Montbrun began with their birth. Many of d'Artagnan's disclosures are more like confidences between intimate friends, especially concerning his relationship with women and his sexual performance, suggesting that the Musketeer had no idea that what he was saying to Courtilz was destined to appear in print.

Throughout his imprisonment, d'Artagnan was constantly reminded by his jailer, Saint-Mars, that if he disclosed his identity to any other person he would immediately be killed. D'Artagnan seems to have taken this threat literally. A cashier locked up for embezzlement was allocated the room below d'Artagnan, and the pair held a conversation by shouting up and down a common fireplace chimney. Asked to reveal his name, d'Artagnan replied that it would cost both of them their lives if he did so. It sees unlikely that d'Artagnan told Courtilz directly who he was, but given the extent of the prisoner's knowledge about the erstwhile captain of the Musketeers, Courtilz must surely have guessed. No doubt Courtilz intended to ask d'Artagnan what had happened to him during and after the siege of Maastricht, but to do so before he had put the finishing touches to his initial account of d'Artagnan's earlier life risked losing his trust. Courtilz was released from the Bastille before he could press him further.

Courtilz' biography was published anonymously under the

title of *Mémoires de M. D'Artagnan, Capitaine-Lieutenant de la première Compagnie des Mousquetaires du Roi*. The subtitle claimed that the work included '*Particulières et Secrettes {sic} Qui se sont passées sous le Regne de Louis le Grand*' ('Peculiarities and Secrets which have happened during the Reign of Louis the Great [XIV]'). All three volumes of the first edition carry the year 1700 in Roman numerals, although the third volume almost certainly did not appear until the following year. The title-page claimed that the work had been printed in Cologne but this was probably a ruse to make it difficult for Louis XIV's agents to track down the printer. He is given as Pierre Marteau and in later editions as Pierre Rouge, but both names were false, the invention of the Elzeviers, a family of Dutch printers based in Leiden.

In 1701, Courtilz and d'Artagnan were reunited within the walls of the Bastille, but scarcely in a way that Courtilz would have wished. A police report indicated that although Courtilz had managed to 'enter Paris whenever he wished by secret routes', he had been under surveillance for some time. The police, actively looking for Courtilz since the publication of the first two volumes of d'Artagnan's memoirs, had an informant in Rotterdam who kept them apprised of Courtilz's movements. Although the informer's letters were unsigned, German historian Herman Runge believed him to be Courtilz's old adversary, Bayle.

After returning to Paris, unaware they were being watched, Courtilz, his sister-in-law and his brother took rooms in the rue de Cléry on the second floor above an upholsterers and openly hawked copies of his books around the shops on the quai des Augustins. The police may have delayed making their move until they could be certain of seizing all of Courtilz's unpublished material as well as the writer himself; finally on 27 July Courtilz was rearrested, returned to the Bastille and locked in the Bertaudière Tower. Instead of the comfortable room provided for his earlier imprisonment, the author of d'Artagnan's memoirs was thrown in the lower dungeon, where he was to remain chained in solitary confinement among the rats and the squalor for more than nine years. Saint-Mars took no more chances with the biographer who had produced three volumes on the captain of the Musketeers, telling his story to 1673: what if it were to be brought up to date in a fourth?

D'Artagnan also remained in the Bertaudière Tower, but on 6 March he had been moved – perhaps as part of Saint-Mars' regular security measures – from the third floor. He was switched to one of two cells on the second floor and, in recording this in his journal, Du Junca said two other inmates were imprisoned 'with the ancient prisoner, both well locked in'. Historian Frantz Funk-Brentano believed this to mean that they were all sharing one cell, and that this was an indication of the declining importance of the Mask. However, his fellow historian Jean-Christian Petitfils thought it was simply a careless note, and that Du Junca intended to say that they were sharing a different cell to the Mask but on the same floor.

In September, an Italian prisoner escaped from the Bastille. The mortified Saint-Mars wrote to Pontchartrain expressing his profuse apologies but he need not have worried. The king, who often made Saint-Mars welcome at court, was concerned only about d'Artagnan. Pontchartrain replied from Versailles on 18 September:

> I have read your letter to the King; you need not take so much to heart the escape of the sieur Boselli; it's unfortunate, but it's not the first time something like this has happened at the Bastille. His Majesty is too persuaded of your faithfulness and zeal to believe this accident happened as a result of your negligence, since every [precaution] that can be taken has been taken by you. So you should calm yourself and you can come to see the king whenever you wish. He will receive you with his customary kindness.

During 1701 Pontchartrain handed over responsibility for d'Artagnan to Michel Chamillart, the new war minister. The following year Chamillart was also responsible for persuading one of his spies, Constantin de Renneville, to return from Holland to France, with the promise of a pension and a fresh assignment. However, on 16 May 1702 Renneville, a Protestant from Normandy, was arrested as a double agent and taken to the Bastille.

Renneville wrote prolifically during his imprisonment, writing in the spaces between the lines of type in books, a small bone for a pen, and soot deposits from a lamp mixed with red wine to make ink. For much of his sentence he was treated extremely harshly, which means that the cameos of his tormentors he preserved for later publication were scarcely objective but, for all that, they seem to have a solid basis of truth. He said Saint-Mars was a 'thin little old man, very deaf, whose head and hands and whole body shook constantly'. Saint-Mars' nephew, Formanoir de Corbé, was equally small, 'bent double with knock-kneed legs . . . unpleasant-looking and very shabbily dressed', dirty, unshaven, with rotten teeth and a deformed body, constantly answering his uncle back. Corbé had with him his illegitimate son, Jacques la France, described by Renneville as 'one of the most vicious and evil characters' in the entire prison. The chief turnkey, L'Ecuyer, could neither read nor write. He had a hump back and no neck, with a dark red face 'like the mask of a devil in an opera'. His subordinate, Antoine Ru, stole the prisoners' food, never washed or changed his clothes, had unkempt hair and smelt 'worse than the dirtiest goat'.

The guard appointed to look after d'Artagnan, Jacques Rosargues, known as 'the major' but actually a sergeant, was perpetually drunk, his face bloated and discoloured, ugly and ignorant; he was called by Renneville 'the monster'. The prisoners' confessor, Abbé Giraut, was 'Saint-Mars' pet'. Coughing continuously, a notorious lecher, he easily manipulated the governor. The abbé recommended the appointment of Abraham Reilhe as the Bastille's surgeon, although he had been a barber pure and simple in a regiment of foot, and proved completely incompetent. Apart from Reilhe, all of them had worked for Saint-Mars on Sainte-Marguerite, and some for much longer. When Renneville arrived at the Bastille, L'Ecuyer had been with the governor for thirty-two years, Rosargues for thirty-one, and Corbé for eighteen. Those of Saint-Mars' staff with any talent had been promoted to other prisons, leaving the dregs behind.

Chamillart apparently had a twinge of conscience, because he put in a good word for Renneville, who at first was given good food and a comfortable room. He had breakfast with Saint-Mars, whom Renneville said was dirty, unshaven, and wore a threadbare coat, frayed trousers, a decaying wig and a decrepit hat. The governor swore continuously and told Renneville some fantastic tales of his early exploits as a Musketeer, including one when he said he had picked a quarrel with some Dutchmen, killed four and disarmed three. Saint-Mars also claimed to have won a joust in Lisbon and a bullfight in Madrid, and he invited Renneville to join him on his forthcoming expedition to India to rescue a princess. At seventy-six, he was already showing severe signs of physical and mental deterioration.

Chamillart himself could scarcely have failed to notice Saint-Mars' condition, which called into serious question his ability to look after d'Artagnan. A governor who impulsively invited Renneville on an expedition to India was just as capable of deciding to take his secret prisoner with him as well. Probably after consulting the king, with whom he played billiards three evenings a week, Chamillart decided it was time to remove d'Artagnan from Saint-Mars' charge. His opportunity came on 10 November 1703, when Saint-Mars' younger son Bénigne, aged twenty-four, was badly injured in a cavalry charge at the Battle of Spire on the Rhine and taken to a field hospital at Landau. Saint-Mars set out to see his son the moment the news reached him. He allowed his son's leg to be amputated on 23 November because gangrene had set it, but, having lost a lot of blood, Bénigne did not survive the operation.

While Saint-Mars was away, d'Artagnan also died. At least, this was what Du Junca noted in his journal on Monday, 19 November:

The unknown prisoner, always wearing a black velvet mask
. . . died today at ten o'clock in the evening, having felt just
a little unwell after Mass the previous day. As death took him
unawares, he did not receive the sacraments, but our chaplain,
Monsieur Girault [sic], exhorted him to confess his sins before
he died.

Hitherto historians have given equal weight to each entry in
Du Junca's journal, failing to distinguish between the primary
sources, where he witnessed and participated in actual events,
and the secondary sources, where he was told about what
had happened by others. In 1703 Du Junca had no access to
d'Artagnan and, unlike his description of the Mask's arrival at
the Bastille five years previously, this account of his death and
burial was based entirely on hearsay. It cannot be reconciled
with other contemporary evidence, which points to d'Artagnan
remaining very much alive. Renneville found Du Junca
'helpful, agreeable, and honest', which set him apart from
the motley crew employed by Saint-Mars, who would have
had no compunction about deceiving Du Junca and faking
d'Artagnan's death for a second time, if the price were right.
It was the only way Chamillart could make certain Saint-Mars
would not make a fuss about losing his most prized prisoner,
and embarrassing the king.

The following day, as darkness fell, the funeral procession
for the fake burial left the Bastille by the little postern gate.
They passed beneath the sombre towers of the fortress, their
way lit by torches. Any stray passers-by gave them a wide
berth. Afterwards Du Junca added two further comments to
his journal.

This unknown prisoner, who has been in custody for such a long
time, was buried at 4 o'clock in the Saint Paul's cemetery in our
parish. In the register of deaths they also gave him a name of
little account that Major Rosargues and M. Reil [sic] certified
by signing the register.

Then, in a postscript: 'I have since learned that on the register he was called M. de Marchiel and that forty livres were paid for his burial.'

Later the writer Germain de Saint-Foix, whose shortcomings as a dramatist were rarely exposed because of his reputation as a duellist, was told by prison officers that the body interred at Saint-Paul's cemetery was definitely not that of the Mask. He said, 'The day after the burial someone bribed the gravedigger to exhume the body, and when they opened the coffin, in place of the head they found a large stone.' This elaborate chicanery was designed to convince Du Junca that the Mask was dead, and to persuade the governor, too, on his return.

Saint-Mars, distraught at the death of his son, had no reason to suspect that d'Artagnan's death was anything but genuine. To aid the deception, the Musketeer was moved to a different cell, possibly in the Well Tower. It may have been here that Renneville accidentally caught sight of d'Artagnan in 1705, when the jailer's staff bundled him out of a room containing the secret prisoner. D'Artagnan was made to turn his back, so Renneville saw neither his face nor the mask, although he could have glimpsed the knot and broad strands of black velvet behind his head that kept it in place. Afterwards the garrulous turnkey, Ru, told the curious Renneville that the mystery man 'had been a prisoner for thirty-one years and had been brought with him by Monsieur de Saint-Mars from the island of Saint[e]-Marguerite'. 'Thirty-one' was clearly not an approximation and it correctly dated the year d'Artagnan arrived at Pignerol as 1674.

Because Renneville had asked questions about the mysterious prisoner, he was thrown into one of the Bastille's worse dungeons, put on bread and water, and made to sleep on the stones and mire of his cell. By the time his special punishment ended, his nose had swollen to the size of a cucumber, half his teeth had fallen out, his mouth was a mass of sores, and his bones came through his skin in more than twenty places. After eleven years in the fortress, he was sent into exile. Renneville settled in England, where King George I in due course would provide the pension that France had denied him. He set about writing an account of his experiences, entitled in brief the 'French Inquisition, or the History of the Bastille'. It is particularly meticulous in its use of names, events and dates. Soon after his book appeared in print – with its reference to seeing the masked prisoner in 1705, two years after d'Artagnan's second supposed death – Renneville was attacked in a London street by three cut-throats, whom, however, he 'bravely repulsed'.

Meanwhile, Chamillart sent a strong rebuke to Du Junca, stating, 'the king does not approve of your conduct', for asking other prisoners questions about the Mask. Du Junca, suffering from a mysterious illness, abandoned his journal on 26 August 1705 and died just under a year later. Saint-Mars' nephew, Corbé, was strongly suspected of giving him poison, perhaps because Du Junca had come close to finding out the truth.

Saint-Mars survived in office for a further two years but, becoming increasingly senile, he had already relinquished most of his duties to Charles de Fournières, sieur de Bernaville. A man with a reputation for brutality in a brutal age, Bernaville was first employed as a liveried retainer, then successively as a gamekeeper, a cook, chief turnkey, lieutenant and, from 1701, jailer of the equally notorious Paris prison at Vincennes. When Saint-Mars breathed his last at 5 p.m. on the evening of 26 September 1708, aged eighty-two 'or thereabouts', Bernaville slipped seamlessly into his place.

After Chamillart lost his post as war minister in June 1709, responsibility for the Bastille returned to Pontchartain. On 10 February 1710, Pontchartain, although careful not to be specific, reminded Bernaville that preserving 'the secret and the mystery' was one of his primary duties and told him to warn the prisoner's confessor of the need to keep the 'inviolable and impenetrable secret'.

Under Bernaville's callous regime, d'Artagnan was never seen again. He may have descended further and further into the hell of the dank dungeons in the lower Bastille, perhaps chained to the wall and locked again in his steel mask, his dish and water cup filled once a day by his turnkey through a slot in his cell door, their subsequent use the only sign that he still lived. This was the domain of lizards, toads and giant rats, scurrying across the stone floor. A prisoner here had straw for his furniture, no sanitation, not even a bucket, and his own stench disguised the foul air that he breathed. All humanity gone, he soon gave up hope, for he was no longer of this earth.

D'Artagnan probably died in January 1711, aged about eighty-eight. As a second funeral might have provoked awkward questions, he was almost certainly buried at night in the garden of the Bastille. His biographer, Courtilz, no longer considered a threat once the Iron Mask was dead, was released a few days later. After his second, long and extremely harsh term of imprisonment, including three years in a cell too small for him to stand upright, Courtilz's health was shattered. His third marriage of 4 February that year to the widow of one of his loyal booksellers was in expectation of death, to keep his property out of the clutches of the state. However, Courtilz lingered on; bedridden and unable to write, he expired the following May in the rue de Hurepois. Whatever d'Artagnan had told him of his second life in prison died with him.

René de Launay, who joined the prison staff as second-in-command on 10 August 1710, and who would succeed Bernaville as governor in 1718, recalled the orders given to strip the Mask's cell when he finally succumbed. They were told to burn everything that he had used.

Even the walls of his cell were scraped and whitewashed and the floor tiles pulled up and replaced, so much was it feared that he had found a means of hiding some message or sign, the discovery of which might reveal his name.

In the prison register, leather-bound, locked with a key kept by the governor, a single page was torn out: the page where the Mask's entry should have appeared. The servants of the Sun King believed they had left no loose ends.

However, the death of the Mask did not remain a secret

for more than a few months, thanks to Elizabeth, Princess of the Palatinate, second wife of Louis XIV's brother, Philippe. Elizabeth was one of the few who dared to stand up to Louis. She also wrote long, brutally candid letters, hundreds of them, spending up to twelve hours a day at her desk. Much of her correspondence attacked the morals and hypocrisy of the court. The princess loathed Athénaïs de Montespan for producing illegitimate royal offspring, whom she described as 'mouse droppings among the pepper', and Françoise de Maintenon for bringing them up and replacing Athénaïs in the king's bed. Elizabeth was very well informed and sufficiently self-assertive to worm the most confidential information out of court officials. On 11 October 1711, in a letter to her aunt, the Electress of Hanover and mother of the future George I, she mentioned the latest story she had heard:

> A man remained long years in the Bastille and has died there, masked. At his side he had two musketeers ready to kill him if he took off his mask. He ate and slept with the mask on. No doubt there was some reason for this, for otherwise he was well treated and lodged, and given everything he wished for. He went to communion masked; he was very devout and read continually. No one has ever been able to learn who he was.

The Princess of the Palatinate's private letter, written in German, created only the tiniest ripple on the surface. Just over two years previously, following the death of police chief La Reynie, Louis XIV and Françoise de Maintenon had burned what they erroneously thought were the only copies of 'the particular facts', the particularly disagreeable facts, about Athénaïs de Montespan and the Affair of the Poisons. Perhaps the bonfire also included documents that alluded to the most dangerous fact of all, that the Sun King had no right to his throne, which had doomed d'Artagnan to perpetual imprisonment. The great secrets of state were safe for the moment, but the Mask still had a vital part to play in the events that would lead to the fall of the French monarchy.

EPILOGUE

REVENGE OF THE MASK

        ৱ   ৶

s d'Artagnan's corpse slowly crumbled to dust beneath the roses of the Bastille, his cause found an unexpected champion in Voltaire, the firebrand philosopher. Born François Marie Arouet at Paris on 21 November 1694, the son of a notary, Voltaire was one of the leaders of the Enlightenment, the name given by writers, philosophers and scientists to the period when they believed they were replacing the 'ignorance' of the past with the 'light' of truth. These thinkers were the *philosophes*, a heterogeneous mix of people who pursued a variety of intellectual interests: literary, mechanical, philosophical, scientific and sociological. They challenged established ideas, and by implication the Establishment itself.

Many of the *philosophes* were imprisoned for their beliefs but Voltaire gave his government other excuses to put him under lock and key. In 1713, as a young man in the diplomatic service, he was sent home from The Hague in disgrace by the French ambassador to the Netherlands for having an affair with a Protestant émigré. Voltaire had to fall back on his literary talents to earn a living and quickly became recognized in the Paris salons as a brilliant and sarcastic writer. His anonymous lampoon accusing the French Regent Philippe II, duc d'Orléans, of incest resulted in Voltaire's imprisonment in the Bastille for eleven months, from 16 May 1717 to 10 April 1718. When some of Voltaire's friends succeeded in persuading the regent that he was not the author of the libel, if indeed a libel it were, the regent ordered his release. Curious to meet the young upstart, he ordered that Voltaire be brought before him. While Voltaire waited in the regent's ante-chamber, a violent storm erupted over Paris. Voltaire, pointing towards the black clouds, exclaimed, 'If the regent were in charge up there as well, things could not be any worse than this.' An official told the regent what Voltaire had said and added, 'Here is young Arouet, whom you have just released from the Bastille, and whom you will send straight back there.' Fortunately for Voltaire, the regent was highly amused and gave him a gift of money. 'I thank your royal highness for taking care of my board,' said Voltaire, 'but I must request that you do not again provide me with lodging.'

During Voltaire's visit to the Bastille, where he was less of a prisoner, more of an honoured guest, he learned for the first time about the mystery of the Man in the Iron Mask. Saint-Mars' immediate circle had long since died or departed, but several of the older warders and, of course, old lags, remained to give Voltaire a hefty dose of hearsay.

In April 1726 Voltaire and the Bastille became briefly reacquainted. He fell out with a chevalier from a prominent noble family, who disliked his newfound popularity at court and accused him of being a parvenu. Voltaire retaliated with a series of witty epigrams, and the chevalier's servants gave him a beating, whereupon Voltaire challenged the nobleman to a duel. This was too much for the authorities, who threatened to send Voltaire back to the Bastille. He eschewed so many opportunities to avoid imprisonment that it seemed he was determined to return to, and research further, the final prison of the Mask. Voltaire was released after a fortnight when he agreed to leave France and go to England.

Voltaire stayed outside France until October 1728. He returned, not to launch a fresh literary assault on the government but to participate in a financial coup. One of his friends, a mathematician, worked out that the prizes in the national lottery exceeded by some margin the value of the tickets for sale and Voltaire joined the syndicate that bought almost all of them up. His share of the winnings was about 500,000 livres, an enormous sum.

Although Voltaire had now achieved financial independence for the rest of his life, allowing him to write whatever he wished, he still faced one major obstacle: censorship in France had reached a new level of intensity. The law of 28 January 1723, 'on pain of exemplary punishment', forbad anyone to own an unauthorized press or to sell any unauthorized book. Voltaire's prolific output came to be seen as an attack on French political and ecclesiastical institutions and twice he was obliged to flee abroad.

Voltaire bided his time. He had begun work on his history of the century of Louis XIV. In October 1738 he corresponded with the secretary of the French Academy, who helped him to fill several gaps and asked him whether he knew the story of the Mask. 'I am well enough informed about the adventure of the Man in the Iron Mask, who died at the Bastille,' wrote Voltaire, reassuringly. 'I have spoken to some people who looked after him.' In another letter, written a few months later, he added,

> I have noted what was said to former mistresses, valets, great nobles and others; I have recorded the facts on which they agree; I have left the rest as anecdotal talk . . . I have investigated the man in the mask.

Voltaire's history was a long time appearing in print, however, a reflection perhaps of even tighter censorship. In 1744, when all the various edicts against censorship were collated, they filled a huge volume. For subversive writers like Voltaire, the only solution was to publish abroad. Early the following year an anonymous book was printed in Amsterdam entitled *Mémoires secrets pour servir à l'histoire de Perse*, a parody of historical events in France. This told the story of two supposedly Persian princes, one legitimate, the other not. Their father, the king, imprisoned the illegitimate prince for life in an island fort and later in a strong citadel. He was forced to wear a mask to keep his identity secret. When rumours of what this fanciful tale really meant reached the French court, Voltaire was present, briefly basking in favour. On 27 March 1745, he was appointed 'official historian' to Louis XV, which was deliciously ironic because Voltaire himself almost certainly had written the so-called 'History of Persia'. The hunt for the identity of the author intensified in 1749 when the third edition appeared with a key at the front and a table at the back which, if put together, matched the fictitious characters to real people and places, including Louis XIV as the 'legitimate prince', the island to Sainte-Marguerite and the citadel to the Bastille.

As suspicions grew at court of his involvement in the 'History of Persia', in June 1750 Voltaire left for Prussia, accepting the patronage of Frederick the Great. It was from Berlin in 1751 that he finally published, under a false name, *Le Siècle de Louis XIV*. In a chapter entitled 'Incidents and Anecdotes', the story of the Iron Mask first appeared in print. After a reference to the death of Mazarin in March 1661, Voltaire continued:

> Some months after the death of that minister, an event occurred that is without parallel, and what is stranger, all historians omit to mention it. An unknown prisoner, of height above the ordinary, young and of an extremely handsome and noble appearance, was conveyed with the utmost secrecy to the castle on the island of Sainte-Marguerite lying in the Mediterranean off Provence. On the journey the prisoner wore a mask, the chin-piece of which had steel springs to enable him to eat while wearing it, and his guards had orders to kill him if he took it off. He remained on the island until a trusted officer called Saint-Mars, governor of Pignerol, who was made governor of the Bastille in 1690, went in that year to Saint[e]-Marguerite, and brought him to the Bastille still wearing his mask.

For all its flawed chronology, Voltaire had the essential facts correct. In an enlarged edition of his history published the following year, Voltaire stated that Chamillart was the last minister to know the identity of the Mask. Chamillart's son-in-law had told Voltaire that the minister's only comment on the subject was that the prisoner 'knew all of Monsieur Fouquet's secrets'. This aptly described d'Artagnan, but Voltaire, lacking any other information, never made the connection.

The egos of Frederick and Voltaire were too large for the relationship to last and in March 1753 they parted, never to meet again. From other, more welcoming, German principalities, Voltaire devoted much of that year to completing a supplement to his history. Stung by criticism of the lack of sources for his story of the secret prisoner, Voltaire made a spirited defence of 'hearsay' evidence. He said:

A large part of history is founded only on gathered and compared hearsay . . . The history of the man in the iron mask is not demonstrated like a Euclidian proposition; but the large number of testimonies which confirm it – that of old men who have heard ministers speak of it – make it for us more authentic than any particular fact of the last four hundred years of Roman History.

In a further reference to the identity of the Mask, 'this so illustrious and ignored captive', Voltaire said, 'I am a historian; I am not a soothsayer.' He simply observed 'He was a prisoner of utmost importance, and one whose destiny had always been kept secret.'

In January 1754, Voltaire received word via Louis XV's mistress, Madame de Pompadour, that he would not be allowed to return to anywhere but the furthest extremities of France. His exile was imprecise, indefinite and irrevocable: an oral sentence from the king that specified nothing, and against which there was no appeal. No historian has supplied a convincing explanation for Voltaire's banishment, but its juxtaposition to his *Siècle de Louis XIV* and its supplement was of huge significance. Louis XV probably knew the identity of the Mask but could scarcely reveal the truth in order to prove that the secret prisoner had not been the real King of France. The mistaken direction of Voltaire's innuendo gave him just as much cause for concern. Voltaire's purported 'History of Persia' and the imprisonment in a mask of a rival prince, combined with what had been unearthed about the Man in the Iron Mask, took Louis XV in a direction he decidedly did not wish to go. It called into question the legitimacy of his particular Bourbon line, if not of the whole Bourbon dynasty.

In 1763, from the comparative safety of his home close to the Swiss frontier, Voltaire risked returning to the subject of the Mask. In his *Essai sur l'histoire générale*, he accurately described the short stay of the masked man at the Château de Palteau during his transfer from Saint-Marguerite to the Bastille. His account was based on information he had received in a letter from Saint-Mars' great-nephew.

The discovery in 1769 of Du Junca's journal written at the Bastille may have stung Voltaire into a further mischievous sally. A year later, in *Questions sur l'encyclopédie*, the huge collected work of Enlightenment thinking, he said of the Mask,

> If he were permitted to speak to his doctor only with a mask on, it was for fear he would be recognized, his features bearing some true striking resemblance [to someone] . . . The one who writes this article knows . . . and will say no more.

In 1771, contributing to a new volume of the *Encyclopédie*, Voltaire finally nailed his colours to the mast. He identified the origins of the masked prisoner, albeit disguising his remarks as those of the *Encyclopédie* 'editor', who, judging by the sycophantic nature of his prose, was none other than Voltaire himself. The editor conjectures:

> From the way whereby M. de Voltaire has recounted the matter, that this famous historian is as much convinced as him of the suspicion he is going to reveal . . . The man with the iron mask was, undoubtedly, a brother and an elder brother of Louis XIV . . . The queen must have imagined that it was her fault that Louis XIII had no heir. The birth of the Iron Mask showed her that was not the case. . . . but the queen and the Cardinal, equally convinced of the necessity of hiding the existence of the Iron Mask from Louis XIII, had the child raised secretly.

It remained a secret from Louis XIV until Mazarin's death. But this Monarch, upon hearing that he had a brother, and an elder one at that, whom his mother could not disown and who, perhaps, bore the features which betrayed his origin, further reflected that this child born during wedlock could not, without inconvenience and a terrible scandal, be declared illegitimate after Louis XIII's death. Louis XIV . . . must have judged he could not use a wiser means to entomb in oblivion the living proof of an illegitimate love . . .

Stripped of its uncharacteristic verbiage, a reflection perhaps of the risk Voltaire felt he was taking in making his theory public, Voltaire claimed that Anne of Austria, unable to conceive a child by Louis XIII, thought herself sterile and, having taken a lover, found otherwise. The child, he claimed, was raised in secret to manhood until Louis XIV, told by Mazarin of his existence, and fearing that the resemblance gave away the truth, had his elder brother imprisoned in an iron mask.

In 1777 Voltaire, planning a new edition of his history of the century of Louis XIV and trying to avoid censorship, sent an open letter to 'the government minister' – apparently unaware of whom that might be whose seal of approval was needed for it to be published in France. After refuting various criticisms of his earlier editions, Voltaire added a comment about the Mask:

This matter so incredible and so true, this unique matter was called into question . . . Today there's only one man who knows the identity of the poor unfortunate whose experience still terrifies us, and this august man stands too far above the rest to be quoted.

Voltaire fell back on unattributed sources because he lacked any significant evidence that the Mask had been the elder brother of Louis XIV, which made later historians hugely indignant. Funck-Brentano said 'With a boldness of imagination which today would be envied by the cleverest journalistic inventor of sensational paragraphs, Voltaire started this monstrous hoax on its vigorous flight.' Tigue Hopkins accused Voltaire of stimulating his audience by an attractive hint or two . . . So, without the least embarrassment on the author's part, the horrid hoax is launched . . . On Voltaire's part not an ounce of proof was ever offered . . . since none was ever in existence.

After Voltaire's involvement in the story about the Mask had become apparent, the drip-feed of information particularly discomfited the *ancien-régime* because of his extraordinary international influence. Voltaire liked to think of himself, as he put it, as the *maître d'hôtel de l'Europe*. He knew everyone and everyone knew him.

In 1778, at the age of eighty-three, Voltaire was persuaded to return to Paris, which he had not seen for twenty-eight years. The French authorities tried to prevent his visit but were confounded by the lack of any documentary evidence that he had ever been sent into exile. Voltaire was overwhelmed by the warmth of the welcome he received but the frenetic atmosphere proved fatal. He fell seriously ill and on 30 May declined the last rites of the Catholic Church. His sardonic refusal as the end drew nigh to deny the existence of the Devil – 'Is this a time to make enemies?' – may be apocryphal, but Voltaire would have said it had he thought of it.

In that same month, the number of prisoners held in the Bastille reached twenty-seven, the highest number under Louis XVI. By December 1778, it was back to nine, making the average number for the reign just sixteen. Nor were all the prisoners in the high-security or high-born categories usually incarcerated in the Bastille. Many were simply transferred there when the nearby fortress of Vincennes was closed in February 1784 for lack of custom.

However, the Bastille's overheads remained as high as ever. The salary of the governor, Bernard de Launay, who had succeeded his father, was increased to 60,000 livres a year, to compensate for the lower profit he made out of his prisoners. Little wonder that France's finance minister recommended the Bastille be closed 'for the sake of economy'. In 1784 the chief architect of Paris drew up a scheme for seven of its eight towers to be knocked down and a circular, colonnaded place Louis XVI to be opened up on the site of the old fortress. In 1788 the king's lieutenant at the Bastille wrote two reports proposing its closure, demolition and the sale of the vacant lot by auction for the benefit of the crown. Early in 1789 the lieutenant of the Paris police, accompanied by a senior judge from the Parlement, made an inspection of the Bastille with the specific intention of transferring the prisoners and arranging its destruction. On 8 June, the treasury minister presented to the Royal Academy of Architecture 'a plan for a monument on the site of the Bastille'.

If these proposals had been common knowledge in 1789, the storming of the Bastille might never have taken place. However, by then the French royal family was losing the propaganda battle. At the heart of its difficulties once again were its sexual shortcomings. In short, for Louis XIII and Anne of Austria, read Louis XVI and Marie Antoinette. The king fell asleep without touching his bride on their wedding night; she comforted herself with a gigantic spending-spree and became known as 'Madame Deficit'.

Louis finally did father the dauphin but, whereas under previous regimes salacious gossip rarely left the confines of the court, unfortunately for the royal couple, it now found its way to the pamphleteers in intimate detail. Their pamphlets alleged that the king was impotent and had been cuckolded by his younger brother, while Marie Antoinette was accused of being a compulsive nymphomaniac with both sexes, of having syphilis, of being a debauched woman completely without morals. The king and queen had a serious problem with their public image that threatened to undermine the monarchy.

That was scarcely surprising: the nobility, whose coaches and wagons were immune from any searches, were embroiled in the traffic of forbidden publications. They transported them in bulk by barges on canals and fishing boats on rivers to meet the eager demand in the provinces, seeing this as a wonderful opportunity to stir up trouble and make a small fortune at the same time. The court itself, whether residing in Paris, Fontainebleau or Versailles, proved to be one of the biggest customers: a series of portable bookshops, rather like those to be found along the banks of the Seine in the capital today, moved with it. Printing prices had more than doubled in less than two years, a reflection of the changing balance between supply and demand. Far more people, too, could read what was written. Literacy in France increased from about 30 per cent of the population in 1650 to about 50 per cent by 1780.

While it would be an exaggeration to ascribe the French Revolution to the power of the press, by bankrolling the most radical of writers and circulating their work, the nobility were exposing to ridicule both the established class system and the Establishment itself. Mirabeau, who was to become, like Voltaire, a patriot hero of the Revolution, understood that better than anyone.

Honoré-Gabriel Victor Riqueti, comte de Mirabeau, was born on 9 March, 1749, at the Château de Bignon in the Ile-de-France. After a difficult birth, Mirabeau emerged with a twisted foot and a malformed tongue. The doctor said that the baby 'will certainly have difficulty in speaking'. As a prediction of the capabilities of probably the greatest orator France has ever produced, it was somewhat wide of the mark. Mirabeau was not handsome. 'Your nephew is ugly as Satan,' wrote the marquis de Mirabeau to his brother. His son was soon left further marked by smallpox, creating an appearance of compelling fascination to women throughout his life. The young Mirabeau was to serve time in four different prisons, primarily for seducing the wives of prominent nobles.

With the French government bankrupt and many of its people starving, in order to raise money Louis XVI was forced in 1789 to recall the assembly of nobles, clergy and commoners, known as the Estates General, for the first time since 1614. Despite his noble title, Mirabeau found his vocation as a champion of the people and was elected as a delegate to represent Aix-en-Provence. He became the unofficial spokesman for the commons, the Third Estate and, when they were ordered to disperse, Mirabeau inspired them to refuse 'except by force of bayonets'. The king then agreed to the formation of a National Assembly.

The honeymoon did not last. On 10 July 1789, the king was persuaded to dissolve the Assembly and use the army to take control of his capital. However, the soldiers occupying the centre of Paris would not obey their officers and were withdrawn to the outskirts; on 14 July this left the governor of the Bastille facing a crowd of students, old soldiers and local tradesmen, among them brewers, cabinetmakers, cobblers and wine merchants, most of whom had never held a musket. Whereas the wily Saint-Mars would either have promptly surrendered without firing a shot or have wreaked havoc with his cannon, the pathologically indecisive Launay managed to do neither. After initial resistance, he unlocked the gates and lowered the drawbridge; the enraged mob, who had lost eighty-three of their number in the exchange of fire, poured into the prison, took him outside and killed him with swords and bayonets.

In the passion of the moment, the prisoners were forgotten. The keys to their cells were already being paraded in the streets, so the inmates had to be released without them, by battering down the doors. There were only seven prisoners, a fact the Assembly found so incredible that four days later the Paris deputies interrogated the four turnkeys independently, to avoid collusion, to discover what had happened to the remainder. The turnkeys stuck to their story. The seven prisoners consisted of four forgers; a count imprisoned for incest by his own family; an Irishman who believed himself, depending on the day of the week, to be either Julius Caesar or Jesus Christ; and finally a man found to be completely insane, who had to be shut up in another prison.

So the great symbol of royal absolutism fell to the people. An enterprising builder, Pierre-François Palloy, who had just completed the new Paris meat market, made sure that the fortress was also demolished. The names of the heroic attackers were on everyone's lips within hours, among them a man called 'Pallet', who may have been on the run from the police, and who just as promptly disappeared. Palloy took his place and quickly spun a yarn about his role in the assault, describing how bullets from the defenders had passed through his tricorn hat. As 'Patriot' Palloy, with impeccable credentials, he turned up the following morning and began recruiting labourers to work on the site; at the end of the day he had 800. By no means all the Paris electors wanted the Bastille torn down; many thought it should be occupied by the militia in case of attack. However, Mirabeau fanned fears that the Bastille might be retaken by troops from the Château of Vincennes, pretending to take seriously rumours of a secret underground passage said to emerge in the darkest recesses of the prison. He made a great show of inspecting the lower floors and passageways, knocking on walls to see if he could find a concealed entrance. This was enough for the Paris electors: they voted immediately to dismantle the Bastille. The following morning, 16 June 1789, with Palloy's encouragement, Mirabeau climbed one of the towers, swung a pickaxe at the battlements and to rapturous applause sent the first stone crashing to the courtyard below.

One of Mirabeau's acolytes, Michel de Cubières-Palmezeaux, also arrived at the Bastille on the morning of 16 July. Cubières fancied himself as the poet of the Revolution. What he lacked in quality he compensated in quantity and by 1788 he had written sixty volumes of prose and verse, twenty-eight pieces in January of that year alone.

Cubières had just returned to Paris from a trip to Venice with another poet, Fanny de Beauharnais. According to those in the know, Cubières was 'a little less than her husband, a bit more than her collaborator'. Fanny's charms had ensured that Cubières would miss the storming of the Bastille but, with the prison still smouldering, he made up for lost time. It was an opportune moment to go into print, as the regime's fourteenth and last lieutenant of police relinquished his remaining powers on 16 July, ending censorship entirely.

With Mirabeau's encouragement, Cubières brought out that day *Voyage à la Bastille*, the earliest commentary on the fall of the great fortress, beating by twenty-four hours the initial number of the *Révolutions de Paris*. Cubières was the first to report the decision to pull down the Bastille. He also described Mirabeau's appearance that morning in the innermost courtyard, as ever with a pretty woman on his arm, showing her the cell where the orator untruthfully claimed he himself had once been imprisoned.

Cubières noted that Mirabeau was 'harvesting' a great number of interesting documents. One of the large chambers in the Bastille had contained records of the prison, carefully filed in boxes in date order. Many of these boxes were hurled off the battlements by the attackers into the courtyard below. Helpful citizens loaded many of the scattered papers into Mirabeau's coach. The same afternoon he made a speech to the Assembly, exhorting them to 'save the papers . . . the title-deeds of an intolerable despotism . . . [from] being plundered'. Mirabeau omitted to mention that he was foremost among those doing the plundering. The ten commissioners sent by the Assembly to protect the documents were predictably too late: they found empty boxes and an 'immense heap of papers in complete disorder'.

The story of the Iron Mask and its potential further to undermine the monarchy was a gift to those, like Mirabeau, who wanted to curb the monarchy's political power. Just in case the Bastille's records showed the Mask to be someone of no consequence, Mirabeau made sure nothing would be found that had any relevance to the 'illustrious prisoner'. The moment had come to make use of the legend. Cubières asserted in his *Voyage à la Bastille* that the identity of the Mask had been disclosed to him 'a long time previously' but it is far more likely that Mirabeau was his source and that Mirabeau persuaded him to publish the most dramatic solution for the first time.

According to Cubières, the birth of Louis XIV on 5 September 1638 had been unexpectedly followed by that of a twin brother much later in the day, at 8.30 p.m., while Louis XIII was at supper; fearing that two claimants to the throne would provoke civil war, the king hid the birth of the second child and later imprisoned him in an iron mask.

Although, as Mirabeau surely intended, the theory of the twin would gain an almost unstoppable momentum, it had no basis in fact. The practical problem for its advocates was to find a credible time, during a hectic day of universal rejoicing at court, when Louis XIII could have returned to his wife's bedside for the second birth, unnoticed. The earliest time unaccounted for was more than nine hours after the birth of Louis XIV and the longer the interval between the births, of course, the more medically doubtful the second became. It seems extremely improbable that such a sensational development in the goldfish bowl of the court could really have remained undetected or indeed that any attempt to keep it a secret would ever have been made. Infant mortality was so high that the birth of a second son to Anne of Austria would have been more welcome than feared. By suppressing news of the second birth, were it subsequently discovered, Louis XIII would have risked adverse conclusions being drawn about the first, already the subject of speculation that cast serious doubts on his son's legitimacy. The fact that the future Louis XIV was almost certainly a bastard was a sufficient problem in itself, without adding the fantastic dimension of the clandestine birth of a twin subsequently hidden from sight.

As to how Mirabeau himself first had the idea, the spirit of Voltaire was surely hovering overhead. Voltaire had suggested the Mask was an elder brother of Louis XIV but a little lateral thinking led just as readily to his twin. As early as 2 July 1780, an uncensored news-sheet, the *Journal de Paris*, had discussed Voltaire's solution at length and highlighted the mysterious prisoner's 'altogether too striking resemblance' to Louis XIV. As with any claim hostile to the Bourbons put forward in the frenetic atmosphere of revolutionary Paris, citizens were eager to believe it, not inclined to subject it to forensic examination. The theory's significance lay not in its substance, but in its timing. Mirabeau wanted to bring the monarchy down to size rather than to its knees, and on 15 July 1789 it would have taken only a word from the great orator to ensure that Cubières inserted the legend into his otherwise spontaneous pamphlet.

From 16 July a pass had to be purchased to visit the Bastille, already a huge attraction, the desire to see inside it made all the more frantic by the knowledge that the fortress would soon disappear for ever. Mirabeau thought that the visitors should be given something more to see than empty rooms. He found a willing accomplice in Palloy, who was already sure of a fine profit from miniature Bastilles made out of rubble from the prison, and supplied to eager municipalities throughout France. Workmen brought to Palloy various pieces of junk they came across and Mirabeau's vivid imagination helped the builder to convert them into artefacts of terror. An old suit of armour became an 'iron corset' designed to squeeze its victim to an agonizing death; the toothed component of a clandestine printing press was labelled as a hideous torture device. Within a day or two, the skeleton in the Bourbons' cupboard had become a real skeleton of the Man in the Iron Mask, attached to rusting chains. On 22 July a mass-produced broadsheet carried as its banner headline 'Skeleton of the Iron Mask found by the Nation' above a woodcut depicting the scene. The story beneath described the discovery of the skeleton, with chains around his neck, hands and feet and an iron mask by his side. Hitherto supposed to be pure invention, the broadsheet almost certainly was a faithful description of Mirabeau and Pallot's imaginative tableau created for the benefit of the tourists. None of this so-called evidence, not even the mask, survived the first few weeks of the Revolution, when it had served its purpose.

Echoing as it did across more than a century, built up first by Voltaire, then by Mirabeau and his cronies for all it was worth, the legend helped to confirm the worst prejudices of the people at what proved to be a pivotal moment. The campaign against absolutism and tyranny, given wings by the storming of the Bastille, found a focal point in the cruel account of the Man in the Iron Mask. Although it would have mortified d'Artagnan had he known the part he would eventually play, the French Revolution became the real Mask's bloody revenge on a regime that had presided over one of the most shameful episodes in history, with the familiar tyrant's plea that it was for the good of the state.

Alexandre Dumas gave d'Artagnan a more agreeable form of immortality in the King's Musketeers, sword in hand, alongside Aramis, Athos and Porthos, one for all and all for one. Leaving Queen Anne's lover, their captain, Tréville, almost forgotten in the supporting cast, in his Musketeers trilogy Dumas made the Iron Mask the legitimate twin brother of Louis XIV, not out of conviction but because he believed it to be 'incontestably the most dramatic' solution. Ironically a far more dramatic and true story eluded the great writer: that of his hero's terrible fate, because d'Artagnan had discovered France's most dangerous secret.

Appendix

& &

Prison Plans

The steep, rising streets of the fortress town of Pignerol led to the almost impregnable donjon or keep on the left of the plan. In 1674 the Man in the Iron Mask was brought into the donjon on a precarious mountain path that led to the concealed postern gate or 'Fausse Porte' (right of B).

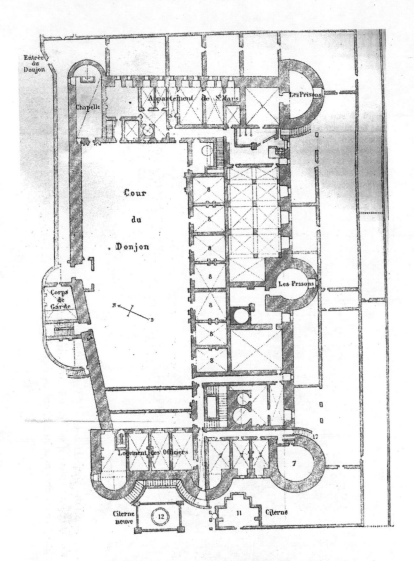

The donjon at Pignerol, as it was in 1675, when it held three important state prisoners, Nicolas Fouquet, the comte de Lauzun, and the Man in the Iron Mask. In the Angle Tower, next to jailer Saint-Mars' apartment, Fouquet lived on the top floor and Lauzun on the floor below, joined by a common chimney. The Mask's cell was on the top floor of the Lower Tower, right of centre.

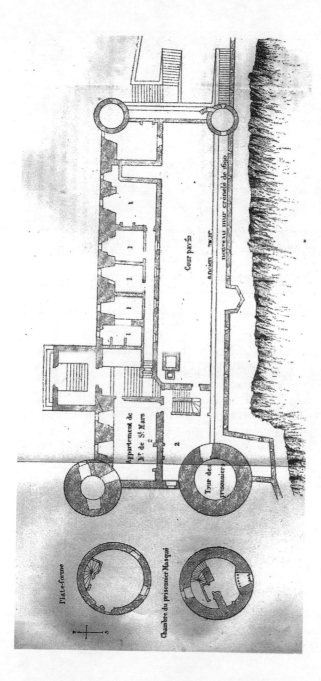

In 1681 Fouquet and the Man in the Iron Mask, both officially dead, were moved to the remote Alpine fort of Exilles. They were held in the old Roman tower, which was accessible only via jailer Saint-Mars' apartment (top left of the main plan). Fouquet was given the higher and larger room, called the 'Plateform' or platform; the Iron Mask had the cell on the floor below.

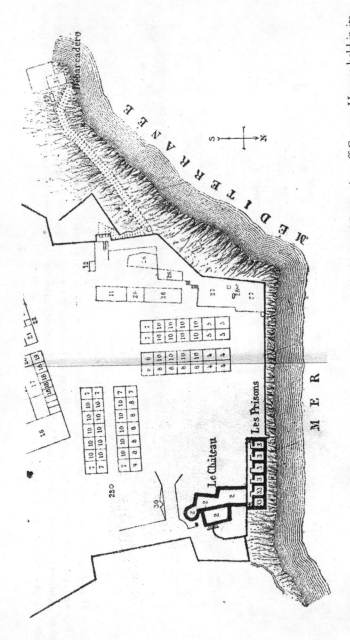

After Fouquet's death in 1687, the Iron Mask was moved to the island of Sainte-Marguerite, off Cannes. He was held in its Fort Royal prison in a row of cells ('Les Prisons' on the plan) overlooking the sea. His cell was the second from the left. His jailer, Saint-Mars, lived close by in 'Le Chateau'.

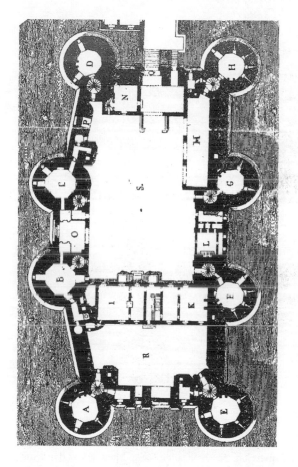

When Saint-Mars was appointed governor of the Bastille in 1698, the Mask went with him to Paris. He was taken initially to a ground floor room in the Basinière Tower (H), then accommodated more permanently on the top floor of the Bertandière Tower (G). After November 1703, the Mask may have been moved to the Well Tower (E), as far as possible from the outer courtyard and the apartment of governor Saint-Mars, who believed his prisoner had died. Courtilz initially had a ground floor room in the Chapel Tower (B) and was allowed to move freely about the prison. Following his re-arrest in 1701, Courtilz was held in a grim dungeon on the lowest level of the Bertandière Tower.

FACSIMILES

Louvois, the war minister responsible for state prisoners, sent a huge volume of orders and questions to their jailer, Saint-Mars. After dictating this letter, dated 10 July 1680, Louvois added five lines at the bottom in his own handwriting before sealing the dispatch. Louvois wanted to know how Eustache Danger had succeeded in obtaining poisons at Pignerol. This was the last time Danger was mentioned, reinforcing the conclusion that he had committed suicide and could not be the Man in the Iron Mask.

Les mousquetaires ont été conduits a l'audian
de congé du Roy par le mareschal de duras
mareschal d'estrées etant malade [14 vernon]
les magnificences et les beautés de versaill...
de la [...] jusqu'a bayonn...
[...] les princes [...]

...de cinq mars a transporté par ordre
du Roy un prisonnier d'estat de pignerol a...
isles de Ste marguerite personne ne sait q...
il est il y a deffenses de dire son nom et ordre de...
s'il l'avoit prononcé on en a conduit d'autres
pignerol, et celuy la sans doute de la sorte
[...] un homme qui [...] celuy cy estoit enfe...
dans une chaise a porteurs ayant un masqu...
[...] sur le visage et tout ce qu'on a pu [...]
de cinq mars est que ce prisonnier estoit dep...
longues années a pignerol et que tous les q...
que le public croit morts ne le sont pas, [...]
[...] de la tour de [...] dans [...]
cette translation ne marqueroit elle point [...]
[...] de la [...] a pignerol au [...]
[...] en de [Louis?] est arrivé malade de la [fie]
double fievre quelques autres [...] d'une [...]
fondüe le quinquina ne luy a pas fait...
le bon effet que l'on en attendoit il a mandé...
de villeneuve qui est inspecteur general des b...
sa majesté a dit à made de maintenon [...]
de plus dames de la cour que [...]
ne luy faisoit jamais que très a propos de [...]
justes il estoit dans la volonté de la luy accor...
toutes [...] elle en a recu de grandes felicita...
par le chemin des principales personnes de [...]

In September 1687 a clandestine newsletter, circulated among revisionist clergy, carried the first eye-witness sighting of the Man in the Iron Mask, on his way to Sainte-Marguerite. It reports in lines 14–15 that he had been seen by a priest at Grasse with 'un masque d'acier', 'a steel mask', covering his face. His jailer, Saint-Mars, let slip a highly significant clue to his identity. In lines 18–19 Saint-Mars is quoted as saying, 'All the people one believes to be dead are not.'

DE MR. D'ARTAGNAN.   11
bien de la peine à le faire, parce qu'il me sembloit
qu'il n'auroit pas trop bonne opinion de moi,
quand il sçauroit que je serois revenu de-là, sans
tirer raison de l'affront que j'y avois reçû.
    Je fus loger dans son quartier, afin d'être plus
près de lui. Je pris une petite chambre dans la ruë
des Fossoïeurs, tout auprès de St. Sulpice, il y
avoit pour enseigne le Gaillard-Bois, il y avoit
des jeux de boule, comme je crois qu'il y en a encore, & elle avoit une porte qui perçoit dans la
ruë Ferou, qui est au derriere de la ruë des
Fossoïeurs. Je fus dès le lendemain matin au
lever de Mr. de Treville, dont je trouvai l'Anti-
chambre toute pleine de Mousquetaires. La plû-
part étoient de mon Païs, ce que j'entendis bien
à leur langage ; ainsi me croyant plus fort
de moitié que je n'étois auparavant, de me
trouver ainsi en païs de connoissance, je me mis à
accoster le premier que je trouvai sous ma main.
J'avois emploié une partie de l'argent de Montigré
à me faire propre, & je n'avois pas aussi oublié la
coûtume du Païs, qui est, quand on auroit pas un
sou dans sa poche, d'avoir toûjours le plumet sur
l'oreille & le ruban de couleur à la cravate. Celui
que j'accostai s'appelloit Portos, & étoit voisin de
mon Pere de deux ou trois lieuës. Il avoit encore
deux Freres dans la Compagnie, dont l'un s'appelloit Athos, & l'autre Aramis. Mr. de Treville les
avoit fait venir tous trois du païs, parce qu'ils y
avoient fait quelques combats, qui leur donnoient
beaucoup de réputation dans la Province. Au reste
il étoit bien-aise de choisir ainsi ces gens, parce
qu'il y avoit une telle jalousie entre la Compagnie
des Mousquetaires, & celle des Gardes du Cardinal de Richelieu, qu'ils en venoient aux mains
tous les jours.
    Cela n'étoit rien, puisqu'il arrive tous les jours
que des particuliers ont querelle ensemble, prin-ci-
palement quand il y a comme assaut de réputation
                                    entr'eux.

Alexandre Dumas never admitted his inspiration for The Three
Musketeers was the Memoirs of Monsieur d'Artagnan, published in 1700,
144 years previously. On page eleven d'Artagnan's biographer, Courtilz,
makes the first reference (lines 25–8) to 'Portos', Athos and Aramis. The
Captain of the Musketeers, Tréville, hears of their reputation as duellists
and summons them to Paris to fight Cardinal Richelieu's Guards.

During its demolition the Bastille became a tourist attraction, which prompted the builder in charge, Palloy, and the revolutionary orator Mirabeau, to create an elaborate tableaux showing 'the skeleton' of the Man in the Iron Mask, complete with chains and the mask itself. On 22 July 1789, eight days after the fall of the Bastille, an unquestioning pamphleteer reported their dramatic 'discovery' as genuine.

NOTES AND SOURCES

& ♌

THE VALUE OF MONEY

According to an expert on seventeenth-century currency, Jean Belaubré, the official exchange rate of the period was twenty sous or three écus to the livre, and ten livres to either the gold louis or the pistole. In practice, however, money minted in Paris, such as the gold louis, was worth between 10 and 20 per cent more than other coinage minted at Tours. So while the pistole equalled ten livres Tournois, someone with a gold louis could expect, in return, eleven livres and a handful of sous. The smallest French coin, the denier, used in change, was worth 1/240 of a livre.

The fifty gold louis that d'Artagnan received from the King of France in 1640 must have gleamed in the sunlight, as they were newly minted for the first time that year. They carried the head of the monarch on one side, the *fleur de lys* on the other, which was the symbol also used for the branding of thieves – including, though only in Dumas' imagination, Cardinal Richelieu's secret agent, Milédi. The equivalent of about 550 livres, at a time when Richelieu's personal apothecary lived comfortably on an annual salary of 150 livres, d'Artagnan's royal purse would have financed a spectacular spending spree.

In Louis XIV's reign, a basic pair of shoes cost about four sous; the same as a *pichet* of average quality wine; a meal of bread, mediocre meat and weak beer would have cost five sous; and a candle, twenty sous, which is one livre. This helps to put into context the earnings of Saint-Mars, the jailer of the Iron Mask, who in thirty months between 1678 and 1680 received pay, bribes and bonuses amounting to 75,000 livres. Using the work of Louis XIV's biographer, Vincent Cronin, and a persuasive formula devised by economist John J. McCusker, this can be said in today's terms to amount to more than £400,000, but in some respects – notably household expenditure – with significantly greater purchasing power. In the same thirty months that Saint-Mars received his windfall, a skilled French workman on a six-day week would have earned the equivalent of £4,000.

THE MEANING OF WORDS IN THE
SEVENTEENTH CENTURY

In the letters sent to and by Saint-Mars about his secret prisoners, the meaning of particular words and phrases at the time is of great significance. The authority used throughout this book is the vast thirty-volume work by Paul-Emile Littré, *Dictionnaire de la Langue Française*, begun in 1844 and published in four volumes from 1863 to 1873, with a supplement issued in June 1877. Two other contemporary works have also been used to complement Littré. They are *Observations sur la langue Française* by Margaret Buffon, published in 1668; and the *Dictionnaire universel* by Antoine Furetière, published posthumously in 1696, then revised by Henri Basnage de Beauval in 1701 and by Jean-Baptiste Brutel de La Rivière in 1727.

CHAPTER 1 (pages 1 to 26)

The formidably well-informed eighteenth-century *historienne* Louise de Kéralio, who wrote *Les Crimes des reines de France* ('The Crimes of the French Queens), was convinced of Anne of Austria's adultery with the Duke of Buckingham. This evidence-based accusation carries more weight because the author tested her original sources (some since lost during the French Revolution) vigorously and did not believe there were sufficient grounds to show conclusively that the queen, much later, had a sexual relationship with Mazarin.

Buckingham later fathered a child by Marie de Chevreuse and, during their pillow talk, admitted to her that he had been fortunate enough to '*gourmer*' three queens. *Gourmer*, from *la gourmette*, the bridle, could mean to take the bridle off a tamed filly or to give way completely to one's passions, so either meaning was apt. Besides Anne of Austria, the queens to whom Buckingham referred were Anne of Denmark and Henrietta Maria, the wives of James I and Charles I respectively. Anne of Denmark lived apart from her bisexual husband after 1606 and Charles ostracized Henrietta for three miserable years from 1625, so a sexual relationship between Buckingham and each of the three queens seems entirely plausible.

Queen Anne's confidant, the comte de Brienne, records in his memoirs that he told the duke face to face that France did not want the queen's lover to be 'a foreigner passing through'. Tréville, however, was much more acceptable. Historian Anthony Levi discovered the unpublished extract from La Rochefoucauld's memoirs that identified Tréville as Anne's lover too late to include it in the first publication of his biography of Louis XIV. He agonized over whether to refer to it in later editions, and eventually decided against doing so because he felt it damaged, possibly fatally, his central thesis that Mazarin was the Sun King's father. According to Levi, La Rochefoucauld had included the reference to Tréville in a draft of his memoirs due to be published in Rouen in 1661; but de Wicquefort, one of Mazarin's agents, had it excised and suppressed the entire manuscript after Mazarin's death. Probably with La Rochefoucauld's connivance, a copy of the edited manuscript, without mention of Tréville, was then secretly taken abroad. The French foreign minister, Lionne, acting on Louis' orders, sent de Wicquefort to track it down. He found that the supposed printer, Van Dyck of Cologne, did not exist, traced the manuscript to Brussels, and finally to Amsterdam – but too late to try to prevent a Dutch printer, Elzevier, from publishing it under the title *Mémoires de M.D.L.R.*, in 1662.

The manuscript of Tallemant's later work, entitled *Mémoires pour la régence d'Anne d'Autriche*, which held out the promise of sensational revelations about the queen in the days of her regency, and quite possibly the identity of the real father of Louis XIV, is missing and was almost certainly destroyed. In his *Historiettes* Tallemant's principal source of Louis XIII's active homosexuality, which is material only in that it reinforces the inescapable conclusion that he was not Louis XIV's father, was the indiscreet *premier valet de chambre* Nyert. On one such occasion Nyert found the royal favourite Cinq-Mars being rubbed from head to foot with oil of jasmine, 'oiling himself for combat', just as Louis entered his bedroom.

The comte de Brienne's discovery, recorded in his memoirs, that Anne of Austria was pregnant significantly before she spent a single night in the same bed as the king, is consistent with the evidence. Louis XIII returned from Picardy for a third time on 16 August 1637, having originally been told to expect the birth of the dauphin between 3 and 10 August. On the basis of the latter date, with the benefit of modern day medical knowledge we can place the start of Anne's last normal regular menstrual cycle before conception at about 3 November 1637 and the date of her conception at between the eleventh and fourteenth day thereafter. Anne could have known from about 2 December that she might be pregnant.

CHAPTER 2 (pages 27 to 52)

While in real life d'Artagnan rose through the ranks to become captain of the King's First Musketeers, without Alexandre Dumas he would have remained a minor footnote of history. His destiny changed when

Dumas wrote *The Three Musketeers*. First published in serial form by a Paris newspaper in 1844, when queues formed in the streets to buy the edition carrying the latest episode, it would become one of the most popular books of all time. Dumas relied heavily for his rough drafts on a former history teacher, Auguste Maquet, who worked with the writer on no fewer than eighteen novels and was also responsible for many of Dumas' best ideas, including, he claimed, *The Three Musketeers*. Dumas wrote at an astonishing pace but, like his heroes, he was barely one step ahead of his pursuers, in his case, the desperate newspaper editors already running the serial. 'Some copy, as fast as possible,' beseeched one note from Dumas to Maquet, 'even if it's only a dozen pages . . . Hammer away, hammer away . . . I'm completely dried up.'

During his research on the Musketeers, Maquet came across a reference to the extremely rare work by Gatien de Courtilz de Sandras, first published in 1700, that professed to be the autobiography of the long-forgotten d'Artagnan. The Marseilles municipal library owned a copy of the first volume, which Dumas deviously acquired while passing through the port on his return from Italy. He seduced a lady whose awe-struck brother just happened to be the city librarian and the book, borrowed by Dumas and passed on unread to Maquet, remains unreturned to this day.

Like most historians, Maquet concluded that the *Mémoires de Monsieur d'Artagnan* were largely apocryphal. Dumas made no direct mention of Courtilz in his preface to *The Three Musketeers* and instead purported to have discovered in the Royal Library an unknown and entirely fictitious manuscript entitled *Mémoires du Comte de la Fère*. Dumas even specified the earliest pages of the document, 20, 27 and 31, on which, he claimed, could be found historical references to Aramis, Athos and Porthos. It successfully diverted attention from the fact that Courtilz, not Dumas, is the first to mention the Three Musketeers. Courtilz introduces them, rather imprecisely, at the beginning of his second chapter   written, of course, as though by d'Artagnan himself: 'Porthos . . . lived two or three leagues from my father's house. Beside himself, two of his brothers belonged to the company of the Musketeers; one was named Athos and the other Aramis.'

The Three Musketeers were members of the same extended family network but not brothers, a mistake that for a long time helped to consign Courtilz to the dustbin of historical literature. However, when, finally, Dumas' imaginary source, the *Memoirs of the comte de la Fère*, was shown not to exist, the great writer, cornered, claimed to have invented the Three Musketeers himself. In 1864, in a feature entitled 'Le pays natal' (The [my] native land) for the *Journal littéraire de la semaine*, Dumas brazenly stated that '*Athos, Porthos et Aramis n'avaient jamais existé, et qu'ils étaient tout simplement des bâtards de mon imagination, reconnus par le public.*' ('Athos, Porthos and Aramis never existed and they were quite simply the bastards of my imagination, acknowledged [as such] by the public.') This impression was reinforced by the way Dumas embellished their characters: there is no evidence, for example, that Porthos was a particularly strong man, but Dumas bestowed upon him the renowned strength of his own father, the Revolutionary general Thomas-Alexandre Dumas, who could lift barn doors off their hinges single-handed. Porthos, Athos and Aramis continued to be regarded as pure fiction for nearly another twenty years.

In the early 1880s, however, Jean-Baptiste Étienne de Jaurgain, a historian eager to preserve the culture and traditions of his native Béarn, began to collate and study its genealogical documents. Like Dumas with Maquet, Jaurgain had an indefatigable assistant, Armand de Dufau de Maluquer, a civil servant from Pau, who made most of the key findings. In 1883–4 Jaurgain published their joint research in an obscure periodical, the *Revue de Béarn, Navarre et Lannes*, and later with many additions in book form as *D'Artagnan, Troisvilles et Les Trois Mousquetaires*, showing the Three Musketeers and Tréville to be flesh and blood.

These works have been supplemented by material from the archives of the Pyrénées-Atlantiques (formerly Basse-Pyrénées), the municipal archives of Pau and the archives of Castetbon, which describe Tréville's meteoric rise from obscurity. By 1637 Tréville already had an illegitimate daughter, Françoise, with Gracianne d'Etchandy from the noble house of Biscayburu de Saugis, who lived on his estate at Troisvilles. Jaurgain found in his own family archive a copy of Françoise's deathbed confession to a priest, dated 4 April 1688; but its present whereabouts is unknown.

Jaurgain showed rather less interest in d'Artagnan because he was a Gascon from the adjoining French province, not a Béarnais. It was left to one of France's most distinguished historians, Charles Samaran, to write in 1912 the first modern biography of d'Artagnan. Samaran was astonished by the extent to which many of the purported inventions of Courtilz dovetailed completely with known events in the period. He concluded that Courtilz, despite some undeniable errors, should be judged by the same standards as other unsupported sources relied upon by historians: on the balance of probabilities, and that yardstick has been followed throughout this book.

D'Artagnan was born about 1623, probably at Chateau Castelmore. The exact date has been lost because the registry for the period 1600–62 kept at Saint-Germier de Meymes, the parish church of the chateau, mysteriously disappeared in the late seventeenth century. Known formally as Monsieur d'Artagnan, he called himself simply 'Artaignan', but this book does not attempt the impossible of correcting Dumas, so d'Artagnan he remains. D'Artagnan's marriage certificate, preserved in the Bibilothèque Nationale, shows his real name to be Charles-Ogier Batz-Castelmore. One of his older brothers was also called Charles, so, on the face of it, even Charles-Ogier was an odd and confusing name for his parents to choose. It was, however, common practice at the time to use a favoured Christian name more than once among siblings, and in due course both d'Artagnan's own children would be baptized Louis.

Charles, the elder brother, makes a fleeting appearance in the Musketeers' roll for 10 March 1633. Some historians have argued that he and Charles-Ogier were one and the same person, and therefore born much earlier, pointing to the inventory of Château Castelmore made after the death of d'Artagnan's father, Bertrand de Batz, in June 1636. The older Charles is mentioned among the beneficiaries, but not Charles-Ogier, the real d'Artagnan; his brother Charles is recorded as absent from the reading of the will, 'in the King's service', and soon afterwards he disappears without trace, probably a casualty of war. As d'Artagnan was still a child, aged about thirteen, a long way down the pecking order in terms of any prospective inheritance, there seems no particular significance in the lack of any reference to him. A further indication that he was born about 1623 comes from Courtilz, who gives d'Artagnan's age as thirty, or nearly thirty, in July 1653. D'Artagnan's compulsory apprenticeship in the guards from 1640 to 1644 would have been entirely unnecessary were he previously a Musketeer in the 1630s.

Neither Samaran nor Jaurgain paid much attention to d'Artagnan's arrival in Paris and Courtilz's account, in Volume 1 of the *Memoirs*, of the multiple duel between Cardinal Richelieu's Guards and the King's Musketeers. Yet everyone involved on one side or the other was real and present in the French capital in May 1640. Some of the detail Courtilz supplies of a fight that was as much farcical as heroic is simply too bizarre to have been invented Jussac's last-minute attempt to find an opponent for d'Artagnan that ended in the recruitment of a prospective churchman in a cassock would have been rejected by Dumas for his novel as far too implausible. R.P. Daniel, in an history of elite French forces first published in 1719, says Courtilz's story of Louis XIII's clandestine meeting with d'Artagnan and the Three Musketeers is eminently plausible, because 'it was a real pleasure for the king to learn his musketeers had manhandled the cardinal's guards.' Humbert de Gallier, in his book on *Auberges et Salons*, confirms that d'Artagnan, Athos and Tréville were drinking companions at the Bel Air tavern in Paris.

The seventeenth-century storyteller, Charles Perrault, visited some of the nobility of Gascony and Béarn, and their Spartan circumstances inspired his version of Cinderella and her impecunious father, Baron Hardupp. Perrault introduced the glass slipper into the fairy tale entirely by accident. He confused 'vair', the word in the local dialect meaning 'animal fur', the source of most local footwear, with 'verre', French for 'glass'.

CHAPTER 3 (pages 53 to 73)

Tréville's opposite number in Richelieu's Guards, the blundering François Dauger de Cavoie, ran out of luck at the siege of Bapaume in 1641: struck by shell fragments, he died from his wounds, leaving his widow to bring up their nine young children. His third son, Eustache Dauger de Cavoie, a scandalous reprobate, was put forward in 1932 by the historian Maurice Duvivier as the logical solution to the mysterious Eustache Dauger, imprisoned at Pignerol in 1669. Alas for Duvivier's brilliantly constructed analysis, within a matter of months, Eustache Dauger de Cavoie was shown to be in another prison, Saint-Lazare, at the time, making it impossible, despite the extraordinary coincidence of names, for him to be the Man in the Iron Mask.

Most of the characters in Rostand's celebrated play, *Cyrano de Bergerac*, set partly on the battlefield and partly in the wild Paris of 1640, are based on real people and events. The actor chased off stage by Cyrano, Monfleury, was as popular as Molière, and enormously fat. Lignière, the drunken writer of epigrams, became an acolyte of the much better-known satirist, Nicolas Boileau. Cyrano's supposedly single-handed defence of Lignière against a mere one hundred assassins was described by historian Gilles Ménage in a contemporary account published two years after his death in 1694. The poet's wealthy cousin, Roxane, was actually called Madeleine Robineau, and Christian was Christophe de Champagne, baron de Neuvillette. In the play Cyrano enables Christian to win Roxane's hand by writing love letters on Christian's behalf that secretly expressed Cyrano's own feelings for her. As d'Artagnan could scarcely string two sentences together and in June 1640 had money to spare, he was as likely a customer as Christian for Cyrano's literary skills to help him pay court to titled Parisian ladies. Roxane herself would not have interested d'Artagnan because in real life she proved rather less of a catch, suffering from such an excess of facial hair that even Cyrano conceded she looked 'a fright'. Cyrano was probably never in love with Roxane in the physical sense, because he had a male lover and constant companion, Charles D'Assouci, a musician and poet.

If Cyrano also helped Christian with his billets-doux, it must have been some years earlier, because by 1640 Christian was already married to Roxane and no longer needed Cyrano's romantic services. The baron was killed at Arras on the opening day of the siege and Roxane, grief stricken, entered the Paris convent of the Filles de la Croix in the rue de la Charonne. When Cyrano was mortally injured in 1655, lingering on for many months, Roxane looked after him until his death on 28 July. Roxane died at the convent in 1657 and her biography, written by the barefoot Carmelite friar, Father Cyprien, was published in 1660.

Cyrano and d'Artagnan were both exceptional swordsmen and both took offence easily. Cyrano, aged twenty-one in 1640, was fighting on average four or five duels a week. At seventeen, d'Artagnan would have been in action just as frequently by inclination, had he not received strict instructions from Tréville to keep out of trouble. Such fire-eating duellists would have been hard put to resist the temptation to challenge each other, and historian Adhémar de Montgon believed they did so out of sheer boredom. In this period Cyrano suffered his only recorded defeat in a duel, so it was perhaps at the hands of d'Artagnan himself. An unnamed 'Gascon cadet', a description that fits d'Artagnan perfectly, wounded Cyrano in this mysterious encounter. The first volume of Courtilz's memoirs of d'Artagnan is subtitled 'The Cadet' and Rostand uses the same expression in his celebrated play about Cyrano.

Richelieu's biographer, Louis Auchincloss, says that Louis XIII had a 'nasty temper'. When Louis and Richelieu fell out furiously, according to Courtilz, over the skirmishes between the King's Musketeers, d'Artagnan and the Cardinal's Guards, the courtier quick and bold enough to interpose himself was the comte de Nogent, François de Noailles. The incident probably happened early in 1642, shortly after Nogent returned to court at the end of his term as ambassador to the Holy See in Rome, and had been appointed a captain of the guard.

CHAPTER 4 (pages 74 to 85)

Richelieu's Army, War, Government and Society in France, 1624–42, a tour de force by David Parrott, makes it easy to understand why the cardinal never found the time to dispose of d'Artagnan as one might a bothersome bluebottle. Richelieu had to oversee a chaotic army, which, as Parrott puts it, was akin to a bathtub with the tap running and the plug out, every new recruit matched by a new desertion. The captains went on leave when they liked and saw no reason to obey orders; because they were paying for their regiments, they believed they had a right to decide how their men were used.

For two such captains, Tréville and his brother-in-law Essarts, and their involvement in the plot to kill Richelieu in 1642, see the notes appended to the 1967 collection of Tallemant's *Historiettes*, edited by Antoine Adams. Queen Anne's betrayal of the royal favourite and the secret treaty with Spain to the cardinal is recounted in detail by Philippe Erlanger in his biography of Cinq-Mars. Richelieu was always disposed to believe that Tréville and his immediate associates were guilty: twelve years earlier, in 1630, Tréville and some of his men had been implicated in a similar plan to assassinate the cardinal on the Day of Dupes.

In the *Memoirs*, d'Artagnan's lover, Lady Percy, Duchess of Carlisle and Richelieu's secret agent, is known only as Milédi. Courtilz ostentatiously leaves a blank space for her real name and later refers to her as 'the daughter of a peer of England'. Charles Carlton, in his biography of Charles I, says that Lucy Percy's role as an amorous *agent provocateur* began before she entered Richelieu's employ: the Duke of Buckingham tried to introduce Lucy into Charles I's bed. Antoine-Marie Roederer, in his 1832 *Intrigues politiques and galantes de la cour de France*, describes her as Richelieu's 'most dangerous spy'. Dumas drew on Roederer for the main plot of *The Three Musketeers*, but Lucy's theft of Queen Anne's diamond studs – a foolish gift to Buckingham – involved the Musketeers only in Dumas' imagination: in 1625 Athos, Aramis and Porthos were children and d'Artagnan still a babe in arms. Lady Percy's well-documented warning to Francis Pym in January 1642 that Charles I was on his way to arrest him and the rest of the Five Members at the House of Commons, enabling them to time their escape down-river to perfection, appears in the memoirs of Sir Philip Warwick, secretary to the English Treasury, which were discovered after his death on 25 January 1682.

D'Artagnan probably first met Lucy Percy in London during the summer of 1643 after she had been banished from royal circles for her treachery. If Sir Thomas Suckling's highly salacious poetry is to be believed, Lucy was scandalously promiscuous, and could well have begun a sexual relationship with d'Artagnan. Courtilz refers to the Gascon's subsequent visit to King Charles' court at Oxford, as a member of the comte d'Harcourt's deputation. This largely forgotten diplomatic mission to England is mentioned by Veronica Wedgwood in *The King's War 1641–1647*, quoting a contemporary tract, the *Parliament Scout*. D'Artagnan did not look the part and was perhaps fortunate that the attention of the Parliamentarians was diverted by their discovery of a Catholic spy in Harcourt's party: the queen's favourite, Wat Tyler, who was imprisoned in the Tower of London. Courtilz subsequently places d'Artagnan at the first Battle of Newbury, which has been neglected by most historians and seems far too obscure a battle to be a random choice by his biographer.

Courtilz also describes the attempt in December 1643 to kill d'Artagnan and the Three Musketeers at the Saint-Germain fair, and the strong suspicion that Lucy Percy was behind it. The death of Athos is recorded in a mortuary register at Saint-Sulpice and was first discovered by the historiographer Augustus Jal.

CHAPTER 5 (pages 86 to 111)

The military historian Pinard lists the campaigns in which d'Artagnan took part with the Musketeers. His vast eight-volume work, *Chronologie historique-militaire*, drew on the seventeenth-century records of the Dépôt de la Guerre, which unfortunately did not survive the French Revolution. Although it has been suggested that Pinard relied upon Courtilz in crediting d'Artagnan with various feats of arms, his opus magnus was published between 1760 and 1766, at a time when Courtilz's biography of d'Artagnan had long since been discredited and was almost forgotten. It seems reasonable to regard Pinard in the main as independent corroboration.

There is a curious connection between the arrest, on Anne of Austria's orders, of the father of the Paris Parlement, Pierre Broussel, in which d'Artagnan was involved and which led to the civil war of the Fronde, and the Grande Mademoiselle's turning of the Bastille's guns on the royal troops to save the Prince of Condé's rebel army from defeat in front of the gates of Paris. The governor of the Bastille, Jerome de Louvières, was Broussel's son and welcomed the opportunity to revenge himself on the Queen Regent. Much later, the Grande Mademoiselle, afraid of Louis XIV's reaction, tried to pretend she had left the Bastille before the cannonade began, but both Madame de Motteville and Paul Gondi, Cardinal de Retz, said she personally gave the command to fire and there is little doubt this was what cousin Louis believed.

Courtilz explains the duplicitous circumstances in which Besmaux unexpectedly became one of Jerome's successors as governor of the Bastille. Charles Samaran, in a short account of Besmaux's life, first published in 1965 by the Society of Parisian History, confirms that not long previously Besmaux had been in disgrace and that d'Artagnan interceded with Mazarin on his behalf. As governor, Besmaux was an important witness to both the civil marriage ceremony between d'Artagnan and Anne-Charlotte de Chanlecy at the Louvre on 5 March 1659 and to the religious service on 3 April held in the nearby Church of Saint André-des-Arts. Almost none of d'Artagnan's family attended either ceremony. Sylvie Monin, in her *Les Artagnan en Bourgogne*, points out that d'Artagnan could not remember his late father Bertrand's Christian name and wrongly recorded it in the church register as Antoine, scarcely an auspicious start to this short-lived union.

CHAPTER 6 (pages 112 to 139)

An anonymous contemporary eyewitness account, *Rélation des magnificences faites par M. Fouquet a Vaux-le-Vicomte lorsque le roi alla*, has survived of Nicolas Fouquet's great party at his newly completed chateau in 1661, held in the presence of the king. At the time, Fouquet clearly believed he was untouchable. Historian Innes Marat describes Fouquet, the over-mighty subject, as follows: 'The superintendant is not accountable. No one can ask to see his accounts, not even the King. He justifies his administration only when it suits him.' Perhaps Fouquet's biggest miscalculation was his attempted seduction of Louise de La Vallière, unaware of her new relationship with the king, by offering her a large sum of money to prostitute herself. The story is told by Gabrielle Basset d'Auriac, in *Les deux pénitences de Louise de La Vallière*.

When Louis chose d'Artagnan to arrest Fouquet, the Gascon claimed to be ill. Courtilz makes no mention of his illness, although the remainder of his account of what happened at Nantes is consistent in every respect with other sources. Instead, Courtilz refers to a conversation with Colbert in which d'Artagnan said he would have been grateful if the king had chosen someone else. 'M. Colbert, who was quick and smart, immediately enquired if I was a pensioner of the Superintendant like many others, since I now excused myself from obeying the King's orders.' It seems probable that d'Artagnan's illness was exaggerated, at the very least. When d'Artagnan could not afford to pay his rent, the money to do so came from a friend of Fouquet, Nicolas Hullot, whose father Pierre owned the property in the rue du Bac leased by d'Artagnan. It may be that Colbert knew that directly or indirectly d'Artagnan was under an obligation to Fouquet, whether or not the Gascon himself was fully aware of the circumstances. Paul Morand, biographer of Fouquet, relates how d'Artagnan bungled his arrest and had to send a deputation that included his quartermaster sergeant, Saint-Mars, to reassure the king. This was almost certainly the first time Louis met Saint-Mars and it led to his subsequent appointment as Fouquet's jailer at Pignerol. Saint-Mars was also part of d'Artagnan's troop of Musketeers who guarded Fouquet at the Bastille. When the court officials came to give Fouquet the trial verdict, fearful of his reaction, they asked for personal protection; d'Artagnan summoned Saint-Mars. Courtilz provides the bizarre, and, as it would prove, highly significant, account of how governor Besmaux put his young wife in a huge mask to discourage the attentions of the Musketeers.

Le Tellier's instructions to d'Artagnan to undertake a secret journey in May 1664 appear in the Fouquet section of the Archives of the Bastille. The letter from d'Artagnan's sister referring to his visit is in the local

Archives de Castetbon. This was probably the only occasion on which d'Artagnan returned to Château Castlemore, although on 26 April 1660 he had passed within a few kilometres when escorting the king to the marriage negotiations that took place on the Spanish frontier.

Samaran examines the relationship between d'Artagnan and Fouquet in an extended essay for *La Revue de Paris*, published in 1912. The *Journal* of honest judge Ormesson is another reliable source of how d'Artagnan became increasingly sympathetic towards Fouquet. D'Artagnan told Ormesson on 27 July 1664 that he would not reveal the conversations between Fouquet and his lawyers, a decision highly provocative to the king and to Pierre Séguier, the trial president. Chancellor Séguier's extraordinary fit of temper, when he destroyed 172 other judgments brought to him to sign, is recorded in Lemoine's *Lettres sur la cour de Louis XIV*.

CHAPTER 7 (pages 140 to 158)

The attack on the convent of Chelles, just to the east of Paris, which led indirectly to d'Artagnan being made captain of the King's First Musketeers, is described by Bryan Bevan in his biography of Hortense Mancini. After a lengthy lawsuit, Hortense's husband, Armand, convinced a court to strip her of all her property rights. Hortense fled to England, where she became Charles II's mistress, and never returned to France.

Louis XIV's successive affairs with three of the Mancini sisters were said to have prompted Queen Maria-Theresa's ill-judged coupling with her black page, Nabo, a dwarf seventy centimetres tall, which resulted in the birth of a baby on 16 November 1664. Historian Pierre-Marie Dijol concluded that for committing so heinous a crime, Nabo was locked in the iron mask. Jean-Christian Petitfils, the most erudite of modern French historians, points out in his painstaking work, *Le Masque de fer*, that Nabo (whose real name was Augustin) does not match any of the contemporary descriptions of the Mask as someone above average in height.

The amusing episode where Queen Maria-Theresa was forced to spend the night in a peasant's cottage in Flanders together with Louis and three of his mistresses, Henrietta Stuart, Louise de La Vallière and Athénaïs de Montespan, took place in April 1670 and is described by Prince Michael of Greece in his biography of the king. Louis' affair with Henrietta had begun in May 1661, with Louise in July 1661, and with Athénaïs in July 1667; it is difficult to decide when he finally ceased to go to each of their beds. The king's obsession with sex is well documented and may even have been understated. Historian Lisa Hilton says the king 'made love the way he ate, with a capacity that would have finished most men'.

The Princess of the Palatinate describes her brother-in-law's desires with a Teutonic detachment: 'Everything was grist to his mill, provided it was female; peasant girls, gardeners' daughters, chambermaids, ladies of quality, so long as they pretended they were in love with him.'

Before and after most of the other concubines, came Athénaïs' personal maid and confidante, Claude de Vin des Oeillets. The daughter of a prominent Parisian actress, Oeillets boasted to Primi Visconti that she regularly enjoyed 'carnal relations with the King'. Noted Visconti: 'She seems quite proud of the fact that she had had several children by him. Not that she is such a beauty, but the King often found himself alone with her when his mistress was unwell or busy . . .' Louis, if kept waiting, clearly had a libido with a mind of its own.

There is some dispute over the sex of Athénaïs' first illegitimate child by Louis, and whether this was in fact the infant smuggled past the sleeping Maria-Theresa by the comte de Lauzun; but he probably performed this sterling service on more than one occasion. Sadly, not in question is that the lovers' first child was born 'with a head so huge, the neck could not support it' and the baby died in 1672, aged three. Of the seven children born to Louis and Athénaïs, three died very young and three more had deformities.

Their governess, Françoise Scarron, attracts an unusual level of disagreement among historians, many of whom remain convinced of her piety and virtue. Of course, the more influential Françoise became at court, the more her enemies had cause to slander her. However, corroborative evidence exists of her adultery with the marquis de Villarceaux and the compromising picture of her that he painted. On 17 February 1661 the Dutch scholar, Christian Huyghens, put a note in his *Journal* about an interesting visit to Paris: 'Went to see the Abbé Boisrobert. He showed me the portrait of Ninon de l'Enclos naked in her bedroom, and the one of Madame Scarron painted by M. de Villarceaux.' At the time Françoise was of passing interest only to a few *salonières*. Once Françoise's ambitions seemed at serious risk of being frustrated by revelations of her past indiscretions, the more ruthless side of her character came to the fore, and, as d'Artagnan found to his cost, anyone who stood in her way was vulnerable. As Françoise's biographer Charlotte Haldane says, 'If she was not in love with . . . any man, not even the King, she was undoubtedly in love with Power.'

CHAPTER 8 (pages 159 to 178)

Étienne Martin's activities in England between December 1668 and July 1669, and the attempts to lure him back to France, are described by Aimé-Daniel Rabinet in *La Tragique Aventure de Roux de Marcilly*, the

Huguenot spy who employed the fake valet. The dates of dispatches filed in the French Foreign Ministry Archives, the Affaires Etrangères, and in the English State Papers, reconcile only when the different calendars in operation on the respective sides of the Channel are taken into account. While Britain continued to abide by the Julian calendar until 1752, its Continental neighbours gradually adopted the calendar reformed by Gregorian III in 1582. By 1669, this was ten days behind the date still in use the British Isles and in most of the Dutch United Provinces. To avoid confusion, the Gregorian calendar has been used in this book for all events taking place on the Continent and both calendars for the period of Martin's activities in England.

If, as Roux claimed, the Committee of Ten plotting an insurrection against Louis XIV's regime had met, they probably did so early in 1669, when Roux believed he had a promise of English support for his plan to bring the Swiss cantons into the conspiracy. Their meeting may have been held in London, seen as a safe haven: Charles II had made clear his unwillingness to arrest anyone wanted for questioning in France, refusing even to apprehend the most notorious fugitive from justice, the notorious poisoner, the marquise de Brinvilliers. Martin was already making plans to disappear and this would have been his ideal opportunity to bribe one of the conspirators, David Eustache, the pastor of Montpellier, to lend him his identity, thereby ensuring that he would be helped by the Protestant communities wherever he went. Augustin and Claude Cochin, writing in the 1913 bulletin for the Society of French History, uncovered a Vatican scheme to undermine the Huguenot exodus from France. In March 1668 the papal nuncio to the court of Louis XIV, Bargellini, had compiled for the pope a list of 'fifty to sixty Huguenot ministers' whom he believed would convert to Catholicism if the stakes were high enough. He considered a budget of 1,500,000 livres would be sufficient to buy pensions for the key priests, including Eustache, who had been married three times, and whom Bargellini described as 'avaricious and vain'.

There is no surviving record in the English State Papers of valet Martin's final departure from Dover in July 1669 using Eustache's identity, but in the 'Domestics' section is a note of the issue of an earlier passport for Roux de Marcilly and one other person, for 'a return journey to the continent from any port', suggesting that checks on travellers and the travel papers themselves were often rudimentary.

CHAPTER 9 (pages 179 to 201)

Some of the most eminent historians have failed to unravel the various confrontations between Lauzun and both Athénaïs de Montespan and Louis XIV. Even the perceptive biography of Lauzun by Mary F. Sandars, *Lauzun: Courtier and Adventurer*, published in 1908, confuses the chronology of events. The most reliable sources are dispatches by the Venetian ambassador, Sagredo, quoted by Ravaisson; supplemented by the memoirs of two courtiers, the Abbé de Choisy and Charles-Auguste, marquis de la Fare.

Madame de Sévigné's letters, particularly one of 26 December 1672 recording an earlier dinner table conversation with Françoise Scarron, are a useful insight on how Louis XIV became increasingly exasperated with Lauzun and how Françoise skilfully fanned the flames. However, it was Lauzun's refusal to apologize to Athénaïs, and not his rumoured marriage to the Grande Mademoiselle or his outbursts in the presence of the king, that finally caused him to be sent to Pignerol in December 1671. The duc de Gramont, who many years previously had invited the teenage Lauzun into his household and felt protective towards him, demanded to know what had taken place and was told privately this version of events. According to Tallemant, soon after making a nuisance of himself with the king, Gramont became the subject of vicious lampoons accusing him of being a homosexual and of cowardice in the face of the enemy.

Gramont had married one of Richelieu's nieces, was well liked by the cardinal, and remained steadfast to Anne of Austria and Mazarin, so much so that when the royal family fled from Paris in 1649, Mazarin gave Gramont personal charge of the young king. The duke knew more than most about what happened backstairs in the royal household, particularly the circumstances of the conception and birth of Louis XIV. However, Gramont's biographer, Petitot, admits that he was far from personally astute, making it likely that he gave Lauzun sensitive information without appreciating its significance.

D'Artagnan had enjoyed a similar close relationship with his old captain, Tréville, who must have been tempted on several occasions to complain to a sympathetic ear about his treatment by his lover, Queen Anne. Thrown together by circumstances on the road to Pignerol, d'Artagnan and Lauzun had every opportunity to compare notes, and to reach the private conclusion that Louis had no right to sit on the French throne.

The surviving letters sent by and to the jailer of the Mask, Saint-Mars, almost 150 in total, reside partly in the modern section of the Service Historique de l'Armée de Terre, at the Château de Vincennes, embracing the former archives of the Dépôt de la Guerre; and partly in the Bastille Archives at the Bibliothèque Nationale, in Paris. Some originals are missing, or, more probably, misfiled, or are now almost unreadable; we know of them and their contents only because they were referred to, or reproduced, in some rare French historical works. These include *Le véritable homme dit au Masque de fer* by St-Mihiel, as early as 1790; Pierre Roux-Fazillac's *Recherches historiques et critiques sur l'Homme au masque de fer*, published, like the good revolutionary he was, in Year IX of the new order (1800); two books by Joseph Delort, *L'Homme au masque de fer* (1825) and *Histoire de la Detention des Philosophes* (1829); and the single most important book published on the subject, Major Théodore Iung's *La Vérité sur le Masque de fer* (1872).

In 1871, the Prussians had swept all before them and occupied Paris, making the French army an unpromising career for ambitious officers. Major Iung got himself noticed by burrowing deep into the archives of the War Office, and produced an exceptional breadth of information, much of it of hidden significance, about the prisons of the Iron Mask and their reluctant occupants. When his book was published, Iung was promoted colonel, and later to brigadier-general.

The letters in the Bastille Archive show that Saint-Mars' formidable wife, Marie-Antoinette, made frequent visits to Paris. For a long time her husband was forbidden to leave Pignerol and it was too dangerous for her to travel alone. Saint-Mars usually had to obtain permission from Louvois for one of his prison officers to accompany her to the capital, a much sought-after trip. Marie-Antoinette's favourite escort was Zachée de Blainvilliers, the jailer's young cousin; on 25 March 1675, for example, Louvois gave him permission to travel with her. No doubt Louvois would have sorely tempted to refuse, as almost the last person he wanted to see in Paris was his jailer's formidable spouse, but the war minister knew that Madame de Saint-Mars could make life very difficult for him through her sister, his mistress.

CHAPTER 10 (pages 202 to 217)

The infamous red casket that led to the sensational pursuit of the marquise de Brinvilliers was opened on 18 August 1672 but the full significance of Étienne Martin's involvement did not emerge until after the marquise's arrest in Liege on 25 March 1676. At her first interrogation back in Paris in April 1676, recorded in the fourth volume of the Archives of the Bastille, Brinvilliers admitted her link with Martin and confessed that she had urged him to go into hiding for their mutual safety. For Martin the price of Louvois's protection was returning, when things got too hot to handle, to Pignerol, which explains his efforts to downplay his involvement in the scandal. It was a risk worth taking for Martin (who as a former *greffier* knew his way around the legal system) so long as the principal suspect remained at large. The greater the hue and cry against the marquise, the more attractive Pignerol must have seemed to Martin as a place of refuge, leading his jailer Saint-Mars to observe laconically to Louvois that that this was a prisoner who gave him no trouble. Louvois communicated with Martin in cypher and many of the minister's instructions have survived; but apart from a heading with Martin's name, they consist of endless numbers. Lacking the nomenclature, the system key that matched numerical sequences to people and places, cryptographers so far have been unable to crack the code.

Étienne Martin is the fourth name on the list drawn up in 1661 of Fouquet's associates to be arrested, a document held at the Bibliothèque Nationale in Paris and in particular among the Archives of the Bastille, an important source concerning Martin's various activities, Fouquet's imprisonment, Saint-Mars' role as jailer and the ring of Paris poisoners. The archives had a long period of gestation. In 1749 Henri Godillon, called Chevalier, a major on the staff of the Bastille, began to catalogue its large collection of documents. It seems likely that Chevalier was the anonymous source of the important account of how the Mask's cell was stripped after his death to ensure no message had been left behind for posterity. Between his more mundane duties, Chevalier spent a remarkable thirty-eight years on his task, and it was still incomplete when he died in 1787.

After the fall of the Bastille in July 1789, heralding the start of the French Revolution, Chevalier's original records were in chaos; many fell into the hands of booksellers, and some found their way to the Russian Imperial Court at St Petersburg, only to suffer the ravages of a second people's revolution in 1917. Even so, in April 1797 more than 600,000 items were handed over to the Library of the Arsenal, whose staff recoiled in dismay and sealed them in a disused basement. Here they remained, gathering cobwebs, for more than forty years, until they were rescued by a young librarian called François Ravaisson. In 1840, while investigating an unpleasant smell in his little kitchen, he asked the workmen to raise the slabs that made up the floor. Beneath it was a heap of old papers and Ravaisson pulled out a *lettre de cachet* signed by Louis XIV. It was the first of a veritable treasure trove of documents that Ravaisson painstakingly catalogued over the next thirty years. Many of the yellowing registers of prisoners still contain blackened holes caused by a half-hearted attempt to burn them during the attack on the Bastille.

Ravaisson found several documents relating to Martin, although he did not appreciate their significance. After his release from the Bastille in

1661, Martin blended perfectly into the background in the quiet town of Montauban, where he lived in the prophetically named rue Perdu (the Street of the Lost) with the widow Vinet. Martin called himself Marc-Antoine de Saint-Martin while in Montauban, but, like many of the names he is known to have used, it was probably false. He used the identity of the real and harmless Étienne Martin, who had married a certain Jeanne Villeroy in Brittany on 10 September 1643. The fake Martin also had papers that declared him to be the sieur de Breuil, on the lowest level of nobility. These, however, may have been genuine because Martin's cousin was someone with proven noble antecedents: Madeleine Bertrand de Breuil, the unsuspecting wife of Gaudan de Sainte-Croix, another link in the deadly chain of murderers and poisoners. Sainte-Croix and Martin helped the notorious marquise de Brinvilliers to dispose of several members of her family. While imprisoned in the Bastille, Sainte-Croix shared a cell with the Italian poisoner, Niccolo Eggidi, and received visits from the high priestess herself, La Voisin, one of his sexual partners. Both Eggidi and Sainte-Croix, mistakenly classed as low-risk category prisoners, had the run of the Bastille in 1663 when d'Artagnan arrived with Fouquet; Sainte-Croix was known to d'Artagnan, who treated him cordially as a fellow Gascon. As La Voisin was a regular visitor to the Bastille, Fouquet was ideally placed to conspire with three of the most infamous poisoners in French history, all of whom had links with Étienne Martin.

CHAPTER 11 (pages 218 to 228)

The incredible escape of two Bastille prisoners in September 1673 prompted an anxious Louvois to move the Mask from Paris to Pignerol. Boissière, from Beauvais, had been sent to the Bastille on 22 June 1673, less than three months previously, for some minor misdemeanour, possibly duelling. Baudouin had been incarcerated since 28 August 1668, his family raising the money to pay for him to occupy one of the more comfortable cells. The prisoners were never recaptured. The interest in their feat heightened the rumours that the Bastille still held a much more mysterious state prisoner, said by some to be the actor Molière.

In 1883 a pamphlet published by Anatole Loquin would revive the improbable hypothesis that Molière had not died but instead had been spirited away to the Bastille, his identity hidden in an iron mask. According to Loquin, the king had agreed to his secret imprisonment, fearing that Molière's trial for incest would reflect badly on the monarchy.

Although the Molièristes poured scorn on his findings, Loquin persisted, first in two pamphlets published in Bordeaux in 1896 and 1899, then in a book printed in 1900. Seventy years later, historian Marcel Diamont-Berger revived the theory, attributing the pressure put on the king to disown the playwright, and Molière's subsequent fate, to the appointment in January 1671 of a Catholic zealot as archbishop of Paris. Diamont-Berger also remarked on the absence of a signature or of any witnesses in the official record of Molière's burial and on the arrival at Pignerol not long afterwards of an unidentified prisoner. In view of the notoriously poor state of his health, however, it is extremely unlikely that Molière could have survived in prison for more than thirty years. Rather, the Catholic Church may have arranged for him to be buried in unconsecrated ground, as a petty retribution after death for his ridiculing of them in life. The year when the rumour about a mysterious prisoner began, 1673, and not Molière himself, was the real clue.

The identity of the prisoner who was brought to Pignerol on 7 April 1674 has always been the subject of heated debate among historians. Iung believed him to be Louis Oldendorf, a nobleman from Lorraine involved in Roux's conspiracy against Louis XIV. However, Jean-Christian Petitfils showed that while Oldendorf had been arrested and taken to the Bastille in 1673, he was released from there in April 1679, taken to Dunkerque and deported to the United Provinces. Oldendorf was never at Pignerol.

Petitfils believed the prisoner who arrived in 1674 to be a Jacobin monk, whom he named 'Lapierre', or La Pierre, based on a reference in Saint-Mars' expense accounts. There is proof, however, that Lapierre was already at Pignerol. On 9 December 1673, in a letter to Louvois, Saint-Mars refers to him by name as the prisoner who had been pressing for some time to be allowed to write to the war minister about his sentence. This leaves just one credible candidate, revealed in Chapter 14, to be the man who arrived at the fortress on 7 April 1674 under the tightest possible security.

Saint-Mars' first reference to a Jacobin monk appears in a letter dated 2 May 1676, confirming that his presence at Pignerol was not a secret, whereas that of the prisoner who arrived two years earlier clearly was. In 1676 Louvois had no recollection of the Jacobin priest and was obliged to ask Saint-Mars about him, a highly improbable lapse of memory if he had been the prisoner whose transfer to Pignerol was on the war minister's direct orders two years previously. Much later, in January 1694, Saint-Mars was asked whether he knew the identity of the prisoner still at Pignerol 'who has been there longest', because he had just died, but Saint-Mars had no idea of his name. This was almost certainly the monk.

The Jacobin has been proposed by some historians as the unknown arrival in 1674 on the doubtful premise that this filled the sole gap in Pignerol's records, whereas in fact there are several other inmates for whom information is incomplete. For example, even Petitfils' meticulous list of the prisoners at Pignerol during the tenure of Saint-Mars omits Caluzio, held at the donjon for two days for interrogation in 1673 and then elsewhere in the town. If there had been any direct evidence that the mysterious prisoner who arrived on 7 April 1674 was the Jacobin monk, then surely Iung would have found it. The exceptional security arrangements for the prisoner reinforce the conclusion that it was not the Jacobin who joined Fouquet and Lauzun behind the walls of Pignerol.

Lauzun's mysterious letter to Louvois on 27 January 1680, saying that he had secret information that only his friend Henri de Barrail could safely pass on to the war minister, hitherto has never been adequately explained. Some historians speculate that Lauzun was trying to arrange a marriage between his niece, the daughter of his sister, the comtesse de Nogent, and Louis-François-Marie Le Tellier de Louvois, the marquis de Barbezieux, Louvois' son. Lauzun's niece was also his designated heir. Had Lauzun after all been permitted to marry the Grande Mademoiselle, who was beyond child-bearing age, Barbezieux stood to inherit her vast estates by marrying Lauzun's niece. This was sufficient bait, in such a hypothesis, for Louvois to support both Lauzun's release from Pignerol and his controversial union with the king's cousin. However, in his letter to the war minister, Lauzun said that if Louvois did not allow Barrail to come, he would have to 'entrust' the information to his sister. If this information really related to the marriage proposal, far from putting pressure on Louvois to agree to Barrail's visit, it would have been a positive incentive for him to refuse. Mary Sandars acknowledges that Madame de Nogent was 'on very friendly terms' with Louvois, so she was far more likely than Barrail to arrange matters to the minister's advantage. Lauzun had already been given a much better opportunity to make this proposal, in November 1677, when Louvois had agreed that Madame de Nogent and a lawyer, Isarn Grèzes, could visit him at Pignerol to settle family affairs arising from the death of Lauzun's elder brother.

Grèzes made a meticulous record of the visit, from the moment they arrived to find the fortress town's gates firmly shut at eight on a Sunday morning because the governor, the marquis d'Herleville, was testing his troops' readiness to repel a surprise attack. The only mention Lauzun made of his niece to his visitors was to enquire after her health, and it seems highly implausible that he would deliberately languish in jail for a further three years if he already believed he had a way out. As, in January 1680, Barbezieux was still only eleven years old, such a marriage in any event could not have taken place for some time, giving Lauzun – as Louvois would have been well aware – every opportunity after his release to alter his will or arrange for his niece to marry someone else. Louvois would also have been hard put to explain to Louis XIV and his family why he was suddenly supporting Lauzun's marriage to the Grande Mademoiselle, having vehemently opposed it; and the minister must have known that any betrothal involving Barbezieux, Mademoiselle's millions and Lauzun's niece and heir would become public knowledge before long. Both Lauzun and Louvois surely would have rejected the idea as unfeasible, leaving Lauzun's discovery of the identity of the Mask as the only credible explanation for his letter, hinting at the real trump card he had to play.

CHAPTER 12 (pages 229 to 244)

The Affair of the Poisons often causes confusion, but Anne Somerset's superbly researched account emphasizes this pivotal point: in January 1680, when the scandal broke over the heads of the good and the great, it related to events that had begun as far back as 1666. Many from the court's inner circle, including Lauzun, would have known at the time what was alleged to have taken place and who was involved.

At first, most people in authority had mistakenly believed the ringleader of the poisoners, La Voisin, to be a harmless charlatan. They could see that her second husband, the retired jeweller Antoine Monvoison, remained in excellent health despite persistent rumours that she was conspiring with her sorcerer lover, Le Sage, to dispose of him. They did not appreciate that La Voisin's housemaid, Margot, had discovered the poisoners' plans. The maid had a soft spot for Antoine and stole the antidote for the poison from Le Sage's bag. Margot regularly mixed it into Antoine's food and once, when she had no time to do this, knocked over his bowl of deadly bouillon before he could plunge his spoon into it.

However, behind such episodes, reminiscent of a Molière comedy, lay the more serious menace of Olympe Mancini's visits to La Voisin. Olympe wanted to dispose of those she saw as her main rivals for Louis' affections and 'malevolently tried to harm both Henrietta . . . and Louise de La Vallière'. Later Henrietta Stuart would die in suspicious circumstances, but Olympe reserved her real venom for Louise and the king. According to La Voisin's testimony after her arrest, Olympe, believing she could not regain her place in Louis's heart and thereby revenge herself on Louise de La Vallière, flew into a rage and said 'she would carry her vengeance to even greater lengths. She would do away with both one and the other.'

Not long afterwards, Louise, alone at her modest two-storey house in the Palais-Royal gardens, was awoken by her pet dog and heard someone trying to force open the window of her maid's room. She raised the alarm but the intruders made good their escape, leaving hooks and a rope ladder against the outside wall. When Louise informed the king, he arranged a guard of Musketeers day and night on the property and ordered his own food tasters to protect her from poison. Louis knew the intended means and may have suspected that Olympe was behind the abortive attempt.

Although ignorance of the medical causes of death accentuated the fear that poison might be the cause, nothing could be proved. Forensic pathology was unknown: the Marsh Test for arsenic would not be invented until 1838. However, Olympe was often around when her enemies died in suspicious circumstances.

Athénaïs de Montespan was first implicated by the poisoners in September 1668, when Le Sage was accused of sorcery and stunned the court by revealing her relationship with La Voisin. He also alleged that Athénaïs had already taken part in a Black Mass 'for the purpose of causing the death of Madame de La Vallière', adding that for such ceremonies to be effective, they had to be repeated twice in quick succession; but that Athénaïs told him she had not got the time. For the mistress *en titre*, in her prime at twenty-five, in great demand at court, this inability to find a gap in her crowded social diary for two more perverted Masses has a ring of truth, almost of gallows humour, about it.

CHAPTER 13 (pages 245 to 257)

Despite the extraordinary security measures taken to seclude the Mask and Fouquet at the fort of Exilles, dogged supporters of the theory that at least one of the inmates guarded by Saint-Mars was only a valet, either 'Eustache Danger' or La Rivière or indeed both, rely upon a letter from Louvois to Saint-Mars dated 14 December 1681. The minister referred disparagingly to the prisoners and said that the clothes Saint-Mars proposed to provide them must last three or four years. However, in this context Louvois used the phrase *'faire habiller'*, where *faire* was a causative verb, as in *'Je le fis arreter'*, 'I had him arrested.' The causative indicates that a third party was going to perform the action, and it is highly unlikely Louvois meant that Saint-Mars could go to the expense of having a tailor make new clothes, given that the minister was concerned about the cost. No mention was made of the purchase of new clothes, so if someone else were to be involved, it was surely in the context of making existing clothes do. Expenses Saint-Mars incurred immediately afterwards 'for your prisoners', reimbursed by Louvois on

31 December, may well have been for a seamstress to make repairs and alterations.

Significantly, the jailer already had in his possession Count Mattioli's fine array of garments, originally brought to Pignerol by his luckless valet, who had suffered the same imprisonment as his master. Saint-Mars took them to Exilles on Louvois' express instructions, despite the fact that their owner remained behind. In his July 1681 letter to d'Estrades, Saint-Mars had stated that Mattioli would not be going with him. Louvois' order concerning Mattioli's clothing made sense only if, in the Alice in Wonderland environment of such prisons, the social status of at least one of Saint-Mars' two prisoners still required him to be supplied with clothes of this quality. Fouquet's own expensive wardrobe had been returned to his family, because he was supposed to be dead.

Until Saint-Mars' letter of June 1681 to ambassador Estrades was discovered, making it clear that Mattioli would remain at Pignerol when the jailer moved to Exilles, most French historians were convinced that his secret prisoner on Sainte-Marguerite was the Italian count. Some still persisted with this conclusion, relying on a letter from Saint-Mars to Barbezieux dated 6 January 1696, in which he referred to his *ensien prisonnier*. They interpreted this as meaning his 'former prisoner', and argued that Mattioli, left behind at Pignerol, had returned to Saint-Mars' tender care at Sainte-Marguerite. In the seventeenth century, the adjective *'ensien'* or in its modern spelling, *'ancien'*, usually indicated 'long-standing', but in the right context, its positioning could also mean a ranking officer by virtue of seniority. Saint-Mars, with his fastidious attention to protocol, could have used it to describe the much higher-ranking prisoner in his care.

Mattioli did indeed rejoin Saint-Mars at Sainte-Marguerite, but not until April 1694, when Pignerol was threatened by Savoy. The arduous journey through the mountains took a heavy toll on Mattioli, who died soon after his arrival at Sainte-Marguerite. He was not the prisoner in the steel mask transferred from Exilles in 1687, and glimpsed at Grasse. Saint-Mars would scarcely have employed Italian porters to carry an Italian.

CHAPTER 14 (pages 258 to 283)

The heavy casualties needlessly suffered by the King's Musketeers at the siege of Maastricht in 1673 when d'Artagnan was ordered to mount a night attack, reinforce the conclusion that Louis XIV and Louvois were doing their best to give their troublesome commander a hero's funeral. The correct parallel for the King's Musketeers would have been

Napoleon's Imperial Guard, ever present on the battlefield but only used *in extremis*, which certainly did not apply to the military situation at Maastricht, whose surrender was only a matter of time.

The alleged eyewitness account by Lord Alington of d'Artagnan's fall at Maastricht is reproduced by Winston Churchill in his biography of the Duke of Marlborough. The eighteenth-century editor of *The Extinct Peerage of England*, Solomon Bolton, supplies the insalubrious background of William Lord Alington, both an Irish and an English peer, whose line died out in 1692. Alington, often confused by historians with Lord Arlington, one of Charles II's ministers, had an Irish peerage arising out of his estate near Killard, on the western coast of Ireland in what is now County Clare, but this consisted of little more than a run-down manor and a few miserable villages surrounded by bog. Alington married three times: two of his wives died in suspicious circumstances, and he may well have been murdered by the third. Meanwhile, in 1682, Charles II made him the second Baron Alington and appointed him constable of the Tower of London. In 1685, a few days before the death of the king, Alington was strongly suspected of being involved in the mysterious death of the Earl of Essex, a prisoner in the Tower, found with his throat cut.

As to the evidence of Saint-Mars' unexpected arrival in Maastricht at the end of the siege, the original of Saint-Mars' coded report to Louvois about d'Artagnan dated 20 July 1673 is missing. However, it could easily have been misfiled later because Louvois' reply, sent from Nancy and dated 4 August, confusingly refers to Saint-Mars' letter as 'your letter of twentieth of this month', that is, August 1673. In 1868 Ravaisson published Louvois' response to Saint-Mars of 4 August, although without realizing its importance, in Volume 3 of the Bastille Archives. At the time Ravaisson clearly had in his possession the original of Louvois' reply, now also missing, because he made a note to the effect that Louvois had written his letter in the last few days of July (hence its reference to 'this month') but had delayed sending it.

The first direct evidence of the metal mask was announced by Stanislas Brugnon in 1987, at a symposium of historians in Cannes. His report of this exceptional discovery, included in a compendium of the papers given at the conference, was particularly coy, perhaps because in the strictest sense it was not a new discovery at all. In 1963 a theology professor from Montpellier, Xavier Azéma, had published a biography of Louis Fouquet, concentrating on his contribution to the Jansenist movement. In a footnote he quoted from the ecclesiastic newsletter of 4 September 1687 he had found at the Bibliothèque Sainte-Geneviève in Paris, including its reference to the prisoner 'with a steel mask on his face', but was unaware of its importance. It was rather galling for the finest historians in France to have to admit that the evidence had been right under their noses for a quarter of a century. If Du Junca saw the metal mask when d'Artagnan arrived at the Bastille, then he knew better than to include it in his journal. His and other references to a velvet mask were either circumstantial or hearsay evidence, making the 1687 eyewitness account of a metal mask of supreme importance.

The belated discovery also undermined the central conclusion of a British historian resident in France, John Noone, in his considerable work, *The Man Behind the Iron Mask*. At Cannes Noone had argued that the whole story of the mask had been invented by Saint-Mars to boost his own importance. At the next symposium of historians, held in Pignerol (now Pinerolo) itself in 1992, Noone admitted 'I am no longer sure it was just a bluff.'

The full significance of the newsletter lay not just in establishing the existence of the metal mask, but in its report of what Saint-Mars had said previously, in an unguarded moment, about his prisoners at Pignerol and Exilles. In observing that 'all the people one believes to be dead are not', the jailer eliminated all the credible alternative candidates. First, by using the plural, he allowed for the possibility that before the transfer to Sainte-Marguerite, he had more than one such prisoner in his charge. Second, if people believed them to be dead, they had to be well-known to attract any comment, and for their supposed deaths to have been widely reported. Third, for their imprisonment to remain undetected, they could only be held in the utmost secrecy. Only Nicolas Fouquet and d'Artagnan meet these essential criteria.

The newsletter also referred to the suicide of a prisoner at Pignerol, which many historians claim to be Lauzun's Béarnais valet, Heurtaut. An anonymous court journal found by Ravaisson confirms that in August 1672 Heurtaut committed suicide after his arrest to avoid interrogation, but not that he was ever held in the Pignerol dungeon. Saint-Mars' report to Louvois said simply that Heurtaut, having opened his veins and lost a lot of blood, was nonetheless 'still alive', and implies that doctors had to go down into the town to keep him that way, although they did not succeed for long. It is also doubtful whether the writer would recall in 1687 an event that occurred as much as fifteen years previously. Its reference to a suicide was far more likely to mean that of Étienne Martin alias Eustace Danger, inside the Pignerol donjon itself, in June 1680, and this is the obvious explanation for the absence of any reference to Danger in later correspondence.

It was a little over a year after the newsletter appeared, while the secret prisoner remained on Sainte-Marguerite, that Louis XIV lost his temper with Louvois and attacked him with glowing fire tongs. Although the exact date of the incident is unknown, it took place in the winter of 1688–9. Nicholas Fouquet's friend, the comte de Brienne's son Louis-Henri de Loménie, later a confidant of the king, refers to it in his memoirs; Prince Michael of Greece, in his biography of Louis XIV, states that Françoise de 'Maintenon threw herself between them'. The evidence is persuasive that the king's anger was not prompted by Louvois authorizing atrocities of which he disapproved. Levi confirms that Louis regularly had the details of such activities read to him; for example, in April 1686, when General Catinat laid waste the villages of the Angrogne valley in Piedmont and reported, 'The countryside is completely deserted; there is no one left at all, neither people nor beasts.' On 14 November 1688, Louvois wrote to the French commander, 'The King has seen with pleasure that you have burned Coblenz and done every possible damage to the Elector's palace.' The order to destroy Mannheim and Heidelberg on 13 January 1689 was followed by another on 21 May to destroy Spire, Worms and Oppenheim, several months after the fire tongs affair. Levi says that Louis picked 'his own evil genius, Louvois' and 'had ample opportunity to reign in . . . [his] excessive aggressivity', but failed to do so.

If Louvois, under threat of dismissal, disclosed the identity of his mysterious prisoner and his knowledge that Tréville was the king's real father, Louis' fear of personal humiliation may explain his sudden and untypical loss of control. The whole panoply of court depended for its credibility on the premise that the monarch sat at the right hand of God. For his acolytes, worshipping the bastard son of a Musketeer, and one whose mistress had influenced his libido with black magic potions, would have been a different proposition altogether. As historian Frances Mossiker puts it in her book on *The Affair of the Poisons*, the Sun King 'could not withstand ridicule. Better an ogre than a figure of fun. His imposing image might dissolve at one titter of laughter were the story to get out that this cock of the international walk was crowing on a craw full of aphrodisiacs; hand-fed for years by his mistresses on a mash of blister beetles, cocks' combs, and cocks' testicles.' In his history of seventeenth-century France, Warren Lewis concludes that 'Ridicule was perhaps the only thing in the world that Louis feared.'

The Italian spy, Caluzio – who perhaps came closest to the truth about the Mask before his arrest in 1673 – did not languish long in prison at Lyon. Loyauté, Louvois' *commissaire de guerre* at Pignerol, was ordered to collect Caluzio. He planned to take with him a number of soldiers from the main Pignerol garrison but on 2 September Saint-Mars, by then back in its donjon, warned Louvois that Loyauté could not count on the loyalty of the escort, whom he said were quite likely to desert and free Caluzio as they did so. Instead, Saint-Mars sent his own men to Lyon with Loyauté to supervise the prisoner. Even though Caluzio had learned little at Maastricht, and there was enough evidence of his espionage to keep him behind bars at Pignerol indefinitely, Louvois wanted him out of France. Caluzio was released at the end of the year, given a large sum of money and turned into a French secret agent in northern Italy, a task he accomplished so effectively that he was later ennobled as the sieur de Caluze.

Creating the mask worn by d'Artagnan would have been no easy task with the technology of the time. To make steel, small pieces of iron were packed into a heavy, non-metallic, heat-resistant vessel and heated to a high temperature for many hours or even days. The time spent at a high temperature allowed the iron to absorb the carbon, a procedure now known as cementation. The pieces that emerged from this process were steel, an alloy – that is to say a mixture – of carbon and iron. Once several small chunks of steel had been produced, they were reheated in the forge and welded together to form larger pieces. The steel was folded back on itself to build up the mass as the piece being worked on lengthened and became thinner. This crude steel was often improved by hammering.

However, the monstrous steel mask Besmaux devised for d'Artagnan could not have been created using only this basic methodology. If it had been made in this way, the two parts would not have fitted together and the mask would have been impossibly hot and heavy for the wearer to survive in it for long. Constructing a strong, lightweight mask in two or three complementary steel sections would have required knowledge of a damascene technique, a kind of compound technology developed in Damascus but successfully adapted for mass production in the Spanish weapons factory at Toledo, where two different kinds of steel were assembled in layers, then forged into the final product.

The disadvantage of the damascene technique was the sensitivity of such a procedure. Overheating the metal ruined the steel, under-heating it meant that the welds would not be sound. Metalsmiths kept to themselves the particular method they used for quenching, that is, cooling the metal suddenly in water, before reheating it slowly in order to manipulate the object into its final form, while minimizing the stresses in the finished castings. The Bastille governor Besmaux had the resources to find a Spaniard who knew the secret and would not recognize d'Artagnan, and the money to tempt him to Paris.

CHAPTER 15 (pages 284 to 304)

Courtilz told only one of his biographic subjects his intention to go into print. He defended his subsequent duplicity by giving as an example his 1676 *Mémoires du sieur de Pontis*, about a former army captain, who was unwilling to add to his story after he learned of Courtilz's intention to publish it.

The third edition of Courtilz's memoirs contains a portrait of d'Artagnan opposite the title-page, the only known version of the original work to do so. It shows d'Artagnan carrying a marshal's baton, an honour he coveted but never achieved, so the picture is probably not a genuine likeness. Courtilz did not supply the illustration, because he was back in the Bastille at the time, languishing in a dungeon. To illustrate his own work on d'Artagnan, Samaran searched for the portrait in the archives of the best engravers in Paris, but was unable to find the original. D'Artagnan could never afford a court artist to paint his picture: the inventory of his sparse belongings shows that they included three paintings, of Mazarin, Anne of Austria and Louis XIV, but not one of himself. However, a portrait of d'Artagnan did once exist, and hung in the grand salon of his father-in-law, Charles de Hénin-Liétard, governor of Chalon sur Saône. Late in the reign of Louis XIV it mysteriously disappeared.

The first detailed study of Courtilz appears in a work by the American professor, Bejamin Woodbridge, published in 1925. Woodbridge devoted almost forty pages to an analysis of d'Artagnan's memoirs and was the first to confirm Courtilz's confinement in the Bastille at the same time as the Mask. It was Courtilz's second wife, Louise Pannetier, who smuggled the manuscript out of the fortress. In his private papers, Woodbridge states his conviction that one of the biographies by Courtilz that established the pattern for the work on d'Artagnan, the *Memoirs of J. B. de La Fontaine*, was based entirely on what Fontaine had told him while he was a fellow inmate at the Bastille.

EPILOGUE (pages 305 to 320)

Although the medical basis of the myth that the Man in the Iron Mask was Louis XIV's near-identical brother, the purported birth of twins to Anne of Austria nine hours apart is not impossible – in 1970 an interval of 72 days between the birth of twins was recorded in Germany – in the seventeenth century the statistical odds would have been extremely high against the second of twins surviving a significant delay. In France four out of ten children did not live long after birth, without taking into account the added problem of twins. Rydhstrom and Ingermarsson reported in the *American Journal of Obstetrics and Gynecology* their findings concerning the impact on second twin perinatal mortality of a long interval between the vaginal birth of the first and second twin. They concluded that in the absence of modern foetal and uterine monitoring, the inter-delivery impact was significantly higher at intervals of thirty minutes or more. Only after 1673, when physician Jules Clement was appointed to the court of Louis XIV, was any substantive progress made in the study of obstetrics. Previously the task of delivering the heir to the throne was left entirely to midwives, whom historian Warren Lewis observed to believe that 'pain at childbirth could be minimised by placing the husband's hat on the woman's belly,' and who relieved the trauma of birth by wrapping the mother's loins 'in the fleece of a newly killed black sheep'.

Although Voltaire never put forward the theory of the twin, preferring the solution of an elder brother of Louis XIV as the Man in the Iron Mask, throughout his life he kept the Bourbons on tenterhooks, wondering what scurrilous information he would reveal next. Voltaire's references to the Iron Mask remained tantalizingly obscure, but there is little doubt that he knew exactly what he was doing. He deliberately released snippets about the Mask at regular intervals in order each time to gauge their effect. For a long time Voltaire sheltered behind his anonymity. The great American attorney of the nineteenth century, Clarence Darrow, mounted a vigorous defence of his strategy. 'More than one hundred names were used by Voltaire in the course of his long literary career', wrote Darrow. 'No doubt some men would have been burned with the first pamphlet that they wrote, but not Voltaire. He preferred to live to an old age and dodge and flee and deny and lie and still pour forth upon the world the greatest mass of rebellious literature that ever came from the pen of man.'

Voltaire disingenuously criticized his own so-called *History of Persia*, an anonymous parody of Louis XIV's reign, hoping to put his accusers off the scent. However, the book contained the story of the silver dish thrown out of his cell window by the secret prisoner and found by a fisherman, which points directly to Voltaire, who received it first-hand from the retired *commissaire de guerre* at Cannes. The financial assistance Voltaire gave to the chevalier de Mouhy, author of the first *Masque de Fer* novel, is confirmed by Charles Monsolet in a book about forgotten men, published in 1857. Voltaire's pension did not ensure the chevalier's loyalty. Sent to the Bastille for breaking the censorship laws, Mouhy gained his freedom after a few weeks by agreeing to become a police informer, and probably told the authorities enough about Voltaire's clandestine activities to prolong the philosopher's enforced exile.

After the fall of the Bastille, when Mirabeau and Palloy set up an

Iron Mask tableau to captivate gullible tourists, complete with a masked skeleton still in his chains, there were plenty of chains to choose from: they had been stockpiled for years. Under the unrealized scheme to replace the Bastille with a square and adorn it with a statue of Louis XVI, the pedestal was intended to be formed by a mound of old chains and bolts from the prison. The iron mask Mirabeau used may well be the one that was later sold for scrap at Langres, and resides in the town museum, but it has no locking mechanism and was never worn by d'Artagnan. The skeleton was probably assembled from a huge collection of bones Palloy found in the cellars. The Academy of Sciences set up a commission to examine them, which dubiously concluded 'the corpses testified to the fact that they had been secretly executed.' In a debate on the human remains in the Assembly, Mirabeau had a field day. 'The [king's] ministers were lacking in foresight,' he said, 'they forgot to eat the bones!'

LOOSE ENDS

Louise de La Fayette, whom Louis XIII visited on the fateful stormy night in Paris in December 1637, never returned to court. She came into a mysterious windfall that in 1657 enabled her to found a convent of her order at Chaillot, where she was mother superior until her death in January 1665.

The Gaillard Bois inn, D'Artagnan's first lodging in Paris, started to collapse into the street in 1933 and had to be demolished

There could be no more eloquent proof of the injustice of Louis XIV's France than the fate of La Voisin's heroic maid, Margot. Having saved the husband of her wicked employer from poisoning, she was interrogated by police chief La Reynie. Although Margot was innocent of any crime, for fear of what she knew, the king had her imprisoned for the rest of her life in the impenetrable fort des Bains, near the Pyrenean village of Amélie-les Bains.

Louis XIV's finance minister, Jean-Baptiste Colbert, suffered for fifteen years from the stomach pains inflicted by the poisoners. His death on 6 September 1683 was the signal for Louis to release the purse strings on the construction of Versailles. In December 1688 the comte de Lauzun played the Scarlet Pimpernel in reverse and rescued the Queen of England and the infant Prince of Wales from a rebellious London, forcing Louis to welcome him back at court. Lauzun would live to be ninety, dying in Paris on 19 November 1723. Another to be rehabilitated after disgrace was the comte de Jussac, who survived the 1640 duel with the Musketeers to become the irascible tutor of Louis XIV's son by Athénaïs de Montespan, the duc de Maine. In saving the cowardly young duke's life, Jussac was killed, aged seventy, at the Battle of Fleurus on 12 July 1690.

It was Athénaïs who enticed Jussac out of retirement to take part in the battle at the duc de Maine's side. She was last seen at Versailles in 1692 and instead flitted about France – 'I am not surprised she has run off to the country,' said the unforgiving Françoise de Maintenon – burning candles all night to keep away the Devil. She died from an over-vigorous emetic, vomiting incessantly, at Bourbon on 27 May 1707. Her perpetual rival Louise de La Vallière survived her by three years, dying at the Carmelite convent in Paris on 6 June 1710. Louis XIV died at Versailles from gangrene on 1 September 1715, burning papers in his final days with the aid of Françoise. She was with him to the last before retiring to Saint-Cyr, where she died on 15 April 1719, not long after receiving a visit from the curious Peter the Great.

Louis would never give Louvois' son, Barbezieux, the status of a minister of state. A notorious debauchee, Barbezieux died suddenly, aged thirty-three, in his office at Versailles on 5 January 1701. Both d'Artagnan's sons joined the army, but it was his young cousin, Pierre, who gained the marshal's baton that d'Artagnan once coveted for himself. At the Battle of Malplaquet on 11 September 1709, Pierre de Montesquiou d'Artagnan had five horses shot from under him, in true family tradition, but rallied his troops and saved the French army from rout. The last of the war ministers to know the identity of the Mask, Michel Chamillart, was dismissed in 1709, made a scapegoat for the French defeats. Chamillart, rather than Louis XIV, may have been the one to hand on the secret to the Bourbon family before his death on 14 April 1721.

Although it would be of little comfort to Louis XVI and Marie Antoinette, destined in 1793 to climb the steps to the guillotine, the main proponents of the fantastic theory of the royal twin in the iron mask did not prosper. Mirabeau died from liver disease on 2 April 1791. As a Hero of the Revolution, he was buried in the Pantheon, until he was found to have advised the royal family to flee or fight, whereupon his remains were disinterred and thrown onto a public cemetery. The poet Cubières became an acolyte of Marat but in July 1793 an idealistic young assassin, Charlotte Corday, put an end both to Marat and to Cubières' unlamented literary career. His mistress, Fanny, achieved a more memorable niche in history as the nymphomaniac aunt of Napoleon's future empress, Joséphine Beauharnais. 'Patriot' Palloy was arrested in February 1794 and, although he bribed his way out of prison, the builder's credentials as a diehard revolutionary were discredited. Palloy ended his days at Sceaux in 1835, after a miserable existence eking out a small pension, ironically awarded for his imaginary role in the taking of the Bastille.

Of the four prisons of the Man in the Iron Mask, only one survives. The dismantled Bastille has given its name to a Paris square. In 1696 Pignerol was handed back to Savoy, after its fortifications, including the donjon, had been razed to the ground, so effectively that scarcely a trace remains. The ravages of time have accounted for Exilles, now also on the Italian side of the border, and whose seventeenth-century fort has long been replaced by another that is little more than an empty shell. However, the Mask's cell can be visited on the island of Sainte-Marguerite. Soon after the author suggested to the authorities that a forensic examination of its crumbling walls might give up the prisoner's secret, the cell was replastered and, perhaps with unconscious irony, given several coats of whitewash.

The beautiful chateau of Elizabea de Tréville, built with the help of money from Nicholas Fouquet, passed to distant cousins when Tréville's two legitimate sons died without issue, Armand-Jean de Peyrer in 1700 and Joseph-Henri de Peyrer in 1708. Joseph-Henri had been elected a member of the French Academy in 1704, but Louis XIV forced the Academy to replace him, perhaps not wishing to associate too closely with someone who could well have been his half-brother. The original of Tréville's portrait by Le Nain was sold at auction in Paris about 1954 and has never been seen since.

BIBLIOGRAPHY

❧ ❧

ORIGINAL SOURCES

Archives des Basse-Pyréneés, Pau
Mss B9, B3080, C730, C731
de Béarn: Extrait du Recueil Official Dressé par Ordre de Louis XIV,
[undated]

Archives Communales, Pau
Mss B11, GG 1, 21–4
Registres Paroissiaux relatifs aux Baptêmes, Mariages, Vêtures,
Noviciats et Sépultures dans les Églises et Couvents de la Ville de Pau
(1553–1792)

Archives de Castetbon
Mss *État civil*

Bibliothèque Nationale, Paris
Mss Mélanges Colbert, Vol 291–307
Dellecourt, Philippe-Joseph, 'Anecdote curieuse et aventure très singulière
    d'un citoyen de Paris, dans les dernites [sic] troubles de cette capitale,
    depuis le 13 juillet, jusqu'à l'arrivée du Roi, le vendredi 17 du même
    mois', microfiche (1993) extract from Les archives de la Révolution
    française, Num. BNF 6.2.913 [1789]
Humbert, Jean-Baptiste, 'Journée de Jean-Baptiste Humbert, horloger,
    qui, le premier, a monté sur les tours de la Bastille', microfiche (1993)
    extract from Les archives de la Révolution française, Num. BNF
    6.2.830 [1789]
Le Grand, Jérôme, 'Louis XIV et le masque de fer, ou Les princes
    jumeaux: tragédie en cinq actes et en vers', Théâtre de Molière,
    microfiche (1991) extract from Les archives de la Révolution française,
    Num. BNF 12.239 [24 September 1791]

Bibliothèque de l'Arsenal, Paris

'Édict . . . portant attribution à la compagnie des mousquetaires à cheval de la Garde du Roy, et à celle des Gardes de la Royne, des mesmes privilèges, franchises et exemptions, dont jouyssent les officiers commançaux de la Maison du Roy. Vérifié en la Cour des Aydes, le 4 juin 1644', edict of the Queen-Regent, Anne of Austria, December 1643, printed by Rocolet of Paris, 1644

'Extraits des procès-verbaux, des scellés et inventaires faits dans les maisons de M. Foucquet et de ses commis', Fontainebleau, 14 September 1661

'Lettres de commission aux maîtres des requêtes y nommés, pour se réunir à l'Arsenal et juger en dernier ressort Marie Maret et ses complices, impliqués dans une affaire de poison', Saint-Germain-en-Laye, 7 April 1679

'Lettres portant ampliation des pouvoirs des commissaires pour juger tous procès de sacrilège et fausse monnaie auxquels les conduira l'enquête sur l'affaire susdite', Saint-Germain-en-Laye, 24 February 1680

Mss series 10,330–438

Service Historique de l'Armée de Terre, Vincennes
Mss series A1 301-1243

Bibliothèque Sainte-Geneviève, Paris
Mss Vol 1/477

Private Collectors
Journal de Paris, No. 184, 2 July 1780, with an article by M. Gallimare on Voltaire and the Man in the Iron Mask

La Rochefoucauld, François VI duc de, unpublished extracts from his Mémoires (written c.1640)

PRINTED PUBLICATIONS

The publication year indicates that of the edition consulted, not necessarily of the earliest edition. Some early publishers are unknown. Names in parentheses indicate authors' pseudonyms. Copies of the works listed are held as follows: Bibliothèque de l'Arsenal (BA), Bodleian Library (BL), Bibliothèque Nationale (BN), Voltaire Library (VL); everything else is in the author's collection.

Articles in Collective Works
'Le masque de fer', *Les Cahiers de l'Histoire*, No 2, April 1960

Symposium presentations, Pinerolo, 28–9 September 1974, 'La Maschera di Ferro e il suo Tempo', Pinerolo: Artistica Savigliano, 1976, BA

Symposium presentations, Cannes, 12–13 September 1987, 'Il y a trois siècles le Masque de fer', Cannes: Ville de Cannes, 1988

Symposium presentations, Pinerolo, 13–15 September 1991, 'La Maschera di Ferro e il suo Tempo', Pinerolo, 1992

'Louis XIV', *Historama*, No 36, July–August 1995

'Le grand secret du Masque de Fer' (ed. Claude Dabos), *Top Secret*, No 3, January 2006

Notable individual contributions are listed under the author's name below.

Individual Works

Allemand, l'Abbé, *Nouveau choix de letters de Madame de Sévigné*, Tours: Mame, 1886

Almeras, Henri d', *Alexandre Dumas et les Trois Mousquetaires*, Paris: Societé Française d'Editions Littéraires, 1929

Amato, Claude, *L'homme au masque de fer: la solution à une énigme dédalienne*, Nice: Bénévent, 2003, BA

Ambelain, Robert, *La Chapelle des Damnés: la véritable affaire des poisons, 1650–1673*, Paris: Laffont, 1983

Amiel, Olivier (ed.), *Lettres de la Princesse Palatine (1672–1722)*, Paris: Mercure, 1981

Anonymous, *Rélation des magnificences faites par M. Fouquet a Vaux-le-Vicomte lorsque le roi alla*, Paris, c.1665, BA

Anonymous, *Histoire du fils d'un roi, prisonnier à la Bastille, trouvée sous les débris de cette forteresse*, Paris: rue de Chartres, 1789, BA

Anonymous, 'L'Homme au masque de fer', critique of books by Delort & George-Agar Ellis on the Iron Mask, *Edinburgh Review*, 1826

Anonymous, *L'Homme au masque de fer dévoilé, d'après une note trouvée dans les papiers de la Bastille*, Paris: Maradan, c. 1879, BA

Anonymous, 'Un romancier oublié: Gatien Courtilz de Sandras', *Révue de deux mondes: Recueil de la politique, de l'administration et des moeurs*, 1897

Anonymous, 'Louis XIV a-t-il fait empoisonner Louvois?', *Historama*, No 265, December 1973

Anonymous, 'The Three Guardsmen', *Blackwood's Magazine*, Vol. 57, January 1845

Aron, Mélanie (ed.), *Les mémoires de Madame de Motteville: du dévouement à la dévotion* (first published Amsterdam, 1723), Nancy: Presses Universitaires, 2003, BA

Arrèse, Pierre-Jacques, *Le Masque de fer: l'enigme enfin résolue*, Paris: Laffont, 1969

Ashley, Maurice, *Louis XIV and the Greatness of France*, London: Hodder and Stoughton, 1946

Ashley, Maurice, *The Golden Century: Europe 1598-1715*, London: Weidenfeld and Nicolson, 1969

Auchincloss, Louis, *Richelieu*, London: Michael Joseph, 1973

Audiat, Pierre, *Madame de Montespan*, Paris: Fasquelle, 1938, BA

Audiat, Pierre, 'Fou[c]quet a-t-il été le Dreyfus du dix-septième siècle?', *Le Figaro Littéraire*, 19 May 1956

Augustin-Thierry, A. (ed.), *Mémoires de Robert Challes: écrivain du Roi*, Paris: Plon, 1934

Auriac, Gabrielle Basset, d', *Les deux pénitences de Louise de la Vallière*, Paris: Librairie Académique, 1924

Avenel, Martial (ed.), *Lettres, instructions diplomatiques et papiers d'état du cardinal de Richelieu*, Paris: Imprimerie impériale, 1853–1874, BA

Azéma, Xavier, *Un prélat Janséniste: Louis Foucquet, évêque et comte d'Agde (1656–1702)*, Paris: Vrin, 1963

Bailly, Auguste, *Richelieu*, Paris: Librairie Arthème Fayard, 1936

Barbery, Bernard, *L' Énigme du masque de fer*, Paris: Monier, 1935

Barine, Arvède, *La Grande Mademoiselle 1627–1652*, New York and London: Putnam, 1902

Barine, Arvède, 'Un géôlier au XVIIe siècle', *La Revue de Paris*, July–August 1905

Barker, Nancy Nichols, *Brother to the Sun King: Philippe, Duke of Orléans*, Baltimore: Johns Hopkins University Press, 1989

Barnes, Arthur Stapylton, *The Man of the Mask, a study in the by-ways of history*, London: Smith, Elder, 1908; revised edn 1912

Barnett, Corelli, *Marlborough*, London: Eyre Methuen, 1974

Bartoli, Camille, *Henri de . . . l'Homme au masque de fer: sa vie et son secret*, Paris: TAC-motifs, 1997

Bassompierre, François de, *Journal de ma vie: Mémoires du Maréchal de Bassompierre*, Paris: J. Morel, 1690, BA

Bastide, Charles, *The Anglo-French Entente in the Seventeenth Century*, London: Bodley Head, 1914

Battifol, Louis, *The Duchesse de Chevreuse: A life of intrigue and adventure in the days of Louis XIII*, London: Heinemann, 1913

Battifol, Louis, *La Vie de Paris sous Louis XIII: l'existence pittoresque des Parisians au XVIIe siècle*, Paris: Calmann-Levy, 1932

Baumont, Stéphane, *D'Artagnan: des siècles d'aventures de cape et d'épée*, Toulouse: Privat, 1999

Beaunier, André, *La jeunesse de madame de La Fayette*, Paris: Flammarion, 1921

Beaupoil, Louis-Clair de, comte de Sainte-Aulaire, *Histoire de la Fronde*, Paris: Baudoin frères, 1827

Behrens, C.B.A., *The Ancien Régime*, London: Thames and Hudson, 1967

Belin, Camille, 'Nicolas de La Reynie, lieutenant-général de police', lecture at the Court of Appeal on 3 November 1874, Limoges: 1874, BA

Bell, Gail, *The Poison Principle*, London: Macmillan, 2002

Bellecombe, M.A. de, 'La Légende du masque de fer', *L'Investigateur*, Vol. 8, 4th series, 1868

Bellecombe, M.A de, 'La Légende du masque de fer', *Revue des Études Historiques*, 1868

Bercé, Yves-Marie, 'Les cadets du Gascogne', *L'Histoire*, No 35, June 1981

Berchet N. and G. Barozzi, *Relazioni degli Stati europei lette al Senato dogli ambasciatori veneti*, Venice: 1857, VL

Bergin, Joseph, *The Rise of Richelieu*, New Haven: Yale University Press, 1991

Bernard, Leon, *The Emerging City: Paris in the Age of Louis XIV*, Durham, NC: Duke University Press, 1970

Besnier, Georges, et al., *Tricentenaire du retour d'Arras et de l'Artois à la France*, Arras: Musée d'Arras, 1954, BA

Bevan, Bryan, *The Duchesse Hortense: Cardinal Mazarin's Wanton Niece*, London: Rubicon, 1987

Billacois, François, *Le Duel dans la société française des xvie–xviie siècles: essai de psychosociologie historique*, Paris: L'École des Sciences Sociales, 1986, BA

Blashfeld, E.H. and E.W., 'The Paris of the Three Musketeers', *Scribner's Magazine*, Vol. 8, No 2, August 1890

Bolton, Solomon, *The Extinct Peerage of England: Containing a Succinct Account of all the Peers whose Titles are Expired; from the Conquest to the Year 1769*, London: Rivington and others, 1769

Bonney, Richard, 'The secret expenses of Richelieu and Mazarin, 1624–1661', *English Historical Review*, 1976

Bonney, Richard, *Society and Government in France under Richelieu and Mazarin, 1624-61*, Basingstoke and London: Macmillan, 1988

Bonvalet, Pierre, 'Quelques remarques à propos de Saint-Mars le cadet', Pinerolo Symposium, 1991

Bordaz, Odile, *D'Artagnan, mousquetaire du Roi: sa vie, son époque, ses contemporains*, Boulogne: Griot, 1995

Bouillevaux, Abbé R.A., *Les Moines du Der*, Montier-en-Der, 1845

Boulenger, Marcel, *Nicolas Fouquet*, Paris: Grasset, 1933

Boutry, Maurice, 'La Trahison du comte Matthioli', lecture given to La Société des Études Historiques on 20 April 1899, published in the Society's *Revue*, Paris: Thorin, 1899

Bouyer, Christian, *La Grande Mademoiselle*, Paris: Albin Michel, 1986

Boyer d'Agen, Auguste-Jean, *Le Masque de fer de l'île Sainte-Marguerite à la Bastille* (first published in *Monde Moderne* and *Armée et Marine*, January 1904), Paris: Juven, 1904, BA

Brégeon, Jean-Joël, 'Une rude gaillarde: la princesse Palatine', *Histoire*, No 21, October 1981

Brel-Bordaz, Odile, *D'Artagnan, mousquetaire du Roi: sa vie, son époque, ses contemporains*, Boulogne: Griot, 1995

Brel-Bordaz, Odile, *D'Artagnan: biographie du capitaine-lieutenant des grands mousquetaires du roy*, Paris: Presses Littéraires, 2001

Brienne, Henri-Auguste de Loménie, comte de, *Mémoires du comte de Brienne, ministre et premier secrétaire d'état, contenant les événemens les plus remarquables du règne de Louis XIII et de celui de Louis XIV, jusqu'à la mort du cardinal Mazarin. Composés pour l'instruction de ses enfans*, Paris: Foucault, 1824

Briggs, Robin, *Early Modern France*, 2nd edn, Oxford: Oxford University Press, 1998

Brugnon, Stanislas, 'Identité de l'homme au masque de fer', Cannes Symposium, 1987

Brugnon, Stanislas, *Réconstitution du registro d'écrou des prisonniers de l'île Sainte-Marguerite: à compter du 30 avril 1687 et jusqu'au 19 mars de l'année 1704*, Paris: S. Brugnon, 1992, BA

Buffon, Margaret, *Observations sur la langue Française*, Paris, 1668, BA

Burckhardt, Carl J., *Richelieu and his Age: His Rise to Power*, London: Allen and Unwin, 1940

Burgaud, Emile, and Étienne Bazeries, *Le Masque de fer, révélation de la correspondance chiffrée de Louis XIV, étude appuyée de documents inédits des archives du dépôt de la guerre*, Paris: Firmin-Didot, 1893

Burke, Peter, *The Fabrication of Louis XIV*, New Haven and London: Yale University Press, 1992

Bussy-Rabutin, Roger de, *Les Amours de Mademoiselle avec Mr. le comte de Lauzun: Augmenté d'une lettre du Roy, & quelques vers sur ce sujet*, Cologne: Baur, 1673, BA

Bussy-Rabutin, Roger de, *Les Mémoires de Messire Roger de Rabutin comte de Bussy, Lieutenant General des Armées du Roy, et Mestre de Camp General de la Cavalerie légère*, Paris: Jean Anisson, 1696, BA

Cabanes, Docteur, *Les Mortes mysterieuses de l'histoire*, Paris: Albin Michel, 1950

Cabanes, Docteur, *Les Indiscrétions de l'histoire*, Paris: Michel, 1956

Caire, Bernard, 'Eustache et son secret', Cannes Symposium, 1987

Caire, Bernard, 'Il était le Masque de Fer: dernièrs découvertes', *Historama*, No 55, September 1988

Calvié, Laurent, *Cyrano de Bergerac dans tout es états*, Toulouse: Anacharsis, 2004

Cardoze, Michel, *Cyrano de Bergerac: libertin libertaire*, Paris: Lattès, 1994, BA

Carlhian-Ribois, Fernand, 'Séjour du "masque de fer" à Briançon', Cannes Symposium, 1987

Carlton, Charles, *Charles I: The Personal Monarch*, London: Routledge and Kegan Paul, 1983

Carré, Henri, *Mademoiselle de La Vallière: de la cour de Louis XIV aux Grandes carmélites, 1644–1710*, Paris: Hachette, 1938, BA

Carré, Henri, *Madame de Montespan: grandeur et décadence d'une favorite, 1640–1707*, Paris: Hachette, 1939, BA

Carré, Henri, *The Early Life of Louis XIV (1638–1661)*, London: Hutchinson, 1951

Cartwright, Julia, *Madame: A Life of Princesse Henrietta, Daughter of Charles I and Duchess of Orleans*, London: Seeley, 1900

Castelbajac, Bernadette, 'Les nuits de la Montespan', *Miroir de l'Histoire*, No 284, 1975

Castelnau, Jacques-Thomas de, *Le Paris de Louis XIII (1610–1643)*, Paris: Hachette, 1928

Castelot, André, 'Buckingham fut-il aimé d'Anne d'Autriche?', *Histoire Pour Tous*, No 2, June 1960

Castelot, André, 'Louis XIII intime, étrange Louis XIII', *Historia*, No 492, December 1987

Champagnac, J.-P., 'Fouquet: du château à la prison', *Miroir de L'Histoire*, No 307, November–December 1978

Charpentier, Colonel, *La Bastille dévoilée ou recueil de pièces authentiques pour servir à son histoire*, Paris: Desenne, 1789

Chartrand, René, *Louis XIV's Army*, London: Osprey, 1988

Chautant, Gisèle, *Croyances et conduites magiques dans la France du XVIIe siècle d'après l'Affaire des poisons*, Villeneuve d'Ascq: Septentrion, 2004, BA

Chéruel, M (ed.), *Journal d'Olivier Le Fèvre d'Ormesson*, Paris, 1861

Chevallier, Pierre, 'Les étranges amours du roi Louis XIII', *Historama*, No 336 and 337, November and December 1979

Childs, John, *Warfare in the Seventeenth Century*, London: Cassell, 2001

Church, William F., *The Greatness of Louis XIV: Myth or Reality?*, Boston: Heath, 1959

Church, William F., *The Influence of the Enlightenment on the French Revolution*, Boston: Heath, 1964

Churchill, Winston Spencer, *Marlborough: His Life and Times*, London: Harrap, 1933

Clément, Pierre, 'Vauban, Louvois et Colbert', *Revue des Études Historiques*, January 1867

Clément, Pierre (ed.), *Lettres, Instructions et Mémoires de Colbert*, Paris: Schiller 1861–7, BL

Cohen, Edgar H., *Mademoiselle Libertine: A Portrait of Ninon de Lenclos* [sic], Boston: Houghton Mifflin, 1970

Constant, Jean-Marie, 'Un attentat manqué contre Richelieu', *Historia*, No 487, July 1987

Corvisier, André, *Louvois*, Paris: Fayard, 1993

Corvisier, André, 'Louvois et Louis XIV partent en guerre', *Historama*, special issue, 1995

Cottret, Monique, 'La Bastille, fabrication d'un mythe', *Historia*, No 487, July 1987

Cottret, Monique, 'Vérité Historique, Vérité Légendaire', Cannes Symposium, 1987

Courtilz de Sandras, Gatien de, *Mémoires du Sieur de Pontis*, Paris, 1676

Courtilz de Sandras, Gatien de, *Les Intrigues amoureuses de la cour de France*, Cologne [in fact The Hague]: Bernard, 1684, BA

Courtilz de Sandras, Gatien de, *Mémoires de J. B. de La Fontaine*, Cologne [in fact The Hague], 1698, BA

Courtilz de Sandras, Gatien de, *Mémoires de M. d'Artagnan, Capitaine-Lieutenant de la première compagnie des Mousquetaires du Roi, contenant quantité de choses Particulières et Secrettes* [sic] *qui se sont passées sous le Règne de Louis le Grand*, Cologne [in fact The Hague]: Marteau, 1700

Courtilz de Sandras, Gatien de, *Mémoires de M. le Marquis de Montbrun, ou l'on voit quelque événements particuliers depuis 1600 jusqu'en 1632*, Amsterdam, 1701, BA

Courtilz de Sandras, Gatien de, *Annales de la Cour et de Paris pour les années 1697 et 1698,* Cologne [in fact The Hague], 1701, BA

Courtilz de Sandras, Gatien, *Memoirs of Monsieur d'Artagnan*, Boston: Little, Brown, 1903

Cousin, Victor, *La Jeunesse de Mazarin*, Paris: Didier, 1865

Cousin, Victor, *Madame de Hautefort*, Paris: Didier, 1868

Cowie, Leonard W., *Seventeenth-Century Europe*, London: Bell, 1961

Cronin, Vincent, *Louis XIV*, London: Collins, 1964

Cubières-Palmezeaux, Michel, *Voyage à la Bastille fait le 16 Juillet 1789 et adresse à Madame de G . . . de Bagnols*, Paris, 1789

Dallemagne, A., 'Un nouveau système sur Le masque de fer', *Revue des Questions Historiques*, July 1873

Davenport, R.A., *History of the Bastille and its Principal Captives*, London: Tegg, 1876

Davidson, Ian, *Voltaire in Exile*, London: Atlantic, 2004

Decaux, Alain, 'Qui était le Masque de fer?', *Historia*, No 255, February 1968

Decker, Michel de, *Madame de Montespan: la Grande Sultane*, Paris: Perrin, 1985

Deloche, Maximin, *La Maison du Cardinal de Richelieu*, Paris: Perrin, 1923

Delorme, Philippe, *Anne d'Autriche: épouse de Louis XIII, mère de Louis XIV*, Paris: Éditions France Loisirs, 2000, BA

Delort, Joseph, *Histoire de la Détention des Philosophes et des gens de lettres à la Bastille et à Vincennes, précédée de celle de Foucquet, de Pellison et de Lauzun, avec tous les documents authentiques et inédits*, Paris: Delaforest, 1829

Delort, Joseph, *Histoire de l'Homme au masque de fer, accompagnée des pièces authentiques et de fac-simile*, Paris: Delaforest, 1825

Des Morgues, Mathieu, *'La tres humble, tres veritable, et tres importante remonstrance au Roy'*, in *Diverses pieces pour la defense de la royne mere du roy*, Paris: 1631

Dessert, Daniel, 'L'argent et le pouvoir: l'affaire Fouquet', *L'Histoire*, No 32, March 1981

Dessert, Daniel, *Fouquet*, Paris: Fayard, 1987

Dessert, Daniel, 'Fouquet, l'argent c'est lui!', *Historia*, No 484, April 1987

Dessert, Daniel, 'Complot: une affaire bien étouffée', interview, *Historama*, No 40, June 1987

Dessert, Daniel, 'Quand les grands s'adonnent aux jeux de l'argent', *Historama*, special issue, 1995

Dessert, Daniel, *Colbert ou Le serpent venimeux, suivi de Mémoires sur les affaires de finances de France pour servir à l'histoire* (using the text of Jean-Baptiste Colbert's *Memoirs*, originally edited by Pierre Clément), Brussels and Paris: Éditions Complexe, 2000, BA

Dethan, George, 'Anne d'Autriche a-t-elle aimé Mazarin?', *Historia*, No 293, April 1971

Diamont-Berger, Marcel, 'La magistrat La Reynie', *Les Cahiers de l'Histoire*, special issue, 1960

Diamont-Berger, Marcel', *C'était l'homme au masque de fer*, Paris: JF Éditions, 1971

Dijol, Pierre-Marie, *Nabo, ou le masque de fer*, Paris: France-Empire, 1978

Dijol, Pierre-Marie, 'L'Homme au Masque de Fer', Cannes Symposium, 1987

Doolittle, James, 'Pattern for Nobility: the Comte de Brienne', *Journal of the Modern Language Association of America*, Vol. 83, No 5, October 1968

Dubois, Cardinal Guillaume, *Secret Memoirs of the Court of France*, London: Smithers, 1899

Duchêne, Roger, *Ninon de Lenclos* [sic]: *La courtisane du Grand Siècle*, Paris: Fayard, 1984

Duchêne, Jacqueline, *Henriette D'Angleterre, duchesse d'Orléans*, Paris: Fayard, 1995

Duclos, Henri, *Madame de La Vallière et Marie-Thérèse d'Autriche, femme de Louis XIV, avec pièces et documents inédits*, Paris: Didier, 1890, BA

Dulong, Claude, *Anne d'Autriche*, Paris: Hachette, 1985

Dumaitre, Paul, *Louis XIV au temps des mousquetaires*, Paris: Nathan, 1971.

Dumas, Alexandre, *Les Mousquetaires: Les Trois Mousquetaires et Vingt Ans Après*, consolidation of the episodes serialised in *Le Siècle*, Paris: Levy, 1850

Dumas, Alexandre, *Taking the Bastille*, London: Collins, 1933

Dunan, Renée, 'Le Masque de fer', preface to his novel, Paris: Bibliothèque des Curieux, 1929

Dunlop, Ian, *Louis XIV*, London: Chatto and Windus, 1999

Dupleix, Scipion, *Histoire générale de France*, Paris, 1621–43, DL

Durant, Will, and Ariel, *The Age of Louis XIV*, New York: Simon and Schuster, 1963

Duvivier, Maurice, *Le Masque de fer*, Paris: Colin, 1932

Dyson, C.C., *Madame de Maintenon: Her Life and Times 1635–1719*, London: Bodley Head, 1910

Ehrlich, Blake, *Paris on the Seine*, London: Weidenfeld and Nicolson, 1962

Elliott, Frances, *Old Court-Life in France*, London: Ward and Downey, 1886

Ellis, George-Agar, *The true History of the State prisoner commonly called the Iron Mask, extracted from documents in the French Archives*, London: Murray, 1826

Emard, Paul, and Suzanne Fournier, *Les Années criminelles de Madame de Montespan*, Paris: Denoël, 1939, BA

Erlanger, Philippe, *Cinq-Mars*, Paris: Librairie Académique Perrin, 1962

Erlanger, Philippe, 'Un troisième centenaire: Anne d'Autriche aima-t-elle Buckingham?', *Historia*, No 230, January 1966

Erlanger, Philippe, *The Age of Courts and Kings: Manners and Morals 1558–1715*, London: Weidenfeld and Nicolson, 1967

Erlanger, Philippe, *Louis XIV*, London: Weidenfeld and Nicolson, 1970

Erlanger, Philippe, 'Les étranges noces de Louis XIII', *Histoire*, No 21, October 1981

Farr, Evelyn, *Before the Deluge: Parisian Society in the Reign of Louis XVI*, London: Owen, 1994

Force, duc de la, *Lauzun: un courtesan du grand roi*, Paris: Hachette, 1919

Force, Piganiol de la, *Nouveau voyage de France avec un itinéraire, et des cartes pour voyages dans toutes les Provinces de ce Royaume*, Paris: Le Clerc, 1775

Fouquet, Nicholas, *Recueil des défenses de M. Fouquet*, Paris, 1665–8, 15 vols, BL [Fouquet published them himself]

Francq, Henry G., *The File of the Man behind the Mask*, Brandon: Brandon University Press, 1984

Fraser, Antonia, *King Charles II*, London: Weidenfeld and Nicolson, 1979

Fraser, Antonia, *Love and Louis XIV: The Women in the Life of the Sun King*, London: Weidenfeld and Nicolson, 2006

Funck-Bretano, Frantz, 'L'Homme au Masque de Velours Noir dit Le Masque de Fer', *Revue Historique*, Vol. 56, 1894

Funck-Brentano, Frantz, *Legends of the Bastille*, London: Downey, 1899

Funck-Brentano, Frantz, *Princes and Poisoners: Studies of the court of Louis XIV*, London: Duckworth, 1901

Funck-Brentano, Frantz, *Légendes et archives de la Bastille*, Paris: Hachette, 1902

Funck-Brentano, Frantz, *Les Lettres de Cachet: Étude suivie d'une liste des Prisonniers de la Bastille (1659-1789)*, Paris: Champion, 1903

Funck-Brentano, Frantz, *Les Secrèts de la Bastille*, Paris: Flammarion, 1932

Funck-Brentano, Frantz, *Le Masque de fer*, Paris: Flammarion, 1933

Funck-Brentano, Frantz, 'L'Homme au masque de fer', *Historia*, No 31, June 1949

Funck-Brentano, Frantz, *Le Drame des poisons*, Paris: Tallandier, 1977

Furnell, Rupert, *The Man behind the Mask*, London: Cassell, 1954

Furetière, Antoine, *Dictionnaire universel, contenant généralement tous les mots françois tant vieux que modernes, & les termes de toutes les sciences et des arts*, The Hague and Rotterdam: Arnout & Reinier Leers, 1690, BA

Gailly, Gérard (ed.), *Mémoires de d'Artagnan: capitaine des grands mousquetaires*, Paris: Jonquières, 1928

Gailly, Gérard (ed.), *Mémoires de d'Artagnan: Capitaine-lieutenant des grands mousquetaires*, Paris: Mercure de France, 1943

Gallier, Humbert, *Auberges & Salons*, Paris: Calmann-Lévy, 1912

Galtier-Boissière, Jean, *Mysteries of the French Secret Police*, London: Stanley Paul, 1938

Gautier, Théophile, *Les Grotesques*, Paris, 1856

Gaxotte, Pierre, *La France de Louis XIV*, Paris: Hachette, 1946

Gay, Pierre, *Mirabeau: l'homme de 89*, Aix-en-Provence: Gay, 1991, BA

Germain, Anne, *Monsieur de Cyrano-Bergerac: biographie littéraire*, Paris: Acatos, 1996, BA

Gibbs, Philip, *The Romance of George Villiers: First Duke of Buckingham*, London: Hutchinson, 1925

Gibson, Wendy, *A Tragic Farce: The Fronde (1648–1653)*, Exeter: Elm Bank Publications, 1999

Gorsse, Pierre de, 'Madame de Maintenon fut-elle toujours prude?', *Histoire Pour Tous*, No 112, August 1969

Goubert, Pierre, *Louis XIV and Twenty Million Frenchmen*, London: Allen Lane, 1969

Gourville, Jean Hérault de, *Mémoires de Gourville*, eds J.F. Michaud and J.J.F. Poujoulat, Paris, 1838

Gramont, Sanche de (ed.), *The Age of Magnificence: Memoirs of the Court of Louis XIV by the Duc de Saint-Simon*, New York: Puttnam, 1963

Griffet, Henri, *Histoire du regne de Louis XIII, roi de France*, Paris: Les libraires associés, 1758

Guénot, Hervé, 'La Bastille: une forteresse, un terrain vague, une place', *Historia*, No 511, July 1989

Haldane, Charlotte, *Madame de Maintenon: Uncrowned Queen of France*, London: Constable, 1970

Hall, Geoffrey F., *Moths Round the Flame: Studies of Charmers and Intriguers*, London: Methuen, 1935

Hall, Geoffrey F., and Joan Sanders, *D'Artagnan: The Utimate Musketeer*, Boston: Houghton Mifflin, 1964

Hardré, Jacques, *Letters of Louvois, François-Michel Le Tellier*, Chapel Hill: University of North Carolina, 1949, BA

Hardwicke, Philip Yorke, Earl of, *Miscellaneous State Papers from 1501 to 1726*, London, 1778, BL

Haristol, Pierre, *Recherches sur le pays Basque*, Bayonne: E Laserre, 1883, BA

Hartmann, Cyril Hughes, *Charles II and Madame*, London: Heinemann, 1934

Hassall, Arthur, *Mazarin*, London: Macmillan, 1903

Hatton, Ragnhild, *Europe in the Age of Louis XIV*, London: Thames and Hudson, 1969

Hatton, Ragnhild, *Louis XIV and his world*, London: Thames and Hudson, 1972

Hillairet, Jacques, *La rue Saint-Antoine*, Paris: Minuit, 1970

Hilton, Lisa, *The Real Queen of France: Athénaïs and Louis XIV*, London: Little, Brown, 2002

Hopkins, Tigue, *The Man in the Iron Mask*, Leipzig: Tauchnitz, 1901

Horne, Alistair, *Seven Ages of Paris: Portrait of a city*, Oxford: Macmillan, 2002

Houyssaye, Amelot de la, *Memoirs*, The Hague, 1737, BA

Huas, Jeanine, *Madame de Brinvilliers: la marquise empoisonneuse*, Paris: Fayard, 2004

Huguet, Charles-Nicolas, *Un grand maréchal des logis de la maison du Roi, le marquis de Cavoye*, Paris: Champion, 1920

Huyard, Etienne, *L'Affaire Fouquet*, Paris: Corrêa, 1937

Iung, Théodore, *La Vérité sur le Masque de fer (les empoisonneurs), d'après des documents inédits des Archives de la guerre et autres dépôts publics (1664–1703)*, Paris: Plon, 1873

Jacob, Louis, *Les Suspects pendant la Révolution 1789–1794*, Paris: Hachette, 1952

Jacob, Paul L. *see* Lacroix, Paul

Jal, Auguste, *Dictionnaire critique de biographie et d'histoire*, Paris, 1867

Jaurgain, Jean de, *Troisvilles, d'Artagnan et les trois mousquetaires: esquisses biographiques et héraldiques, suivies d'une notice sur les deux compagnies de mousquetaires et la liste de leurs capitaines* (first published in *Revue de Béarn, Navarre et Lande*, 1883–4), revised edition, Paris: Champion, 1910, BA

Jouvenel, Henri de, *The Stormy Life of Mirabeau*, London: Harrap, 1929

Judge, H.G., *Louis XIV*, London: Longman, 1965

Julliard, René, *Le vrai d'Artagnan: Pierre de Montesquiou*, Paris: Julliard, 1963

Jusserand, Jean Jules, *A French Ambassador at the Court of Charles II*, London: T. Fisher Unwin, 1892

Kekewich, Margaret Lucille, *Princes and Peoples: France and the British Isles, 1620–1714*, Manchester: Manchester University Press, 1994

Keler, Theodore M.R. von, *The Mystery of Tthe Iron Mask*, Girard, KA: Haldeman-Julius, 1923

Kéralio-Robert, Louise Félicité de, *Les crimes des reines de France, depuis le commencement de la monarchie jusqu'à Marie-Antoinette*, Paris: Prudhomme, 1791

Kleinman, Ruth, *Anne of Austria, Queen of France*, Columbus: Ohio State University Press, 1985

La Porte, Pierre de, *Mémoires de M. de la Porte, premier valet de chambre de Louis XIV,* Geneva, 1756

La Rochefoucauld, François VI duc de la, *Oeuvres*, in *Les grand écrivains de la France*, Paris: Hachette, Vol. 1–4, 1874–1923, BN

La Rochefoucauld, François VI duc de la, *Mémoires*, Paris: Bossard, 1925

Laffargue, André, *En visite chez d'Artagnan et autres mousquetaires gascons et béarnaise*, Marsolan: CTD, 1979

Lacour-Ollé, Christian (ed.), *Silhouettes et Portraits Huguenots: Les Réfugiés*, Nimes: Rediviva, 2001

Lacroix, Paul, *Henry IV et Louis XIII*, Paris: Firmin-Didot, 1886

Lacroix, Paul [Paul L. Jacob], *L'Homme au masque de fer*, Paris: Magen, 1837, BA

Lair, Jules, *Nicolas Foucquet, procureur général, surintendant des finances, ministre d' État de Louis XIV*, Paris, 1980, BA

Laloy, Émile, *Énigmes du Grand Siècle: le masque de fer*, Paris: Soudier, 1913

Laloy, Émile, *Qui était le masque de fer?* (first printed in *Mercure de France*, 15 August 1931, 15 August 1932 and 15 March 1933), Paris: Klincksieck, 1931–3

Lang, Andrew, *The Valet's Tragedy and Other Studies*, London: Longmans, Green, 1903

Langeron, Edouard, *L'Homme au masque de fer. Mémoire lu à la séance publique de l'Académie de La Rochelle, le 26 mars 1870*, La Rochelle: Mareschal, 1870, BA

Langlois, Michel, *Louis XIV et la Cour*, Paris: Albin Michel, 1926

Lanson, Gustave (ed.), *Choix de lettres du xviie siècle*, Paris: Hachette, 1913

Lawrence, Eugene, 'The Man in the Iron Mask', *Harper's New Monthly Magazine*, Vol. 43, June–November 1871

Le Bossé, Michel-Vital, *Le Masque de Fer: c'est la faute à Voltaire*, Condé-sur-Noireau: Corlet, 1991

Le Nabour, Éric, 'La Reynie s'attaque a l'insecurité', *Historama*, special issue, 1995

Le Nabour, Éric, 'Des Affaires des Poisons', *Historama*, special issue, 1995

Le Nabour, Éric, *La Reynie: le policier de Louis XIV*, Paris: Perrin, 1991

Léouzon Le, duc Louis Antoine, *Voltaire et la Police: dossier recueilli à Saint-Pétersbourg parmi les manuscrits français originaux enlevés à la Bastille en 1789*, Paris: Ambroise Bray, 1867

Le Pippre, Octave-Louis-Marie, Commandant, *Dernier Mot sur le Masque de fer*, Paris: Charles-Lavauzelle, 1903, BA

Lebigre, Arlette, *L'affaire des Poisons, 1679–1682*, Brussels and Paris: Éditions Complexe, 2001, BA

Lebossé, Camille, *Maestricht et ses héros, d'Artagnan et Vauban*, Quarré-les-Tombes: Association Promotion Quarré-Morvan, 1993

Lebrige, Arlette, 'Le "Grand Siècle" des empoisonneuses', *L'Histoire*, No 37, September 1981

Lecointe, Paul, *Les Mensonges politiques, ou Révélation des mystères du Masque de fer et de Louis XVII*, Paris: Frey, 1847, BA

Lefebvre, Georges, *The Coming of the French Revolution*, Princeton: Princeton University Press, 1947

Lejeune, Paule, *Les favorites des rois de France*, Paris: Félin, 2004

Letourneur, Louis, *Histoire de l'Homme au masque de fer*, Plancy: Société de St-Victor, 1849, BA

Lever, Evelyne, 'Les femmes ont-elles influencé le roi?', *Historama*, special issue 1995

Levi, Anthony, *Cardinal Richelieu and the Making of France*, London: Constable, 2000

Levi, Anthony, *Louis XIV*, London: Constable, 2004

Lewis, Warren Hamilton, *The Splendid Century: Life in the France of Louis XIV*, New York: Morrow, 1953

Lewis, Warren Hamilton., *The Sunset of the Splendid Century*, London: Eyre and Spottiswoode, 1955

Leynadier, Camille, *Histoire du masque de fer*, Paris, 1876, BA

Littré, Maximilien Paul-Émile, *Dictionnaire de la Langue Française*, Paris: Hachette 1863–77, VL

Liversidge, Douglas, *The Day the Bastille Fell*, London: Franklin Watts, 1972

Lloyd Moote, Alanson, *Louis XIII, The Just*, Berkeley: University of California Press, 1989

Loiseleur, Jules, *Le Masque de fer devant la critique moderne* (first published in *Revue Contemporaine*, 31 July 1867, Vol. 58), Paris: Revue Contemporaine, 1867

Loiseleur, Jules, *Trois énigmes historiques*, Paris: Plon, 1882

Loquin, Anatole [as Ubalde], *L'Homme au masque de fer, c'est . . . Molière, opinion émise par Ubalde et présenté de nouveau par un bouquineur*, Aix-les-Bains, 1893

Loquin, Anatole, *Le Masque de fer et le livre de M. Frantz Funck-Brentano* (first published in *La Gironde*, July 1898), Paris: Libraires Associés, 1899

Loquin, Anatole, *Le Prisonnier Masqué de la Bastille: son histoire authentique*, Paris: Libraires Associés, 1900

Lough, John, 'France under Louis XIV', in *The New Cambridge Modern History, Volume V*, ed. Peter Burke, Cambridge: Cambridge University Press, 1961

Lough, John, *An Introduction to Seventeenth Century France*, London: Longman, 1954; revised 1969

Louvet, Louis, *L'Homme au masque de fer* (first published in *Encyclopédie des gens du monde*, undated), Paris: Treuttel et Würtz, 1842, BA

Lucea, Yannick, 'Pamphlets et pamphlétaires sous la Révolution', *Historia*, No 509, May 1989

Luizet, Jean, *Ce masque de fer qui n'était qu'en velours!*, Paris and Carnac: Grassin, 1991, BA

McCracken, Peggy, *The Romance of Adultery: Queenship and Sexual Transgression in Old French Literature*, Philadelphia: University of Philadelphia Press, 1998

McNair, William A., *In Search of the Four Musketeers*, Sydney: Alpha, 1972

Macdonald, Roger, 'Behind the Iron Mask', *History Today*, Vol. 55, Issue 11, November 2005

Macdonald, Roger, 'More About the Mask', *History Today*, Vol. 56, Issue 1, January 2006

Magne, Émile, *Un Ami de Cyrano de Bergerac, le chevalier de Lignières*, Paris: Sansot, 1920, BA

Magne, Emile, *La Vie quotidienne au temps de Louis XIII*, Paris: Hachette, 1942

Maller-Joris, Françoise, *Marie Mancini: le premier amour de Louis*, Paris: Librairie générale française, 2002, BA

Mancini, Hortense, *Mémoires*, Cologne: Pierre Marteau, 1675, BA

Maquet, Auguste Jules, with Auguste Arnould and Alboize de Pujol, *Histoire de la Bastille et le Donjon de Vincennes*, Paris: Dupont, 1844

Markale, Jean, *La Bastille et l'énigme du Masque de Fer*, Paris: Pygmalion, 1989

Martin, Henri-Jean, *The French Book: Religion, Absolutism and Readership, 1585–1715*, Baltimore and London: Johns Hopkins University Press, 1996

Masini, Clément de, *L'Homme au Masque de Fer*, Paris: Scorpion, 1964

Mast, Marie-Madeleine, *Le Masque de Fer: une solution révolutionnaire*, Paris: Tallandier, 1974

Mauzaize, Jean, *Les Capucins et l'affaire des poisons*, Paris: Amis de Saint François, 1969, BA

Maza, Sarah C., *Private Lives and Public Affairs: The Causes Célèbres of Pre-Revolutionary France*, Los Angeles and London: University of California Press, 1993

Mazarin, Jules Renouard, *Lettres écrits pendant sa retraite hors de France 1651–1652*, notes by J. Ravenel, Paris: 1836, BL

Maze, Jules, 'D'Artagnan, mousquetaire du roi', *Historia*, No 191, October 1962

Ménage, Gilles and Antoine Galland (ed.), *Menagiana, ou Les bons Mots et remarques critiques, historiques, morales et d'érudition de Monsieur Ménage*, Paris: Florentin Delaulne, 1694, BA

Menegazzi, Claudio, *Louis XIV*, Luxemburg: Hasso Ebeling, 1981

Merrick, Jeffery, 'The Cardinal and the Queen: Sexual and Political Disorders in the Mazarinades', *French Historical Studies*, Vol. 18, No 3, Spring 1994

Michael of Greece, Prince, *Louis XIV: The Other Side of the Sun*, London: Orbis, 1983

Michelet, Jules, *Histoire de France*, Paris: Hachette, 1833–67; Vol 14, 1610–1643 is material, BL

Milhes, C. (ed.), annotated reprint of Eugène d'Auriac, *D'Artagnan* (Paris: Baudry, 1847), Paris: Table Ronde, 1993

Miller, John, *Bourbon and Stuart: Kings and Kingship in France and England in the Seventeenth Century*, London: Philip, 1987

Miquel, Pierre, *Au temps des mousquetaires*, Paris: Hachette, 1978

Miquel, Robert [Romi], *Patriote Palloy*, Paris: Éditions de Paris, 1956

Mitford, Nancy, *The Sun King*, London: Hamish Hamilton, 1966

Mongrédien,Georges, *La Vie quotidienne sous Louis XIV*, Paris: Hachette, 1948

Mongrédien, Georges, *Le Masque de Fer*, Paris: Hachette, 1952

Mongrédien, Georges, *Madame de Montespan et l'affaire des poisons*, Paris: Hachette, 1953

Mongrédien,Georges, 'Deux documents inédites sur le Masque de Fer', *Bulletin de la 'Société d'Étude du XVIIe Siecle*, No 17–18, 1953

Mongrédien, Georges, 'Le problème du Masque de Fer', Pinerolo Symposium, 1976

Monin, Sylvie, *Les Artagnan en Bourgogne*, Lyon: L'Association d'Artagnan, 1998

Montaudon, Henri, 'La Vérité sur le Masque de fer, ou Recherches sur l'identité du personnage désigné sous ce titre', *Revue de la Société des Études Historiques*, September–October and November–December 1888

Montbas, Hugues, *La Police Parisienne sous Louis XVI*, Paris: Hachette, 1949

Montesquiou-Fezensac, Pierre duc de, *Le Vrai d'Artagnan*, Paris: R. Julliard, 1963

Montglat, François de Paule de Clermont, marquis de, *Mémoires*, Paris: 1825

Montpensier, Anne-Marie-Louise d'Orléans, duchesse de, *Mémoires* Amsterdam, 1729, BA

Montrésor, Claude de Bourdeille, comte de, *Mémoires pour servir à l'histoire de France*, Paris: 1664, BA

Morand, Paul, *Fouquet ou le soleil offusqué*, Paris: Gallimard, 1961

Morand, Paul, 'L'Arrestation de Fouquet', *Géographia-Histoire*, No 122, November 1961

Morand, Paul, 'Fouquet emprisonné dans la forteresse de Pignerol', *Historia*, No 207, February 1964

Mossiker, Frances, *The Affair of the Poisons*, London: Gollancz, 1970

Mousnier, Roland (ed.), *Richelieu et la culture*, Paris: Colloque de la Sorbonne, 1988

Muller, Josy, *Vauban et Ath, construction de la forteresse, 1668–1674*, Tamines: Duculot-Roulin, 1955

Munck, Thomas, *Seventeenth Century Europe 1598–1700*, London: Macmillan, 1990

Murat, Inès, *Colbert*, Paris: Fayard, 1980

Murat, Inès, 'Que ferait Colbert aujourd'hui?', *Historia*, No 443, October 1983

Nevill, Ralph (ed.), *Memoirs of Monsieur d'Artagnan: Captain Lieutenant of the 1st Company of the King's Musketeers*, London: Nichols, 1898–9

Newman, Bernard, *In the Trail of the Three Musketeers*, London: Herbert Jenkins, 1934

Nichols Barker, Nancy, *Brother to the Sun King: Philippe Duke of Orléans*, Baltimore: Johns Hopkins University Press, 1989

Noone, John, 'Le Masque sous son vrai visage', Cannes Symposium, 1987

Noone, John, *The Man Behind the Iron Mask*, Gloucester: Sutton, 1988

Noone, John, 'The Mask of Steel', Pinerolo Symposium, 1991

Noone, John, *The Man Behind the Iron Mask*, revised edn, Gloucester: Sutton, 1994

Norton, Lucy (ed.), *Historical Memoirs of the Duc de Saint-Simon*, London: Hamish Hamilton, 1967

Norton, Lucy (ed.), *Saint-Simon at Versailles*, London: Hamish Hamilton, 1980

O'Connell, D.P., *Richelieu*, London: Weidenfeld and Nicolson, 1968

Ogg, David, *Louis XIV*, Oxford: Oxford University Press, 1967

Opie, Robert, *Guillotine*, revised edn, Gloucestershire: Sutton, 1996

Oudin, M., *Une page d'histoire. L'homme au masque de fer, lecture faite à la séance publique de la Société des antiquaires de Picardie du 2 juillet 1882*, Amiens: Douillet, 1884, BA

Pagnol, Marcel, *Le Masque de fer*, Paris: Éditions de Provence, 1965

Pagnol, Marcel, 'Enfin la solution de l'énigme? Qui était le Masque de Fer?', *Historia*, No 228, November 1965

Pagnol, Marcel, 'Le Masque de Fer, valet de Fouquet', *Miroir de l'Histoire*, No 201, September 1966

Pagnol, Marcel, 'L' Énigme du Masque de Fer enfin résolue', *Historama*, No 274 and 275, September and October 1974

Pagnol, Marcel, *Le Secret du Masque de Fer*, Paris: Éditions de Provence, 1977

Parker, David, *The Making of French Absolutism*, London: Arnold, 1983

Parrott, David, *Richelieu's Army, War, Government and Society in France, 1624–42*, Cambridge: Cambridge University Press, 2001

Patmore, K.A., *Court of Louis XIII*, London: Methuen, 1909

Patria, Ettore, 'Bénigne de Saint-Mars, geôlier du Masque de Fer', Cannes Symposium, 1987

Patria, Ettore, 'Un Governatore nelle Alpi: Benigno di Saint-Mars tra Pinerolo ed Exiles', Pinerolo Symposium, 1991

Pennington, Donald H., *Europe in the Seventeenth Century*, London: Longman, 1989

Pérez-Reverte, Arturo, *The Dumas Club*, London: Harvill, 1996

Perrault, Charles, *Histoires ou Contes du temps passé*, The Hague, 1749

Perrot, Mauro Maria, 'Pignerol et les études sur le Masque de Fer', Cannes Symposium, 1987

Perrot, Mauro Maria, *La maschera di ferro: il mistero di un volto*, Pinerolo: Alzani, 1998, BA

Petitfils, Jean-Christian, *Le Masque de fer: le plus mystérieux des prisonniers de l'histoire*, Paris: Perrin, 1970

Petitfils, Jean-Christian, 'L'Affaire des Poisons', *Historama*, No 316, March 1978

Petitfils, Jean-Christian, *Lauzun ou l'insolente séduction*, Paris: Perrin, 1987

Petitfils, Jean-Christian, 'Dix ans de prison pour l'insolence: Lauzun à Pignerol', *Historia*, No 488, August 1987

Petitfils, Jean-Christian, *Madame de Montespan*, Paris: Fayard, 1988, BA

Petitfils, Jean-Christian, 'Il était le Masque de Fer: le fin d'une énigme', *Historama*, No 55, September 1988

Petitfils, Jean-Christian, 'Madame de Montespan a-t-elle vraiment voulu empoisonner le roi?', *Historia*, No 505, January 1989

Petitfils, Jean-Christian, *Louis XIV*, Paris: Perrin, 1995, BA

Petitfils, Jean-Christian, 'Louis XIV invente la politique de communication', *Historama*, special issue, 1995

Petitfils, Jean-Christian, 'La lutte sans merci des clans et des côteries de cour', *Historama*, special issue, 1995

Petitfils, Jean-Christian, '"La Révolution de 1661". Mazarin est mort. Vive le Roi-Soleil', *Historama*, special issue, 1995

Petitfils, Jean-Christian, *Le Véritable d'Artagnan* (first published 1981), revised edn, Paris: Tallandier, 1999

Petitfils, Jean-Christian, *Le Masque de fer: entre histoire et légende*, Paris: Perrin, 2003

Pinard, Maurice, *Chronologie historique-militaire*, Paris: Claude Hérissant, 1760–6, Vols 1–8 (8 is unfinished), BN

Pitts, Vincent J., *La Grande Mademoiselle at the Court of France, 1627–1693*, Baltimore: Johns Hopkins University Press, 2000

Plowden, Alison, *Henrietta Maria: Charles I's Indomitable Queen*, Gloucestershire: Sutton, 2001.

Praviel, Armand, *Histoire Vraie des Trois Mousquetaires*, Paris: Flammarion, 1933

Praviel, Armand, *Madame de Montespan: empoisonneuse*, Paris: Alcan, 1934

Prawdin, Michael, *Marie de Rohan: Duchesse de Chevreuse*, London: Allen and Unwin, 1971

Price, Eleanor C., *A Princess of the Old World*, London: Methuen, 1907

Price, Munro, *The Fall of the French Monarchy*, Oxford: Macmillan, 2002

Puchesse, Gustave Bagenault de, 'Les derniers travaux sur l'homme au Masque de Fer', *Revue des Questions Historiques*, January 1870

Puchesse, Gustave Baguenault de, 'Les dix dernières années de l'administration de Mazarin', *Revue des Questions Historiques*, 1883

Pure, Michel de, *Histoire du maréchal de Gassion*, Amsterdam, 1696, BA

Rabinel, Aimé-Daniel, *La Tragique Aventure de Roux de Marcilly*, Toulouse: Privat, 1969

Raillicourt, D. Labarre de, 'L'Homme au Masque de Fer', *Les Cahiers de l'Histoire*, special issue, 1960

Rat, Maurice, 'Le vrai d'Artagnan', *Géographia-Histoire*, No 109, October 1960

Rat, Maurice, 'Masque de Fer? Ou . . . Masque de Velours?', *Géographia-Histoire*, No 110, November 1960

Raulin, G. de, *L'Ile Sainte-Marguerite*, Paris: A. Michel, 1920

Ravaisson François, *Archives de la Bastille: documents inédits/recueillis*, Paris: Durand and Pedone-Lauriel, 1866–1904. Vol. 1. *Règne de Louis XIV (1659–1661)*, published 1866; 2. *Règne de Louis XIV (1661–1668)*, 1868; 3. *Règne de Louis XIV (1661–1664)*, 1868; 4. *Règne de Louis XIV (1663–1678)*, 1870; 5. *Règne de Louis XIV (1678–1679)*, 1872; 6. *Règne de Louis XIV (1679-1681)*, 1873; 7. *Règne de Louis XIV (1681 and 1665–1674)*, 1874; 8. *Règne de Louis XIV (1675–1686)*, 1876; 9. *Règne de Louis XIV (1687–1692)*, 1877; 10. *Règne de Louis XIV (1693–1702)*, 1879; 11. *Règne de Louis XIV (1702–1710)*, 1880; 12. *Règnes de Louis XIV et de Louis XV (1709–1772)*, 1881; 13. *Règnes de Louis XIV et de Louis XV (1711–1725)*, 1882.

Vols 13–19 are not material. Vols published 1868–73 author's collection, rest BA

Regan, Geoffrey, *Royal Blunders*, London: Deutsch, 1995

Renneville, René-Augustin-Constantin de, *The French Inquisition: or the History of the Bastille in Paris, the State-Prison in France, in which is an Account of the Manner of the Apprehending of Persons Sent Thither; and of the Barbarous Usage They Meet with There*, London: Bell and others, 1715

Renson, Daniel (ed.), *Vauban, Ingénieur du Roi-Soleil: les grands personnages de l'histoire*, No 1, Avon: Metawalk, 2004

Reth [Servières, Eugénie baron de], *Véritable Clef de l'histoire de l'homme au masque de fer*, Turin, 1794, BA

Retz, Jean-François Paul de Gondi, Cardinal de, *Mémoires*, Paris, 1717, BA

Richard, Aimé, *Louvois: le bras armé de Louis XIV*, Paris: Tallandier, 1998

Richardson, Joanna, *Louis XIV*, London: Weidenfeld and Nicolson, 1973

Richelieu, Cardinal de, *Mémoires de Richelieu, publiés d'après les manuscrits originaux pour la Société de l'Histoire de France*, Paris: Edouard Champion, 1908–31, BA

Riga, Jean-Étienne, *Le Masque de fer: un ombre au règne du Roi-Soleil*, Brussels: Marabout, 1996

Ripert, Pierre, *Richelieu et Mazarin: le temps des cardinaux*, Toulouse: Privat, 2002, BA

Ritchie, Graeme, 'French History: The Seventeenth Century', in his *France*, London: Methuen, 1937

Ritchie, W.K., *The France of Louis XIV*, Harlow: Longman, 1977

Ritter, Raymond, *Pyrénées, Côte-Basque, Gascogne*, Paris: Lajeunesse, 1952

Robert, Henri, 'Le Masque de Fer', in his *Les Grands Procès de l'Histoire*, Paris: Payot, 1926

Roberts, Keith, *Matchlock Musketeer*, Oxford: Osprey, 2002

Rochete, Charlon de la (ed.), *Histoire secrete du cardinal de Richelieu, ou ses amours avec Marie de Medici et Mme de Combalet*, Paris, 1808, BA

Roederer, Antoine Marie, 'Les Aiguillettes d'Anne d'Autriche' in his *Les Intrigues politiques de la cour de France sous Charles IX, Louis XIII, Louis XIV, le Regent et Louis XV, . . .*, Paris: Charles Gosselin, 1832

Romain, Charles, *Louis XIII: un grand roi méconnu 1601–1643*, Paris: Hachette, 1934

Ross, Michael, *Alexandre Dumas*, Newton Abbot: David and Charles, 1981

Roujon, Jacques, *Louvois et son maître*, Paris: Grasset, 1934

Roux-Fazillac, Pierre, *Recherches historiques et critiques sur l'Homme au masque de fer, d'où résultent des notions certaines sur ce prisonnier. Ouvrage rédigé sur des matériaux authentiques*, Paris: Valade, 1800

Rudé, George, *Paris and London in the 18th Century: Studies in Popular Protest*, London: Fontana/Collins, 1969

Ruggieri, Ève, *L'honneur retrouvé du marquis de Montespan*, Paris: Perrin, 1992, BA

Sackville-West, Vita, *Daughter of France: The Life of Anne Marie d'Orléans, La Grande Mademoiselle*, London: Michael Joseph, 1959

Saillens, E., *Une Source de Cyrano de Bergerac: l'orgueil d'e*, Paris: Mercure de France, 1938, BA

Sainte-André, Claude, *Henriette d'Angleterre et la Cour de Louis XIV*, Paris: Plon, 1933

Saint-Cyprien, R.P, *Rec. des vertus et des écrits de madame la baronne de Neuvillette*, Paris: Denis Bechet, 1660, BA

Saint-Foix, Germain-François Poullain de, *Au sujet de l'homme au masque de fer*, Paris: Duchesne, 1768, BA

Saint-Foix, Germain-François Poullain de, *Réponse de M. de Saint-Foix au R. P. Griffet, et recueil de tout ce qui a été écrit sur le prisonnier masqué*, Paris: Vente, 1770, BA

Sainte-Foix, Germain-François Poullain de, *Essais historiques sur Paris*, Paris: Duchesne, 1776

Saint-Germain, Jacques, *La Reynie et la police au grand siècle d'après de nombreux documents inédits*, Paris: Hachette, 1962, BA

Saint-Mihiel, Jean-Baptiste de, *Le véritable homme dit au Masque de fer, ouvrage dans lequel on fait connaître, sur preuves incontestables, à qui ce célèbre infortuné dut le jour, quand et où il naquit*, Strasbourg. Librairie Académique, second edition with corrections, 1791

Samaran, Charles Maxime Donatien, 'D'Artagnan et Fouquet', *La Revue de Paris*, January–February 1894

Samaran, Charles Maxime Donatien, *D'Artagnan capitaine des mousquetaires du roi: histoire véridique d'un héros de roman*, Paris: Calmann-Lévy, 1912

Samaran, Charles Maxime Donatien, *Un Gascon Gouverneur de la Bastille sous Louis XIV: François de Monlézun, Marquis de Besmaux*, reprinted from the *Bulletin de la Société de l'Histoire de Paris*, 1965

Samaran, Charles Maxime Donatien, *D'Artagnan: capitaine des mousquetaires du Roi*, reproduction of 1912 edition with author's new foreword, Auch: Calmann-Lévy, 1967

Sandars, Mary Frances, *Lauzun: Courtier and Adventurer*, London: Hutchinson, 1908

Savine, Albert, and François Bournand, *Fouquet: superintendant général des finances*, Paris: Louis-Michaud, 1908

Savine, Albert, *Le Beau Lauzun*, Paris: Louis-Michaud, 1909

Scaggion, Guy, and Joseph Arney, *Le premier homme à poser le pied dans la Bastille investie le 14 juillet 1789*, Bordeaux: Les Dossiers d'Aquitaine, 2002, BA

Schmit, J.-A., *Les campagnes de Louis XIII en Lorraine*, Nimes: Rediviva, 1999

Schreiber, Roy E., *The First Carlisle: Sir James Hay, First Earl of Carlisle as Courtier, Diplomat and Entrepreneur 1580–1636*, Philadelphia: Transactions of the American Philosophical Society, Vol. 74, Part 7, 1984

Seward, Desmond, *The First Bourbon: Henry IV of France and Navarre*, London: Constable, 1971

Sewell, Brian, et al., *The Age of Louis XIV*, Winter Exhibition catalogue, London: Royal Academy of Arts, 1958

Shama, Simon, *Citizens: A Chronicle of the French Revolution*, New York: Knopf, 1989

Shennan, J.H., *The Parlement of Paris*, London: Eyre and Spottiswoode, 1968

Shennan, J.H., *Government and Society in France 1461–1661*, London: Allen and Unwin, 1969

Shennan, J.H., *Philippe Duke of Orléans*, London: Thames and Hudson, 1979

Sigaux, Gilbert (ed.), *Mémoires de Monsieur d'Artagnan*, Paris: Mercure de France, 1957

Solnon, Jean-François (ed.), *Mémoires sur la cour de Louis XIV by Primi Visconti, 1673–1681*, Paris: Perrin, 1988, BA

Somerset, Anne, *The Affair of the Poisons: Murder, Infanticide & Satanism at the Court of Louis XIV*, London: Weidenfeld and Nicolson, 2003

Spens, Willy de, *Cyrano de Bergerac: l'esprit de révolte*, Monaco: Rocher, 1989, BA

Spurr, H.A., *The Life and Writings of Alexandre Dumas*, London: Dent, 1902

Steegmuller, Francis, *La Grande Mademoiselle*, London: Hamish Hamilton, 1955

Stokes, Hugh, *Madame de Brinvilliers and her Times 1630-1676*, London: John Lane, 1912

Stone, Lawrence, *The Crisis of the Aristocracy, 1558–1641*, Oxford: Oxford University Press, 1965

Sturdy, D.J., *The D'Aligres de la Rivière: Servants of the Bourbon State in the Seventeenth Century*, Woodbridge: Boydell and Brewer, 1986

Surville, de, Jean, *Le Masque de fer a-t-il été fatal au trône de France, ou les misères d'une dynastie, de 1703 à 1883*, Paris: Auguste Ghio, 1884

Taillandier, Saint-René, *La jeunesse du grand Roi: Louis XIV et Anne d'Autriche*, Paris: Plon, 1945

Tallemant des Réaux, Gédéon, *Historiettes*, ed. Antoine Adam, Paris: Pléiade, 1960–1

Tallemant des Reaux, Gédéon, *Portraits and Anecdotes from his Historiettes*, London: Oxford University Press, 1965

Tapie, Victor-L., *France in the Age of Louis XIV and Richelieu*, Cambridge: Cambridge University Press, 1974

Taulès, chevalier de, *Du Masque de fer, ou Réfutation de l'ouvrage de M. Roux Fazillac, intitulé: 'Recherches historiques sur le Masque de fer', et réfutation également de l'ouvrage de M.J. Delort, qui a pour titre: 'Histoire de l'Homme au masque de fer'*, Paris: Peytieux, 1825, BA

Taulès, chevalier de, *L'Homme au masque de fer, mémoire historique, où l'on réfute les différentes opinions relatives à ce personnage mystérieux, et où l'on démontre que ce prisonnier fut une victime des Jésuites ; Suivi d'une correspondance inédite de Voltaire avec M. de Taulès sur le 'Siècle de Louis XIV', le 'Testament politique du cardinal de Richelieu', etc.*, Paris: Peytieux, 1825

Tawney, Richard Henry, *Business and Politics under James I: Lionel Cranfield as Merchant and Minister*, Cambridge: Cambridge University Press, 1958

Thompson, Harry, *The Man in the Iron Mask: A Historical Detective Investigation*, London: Weidenfeld and Nicolson, 1987

Thompson, Harry, 'La Théorie d'Eustache Dauger de Cavoye', Cannes Symposium, 1987

Tiollais, Madeleine, *Le Masque de fer: enquête sur le prisonnier dont le nom ne se dit pas*, Coudray-Macouard: Cheminements, 2003

Topin, Marius, *The Man with the Iron Mask*, London: Smith, Elder, 1870

Topin, Marius, *L'Homme au masque de fer*, Paris: Dentu, 1870; revised edn 1883, BA

Tour, Geoffroy Tenant de La, *Une étrange aventure. Le 'masque de fer' à Saint-Yrieix.?*, Paris: Orphelins-apprentis d'Auteuil, 1934, BA

Treasure, Geoffrey, *Richelieu and Mazarin*, London: Routledge, 1998

Treasure, Geoffrey, *Louis XIV*, London: Pearson, 2001

Turgeon, F.K., 'Fanny de Beauharnais. Biographical Notes', reprinted from *Modern Philology*, Vol. 30, No. 1, August 1932

Valentin, Antonina, *Mirabeau: Voice of the Revolution*, London: Hamish Hamilton, 1948

Vallot, Antoine, *Journal de la santé du Roi Louis XIV de l'année 1646 a l'année 1711*, ed. J.-A. Le Roi, Paris: 1862, BA

Vergé-Franceschi, Michel, *Colbert: La politique du bon sens*, Paris: Payot, 2003

Vernandeau, Pierre, *Le Médecin de la reyne*, Paris: Denoël and Steele, 1934

Vigny, Alfred de, *Cinq-Mars ou une conjuration sous Louis XIII*, Paris: Levy, 1891

Voltaire [François Marie Arouet] *Oeuvres complètes*, Paris: Garnier, 1875 VL

Voltaire [François Marie Arouet] *Correspondance*, Paris: Gallimard, 1977–92, VL

Vosgien, M., *Dictionnaire Géographique-Portatif, ou Description des royaumes, duchés, comtés, marquisats, villes impériales, ports, fortresses*, Paris: Echard, 1785

Vulliamy, C.E., *Voltaire*, London: Bles, 1930.

Warwick, Sir Philip, *Memoirs of the Reign of King Charles I: containing the most remarkable Occurrences of that Reign, and setting many Secret Passages thereof in a clear Light*, London: Chiswell, 1702

Wedgwood, Cicely Veronica, *Richelieu and the French Monarchy*, London: English Universities, 1949

Wedgwood, Cicely Veronica, *The King's War 1641–1647*, London: Collins, 1958

Weygand, Max, *Turenne: Marshall of France*, London: Harrap, 1930

Wilkinson, Richard, *Louis XIV, France and Europe, 1661–1715*. London: Hodder and Stoughton, 2002

Williamson, Hugh Ross, 'The Man in the Iron Mask', in his *Enigmas of History*, London: Michael Joseph, 1957

Wolf, John B., *Louis XIV*, New York: Norton, 1968

Woodbridge, Benjamin Mather, 'Biographical Notes on Gatien de Courtilz', *Modern Language Notes*, Vol. 30, 1915

Woodbridge, Benjamin Mather, *Gatien de Courtilz*, Baltimore: John Hopkins University Press, 1925

Zuber, Roger, 'Qui ose critiquer le roi?', *Historama*, special edition, 1995

INDEX